Ancient Tales Of Wisdom

JATAKA TALES

FRANCIS & THOMAS

JAICO PUBLISHING HOUSE

Ahmedabad Bangalore Bhopal Bhubaneswar Chennai
Delhi Hyderabad Kolkata Lucknow Mumbai

Published by Jaico Publishing House
A-2 Jash Chambers, 7-A Sir Phirozshah Mehta Road
Fort, Mumbai - 400 001
jaicopub@jaicobooks.com
www.jaicobooks.com

JATAKA TALES
ISBN 81-7224-096-1

First Jaico Impression: 1957
Twenty-third Jaico Impression: 2013

Printed by
Concept Imprint Pvt. Ltd.
Plot No. 51/1/4, Site-4. Industrial Area,
Sahibabad Ghaziabad (U.P.)

INTRODUCTION

The Jataka as we possess it occurs in the second of the three great divisions of the Pali Buddhist scriptures. It consists of 547 Jatakas each containing the life of Buddha during some incarnation in one of his previous existences as a Bodhisatta. Some of the tales occur more than once in a different setting or in a variant version and occasionally several stories are included in one birth. Each separate story is embedded in a framework, which forms the story of the present. This is generally an account of some incident in the life of the historic Buddha, such as an act of disobedience or folly among the brethren of the order, the discussion of a question of ethics, or an instance of eminent virtue. Buddha then tells a story of the past, an event in one of his previous existences, which explains the present incident as a repetition of the former one, or as a parallel case and shows the moral consequences.

All stories contain the Bodhisatta (one being destined to enlightenment) as well as verses occur in all the births. It is these verses which are canonical, the prose being a commentary explaining how the verses came to be spoken.

Although much of the Jataka is merely moral instruction to the unconverted it also expounds teaching which leads to enlightenment, such as the doctrine of impermanence, belief in the Buddha, the rejection of superstitious rites, freedom from lust, hatred and delusion and other bonds which the disciple must break as he advances on the noble path.

The present selection has been made with the purpose of brining together the Jataka stories of the most widespread interest.

Contents

Contents

Contents

Contents

JĀTAKA TALES
THE LITTLE GILDMASTER

Once on a time when Brahmadatta was reigning in Benares in Kasi, the Bodhisatta was born into a gildmaster's family, and growing up, became gildmaster, being called Gildmaster Little. A wise and clever man was he, with a keen eye for signs and omens. One day on his way to wait upon the king, he came on a dead mouse lying on the road; and, taking note of the position of the stars at that moment, he said, "Any decent young fellow with his wits about him has only to pick that mouse up, and he might start a business and keep a wife."

His words were overheard by a young man of good family but reduced circumstances, who said to himself, "That's a man who has always got a reason for what he says." And accordingly he picked up the mouse, which he sold for a farthing at a tavern for their cat.

With the farthing he got molasses and took drinking water in a water-pot. Coming on flower-gatherers returning from the forest, he gave each a tiny quantity of the molasses and ladled the water out to them. Each of them gave him a handful of flowers, with the proceeds of which, next day, he came back again to the flower grounds provided with more molasses and a pot of water. That day the flower-gatherers, before they went, gave him flowering plants with half the flowers left on them, and thus in a little while he obtained eight pennies.

Later, one rainy and windy day, the wind blew down a quantity of rotten branches and boughs and leaves in the king's pleasaunce, and the gardener did not see how to clear them away. Then up came the young man with an offer to remove the lot, if the wood and leaves might be his. The gardener closed with the offer on the spot. Then this apt pupil of Gildmaster Little repaired to the children's playground and in

1

a very title while had got them by bribes of molasses to collect every stick and leaf in the place into a heap at the entrance to the pleasaunce. Just then the king's potter was on the look out for fuel to fire bowls for the palace, and coming on this heap, took the lot off his hands. The sale of his wood brought in sixteen pennies to this pupil of Gildmaster Little, as well as five bowls and other vessels. Having now twenty-four pennies in all, a plan occurred to him. He went to the vicinity of the city-gate with a jar full of water and supplied 500 mowers with water to drink. Said they, "You've done us a good turn, friend. What can we do for you?" "Oh, I'll tell you when I want your aid," said he: and as he went about, he struck up an intimacy with a land-trader and a sea-trader. Said the former to him, "To-morrow there will come to town a horse-dealer with 500 horses to sell." On hearing this piece of news, he said to the mowers, "I want each of you to-day to give me a bundle of grass and not to sell your own grass till mine is sold." "Certainly," said they, and delivered the 500 bundles of grass at his house. Unable to get grass for his horses elsewhere, the dealer purchased our friend's grass for a thousand pieces. Only a few days later his sea-trading friend brought him news of the arrival of a large ship in port; and another plan struck him. He hired for eight pence a well appointed carriage which plied for hire by the hour, and went in great style down to the port. Having bought the ship on credit and deposited his signet-ring as security, he had a pavilion pitched hard by and said to his people as he took his seat inside, "When merchants are being shown in, let them be passed on by three successive ushers into my presence." Hearing that a ship had arrived in port, about a hundred merchants came down to buy the cargo; only to be told that they could not have it as a great merchant had already made a payment on account. So away they all went to the young man; and the footmen duty announced them by three successive ushers, as had been arranged beforehand. Each man of the hundred severally gave him a thousand pieces to buy a share in the ship and then a further thousand each to buy him out altogether. So it was with 20,000 pieces that this pupil of Gildmaster Little returned to Benares.

Actuated by a desire to show his gratitude, he went with one hundred thousand pieces to call on Gildmaster Little. "How did you come by all this wealth?" asked the gildmaster. "In four short months, simply by following your advice." replied the young man; and he told him the whole story, starting with the dead mouse. Thought Lord High Gildmaster Little, on hearing all this, "I must see that a young fellow of these parts does not fall into anybody else's hands." So he married him to his own grown-up daughter and settled all the family estates on the young man. And at the gildmaster's death, he became gildmaster in that city. And the Bodhisatta passed away to fare according to his deserts.

THE KING AND THE STICK-GATHERER

Once on a time in Benares Brahmadatta the king, having gone in great state to his pleasaunce, was roaming about looking for fruits and flowers when he came in on a woman who was merrily singing away as she picked up sticks in the grove. Falling in love at first sight, the king became intimate with her, and the Bodhisatta was conceived then and there. Feeling as heavy within as though weighed down with the bolt of Indra, the woman knew that she would become a mother, and told the king so. He gave her the signet-ring from his finger and dismissed her with these words: "If it be a girl, spend this ring on her nurture; but if it be a boy, bring ring and child to me."

When the woman's time was come, she bore the Bodhisatta. And when he could run about and was playing in the playground a cry would arise, "No-father has hit me!" Hearing this, the Bodhisatta ran away to his mother and asked who his father was.

"You are the son of the king of Benares, my boy." "What proof of this is there mother?" "My son, the king on leaving me gave me this signet-ring and said, 'If it be a girl, spend this ring on her nurture; but if it be a boy, bring ring and child to me.' "Why then don't you take me to my father, mother?"

Seeing that the boy's mind was made up, she took him to the gate of the palace, and bade their coming be announced to the king. Being summoned in, she entered and bowing before his majesty said, "This is your son, sire."

The king knew well enough that this was the truth, but shame before all his court made him reply, "He is no son of mine." "But here is your signet-ring, sire; you will recognize that." "Nor is this my signet-ring." Then said the woman, "Sire, I have now no witness to prove my words, except to make an act of truth. Wherefore, if this child is yours, I pray that he may stay in mid-air; but if not, may he fall to earth and be killed" So saying, she seized the Bodhisatta by the foot and threw him up into the air.

Seated cross-legged in mid-air, the Bodhisatta in sweet tones repeated this stanza to his father, declaring the truth:
Your son am I, great monarch; rear me, Sire!
The king rears others, but much more his child.

Hearing, the Bodhisatta thus teach the truth to him from mid-air, the king stretched out his hands and cried, "Come to me, my boy! None, none but me shall rear and nurture you!" A thousand hands were stretched out to receive the Bodhisatta, but it was into the arms of the king and of no other that he descended, seating himself in the king's lap. The king made him viceroy, and made his mother queen-consort. At the death of the king his father, he came lo the throne by the title of King Katthavahana — the faggot-bearer, — and after ruling his realm righteously. passed away to fare according to his deserts.

KING MAKHĀDEVA'S GREY HAIRS

Once on a time in Mithilā in the realm of Videha there was a king named Makhādeva, who was righteous and ruled righteously. For successive periods of eighty-four thousand years he had respectively amused himself as prince, ruled as viceroy, and reigned as king. All these long years had he lived, when one day he said to his barber,— "Tell me, friend barber, when you see any grey hairs in my head." So one day, years and years after, the barber did find among the raven locks of the king a single grey hair, and he told the king so. "Pull it out, my friend," said the king; "and lay it in my palm." The barber accordingly plucked the hair out with his golden tongs, and laid it in the king's hand. The king had at the time still eighty-four thousand years more to live; but nevertheless at the sight of that one grey hair he was filled with deep emotion. He seemed to see the King of Death standing over him, or to be cooped within a blazing hut of leaves. "Foolish Makhādeva!" he cried; "grey hairs have come upon you before you have been able to rid yourself of the depravities." And as he thought and thought about the appearance of his grey hair, he grew aflame within; the sweat rolled down from his body; whilst his raiment oppressed him and seemed intolerable. "This very day," thought he, "I must renounce the world for a hermit's life."

To his barber he gave the grant of a village, which yielded a hundred thousand pieces of money. He sent for his eldest son and said to him, "My son, grey hairs are come upon me, and I am become old. I have had my fill of human joys, and fain would taste the joys divine; the time for my renunciation has come. Take the sovereignty upon yourself; as for me, I will take up my abode in the pleasaunce called Makhādeva's Mango-grove, and there tread the ascetic's path."

As he was thus bent on becoming a hermit, his ministers drew near and said, "What is the reason, sire, of your becoming a hermit?"

Taking the grey hair in his hand, the king repeated this stanza to his ministers:
Lo, these grey hairs that on my head appear
Are Death's own messengers that come to rob
My Life. 'Tis time I turned from worldly things,
And in the hermit's path sought saving peace.

And after these words, he renounced his sovereignty that

self-same day and became a recluse. Dwelling in that very Mango-grove of Makhādeva, he there during eighty-four thousand years fostered the Four Perfect States within himself, and, dying with ecstasy full and unbroken, was reborn in the Realm of Brahma. Passing thence, he became a king again in Mithilā, under the name of Nimi, and after uniting his scattered family, once more became a hermit in that same Mango-grove, winning the Four Perfect States and passing thence once more to the Realm of Brahma.

THE COLD HALF OF THE MONTH

Once upon a time at the foot of a certain mountain there-were living together in one and the same cave two friends, a lion and a tiger. The Bodhisatta too was living at the foot of the same hill, as a hermit.

Now one day a dispute arose between the two friends about the cold. The tiger said it was cold in the dark half of the month, whilst the lion maintained that it was cold in the- light half. As the two of them together could not settle the question, they put it to the Bodhisatta. He repeated this stanza:

In light or dark half, whensoe'er the wind
Doth blow, 'tis cold. For cold is caused by wind.
And, therefore, I decide you both are right.

Thus did the Bodhisatta make peace between those friends.

THE FEAST FOR THE DEAD

Once upon a time when Brahmadatta was reigning in Benares, a brahmin, who was versed in the three Vedas and world-famed as a teacher, being minded to offer a Feast for the Dead, had a goat fetched and said to his pupils. "My sons, take this goat down to the river and bathe it; then hang a wreath round its neck, adorn it with a five-sprayed garland, and bring it back."

"Very good," said they, and down to the river they took

the goat, where they bathed and adorned the creature and set it on the bank. The goat, becoming conscious of the deeds of its past lives, was overjoyed at the thought that on this very day it would be freed from all its misery, and laughed aloud like the smashing of a pot. Then at the thought that the brahmin by slaying it would bear the misery which it had borne, the goat felt a great compassion for the brahmin, and wept with a loud voice. "Friend goat," said the young brahmins, "your voice has been loud both in laughter and in weeping: what made you laugh and what made you weep?"

"Ask me your question before your master."

So with the goat they came to their master and told him of the matter. After hearing their story, the master asked the goat why it laughed and why it wept. Hereupon the animal, recalling its past deeds by its power of remembering its former existence, spoke thus to the brahmin: "In times past, brahmin, I like you, was a brahmin versed in the mystic texts of the Vedas, and I, to offer a Feast for the Dead, killed a goat for my offering. Ail through killing that single goat, I have had my head cut off five hundred times all but one. This is my five hundredth and last birth; and I laughed aloud when I thought that this very day I should be freed from my misery. On the other hand, I wept when I thought how, whilst I, who for killing a goat had been doomed to lose my head five hundred times, was to-day being freed from my misery, you, as a penalty for killing me, would be doomed to lose your head, like me, five hundred times. Thus it was out of compassion for you that I wept." "Fear not, goat" said the brahmin; "I will not kill you." "What is this you say, brahmin?" said the goat. "Whether you kill me or not, I cannot escape death to-day." "Fear not, goat; I will go about with you to guard you." "Weak is your protection, brahmin, and strong is the force of my evil-doing."

Setting the goat at liberty, the brahmin said to his disciples, "Let us not allow anyone to kill this goat"; and, accompanied by the young men, he followed the animal closely about. The moment the goat was set free, it reached out its neck to browse on the leaves of a bush growing near the top of a rock. And that very instant a thunderbolt struck the rock, rending off a mass which hit the goat on the outstretched neck and tore off its head. And people came crowding round.

In those days the Bodhisatta had been born a tree divinity in that selfsame spot. By his supernatural powers he now seated himself cross legged in mid-air while all the crowd looked on. Thinking to himself, "If these creatures only knew the fruit of evil-doing, perhaps they would desist from killing," in his sweet voice he taught them the Truth in this stanza:
If folk but knew the truth that their existence
Is pain, then living things would cease
From taking life. Stern is the slayer's doom.

Thus did the Great Being preach the Truth, scaring his hearers with the fear of hell; and the people, hearing him, were so terrified at the fear of hell that they left off taking life. And the Bodhisatta after establishing the multitude in the Commandments by preaching the Truth to them, passed away to fare according to his deserts. The people, too, remained steadfast in the teaching of the Bodhisatta and spent their lives in charity and other good works, so that in the end they attained to the city of the gods.

THE MONKEYS AND THE OGRE

In past times, we are told, there was a thick forest on this spot. And in the lake here dwelt a water-ogre who used to devour everyone who went down into the water. In those days the Bodhisatta had come to life as the king of the monkeys and was as big as the fawn of a red deer; he lived in that forest at the head of a troop of no less than eighty thousand monkeys whom he shielded from harm. Thus did he counsel his subjects: "My friends, in this forest there are trees that are poisonous and lakes that are haunted by ogres. Mind to ask me first before you either eat any fruit which you have not eaten before, or drink of any water where you have not drunk before." "Certainly," said they readily.

One day they came to a spot they had never visited before. As they were searching for water to drink after their day's wanderings, they came on this lake. But they did not drink; on the contrary they sat down watching for the coming of the Bodhisatta.

When he came up, he said, "Well, my friends, why don't you drink?"

"We waited for you to come."

"Quite right, my friends," said the Bodhisatta. Then he made a circuit of the lake, and scrutinized the footprints round, with the result that he found that all the footsteps led down into the water and none came up again. "Without doubt," thought he to himself, "this is the haunt of an ogre." So he said to his followers, "You are quite right, my friends, in not drinking of the water; for the lake is haunted by an ogre."

When the water-ogre realised that they were not entering his domain, he assumed the shape of a horrible monster with a blue belly, a white face, and bright-red hands and feet; in this shape he came out from the water, and said, "Why are you seated here? Go down into the lake and drink." But the Bodhisatta said to him. "Are not you the ogre of this water?" "Yes, I am," was the answer. "Do you take as your prey all those who go down into this water?" "Yes I do; from small birds upwards, I never let anything go which comes down into my water. I will eat the lot of you too." "But we shall not let you eat us." "Just drink the water." "Yes, we will drink the water, and yet not fall into your power." "How do you propose to drink the water then?" "Ah, you think we shall have to go down into the water to drink; whereas we shall not enter the water at all, but the whole eighty thousand of us will take a reed each and drink therewith from your lake as easily as we could through the hollow stalk of a lotus. And so you will not be able to eat us." And he repeated the latter half of the following stanza (the first half being added by the Master when, as Buddha, he recalled the incident):

I found the footprints all lead down, none back.
With reeds well drink; you shall not take my life.

So saying, the Bodhisatta had a reed brought to him. Then, calling to mind the Ten Perfections displayed by him, he recited them in a solemn asseveration, and blew down the reed. Straightway the reed became hollow throughout, with out a single knot being left in all its length. In this fashion he had another and another brought and blew down them. (But if this were so, he could never have finished; and accordingly the foregoing sentence must not be understood in this— literal—sense.) Next the Bodhisatta made the tour of the lake, and commanded, saying. "Let all reeds growing here become hollow throughout, Now thanks to the qreat virtues of the saving goodness of Bodhisattas, their commands are always fulfilled. And thenceforth every single reed that grew round that lake became hollow throughout.

(In this *Kappa,* or Era, there are four miracles which endure through the whole Era. What are the four? Well, they are first, the sign of the hare in the moon, which will last through the whole Era; secondly, the spot where the fire was put out as told in the Vattaka Jātaka, which shall remain untouched by fire throughout the Era; thirdly, on the site of Ghatikāra's house no rain shall ever fall while this Era lasts; and lastly, the reeds that grow round this lake shall be hollow throughout during the whole of the Era. Such are the four Era-miracles, as they are called.)

After giving this command, the Bodhisatta seated himself with a reed in his hands. All the other eighty thousand monkeys too seated themselves round the lake, each with a reed in his hands. And at the same moment when the Bodhisatta sucked the water up through his reed, they all drank too in the same manner, as they sat on the bank. This was the way they drank, and not one of them could the water-ogre get; so he went off in a rage to his own habitation. The Bodhisatta, too, with his followers went back into the forest.

THE GUILTY DOGS

Once upon a time when Brahmadatta was reigning in Benares, the result of a past act of the Bodhisatta was that he came to life as a dog, and dwelt in a great cemetery at the head of several hundred dogs.

Now one day, the king set out for his pleasaunce in his chariot of state drawn by white Sindh horses, and after amusing himself all the day in the grounds came back to the city after sunset. The carriage-harness they left in the courtyard, still hitched on to the chariot. In the night it rained and the harness got wet. Moreover, the king's dogs came down from the upper chambers and gnawed the leather work and straps. Next day they told the king, saying, "Sire, dogs have got in through the mouth of the sewer and have gnawed the leather work and straps of your majesty's carriage." Enraged at the dogs, the king said, "Kill every dog you see." Then began a great slaughter of dogs; and the creatures, finding that they were being slain whenever they were seen, repaired to the cemetery to the Bodhisatta. "What is the meaning," asked he, "of your assembling in such numbers?" They said, "The king is so enraged at the report that the leather work and straps of his carriage have been gnawed by dogs within the royal precincts, that he has ordered all dogs to be killed. Dogs are being destroyed wholesale, and great peril has arisen."

Thought the Bodhisatta to himself, "No dogs from without can get into a place so closely watched; it must be the thoroughbred dogs inside the palace who have done it. At present nothing happens to the real culprits, while the guiltless are being put to death. What if I were to discover the culprits to the king and so save the lives of my kith and kin?" He comforted his kinsfolk by saying, "Have no fear; I will save you. Only wait here till I see the king."

Then, guided by the thoughts of love, and calling to mind the Ten Perfections, he made his way alone and unattended into the city, commanding thus, "Let no hand be lifted to throw

stick or stone at me." Accordingly, when he made his
appearance, not a man grew angry at the sight of him.

The king meantime, after ordering the dogs' destruction,
had taken his seat in the hall of justice. And straight to him ran
the Bodhisatta, leaping under the king's throne. The king's
servants tried to get him out; but his majesty stopped them.
Taking heart a little, the Bodhisatta came forth from under the
throne, and bowing to the king, said, "Is it you who are having
the dogs destroyed?" "Yes, it is I." "What is their offence, king
of men?" "They have been gnawing the straps and the leather
covering my carriage." "Do you know the dogs who actually
did the mischief?" "No, I do not." "But, your majesty, if you do
not know for certain the real culprits, it is not right to order the
destruction of every dog that is seen." "It was because dogs
had gnawed the leather of my carriage that I ordered them all
to be killed." "Do your people kill all dogs without exception;
or are there some dogs who are spared?" "Some are spared,
the thorough-bred dogs of my own palace." "Sire, just now you
were saying that you had ordered the universal slaughter of all
dogs wherever found, because dogs had gnawed the leather of
your carriage; whereas, now you say that the thorough-bred
dogs of your own palace escape death. Therefore you are
following the four Evil Courses of partiality, dislike, ignorance
and fear. Such courses are wrong, and not kinglike. For kings
in trying cases should be as unbiased as the beam of a balance.
But in this instance, since the royal dogs go scot-free, whilst
poor dogs are killed, this is not the impartial doom of all dogs
alike, but only the slaughter of poor dogs." And moreover, the
Great Being, lifting up his sweet voice, said, "Sire, it is not
justice that you are performing," and he taught the Truth to the
king in this stanza:

> The dogs that in the royal palace, grow,
> The well-bred dogs, so strong and fair of form,—
> Not these, but only we, are doomed to die.
> Here's no impartial sentence meted out
> To all alike; 'tis slaughter of the poor.

After listening to the Bodhisatta's words, the king said, "Do you in your wisdom know who it actually was that gnawed the leather of my carriage?" "Yes sire." "Who was it?" "The thorough-bred dogs that live in your own palace." "How can it be shown that it was they who gnawed the leather?" "I will prove it to you." "Do so, sage." "Then send for your dogs, and have a little butter-milk and kusa-grass brought in." The king did so.

Then said the Great Being, "Let this grass be mashed up in the butter-milk, and make the dogs drink it.

The king did so;—with the result that each several dog, as he drank, vomited. And they all brought up bits of leather! "Why, it is like a judgment of a Perfect Buddha himself," cried the king overjoyed, and he did homage to the Bodhisatta by offering him the royal umbrella. And the Bodhisatta taught the Truth in the ten stanzas on righteousness in the Te-sakuna-Játaka, beginning with the words:
Walk righteously, great king of princely race.

Then having established the king in the five Commandments, and having exhorted his majesty to be steadfast, the Bodhisatta handed back to the king the white umbrella of kingship.

At the close of the Great Being's words, the king commanded that the lives of all creatures should be safe from harm. He ordered that all dogs, from the Bodhisatta downwards, should have a constant supply of food such as he himself ate; and abiding by the teachings of the Bodhisatta, he spent his life long in charity and other good deeds, so that when he died he was re-born in the world of gods. The 'Dog's Teaching' endured for ten thousand years. The Bodhisatta also lived to a ripe old age, and then passed away to fare according to his deserts.

THE DISCONTENTED OX

Once upon a time, when Brahmadatta was reigning in Benares the Bodhisatta came to life as an ox, named Big Red, on the landowner's estate in a certain hamlet. And he had a younger brother who was known as Little Red. There were only these two brothers to do all the draught-work of the family. Also, the landowner had an only daughter, whose hand was asked in marriage for his son by a gentleman of the town. And the parents of the giri, with a view to furnishing dainty fare for the wedding guests, began to fatten up a pig named Munika.

Observing this, Little Red said to his brother, "All the loads that have to be drawn for this household are drawn by you and me, my brother; but all they give us for our pains is sorry grass and straw to eat. Yet here is the pig being victualled on rice! What can be the reason why he should be treated to such fare?"

Said his brother, "My dear Little Red, envy him not; for the pig eats the food of death. It is but to furnish a relish for the guests at their daughter's wedding, that the family are feeding up the pig. Wait but a little time and the guests will be coming. Then will you see that pig lugged out of his quaiters by the legs, killed, and in process of conversion into curry. And so saying, he repeated this stanza:

Then envy not poor Munika; 'tis death
He eats. Contented munch your frugal chaff,
—The pledge and guarantee of length of days.

Not long afterwards the guests did arrive; and Munika was killed and cooked into all manner of dishes. Said the Bodhisatta to Little Red, "Did you see Munika, dear brother?" "I have indeed seen, brother, the outcome of Munika's feasting. Better a hundred, nay a thousand, times than such food is ours, though it be but grass, straw, and chaff: -for our fare harms us not, and is a pledge that our lives will not be cut short."

THE PEACOCK'S WOOING

Once upon a time, in the first cycle of world's history, the quadrupeds chose the Lion as their king, the fishes the monsterfish Ānanda, and the birds the Golden Mallard. Now the King Golden Mallard had a lovely young daughter, and her royal father granted her any boon she might ask. The boon she asked for was to be allowed to choose a husband for herself; and the king in fulfilment of his promise mustered all the birds together in the country of the Himalayas. All manner of birds came, mallards, peacocks and all other birds; and they flocked together on a great plateau of bare rock. Then the king sent for his daughter and bade her go and choose a husband after her own heart. As she reviewed the crowd of birds, her eye lighted on the peacock with his neck of jewelled sheen and tail of varied hue; and she chose him, saying, "Let this be my husband." Then the assembly of the birds went up to the peacock and said, "Friend peacock, this princess, in choosing her husband from among all these birds, has fixed her choice on you."

Carried away by his extreme joy, the peacock exclaimed, "Until this day you have never seen how active I am"; and in defiance of all decency in the midst of the assembly he spread his wings and began to dance; and in dancing he exposed himself.

Filled with shame, King Golden Mallard said, "This fellow has neither modesty within his heart nor decency in his outward behaviour; I certainly will not give my daughter to one so shameless." And there in the midst of all that assembly of the birds, he repeated this stanza:
A pleasing note is yours, a lovely back,
A neck in hue like lapis lazuli;
A fathom's length your outstretched feathers reach.
Withal, your dancing loses you my child.

Right in the face of the whole gathering King Royal Mallard gave his daughter to a young mallard, a nephew of his. Covered with shame at the loss of the mallard princess, the peacock rose straight up from the place and fled away. And King Golden Mallard too went back to his dwelling-place.

THE FOWLER AND THE QUAILS

Once upon a time when Brahmadatta was king of Benares, the Bodhisatta was born a quail, and lived in the forest at the head of many thousands of quails. In those days a fowler who caught quails came to that place; and he used to imitate the note of a quail till he saw that the birds had been drawn together, when he flung his net over them, and whipped the sides of the net together, so as to get them all huddled up in a heap. Then he crammed them into his basket, and going home sold his prey for a living.

Now one day the Bodhisatta said to those quails, "This fowler is making havoc among our kinsfolk. I have a device whereby he will be unable to catch us. Henceforth, the very moment he throws the net over you, let each one put his head through a mesh and then all of you together must fly away with the net to such place as you please, and there let it down on a thorn-brake; this done, we will all escape from our several meshes." "Very good," said they all in ready agreement.

On the morrow, when the net was cast over them, they did just as the Bodhisatta had told them-they lifted up the net, and let it down on a thorn-brake, escaping themselves from underneath. While the fowler was still disentangling his net, evening came on; and he went away empty-handed. On the morrow and following days the quails played the same trick. So that it became the regular thing for the fowler to be engaged till sunset disentangling his net, and then to betake himself home empty-handed. Accordingly his wife grew angry and said, "Day by day you return empty-handed; I suppose you've got a second establishment to keep up elsewhere."

"No, my dear," said the fowler; "I've no second establishment to keep up. The fact is those quails have come to

work together now. The moment my net is over them, off they
fly with it and escape, leaving it on a thorn-brake. Still, they
won't live in unity always. Don't you bother yourself; as soon
as they start bickering among themselves, I shall bag the lot,
and that will bring a smile to your face to see." And so saying
he repeated this stanza to his wife:

While concord reigns, the birds bear off the net.
When quarrels rise, they'll fall a prey to me.

Not long after this, one of the quails, in alighting on their
feeding-ground, trod by accident on another's head. "Who trod
on my head ?" angrily cried this latter. "I did; but I didn't mean
to. Don't be angry," said the first quail. But notwithstanding
this answer, the other remained as angry as before. Continuing
to answer one another, they began to bandy taunts, saying, "I
suppose it is you single-handed who lift up the net." As they
wrangled thus with one another, the Bodhisatta thought to
himself, "There's no safety with one who is quarrelsome. The
time has come when they will no longer lift up the net, and
thereby they will come to great destruction. The fowler will get
his opportunity. I can stay here no longer." And thereupon he
with his following went elsewhere.

Sure enough the fowler came back again a few days later,
and first collecting them together by imitating the note of a
quail, flung his net over them. Then said one quail, "They say
when you were at work lifting the net, the hair of your head fell
off. Now's your time; lift away." The other rejoined, "When you
were lifting the net, they say both your wings moulted. Now's
your time; lift away."

But whilst they were each inviting the other to lift the net,
the fowler himself lifted the net for them and crammed them in
a heap into his basket and bore them off home, so that his
wife's face was wreathed with smiles.

THE OLDEST OF THE ANIMALS

Once upon a time, near by a great banyan-tree on the

slopes of the Himalayas, there dwelt three friends, — a partridge, a monkey, and an elephant. And they came to lack respect and subordination one to another, and had no ordering of their common life. And the thought came to them that it was not seemly for them to live in this way, and that they ought to find out which of their number was the senior and to honour him.

As they were engaged thinking which was the oldest, one day an idea struck them. Said the partridge and the monkey to the elephant as they all three sat together at the foot of that banyan-tree, "Friend elephant, how big was this banyan when you remember it first?" Said the elephant, "When I was a baby, this banyan was a mere bush, over which I used to walk; and as I stood-astride of it, its topmost branches used just to reach up to my belly. I've known the tree since it was a mere bush."

Next the monkey was asked the same question by the other two; and he replied, "My friends, when I was a youngling, I had only to stretch out my neck as I sat on the ground, and I could eat the topmost sprouts of this banyan. So I've known this banyan since it was very tiny."

Then the partridge was asked the same question by the two others; and he said, "Friends, of old there was a great banyan-tree at such and such a spot; I ate its seeds, and voided them here; that was the origin of this tree. Therefore, I have knowledge of this tree from before it was born, and am older than the pair of you."

Hereupon the monkey and the elephant said to the sage partridge, "Friend, you are the oldest. Henceforth you shall have from us acts of honour and veneration, marks of obeisance and homage, respect of word and deed, salutation, and all due homage; and we will follow your counsels. You for your part henceforth will please impart such counsel as we need."

Thenceforth the partridge gave them counsel, and established them in the Commandments, which he also undertook himself to keep. Being thus established in the Commandments, and becoming respectful and subordinate among themselves, with proper ordering of their common life, these three made themselves sure of re-birth in heaven at this life's close.

THE CRANE AND THE CRAB

Once on a time the Bodhisatta came to life in a certain forest-haunt as the divinity of a tree which stood near a certain lotus-pond. In those days the water used every summer to fall very low in a certain pond, not very big,—which was plentifully stocked with fish. Catching sight of these fish, a certain crane said to himself, "I must find a way to cajole and eat these fish." So he went and sat down in deep thought by the side of the water.

Now when the fishes caught sight of him, they said, "Of what are you thinking, my lord, as you sit there?" "I am thinking about you," was the reply. "And what is your lordship thinking about us?" 'The water in this pool being low, food scarce, and the heat intense,—I was wondering to myself, as I sat here, what in the world you fishes would do." "And what are we to do, my lord?" "Well, if you'll take my advice, I will take you up one by one in my beak, and carry you all off to a fine large pool covered with the five varieties of lotuses, and there put you down." "My lord," said they, "no crane ever took the slightest thought for fishes since the world began. Your desire is to eat us one by one." "No; I will not eat you while you trust me," said the crane. "If you don't take my word that there is such a pond, send one of your number to go with me and see for himself." Believing the crane, the fish presented to him a great big fish (blind of one eye, by. the way), who they thought would be a match for the crane whether afloat or ashore; and they said, "Here's the one to go with you."

The crane took the fish off and put him in the pool, and after showing him the whole extent of it, brought him back again and put him in along with the other fish in his old pond.

And he held forth to them on the charms of the new pool.

After hearing this report, they grew eager to go there, and said to the crane, 'Very good, my lord; please take us across."

First of all, the crane took that big one-eyed fish again and carried him off to the edge of the pool, so that he could see the water, but actually alighted in a Varana-tree which grew on the bank. Dashing the fish down in a fork of the tree, he pecked it to death, — after which he picked him clean and let the bones fall at the foot of the tree. Then back he went and said, "I've thrown him in; who's the next?" And so he took the fish one by one, and ate them all, till at last when he came back, he could not find another left. But there was still a crab remaining in the pond; so the crane, who wanted to eat him up too, said, "Mister crab, I've taken all those fishes away and turned them into a fine large pool covered all over with lotuses. Come along; I'll take you too." "How will you carry me across?" said the crab. "Why, in my beak, to be sure," said the crane. "Ah, but you might drop me like that," said the crab; "I won't go with you." "Don't be frightened; I'll keep tight hold of you all the way." Thought the crab to himself, "He hasn't put the fish in the pool. But, if he would really put me in, that would be capital. If he does *not*, — why, I'll nip his head off and kill him." So he spoke thus to the crane, "You'd never be able to hold me tight enough, friend crane; whereas we crabs have got an astonishingly tight grip. If I might take hold of your neck with my claws, I could hold it tight and then would go along with you."

Not suspecting that the crab wanted to trick him, the crane gave his assent. With his claws the crab griped hold of the crane's neck as with the pincers of a smith, and said, "Now you can start." The crane took him and showed him the pool first, and then started off for the tree.

"The pool lies this way, uncle," said the crab; "but you're taking me the other way." "Very much your dear uncle am I!" said the crane; "and very much my nephew are you!' I suppose you thought me your slave to lift you up and carry you about!

Just cast your eye on that heap of bones at the foot of the tree; as I ate up all those fishes, so I will eat you too." Said the crab, "It was through their own folly that I fishes were eaten by you: but I shan't give you the chance of eating me No; what I shall do, is to kill *you*. For you, fool that you were did not see that I was tricking you. If we die. we will both die together; I'll chop your head clean off." And so saying, he gripped the crane's weazand with his claws, as with pincers With his mouth wide open, and tears streaming from his eyes, the crane, trembling for his life, said, "Lord, indeed I will not eat you! Spare my life!

"Well, then, just step down to the pool and put me in," said, the crab. Then the crane turned back and stepped down as directed to the pool, and placed the crab on the mud, at the water-edge. But the crab, before entering the water, nipped off the crane's head as deftly as if he were cutting a lotus stalk with a knife.

The divinity who dwelt in the tree, marking this wonderful thing, made the whole forest ring with applause repeating this stanza in sweet tones:
Guile profits not your very guileful folk.
Mark what the guileful crane got from the crab!

THE HAUGHTY SLAVE

Once upon a time when Brahmadatta was reigning in Benares, the Bodhisatta came to life again as a landowner. Another landowner, a friend of his, was an old man himself, but had a young wife who had borne him a son and heir. Said the old man to himself, "As soon as I am dead, this giri, being so young as she is, will marry heaven knows whom. and spend all my money, instead of handing it over to my son. Wouldn't it be my best course to bury my money safely in the ground?"

So, in the company of a household slave of his named Nanda, he went to the forest and buried his riches at a certain spot, saying to the slave, "My good Nanda, reveal this treasure to my son after I am gone, and don't let the wood be sold."

After giving this injunction to his slave, the old man died. In due course the son grew up, and his mother said to him, "My son, your father, in the company of Nanda, buried his money. Get it back and look after the property of the family." So one day he said to Nanda, "Uncle, is there any trasure which my father buried?" "Yes, my lord." 'Where is it buried?" "In the forest, my lord." "Well, then, let us go there." And he took a spade and a basket, and going to the scene, said to Nanda. 'Well uncle, where's the money?" But by the time Nanda had got up to the treasure and was standing right over it, he was so puffed up by the money that he abused his master, saying, "You servant of a slave-wench's son! how should you have any money here?"

The young gentleman, pretending not to have heard this insolence, simply said, "Let us be going then," and took the slave back home with him. Two or three days later, he returned to the place; but again Nanda abused him, as before. Without any abusive rejoinder, the young gentleman came back and turned the matter over in his mind. Thought he to himself, "At starting, this slave always means to reveal where the money is; but no sooner does he get there, than he falls to abusing me. The reason of this I do not see; but I could find out, if I were to ask my father's old friend, the landowner." So he went to the Bodhisatta, and laying the whole business before him, asked his friend what was the real reason of such behaviour.

Said the Bodhisatta, "The spot at which Nanda stands to abuse you my friend, is the place where your father's money is buried. Therefore, as soon as he starts abusing you again, say to him, Whom are you talking to, you slave?' Pull him from his perch, take the spade, dig down, remove your family treasure, and make the slave carry it home for you." And so saying, he repeated this stanza:

Methinks the gold and jewels buried lie
Where Nanda, low-born slave, so loudly bawls!

Taking a respectful leave of the Bodhisatta, the young gentleman went home, and taking Nanda went to the spot where the money was buried. Faithfully following the advice he had received, he brought the money away and looked after the family property. He remained steadfast in the bodhisatta's counsels, and after a life spent in charity and other good works he passed away to fare according to his deserts.

THE PIGEON AND THE CROW

Once upon a time when Brahmadatta was reigning in Benares, the Bodhisatta was born a pigeon. Now the Benares folk of those days, as an act of goodness, used to hang up straw-baskets in diverse places for the shelter and comfort of the birds; and the cook of the gildmaster of Benares hung up one of these baskets in his kitchen. In the basket the Bodhisatta took up his abode, sallying out at daybreak in quest of food, and returning home in the evening; and so he lived his life.

But one day a crow, flying over the kitchen, snuffed up the goodly savour from the salt and fresh fish and meat there, and was filled with longing to taste it. Casting about how to have his will, he perched hard by and at evening saw the Bodhisatta come home and go into the kitchen. "Ah!" thought he, "I can manage it through the pigeon."

So back he came next day at dawn, and, when the Bodhisatta sallied out in quest of food, kept following him about from place to place like his shadow. So the Bodhisatta said, "Why do you keep with me, friend?"

"My lord," answered the crow, "your demeanour has won my admiration: and henceforth it is my wish to follow you." "But your kind of food and mine, friend, are not the same," said the Bodhisatta; "My lord," said the crow, "when you are seeking your food, I will feed too, by your side." "So be it, then," said the Bodhisatta; "only you must be earnest." And with this admonition to the crow, the Bodhisatta ranged about pecking up grass-seeds; whilst the other went about turning over cowdung and picking out the insects underneath till he had got his fill. Then back he came to the Bodhisatta and remarked,

"My lord, you give too much time to eating; excess therein should be shunned."

And when the Bodhisatta had fed and reached home again at evening, in flew the crow with him into the kitchen.

"Why, our bird has brought another home with him;" exclaimed the cook, and hung up a second basket for the crow. And from that time onward the two birds dwelt together in the kitchen.

Now one day the gildmaster had in a store of fish which the cook hung up about the kitchen. Filled with greedy longing at the sight, the crow made up his mind to stay at home next day and treat himself to this excellent fare.

So all night long he lay groaning away; and next day, when the Bodhisatta was starting in search of food, cried, "Come along, friend crow," the crow replied, "Go without me, my lord; for I have a pain in my stomach." "Friend," answered the Bodhisatta, "I never heard of crows having pains in their stomachs before. True, crows feel faint in each of the three night-watches; but if they eat a lamp-wick, their hunger is appeased for the moment. You must be hankering after the fish in the kitchen here. Come now, man's food will not agree with you. Do not give way like this, but come and seek your food with me." "Indeed, I am not able, my lord," said the crow. "Well, your own conduct will show," said the Bodhisatta. "Only fall not a prey to greed, but stand steadfast." And with this exhortation, away he flew to find his daily food.

The cook took several kinds of fish, and dressed some one way, some another. Then lifting the lids off his saucepans a little to let the steam out, he put a colander on the top of one and went outside the door, where he stood wiping the sweat from his brow. Just at that moment out popped the crow's head from the basket. A glance told him that the cook was away, and "Now or never," thought he, "is my time. The only question is shall I choose minced meat or a big lump?" Arguing that it takes a long time to make a full meal of minced meat, he resolved to take a large piece of fish and alighted on the colander. "Click" went the colander.

"What can that be?" said the cook, running in on hearing the noise. Seeing the crow, he cried, "Oh, there's that rascally crow wanting to eat my master's dinner. I have to work for my master, not for that rascal! What's he to me, I should like to know?" So, first shutting the door, he caught the crow and plucked every feather off his body. Then, he pounded up ginger with salt and cumin, and mixed in sour butter-milk—finally sousing the crow in the pickle and flinging him back into his basket. And there the crow lay groaning, overcome by the agony of his pain.

At evening the Bodhisatta came back, and saw the wretched plight of the crow. "Ah! greedy crow," he exclaimed, "you would not heed my words, and now your own greed has worked you woe." So saying, he repeated this stanza:
The headstrong man who, when exhorted, pays
No heed to friends who kindly counsel give,
Shall surely perish, like the greedy crow,
Who laughed to scorn the pigeon's warning words.

Then, exclaiming "I too can no longer dwell here," the Bodhisatta flew away. But the crow died there and then, and the cook flung him, basket and all, on the dust-heap.

THE FOOLISH FRIEND

Once upon a time when Brahmadatta was reigning in Benares, the Bodhisatta gained his livelihood as a trader. In those days in a border-village in Kāsi there dwelt a number of carpenters. And it chanced that one of them, a bald grey-haired man, was planning away at some wood, with his head glistening like a copper bowl, when a mosquito settled on his scalp and stung him with its dart-like sting.

Said the carpenter to his son, who was seated near by,—

"My boy, there's a mosquito stinging me on the head; do drive it away." "Hold still then, father," said the son; "one blow will settle it."

(At that very time the Bodhisatta had reached that village in the way of trade, and was sitting in the carpenter's shop.)

"Rid me of it," said the father. "Ail right father," answered the son, who was behind the old man's back, and, raising a sharp axe on high with intent to kill only the mosquito, he cleft his father's head in twain. So the old man fell dead on the spot.

Thought the Bodhisatta, who had been an eye-witness of the whole scene, - "Better than such a friend is an enemy with sense, whom fear of men's vengeance will deter from killing a man." And he recited these lines:
Sense-lacking friends are worse than foes with sense:
Witness the son that sought the gnat to slay,
But cleft, poor fool, his father's skull in twain.

So saying, the Bodhisatta rose up and departed, passing away in after days to fare according to his deserts. And as for the carpenter his body was buried by his kinsfolk.

THE STUPID MONKEYS

Once upon a time when Brahmadatta was king of Benares, a festival was proclaimed in the city; and at the first summoning notes of the festal drum out poured the townsfolk to keep holiday.

Now in those days, a tribe of monkeys was living in the king's pleasaunce; and the king's gardener thought to himself, "They're holiday-making up in the city. I'll get the monkeys to do the watering for me, and be off to enjoy myself with the rest." So saying, he went to the king of the monkeys, and, first dwelling on the benefits his majesty and his subjects enjoyed from residence in the pleasaunce in the way of flowers and fruit and young shoots to eat, ended by saying, "To-day there's holiday-making up in the city, and I'm off to enjoy myself. Couldn't you water the young trees while I'm away?"

"Oh! yes," said the monkey.

"Only mind you do," said the gardener; and off he went, giving the monkeys the water-skins and wooden watering-pots to do the work with.

Then the monkeys took the water-skins and watering-pots, and fell to watering the young trees. "But we must mind not to waste the water," observed their king; "as you water, first pull each young tree up and look at the size of its roots. Then give plenty of water to those whose roots strike deep, but only a little to those with tiny roots. When this water is all gone, we shall be hard put to it to get more."

"To be sure," said the other monkeys, and did as he bade them.

At this juncture a certain wise man, seeing the monkeys thus engaged, asked them why they pulled up tree after tree and watered them according to the size of their roots.

"Because such are our king's commands," answered the monkeys.

Their reply moved the wise man to reflect how, with every desire to do good, the ignorant and foolish only succeed in doing harm. And he recited this stanza:
'Tis knowledge crowns endeavour with success.
For fools are thwarted by their foolishness,
—Witness the ape that killed the garden trees.

With this rebuke to the king of the monkeys, the wise man departed with his followers from the pleasaunce.

THE ROBBERS AND THE TREASURE

Once upon a time when Brahmadatta was reigning in Benares, there was a brahmin in a village who knew the charm called Vedabbna. Now this charm, so they say, was precious beyond all price. For, if at a certain conjunction of the planets the charm was repeated and the gaze bent upwards to the skies, straightway from the heavens there rained the Seven Things of Price, gold, silver, pearl, coral, catseye, ruby and diamond.

In those days the Bodhisatta was a pupil of this brahmin; and one day his master left the village on some business or other, and came with the Bodhisatta to the country of Ceti.

In a forest by the way dwelt five hundred robbers—known as "the Despatchers—"who made the way impassable. And these caught the Bodhisatta and the Vedabbha-brahmin. (Why, you ask, were they called the Despatchers?—Well, the story goes that of every two prisoners they made they used to despatch one to fetch the ransom; and that's why they were called the Despatchers. If they captured a father and son, they told the father to go for the ransom to free his son. if they caught a mother and her daughter, they sent the mother for the money; if they caught two brothers, they let the elder go; and so too, if they caught a teacher and his pupil, it was the pupil they set free. In this case, therefore, they kept the Vedabbha-brahmin, and sent the Bodhisatta for the ransom.) And the Bodhisatta said with a bow to his master, "In a day or two I shall surely come back; have no fear; only fail not to do as I shall say. To-day will come to pass the conjunction of the planets which brings about the rain of the Things of Price. Take heed lest, yielding to this mishap, you repeat the charm and call down the precious shower. For, if you do, calamity will certainly befall both you and this band of robbers." With this warning to his master, the Bodhisatta went his way in quest of the ransom.

At sunset the robbers bound the brahmin and laid him by the heels. Just at this moment the full moon rose over the eastern horizon, and the brahmin, studying the heavens, knew that the great conjunction was taking place. "Why." thought he, "should I suffer this misery? By repeating the charm I will call down the precious rain, pay the robbers the ransom, and go free." So he called out to the robbers. "Friends, why do you take me a prisoner?" "To get a ransom reverend sir," said they. 'Well, if that is all you want," said the brahmin, "make haste and untie me; have my head bathed, and new clothes put on me; and let me be perfumed and decked with flowers. Then leave me to myself." The robbers did as he bade them. And the brahmin, marking the conjunction of the planets, repeated his charm with eyes uplifted to the heavens. Forthwith the Things of Price poured down from the skies! The robbers picked them all up, wrapping their booty into bundles with their cloaks. Then with their brethren they marched away; and the brahmin followed in the rear. But, as luck would have it, the party was captured by a second band of five hundred robbbers! "Why do you seize us?" said the first to the second band. "For booty," was the answer. "If booty is what you want, seize on that brahmin, who by simply gazing up at the skies brought down riches as rain. It was he who gave us all that we have got." So the second band of robbers let the first band go, and seized on the brahmin, crying, "Give us riches too!" "It would give me great pleasure," said the brahmin; "but it will be a year before the requisite conjunction of the planets takes place again. If you will only be so good as to wait till then, I will invoke the precious shower for you."

"Rascally brahmin!" cried the angry robbers, "you made the other band rich off-hand, but want us to wait a whole year!" And they cut him in two with a sharp sword, and flung his body in the middle of the road. Then hurrying after the first band of robbers, they killed every man of them too in hand-to-hand fight, and seized the booty. Next, they divided into two companies and fought among themselves, company against company, till two hundred and fifty men were slain. And so they went on killing one another, till only two were left alive. Thus did those thousand men come to destruction.

Now, when the two survivors had managed to carry off the treasure they hid it in the jungle near a village; and one of them sat there, sword in hand, to guard it, whilst the other went into the village to get rice and have it cooked for supper. But true is the saying:

And greed is verily the root of ruin.

He who stopped by the treasure thought, "When my mate comes back, he'll want half of this. Suppose I kill him the moment he gets back." So he drew his sword and sat waiting for his comrade's return.

Meanwhile, the other had equally reflected that the booty had to be halved, and thought to himself, "Suppose I poison the rice, and give it him to eat and so kill him, and have the whole of the treasure to myself." Accordingly, when the rice was boiled, he first ate his own share, and then put poison in the rest, which he carried back with him to the jungle. But scarce had he set it down, when the other robber cut him in two with his sword, and hid the body away in a secluded spot. Then he ate the poisoned rice, and died then and there. Thus by reason of the treasure, not only the brahmin but all the robbers came to destruction.

Howbeit, after a day or two the Bodhisatta came back with the ransom. Not finding his master where he had left him, but seeing treasure strewn all round about, his heart misgave him that, in spite of his advice, his master must have called down a shower of treasure from the skies, and that all must have perished in consequence; and he proceeded along the road. On his way he came to where his master's body lay cloven in twain upon the way. "Alas!" he cried, "he is dead through not heeding my warning." Then with gathered sticks he made a pyre and burnt his master's body, making an offering of wild flowers. Further along the road, he came upon the five hundred "Despatchers," and further still upon the two hundred and fifty, and so on by degrees until at last he came to where lay only two corpses. Marking how of the thousand all but two had perished, and feeling sure that there must be two survivors, and that these could not refrain from strife, he pressed on to see where they had gone. So on he went till he found the path by which with the treasure they had turned into the jungle: and there he found the heap of bundles of treasure, and one robber lying dead with his rice-bowl overturned at his side. Realising the whole story at a glance, the Bodhisatta set himself to search for the missing man, and at last found his body in the secret spot where it had been flung. "And thus," mused the Bodhisatta, "through not following my counsel my master in his self-will has been the means of destroying not himself only but a thousand others also. Truly they that seek their own gain by mistaken and misguided means shall reap ruin, even as my master." And he repeated this stanza:

Misguided effort leads to loss, not gain;
Thieves killed Vedabbha and themselves were slain.

Thus spake the Bodhisatta, and went on to say,—"And even as my master's misguided and misplaced effort in causing the rain of treasure to fall from heaven wrought both his own death and the destruction of others with him, even so shall every other man who by mistaken means seeks to compass his own advantage utterly perish and involve others in his destruction." With these words did the Bodhisatta make the forest ring; and in this stanza did he preach the Truth, whilst the tree divinities shouted applause. The treasure he contrived to carry off to his own home, where he lived out his term of life in the exercise of ailmsgiving and other good works. And when his life closed he departed to the heaven he had won.

GREAT KING GOODNESS

Once upon a time when Brahmadatta was reigning in Benares, the Bodhisatta came to life again as the child of the queen; and on his name-day they gave him the name of Prince Goodness (Silava). At the age of sixteen his education was complete; and later he came at his father's death to be king, and ruled his people righteously under the title of the great King Goodness. At each of the four city-gates he built an almonry, another in the heart of the city, and yet another at his own palace-gates—six in all; and at each he distributed alms to poor travellers and the needy. He kept the Commandments and observed the fast-days: he- abounded in patience, loving-kindness, and mercy; and in righteousness he ruled the land, cherishing all creatures alike with the fond love of a father for his baby boy.

Now one of the king's ministers had dealt treacherously in the king's harem, this became matter of common talk. The ministers reported it to the king. Examining into the matter himself, the king found the minister's guilt to be clear. So he sent for the culprit, and said, "0 blinded by folly! you have sinned, and are not worthy to dwell in my kingdom; your substance and your wife and family, and go hence." Driven thus from the realm, that minister left the Kāsi country, and entering the service of the king of Kosala, gradually rose to be that monarch's confidential adviser. One day he said to the king of Kosala, "Sire, the kingdom of Benares is like a goodly honeycomb untainted by flies; its king is feebleness itself; and a trifling force would suffice to conquer the whole country."

Hereon, the king of Kosala reflected that the kingdom of Benares was large, and considering this in connexion with the advice that a trifling force could conquer it, he grew suspicious that his adviser was a hireling suborned to him into a trap. "Traitor," he cried, "you are paid to say this!"

"Indeed I am not," answered the other; "I do but speak the truth. If you doubt me, send men to massacre a village over his border, and see whether when they are caught brought before him, the king does not let them off scot-free and even load them with gifts."

"He shows a very bold front in making his assertion. thought the king; "I will test his counsel without delay." And accordingly he sent some of his creatures to harry a village across the Benares border. The ruffians were captured and brought before the king of Benares, who asked them saying, "My children, why have you killed my villagers?"

"Because we could not make a living," said they.

"Then why did you not come to me?" said the king. "See that you do not do the like again."

And he gave them presents and sent them away. Back they went and told this to the king of Kosala. But this evidence was not enough to nerve him to the expedition; and a second band was sent to massacre another village, this time in the heart of the kingdom. These too were likewise sent away with presents by the king of Benares. But even this evidence was not deemed strong enough; and a third party was sent to plunder the very streets of Benares. And these, like their forerunners, were sent away with presents! Satisfied at last that the king of Benares was an entirely good king, the king of Kosala resolved to seize on his kingdom, and set out against him with troops and elephants.

Now in these days the king of Benares had a thousand gallant warriors, who would face the charge even of a rut elephant,—whom the launched thunderbolt of Indra could not terrify, - a matchless band of invincible heroes ready at the king's command to reduce all India to his sway! These, hearing the king of Kosala was coming to take Benares, came to their sovereign with the news, and prayed that they might be despatched against the invader. "We will defeat and capture him, sire," said they, "before he can set foot over the border."

"Not so, my children," said the king. "None shall suffer because of me. Let those who covet kingdoms seize mine, if they will." And he refused to allow them to march against the invader.

Then the king of Kosala crossed the border and came to the middle-country; and again the ministers went to the king with renewed entreaty. But still the king refused. And now the king of kosala appeared outside the city, and sent a message to the king bidding him either yield up the kingdom or give battle. "I fight not," was the message of the king of Benares in reply; "let him seize my kingdom."

Yet a third time the king's ministers came to him and besought him not to allow the king of Kosala to enter, but to permit them to overthrow and capture him before the city. Still refusing, the king bade the city-gates be opened, and seated himself in state aloft upon his royal throne with his thousand ministers round him.

Entering the city and finding none to bar his way, the king of Kosala passed with his army to the royal palace. The doors stood open wide; and there on his gorgeous throne with his thousand ministers around him sat the great King Goodness in state. "Seize them all," cried the king of Kosala; "tie their hands tightly behind their backs, and away with them to the cemetery! There dig holes and bury them alive up to the neck, so that they cannot move hand or foot. The jackals will come at night and give them sepulchre!"

At the bidding of the ruffianly king, his followers bound the king of Benares and his ministers, and hauled them off. But even in this hour not so much as an angry thought did the great King Goodness harbour against the ruffians; and not a man among his ministers, even when they were being marched off in bonds, could disobey the king,—so perfect is said to have been the discipline among his followers.

So King Goodness and his ministers were led off and buried up to the neck in pits in the cemetery, the king in the middle and the others on either side of him. The ground was trampled in upon them, and there they were left. Still meek and free from anger against his oppressor, King Goodness exhorted his companions, saying, "Let your hearts be filled with naught but love and charity, my children."

Now at midnight the jackals came trooping to the banquet of human flesh; and at sight of the beasts the king and his companions raised a mighty shout all together, frightening the jackals away. Halting, the pack looked back, and seeing no one pursuing, again came forward. A second shout drove them away again, but only to return as before. But the third time, seeing that not a man amongst them all pursued, the jackals thought to themselves, "These must be men who are doomed to death." They came on boldly; even when the shout was again being raised, they did not turn tail. On they came, each singling out his prey,—the chief jackal making for the king, and the other jackals for his companions. Fertile in resource, the king marked the beast's approach, and raising his throat as if to receive the bite, fastened his teeth in the jackal's throat with a grip like a vice! Unable to free its throat from the mighty grip of the king's jaws, and fearing death, the jackal raised a great howl. At his cry of distress the pack conceived that their leader must have been caught by a man. With no heart left to approach their own destined prey, away they all scampered for their lives.

Seeking to free itself from the king's teeth, the trapped jackal plunged madly to and fro, and thereby loosened the earth above the king. Hereupon the latter, letting the jackal go, put forth his mighty strength, and by plunging from side to side got his hands free! Then, clutching the brink of the pit, he drew himself up, and came forth like a cloud scudding before the wind. Bidding his companions be of good cheer. he now set to work to loosen the earth round them and to get them out, till with all his ministers he stood free once more in the cemetery.

Now it chanced that a corpse had been exposed in part of the cemetery, which lay between the respective domains of two goblins; and the goblins were disputing over the division of the spoil.

"We can't divide it ourselves," said they, "but this King Goodness is righteous; he will divide it for us. Let us go to him." So they dragged the corpse by the foot to the king, and said, "Sire, divide this man and give us each our share." "Certainly I will, my friends," said the king. "But, as I am dirty, I must bathe first."

Straightway, by their magic power, the goblins brought to

the king the scented water prepared for the usurper's bath.
And when the king had bathed, they brought him the robes
which had been laid out for the usurper to wear. When he had
put these on. they brought his majesty a box containing the
four kinds of scent. When he had perfumed himself, they brought
flowers of diverse kinds laid out upon jewelled fans, in a casket
of gold. When he had decked himself with the flowers, the
goblins asked whether they could be of any further service.
And the king gave them to understand that he was hungry. So
away went the goblins, and returned with rice flavoured with
all the choicest flavours, which had been prepared for the
usurper's table. And the king, now bathed and scented, dressed
and arrayed, ate of the dainty fare. Thereupon the goblins
brought the usurper's perfumed water for him to drink, in the
usurper's own golden bowl, not forgetting to bring the golden
cup too. When the king had drunk and had washed his mouth
and was washing his hands, they brought him fragrant betel to
chew, and asked whether his majesty had any further
commands, "Fetch me," said he, "by your magic power the
sword of state which lies by the usurper's pillow." And
straightway the sword brought to the king. Then the king took
the corpse, and setting it upright, cut it in two down the chin,
giving one-half to each goblin. This done, the king washed the
blade, girded it on his side.

Having eaten their fill, the goblins were glad of heart, and
in their gratitude asked the king what more they could do for
him. "Set me by your magic power," said he, "in the usurper's
chamber, and set each of my ministers back in his own house."
"Certainly, sire," said the goblins; and forthwith it was done.
Now in that hour the usurper was lying asleep on the royal bed
in his chamber of state. And as he slept in all tranquility, the
good king struck him with the flat of the sword upon the belly.
Waking up in a fright, the usurper saw by the lamp-light that
it was the great King Goodness. Summoning up all his courage,
he rose from his couch and said: "Sire, it is night; a guard is set;
the doors are barred; and none may enter. How then came you
to my bedside, sword in hand and clad in robes of splendour?"
Then the king told him in detail all the story of his escape.

Then the usurper's heart was moved within him, and he cried. "0 king, I, though blessed with human nature, knew not your goodness; but knowledge thereof was given to the fierce and cruel goblins, whose food is flesh and blood. Henceforth, I sire, will not plot against such signal virtue as you possess." So saying, he swore an oath of friendship upon his sword and begged the kings forgiveness. And he made the king lie down upon the bed of state, while he stretched himself upon a little couch.

On the morrow at daybreak, when the sun had risen, his-whole host of every rank and degree was mustered by beat of drum at the usurper's command; in their presence he extolled King Goodness, as if raising the full-moon on high in the heavens: and right before them all, he again asked the king's forgiveness and gave him back his kingdom, saying, "Henceforth, let it be my charge to deal with rebels; rule thou thy kingdom, with me to keep watch and ward." And so saying, he passed sentence on the slanderous traitor, and with his troops and elephants went back to his own kingdom.

Seated in majesty and splendour beneath a white umbrella of sovereignty upon a throne of gold with legs *as* of a gazelle, the great King Goodness contemplated his own glory and thought thus within himself: "Had I not persevered, I should not be in the enjoyment of this magnificence, nor would my thousand ministers be still numbered among the living. It was by perseverance that I recovered the royal state I had lost, and saved the lives of my thousand ministers. Verily, we should strive on unremittingly with dauntless hearts, seeing that the fruit of perseverance is so excellent." And therewithal the king broke into this heartfelt utterance:
Toil on my brother, still in hope stand fast;
Nor let thy courage flag and tire.
Myself I see. who, all my woes o'erpast,
Am master of my heart's desire.

Thus spoke the Bodhisatta in the fulness of his heart, declaring how sure it is that the earnest effort of the good will

come to maturity. After a life spent in right-doing he passed
away to fare thereafter according to his deserts.

PRINCE FIVE-WEAPONS

Once upon a time when Brahmadatta was reigning in
Benares, it was as his queen's child that the Bodhisatta came
to life once more. On the day when he was to be named, the
parents enquired as to their child's destiny from eight hundred
brahmins, to whom they gave their hearts' desire in all pleasures
of sense. Marking the promise which he showed of a glorious
destiny, these clever soothsaying brahmins foretold that, coming
to the throne at the king's death, the child should be a mighty
king endowed with every virtue; famed and renowned for
his exploits with five weapons, he should stand peerless in
all Jambudipa. And because of this prophecy of the brahmins,
the parents named their son Prince Five-Weapons.

Now, when the prince was come to years of discretion,
and was sixteen years old, the king bade him go away and
study.

'With whom, sire, am I to study?" asked the prince.

"With the world-famed teacher in the town of Takkasilā in
the Gandharā country. Here is his fee," said the king, handing
his son a thousand pieces.

So the prince went to Takkasilā and was taught there.
When he was leaving, his master gave him a set of five weapons,
armed with which, after bidding adieu to his old master, the
prince set out from Takkasilā for Benares.

On his way he came to a forest haunted by a goblin named
Hairy-grip; and, at the entrance to the forest, men who met him
tried to stop him, saying: "Young student, do not go through
that forest; it is the haunt of the goblin Hairy-grip, and he kills
every one he meets." But, bold as a lion, the self-reliant
Bodhisatta pressed on, till in the heart of the forest he came on

the goblin. The monster made himself appear in stature as tall as a palm-tree, with a head as big as an arbour and huge eyes like bowls, with two tusks like turnips and the beak of a hawk; his belly was blotched with purple; and the palms of his hands and the soles of his feet were blue-black! "Whither away?" cried the monster. "Halt! you are my prey." "Goblin," answered the Bodhisatta, "I knew what I was doing when entering this forest. You will be ill-advised to come near me. For with a poisoned arrow I will slay you where you stand." And with this defiance, he fitted to his bow an arrow dipped in deadliest poison and shot it at the goblin. But it only stuck on to the monster's shaggy coat. Then he shot another and another, till fifty were spent, all of which merely stuck on to the goblin's shaggy coat. Hereon the goblin, shaking the arrows off so that they fell at his feet came at the Bodhisatta; and the latter, again shouting defiance, drew his sword and struck at the goblin. But like the arrows, his sword, which was thirty-three inches long, merely stuck fast in the shaggy hair. Next the Bodhisatta hurled his spear, and that stuck fast also. Seeing this, he smote the goblin with his club; but, like his other weapons, that too stuck fast. And thereupon the Bodhisatta shouted, "Goblin, you never heard yet of me, Prince Five-Weapons. When I ventured into this forest, I put my trust not in my bow and other weapons, but in myself! Now will I strike you a blow which shall crush you into dust." So saying, the Bodhisatta smote the goblin with his right hand; but the hand stuck fast upon the hair. Then, in turn, with his left hand and with his right and left feet, he struck at the monster, but hand and feet alike clave to the hide. Again shouting "I will crush you into dust!" he butted the goblin with his head, and that too stuck fast.

Yet even when thus caught and snared in fivefold wise, the Bodhisatta, as he hung upon the goblin, was still fearless, still undaunted. And the monster thought to himself, "This is a very lion among men, a hero without a peer, and no mere man. Though he is caught in the clutches of a goblin like me. yet not so much as a tremor will he exhibit. Never, since I first took to slaying travellers upon this road, have I seen a man to

equal him. How comes it that he is not frightened?" Not daring
to devour the Bodhisatta offhand, he said, "How is it young
student, that you have no fear of death?"

"Why should I?" answered the Bodhisatta. "Each life must
surely having its destined death. Moreover, within my body is
a sword of adamant, which you will never digest, if you eat me.
It will chop your inwards into mincemeat, and my death will
involve yours too. Therefore it is that I have no fear." (By this,
it is said, the Bodhisatta meant the Sword of Knowledge, which
was within him.)

Hereon, the goblin fell a-thinking. "This young student is
speaking the truth and nothing but the truth," thought he.
"Not a morsel so big as a pea could I digest of such a hero. I'll
let him go." And so, in fear of his life, he let the Bodhisatta go
free, saying, "Young student, you are a lion among men; I will
not eat you. Go forth from my hand, even as the moon from the
jaws of Rāhu, and return to gladden the hearts of your kinsfolk,
your friends, and your country."

"As for myself, goblin," answered the Bodhisatta, "I will
go. As for you, it was your sins in bygone days that caused you
to be re-born a ravening, murderous, flesh-eating goblin; and,
if you continue in sin in this existence, you will go on
from darkness to darkness. But, having seen me, you will be
unable thence-forth to sin any more. Know that to destroy life
is to ensure re-birth either in hell or as a brute or as a ghost or
as a titan. Or, if the re-birth be into the world of men, then such
sin cuts short the days of a man's life.

In this and other ways the Bodhisatta showed the evil
consequences of the five bad courses, and the blessing that
comes of the Five Commandments; and so wrought in diverse
ways upon that goblin's fears that by his teaching he converted
the monster, imbuing him with self-denial and establishing him
in the Five Commandments. Then making the goblin the divinity
of that forest, with a right to receive offerings, and charging
him to remain steadfast, the Bodhisatta went his way, making

known the change in the goblin's mood as he issued from the forest. And in the end he came, armed with the five weapons, to the city of Benares, and presented himself before his parents. In later days, when king, he was a righteous ruler; and after a life spent in charity and other good works he passed away to fare thereafter according to his deserts.

THE BRAHMIN'S SPELL

Once upon a time when Brahmadatta was reigning in Benares, the Bodhisatta came to life as the child of the Queen-consort. When he grew up, he mastered every accomplishment; and when, at his father's death, he came to be king, he proved a righteous king. Now he used to play at dice with his family priest, and, as he flung the golden dice upon the silver dice-board, he would sing this catch for luck:

Tis nature's law that rivers wind;
Trees grow of wood by law of kind;
And, given opportunity,
All women work iniquity.

As these lines always made the king win the game, the priest was in a fair way to lose every penny he had in the world. And, in order to save himself from utter ruin, he resolved to seek out a little maid that had never seen another man, and then to keep her under lock and key in his own house. "For," thought he, "I couldn't manage to look after a girl who has seen another man. So I must take a new-born baby girl, and keep her under my thumb as she grows up, with a close guard over her, so that none may come near her and that she may be true to one man. *Then* I shall win of the king, and grow rich." Now he was skilled in bodily signs; and seeing a poor woman who was about to become a mother, and knowing that her child would be a girl, he paid the woman to come and be confined in his house, and sent her away after her confinement with a present. The infant was brought up entirely by women, and no men-other than himself-were ever allowed to set eyes on her. When the girl grew up, she was subject to him and he was her master.

Now, while the girl was growing up, the priest forbore to play with the king; but when she was grown up and under his own control, he challenged the king to a game. The king accepted, and play began. But, when in throwing the dice the king sang his lucky catch, the priest added,-"always excepting my girl." And then luck changed, and it was now the priest who won, while the king lost.

Thinking the matter over, the Bodhisatta suspected the priest had a virtuous girl shut in his house; and enquiry proved his suspicions true. Then, in order to work her fall, he sent for a clever scamp, and asked whether he thought he could seduce the girl. "Certainly, sire," said the fellow. So the king gave him money, and sent him away with orders to lose no time.

With the king's money the fellow bought perfumes and incense and aromatics of all sorts, and opened a perfumery shop close to the priest's house. Now the priest's house was seven stories high, and had seven gateways, at each of which a guard was set, - a guard of women only, - and no man but the brahmin himself was ever allowed to enter. The very baskets that contained the dust and sweepings were examined before they were passed in. Only the priest was allowed to see the girl, and she had only a single waiting-woman. This woman had money given her to buy flowers and perfumes for her mistress, and on her way she used to pass near the shop which the scamp had opened. And he, knowing very well that she was the girl's attendant, watched one day for her coming, and, rushing out of his shop, fell at her feet, clasping her feet tightly with both hands and blubbering, out, "O my mother! Where have you been all this long time?"

And his confederates, who stood by his side, cried, "What a likeness! Hand and foot, face and figure, even in style of dress, they are identical!" As one and all kept dwelling on the marvellous likeness, the poor woman lost her head. Crying out that it must be her boy, she too burst into tears And with weeping and tears the two fell to embracing one another. Then said the man, "Where are you living, mother?"

"Up at the priest's my son. He has a young wife of peerless beauty, a very goddess for grace; and I'm her waiting-woman." "And whither away now mother?" "To buy her perfumes and flowers." "Why go elsewhere for them? Come to me for them in future," said the fellow. And he the woman betel, bdellium, and so forth, and all kinds of flowers, refusing all payment. Struck with the quantity of flowers and perfumes which the waiting-woman brought home, the girl asked why the brahmin was so pleased with her that day. "Why do you say that, my dear?" asked the old woman. "Because of the quantity of things you have brought home." "No, it isn't that the brahmin was free with his money," said the old woman; "for I got them at my sons." And from that day forth she kept the money the brahmin gave her, and got her flowers and other things free of charge at the man's shop.

And he, a few days later, made out to be ill, and took to his bed. So when the old woman came to the shop and asked for her son, she was told he had been taken ill. Hastening to his side, she fondly stroked his shoulders, as she asked what ailed him. But he made no reply. "Why don't you tell me, my son?" "Not even if I were dying, could I tell you, mother" "But, if you don't tell me, whom are you to tell?" 'Well then, mother, my malady lies, solely in this that, hearing the praises of your young mistresses beauty, I have fallen in love with her. If I win her, I shall live; 'if not, this will be my death-bed." "Leave that to me, my boy," said the old woman cheerily; "and don't worry-yourself on this account." Then-with a heavy load of perfumes and flowers to take with her - she" went home, and said to the brahmin's young wife, "Alas! here's my son in love with you, merely because I told him how beautiful you are? What is to be done?"

"If you, can smuggle him in here," replied the girl, "you have my leave."

Hereupon the old woman set to work sweeping together all the dust she could find in the house from top to bottom; this dust she put into a huge flower-basket, and tried to out with

it. When the usual search was made, she emptier dust over the
woman on guard, who fled away under such ill-treatment. In
like manner she dealt with all the other watchers, smothering
in dust each one in turn that said anything to her. And so it
came to pass from that time forward that, no matter what the
old woman took in or out of the house, there was nobody bold
enough to search her Now was the time! The old woman
smuggled the scamp into the house in a flower-basket, and
brought him to her young mistress. He succeeded in wrecking
the girl's virtue, and actually stayed a day or two in the upper
rooms, —hiding when the priest was at home, and enjoying the
society of his mistress when the priest was off the premises. A
day or two passed and the girl said to her lover, "Sweetheart,
you must be going now." "Very well; only I must cuff the
brahmin first." "Certainly," said she, and hid the scamp. Then,
when the brahmin came in again, she exclaimed, "Oh, my dear
husband. I should so like to dance, if you would play the lute
for me." "Dance away, my dear," said the priest, and struck up
forthwith. "But I shall be too ashamed, if you're looking. Let me
hide your handsome face first with a cloth; and then I will
dance." "All right," said he; "if you're too modest to dance
otherwise." So she took a thick cloth and tied it over the
brahmin's face so as to blindfold him. And, blindfolded as he
was, the brahmin begin to play the lute. After dancing a while,
she cried, "My dear, I should so like to hit you once on the
head." "Hit away," said the unsuspecting dotard. Then the girl
made a sign to her paramour; and he softly stole up behind
the brahmin and smote him on the head. Such was the force of
the blow, that the brahmin's eyes were like to start out of his
head, and a bump rose up on the spot. Smarting with pain, he
called to the girl to give him her hand and she placed it in his.
"Ah! it's a soft hand." said he "but it hits hard!"

Now, as soon as the scamp had struck the brahmin, he
hid; and when he was hidden, the girl took the bandage off the
priest's eyes and rubbed his bruised head with oil. The moment
the brahmin went out, the scamp was stowed away in his
basket again by the old woman, and so carried out of the house.
Making his way at once to the king, he told him the whole

adventure.

Accordingly, when the brahmin was next in attendance, the king proposed a game with the dice; the brahmin was willing; and the king caused the gaming-circle to be drawn. As the king made his throw, he sang his old catch, and the brahmin—ignorant of the girl's naughtiness—added his "always excepting my girl,"—and nevertheless lost!

Then the king, who *did* know what had passed, said to his priest, "Why except her? Her virtue has given way. Ah, you dreamed that by taking a girl in the hour of her birth and by placing a sevenfold guard round her, you could be certain of her. Why, you couldn't be certain of a woman, even it you had her inside you and always walked about with her. No woman is ever faithful to one man alone. As for that girl of yours, she told you she should like to dance, and having first blindfolded you as you played the lute to her, she let her paramour strike you on the head, and then smuggled him out of the house. Where then is your exception?" And so saying the king repeated this stanza:
Blindfold, a-luting, by his wife beguiled,
The brahmin sat,—who tried to rear
A paragon of virtue undefiled!
Learn hence to hold the sex in fear.

In such wise did the Bodhisatta expound the Truth to the brahmin. And the brahmin went home and taxed the girl with the wickedness of which she was accused. "My dear husband, who can have said such a thing about me?" said she. "Indeed I am innocent; indeed it was my own hand, and nobody else's that struck you; and, if you do not believe me. I will brave the ordeal of fire and swear that no man's hand has touched me but yours; and so I will make you believe me." "So be it," said the brahmin. And he had a quantity of wood brought and set light to it. Then the girl was summoned. "Now," said he, "if you believe your own story, brave these flames!"

Now before this the girl had instructed her attendant as

follows: "Tell your son, mother, to be there and to seize my hand just as I am about to go into the fire." And the old woman did as she was bidden; and the fellow came and took his stand among the crowd. Then, to delude the brahmin, the girl, standing there before all the people, exclaimed with fervour, "No man's hand but thine, brahmin, has ever touched me; and, by the truth of my asseveration I call on this fire to harm me not." So saying, she advanced to the burning pile,—when up dashed her paramour, who seized her by the hand, crying shame on the brahmin who could force so fair a maid to enter the flames! Shaking her hand free, the girl exclaimed to the brahmin that what she had sworn was now undone, and that she could not now brave the ordeal of fire. "Why not?" said the brahmin. "Because," she replied, "my asseveration was that no man's hand but thine had ever touched me; and now here is a man who has seized hold of my hand!" But the brahmin, knowing that he was tricked, drove her from him with blows.

Such, we learn, is the wickedness of women. What crime will they not commit; and then, to deceive their husbands, what oaths will they not take—aye, in the light of day—that they did it not! So false-hearted are they! Therefore has it been said:

A sex composed of wickedness and guile,
Unknowable, uncertain as the path
Of fishes in the water,—womankind
Hold truth for falsehood, falsehood for the truth'
As greedily as cows seek pastures new,
Women, unsated, yearn for mate on mate.
Thievish and cruel as a sweet-voiced snake,
They know all tricks wherewith to gull mankind.

THE VALUE OF A BROTHER

This story was told by the Master while at Jetavana, a certain country-woman.

For it fell out once in Kosala that three men were ploughing on the outskirts of a certain forest, and that robbers plundered folk in that forest and made their escape. The victims came, in the course of a fruitless search for the rascals, to where the three men were ploughing. "Here are the forest robbers, disguised as husbandmen," they cried, and hauled the trio off as prisoners to the King of Kosala. Now time after time there came to the king's palace a woman who with loud lamentations begged for "wherewith to be covered." Hearing her cry, the king ordered a shift to be given her; but she refused it, saying this was not what she meant. So the king's servants came back to his majesty and said that what the woman wanted was not clothes but a husband. Then the king had the woman brought into his presence and asked her whether she really did mean a husband.

"Yes, sire," she answered; "for a husband is a woman's real covering, and she that lacks a husband—even though she be clad in garments costing a thousand pieces—goes bare and naked indeed."

(And to enforce this truth, the following Sutta should be recited here:
Like kingless kingdoms, like a stream run dry,
So bare and naked is a woman seen,
Who, having brothers ten, yet lacks a mate.)

Pleased with the woman's answer, the king asked what relation the three prisoners were to her. And she said that one was her husband, one her brother, and one her son. "Well, to mark my favour," said the king, "I give you one of the three. Which will you take?" "Sire," was her answer, "if I live, I can get another husband and another son; but as my parents are dead, I can never get another brother. So give me my brother, Sire." Pleased with the woman, the king set all three   men at liberty; and thus this one woman was the means of saving three persons from peril.

When the matter came to the knowledge of the Brotherhood, they were lauding the woman in the Hall of Truth, when the Master entered. Learning on enquiry what was the subject of their talk, he said, 'This is not the first time, Brethren, that this woman has saved those three from peril; she did the same in days gone by." And, so saying, he told a story of the past.

THE GRATEFUL ANIMALS

Once upon a time Brahmadatta was reigning in Benares. He had a son named. Prince Wicked. Fierce and cruel was he, like a scotched snake; he spoke to nobody without abuse or blows. Like grit in the eye was this prince to all folk both within and without the palace, or like a ravening ogre,—so dreaded and fell was he.

One day, wishing to disport himself in the river, he went with a large retinue to the water side. And a great storm came on, and utter darkness set in. "Hi there!" cried he to his servants; "take me into mid-stream, bathe me there, and then bring me back again." So they took him into mid-stream and there took counsel together, saying, 'What will he do to us when king? Let us kill the wicked wretch here and now! So in you go, you pest'" they cried, as they flung him into the water. When they made their way ashore, they were asked where the prince was, and replied, "we don't see him, finding the storm come on he must have come out of the river and gone home ahead of us."

The courtiers went into the king's presence, and the king asked where his son was. "We do not know, sire," said they; "a storm came on, and we came away in the belief that he must have gone on ahead." At once the king had the gates thrown open; down to the riverside he went and bade diligent search be made up and down for the missing prince. But no trace of him could be found. For, in the darkness of the storm, he had been swept away by the current, and, coming across a tree-trunk, had climbed on to it, and so floated down stream, crying lustily in the agony of his fear of drowning.

Now there had been a gild-merchant living in those days

at Benares, who had died, leaving forty crores buried in the banks of that same river. And because of his craving for riches, he was re-born as a snake at the spot under which lay his dear treasure. And also in the self-same spot another man had hidden thirty crores, and because of his craving for riches, was re-born as a rat at the same spot. In rushed the water into their dwelling-place; and the two creatures, escaping by the way by which the water rushed in were making their way athwart the stream, when they chanced upon the tree-trunk to which the prince was clinging The snake climbed up at one end, and the rat at the other; and so both got a footing with the prince on the trunk.

Also there grew on the river's bank a Silk-cotton tree, in which lived a young parrot; and this tree, being uprooted by the swollen waters, fell into the river. The heavy rain beat down the parrot when it tried to fly, and it alighted in its fall upon this same tree-trunk. And so there were now these four floating down stream together upon the tree.

Now the Bodhisatta had been re-born in those days as a brahmin in the North-West country. Renouncing the world for the hermit's life on reaching manhood, he had built himself a hermitage by a bend of the river; and there he was now living. As he was pacing to and fro, at midnight, he heard the loud cries of the prince, and thought thus within himself: "This fellow-creature must not perish thus before the eyes of so merciful and compassionate a hermit as I am. I will rescue him from the water, and save his life." So he shouted cheerily, "Be not afraid! Be not afraid!" and plunging across stream, seized hold of the tree by one end, and, being as strong as an elephant, drew it in to the bank with one long pull, and set the prince safe and sound upon the shore. Then becoming aware of the snake and the rat and the parrot, he carried them to his hermitage, and there lighting a fire, warmed the animals first, as being the weaker, and afterwards the prince. This done, he brought fruits of various kinds and set them before his guests, looking after the animals first and the prince afterwards. This enraged the young prince, who said within himself, "This rascally hermit pays no respect to my royal birth, but actually gives brute beasts precedence over me." And he conceived hatred against the Bodhisatta.

A few days later, when all four had recovered their strength and the waters had subsided, the snake bade farewell to the hermit with these words, "Father, you have done me a great service. I am not poor, for I have forty crores of gold hidden at a certain spot. Should you ever want money, all my hoard shall be yours. You have only to come to the spot and call 'Snake." " Next the rat took his leave with a like promise to the hermit as to his treasure, bidding the hermit come and call out "Rat." Then the parrot bade farewell, saying, "Father, silver and gold have I none: but should you ever want for choice rice, come to where I dwell and call out 'Parrot'; and I with the aid of my kinsfolk will give you many waggon-loads or rice." Last came the prince. His heart was filled with base ingratitude and with a determination to put his benefactor to death, if the Bodhisatta should come to visit *him*. But, concealing his intent, he said "Come, father, to me when I am king, and I will bestow on you the Four Requisites." So saying, he took his departure, and not long after succeeded to the throne.

The desire came on the Bodhisatta to put their professions to the test; and first of all he went to the snake and standing hard by its abode, called out "Snake." At the word the snake darted forth and with every mark of respect said. Father in this place there are forty crores in gold. Dig them up and take them all." "It is well," said the Bodhisatta: "when I need them, I will not forget." Then bidding adieu to the snake, he went on to where the rat lived, and called out "Rat." And the rat did as the snake had done. Going next to the parrot, and calling out "Parrot," the bird at once flew down at his call from the tree-top, and respectfully asked whether it was the Bodhisatta's wish that he with the aid of his kinsfolk should gather paddy for the Bodhisatta from the region round the Himalayas. The Bodhisatta dismissed the parrot also with a promise that, if need arose, he would not forget the bird's offer. Last of all being minded to test the king in his turn, the Bodhisatta came to the royal pleasaunce, and on the day after his arrival made his way, carefully dressed, into the city on his round for alms. Just at that moment, the ungrateful king, seated in all his royal splendour on his elephant of state, was passing in rightwise procession round the city followed by a vast retinue. Seeing the Bodhisatta from afar, he thought to himself, "Here's that rascally hermit come to quarter himself and his appetite on me. I must have his head off before he can publish to the world the service he rendered me." With this intent, he signed to his attendants, and on their asking what was his pleasure, said, "Methinks yonder rascally hermit is here to importune me. See that the ill-omened ascetic does not look at me, but seize and bind him; flog him at every street-corner: and then march him out of the city, chop off his head at the place of execution and impale his body on a stake."

Obedient to their king's command, the attendants laid the innocent Great Being in bonds and flogged him at every street-corner on the way to the place of execution. But all their floggings failed to move the Bodhisatta or to wring from him any cry of "Oh, my mother and father!" All he did was to repeat this stanza:
They knew the world, who framed this proverb true—
"A log pays better salvage than some men."

These lines he repeated wherever he was flogged, till at last the wise among the bystanders asked the hermit what service he had rendered to their king. Then the Bodhisatta told the whole story, ending with the words,— "So it comes to pass that by rescuing him from the torrent I brought all this woe upon myself. And when I bethink me how I have left unheeded the words of the wise of old, I exclaim as you have heard."

Filled with indignation at the recital, the nobles and brahmins and all classes with one accord cried out, "This ungrateful king does not recognise even the goodness of this good man who saved his majesty's life. How can we have any profit from the king? Seize the tyrant!" And in their anger they rushed upon the king from every side, and slew him there and then, as he rode on his elephant, with arrows and javelins and stones and clubs and any weapons that came to hand. The corpse they dragged by the heels to a ditch and flung it in. Then they anointed the Bodhisatia king and set him to rule over them.

As he was ruling in righteousness, one day the desire came on him again to try the snake and the rat and the parrot; and followed by a large retinue he came to where the snake dwelt. At the call of "Snake," out came the snake from his hole and with every mark of respect said, "Here, my lord, is your treasure; take it." Then the king delivered the forty crores of gold to his attendants, and proceeding to where the rat dwelt, called "Rat." Out came the rat, and saluted the king, and gave up its thirty crores. Placing this treasure too in the hands of his attendants, the king went on to where the parrot dwelt, and called "Parrot." And in like manner the bird came, and bowing down at the king's feet asked whether it should collect rice for his majesty. "We will not trouble you," said the king, "till rice is needed. Now let us be going." So with the seventy crores of gold, and with the rat, the snake and the parrot as well, the king journeyed back to the city. Here, in a noble palace, to the state-story of which he mounted, he caused the treasure to be lodged and guarded; he had a golden tube made for the snake to dwell in, a crystal casket to house the rat, and a cage of gold for the parrot. Every day too by the king's command food was served to the three creatures in vessels of gold,—sweet parched-corn for the parrot and snake, and scented rice for the rat. And the king abounded in charity and all good works. Thus in harmony and goodwill one with another, these four lived their lives; and when their end came, they passed to fare according to their deserts.

THE GREAT DREAMS

This story was told by the Master while at Jetavana about sixteen wonderful dreams. For in the last watch of one night (so tradition says) the King of Kosala, who had been asleep all the night, dreamed sixteen great dreams, and woke up in great fright and alarm as to what they might portend for him. So strong was the fear of death upon him that he could not stir, but lay there huddled up on his bed. Now, when the night grew light, his brahmins and chaplains came to him and with due obeisance asked whether his majesty had slept well.

"How could I sleep well, my directors?" answered the king. "For just *at* daybreak I dreamed sixteen wonderful dreams, and I have been in terror ever since! Tell me, my directors, what it all means."

'We shall be able to judge, on hearing them."

Then the king told them his dreams, and asked what those visions would entail upon him.

The brahmins fell a-wringing their hands! 'Why wring your hands, brahmins?" asked the king. "Because, sire, these are evil dreams." "What will come of them?" said the king. "One of three calamities,—harm to your kingdom, to your life, or to your riches." "Is there a remedy, or is there not?" "Undoubtedly these dreams in themselves are so threatening as to be without remedy: but none the less we will find a remedy for them. Otherwise, what boots our much study and learning?" 'What then do you propose to do to avert the evil?" "Wherever four roads meet, we would offer sacrifice, sire." "My directors," cried the king in his terror, "my life is in your hands; make haste and work my safety." "Large sums of money, and large supplies of food of every kind will be ours," thought the exultant brahmins; and, bidding the king have no fear, they departed from the palace. Outside the town they dug a sacrificial pit and collected a host of fourfooted creatures, perfect and without blemish, and a multitude of birds. But still they discovered something lacking, and back they kept coming to the king to ask for this, that and the other. Now their doings were watched by Queen Mallikā, who came to the king and asked what made these brahmins keep coming to him.

"I envy you," said the king; "a snake in your ear, and you

not to know of it!" "What does your majesty mean?" "I have
dreamed, oh such unlucky dreams" The brahmins tell me they
point to one of three calamities; and they are anxious to offer
sacrifices to avert the evil. And this is what brings them here
so often." "But has your majesty consulted the Chief Brahmin
both of this world and of the world of gods?" 'Who, pray, may
he be, my dear?" asked the king. "Know you not that chiefest
personage of all the world, the all-knowing and pure, the
spotless master-brahmin? Surely, he, the Lord Buddha, will
understand your dreams. Go, ask him." "And so I will, my
queen," said the king. And away he went to the monastery,
saluted the Master, and sat down. "What, pray, brings your
majesty here so early in the morning?" asked the Master in his
sweet tones. "Sir," said the king, "just before daybreak I
dreamed sixteen wonderful dreams, which so terrified me that
I told them to the brahmins. They told me that my dreams
boded evil, and that to avert the threatened calamity they must
offer sacrifice wherever four roads meet And so they are busy
with their preparations, and many living creatures have the
fear of death before their eyes. But I pray you, who are the
chiefest personage in the world of men and gods, you into
whose ken comes all possible knowledge of things past and
present and to be,—I pray you tell me what will come of my
dreams, Lord".

"True it is, sire, that there is none other save me, who can
tell what your dreams signify or what will come of them. I will
tell you. Only first of all relate to me your dreams as they
appeared to you."

"I will, sir," said the king, and at once began this list,
following the order of the dreams' appearance:
Bulls first, and trees, and cows, and calves,
Horse, dish, she-jackal, waterpot,
A pond, raw rice, and sandal-wood.
And gourds that sank and stones that swam,
With frogs that gobbled up black snakes,
A crow with gold-plumed retinue,
And wolves in panic-fear of goats!

"How was it, sir, that I had the following one of my dreams? Methought, four black bulls, like collyrium in hue, came from the four cardinal directions to the royal courtyard with avowed intent to fight; and people flocked together to see the bull-fight, till a great crowd had gathered. But the bulls only made a show of fighting, roared and bellowed, and finally went off without fighting at all. This was my first dream. What will come of it?"

"Sire, that dream shall have no issue in your days or in mine. But hereafter, when kings shall be niggardly and unrighteous and when folk shall be unrighteous, in days when the world is perverted, when good is waning and evil waxing apace,—in those days of the world's backsliding there shall fall no rain from the heavens, the feet of the storm shall be lamed, the crops shall wither, and famine shall be on the land. Then shall the clouds gather as if for rain from the four quarters of the heavens; there shall be haste first to carry indoors the rice and crops that the women have spread in the sun to dry, for fear the harvest should get wet; and then with spade and basket in hand the men shall go forth to bank up the dykes. As though in sign of coming rain, the thunder shall bellow, the lightning shall flash from the clouds,—but even as the bulls in your dream, that fought not so the clouds shall flee away without raining. This is what shall come of this dream. But no harm shall come there from to you; for it was with regard to the future that you dreamed this dream. What the brahmins told you, was said only to get themselves a livelihood." And when the Master had thus told the fulfilment of this dream, he said, "Tell me your second dream, sire."

"Sir," said the king, "my second dream was after this manner: Methought little tiny trees and shrubs burst through the soil, and when they had grown scarce a span or two high, they flowered and bore fruit! This was my second dream what shall come of it?"

"Sire," said the Master, "this dream shall have its fulfillment in days when the world has fallen into decay and when men are shortlived. In times to come the passions shall be strong; quite young girls shall go to live with men, it shall be with them after the manner of women, and they shall conceive and bear children. The flowers typify their issue, and the fruit their offspring. But you, sire, have nothing to fear there from Tell me your third dream, 0 great king."

"Methought, sir, I saw cows sucking the milk of calves which they had borne that selfsame day. This was my third dream. What shall come of if?"

"This dream too shall have its fulfilment only in days to come, when respect shall cease to be paid to age. For in the future men, showing no reverence for parents or parents-in-law, shall themselves administer the family estate, and, if such be their good pleasure, shall bestow food and clothing on the old folks, but shall withhold their gifts, if it be not their pleasure to give. Then shall the old folks, destitute and dependent, exist by favour of their own children, like big cows suckled by calves a day old. But you have nothing to fear therefrom. Tel! me your fourth dream."

"Methought, sir, I saw men unyoking a team of draught-oxen, sturdy and strong, and setting young steers to draw the load; and the steers, proving unequal to the task laid on them, refused and stood stock-still, so that wains moved not on their way. This was my fourth dream. What shall come of it?"

"Here again the dream shall not have its fulfilment until the future, in the days of unrighteous kings. For in days to come. unrighteous and niggardly kings shall show no honour to wise lords skilled in precedent, fertile in expedient, and able to get through business; nor shall appoint to the courts of law and justice aged councillors of wisdom and of learning in the law. Nay, they shall honour the very young and foolish, and appoint such to preside in the courts. And these latter, ignorant alike of state-craft and of practical knowledge, shall not be able to bear the burden of their honours or to govern, but because of their incompetence shall throw off the yoke of office. Whereon the aged and wise lords, albeit right able to cope with all difficulties, shall keep in mind how they were passed over, and shall decline to aid, saying: 'It is no business of ours; we are outsiders: let the boys of the inner circle see to it.' Hence they shall stand aloof, and ruin shall assail those kings on every hand. It shall be even as when the yoke was laid on the young steers, who were not strong enough for the burden, and not upon the team of sturdy and strong draught-oxen, who alone were able to do the work. Howbeit you have nothing to fear therefrom. Tell me your fifth dream."

"Methought, Sir, I saw a horse with a mouth on either side, to which fodder was given on both sides, and it ate with both its mouths. This was my fifth dream. What shall come of it.?"

"This dream too shall have its fulfilment only in the future, in the days of unrighteous and foolish kings, who shall appoint unrighteous and covetous men to be judges. These base ones, fools, despising the good, shall take bribes from both sides as they sit in the seat of judgment and shall be filled with this twofold corruption, even as the horse that ate fodder with two mouths at once. Howbeit, you have nothing to fear therefrom. Tell me your sixth dream."

"Methought, sir, I saw people holding out a well-scoured golden bowl worth a hundred thousand pieces, and begging an old jackal to stale therein. And I saw the beast do so. This was my sixth dream. What shall come of it?"

"This dream too shall only have its fulfillment in the future. For in the days to come, unrighteous kings, though sprung of a race of kings, mistrusting the scions of their old nobility, shall not honour them, but exalt in their stead the low-born; whereby the nobles shall be brought low and the low-born raised to lordship. Then shall the great families be brought by very need to seek to live by dependence on the upstarts, and shall offer them their daughters in marriage. And the union of the noble maidens with the low-born shall be like unto the staling of the old jackal in the golden bowl. Howbeit, you have nothing to fear therefrom. Tell me your seventh dream."

"A man was weaving rope, sir, and as he wove, he threw it down at his feet. Under his bench lay a hungry she-jackal, which kept eating the rope as he wove, but without the man knowing it. This is what I saw. This was my seventh dream. What shall come of it?"

"This dream too shall not have its fulfillment till the future. For in days to come, women shall lust after men and strong drink and finery and gadding abroad and after the joys of this world. In their wickedness and profligacy these women shall drink strong drink with their paramours; they shall flaunt in garlands and perfumes and unguents; and heedless of even the most pressing of their household duties, they shall keep watching for their paramours, even at crevices high up in the outer wall; aye, they shall pound up the very seed-corn that should be sown on the morrow so as to provide good cheer;— in all these ways shall they plunder the store won by the hard work of their husbands in field and byre, devouring the poor men's substance even as the hungry jackal under the bench ate up the rope of the rope-maker as he wove it. Howbeit, you have nothing to fear therefrom. Tell me your eighth dream."

"Methought, sir, I saw at a palace gate a big pitcher which was full to the brim and stood amid a number of empty ones. And from the four cardinal points, and from the four intermediate points as well, there kept coming a constant stream of people of all the four castes, carrying water in pipkins and pouring it into the full pitcher. And the water overflowed and ran away. But none the less they still kept on pouring more and more water into the overflowing vessel, without a single man giving so much as a glance at the empty pitchers. This was my eighth dream. What shall come of it?"

'This dream too shall not have its fulfilment until the future. For in days to come the world shall decay; the kingdom shall grow weak, its kings shall grow poor and niggardly: the fore-most among them shall have no more than 100,000 pieces of money in his treasury. Then shall these kings in their need set the whole of the country-folk to work for them;—for the king's sake shall the toiling folk, leaving their own work, sow grain and pulse, and keep watch and reap and thresh and garner; for the kings' sake shall they plant sugarcanes, make and drive sugar-mills, and boil down the molasses; for the kings' sake shall they lay out flower-gardens and orchards, and gather in the fruits. And as they gather in all the diverse kinds of produce, they shall fill the royal garners to overflowing, not giving so much as a glance at their own empty barns at home. Thus it shall be like filling up the full pitcher, heedless of the quite-empty ones. Howbeit, you have nothing to fear therefrom. Tell me your ninth dream."

"Methought, sir, I saw a deep pool with shelving banks ail round and overgrown with the five kinds of lotuses. From every side two-footed creatures and four-footed creatures flocked thither to drink of its waters. The depths in the middle were muddy, but the water was clear and sparkling at the margin where the various creatures went down into the pool. This was my ninth dream. What shall come of it?"

"This dream too shall not have its fulfilment till the future. For in days to come kings shall grow unrighteous; they shall rule after their own will and pleasure, and shall not execute judgment according to righteousness. These kings shall hunger after riches and wax fat on bribes; they shall not show mercy, love and compassion toward their people, but be fierce and cruel, amassing wealth by crushing their subjects like sugarcanes in a mill and by taxing them even to the uttermost farthing. Unable to pay the oppressive tax, the people shall fly from village and town and the like, and take refuge upon the borders of the realm; the heart of the land shall be a wilderness, while the borders shall teem with people,—even as the water was muddy in the middle of the pool and clear at the margin. Howbeit, you have nothing to fear therefrom. Tell me your tenth dream."

"Methought, sir, I saw rice boiling in a pot without getting done. By not getting done, I mean that it looked as though it were sharply marked off and kept apart, so that the cooking went on in three distinct stages. For part was sodden, part hard and raw, and part just cooked to a nicety. This was my tenth dream. What shall come of it?"

"This dream too shall not have its fulfilment till the future. For in days to come kings shall grow unrighteous; the people surrounding the kings shall grow unrighteous too, as also shall brahmins and householders, townsmen, and country-folk; yes, all people alike shall grow unrighteous, not excepting even sages and brahmins. Next, their very tutelary deities—the spirits to whom they offer sacrifice, the spirits of the trees, and the spirits of the air—shall become unrighteous also. The very winds that blow over the realms of these unrighteous kings shall grow cruel and lawless; they shall shake the mansions of the skies and thereby kindle the anger of the spirits that dwell there, so that they will not suffer rain to fall-or, if it does rain, it shall not fall on all the kingdom at once, nor shall the kindly shower fall on all tilled or sown lands alike to help them in their need. And, as in the kingdom at large, so in each several district and village and over each separate pool or lake, the rain shall not fall at one and the same time on its whole expanse; if it rains on the upper part, it shall not rain upon the lower; here the crops shall be spoiled by a heavy downpour, there wither for very drought, and here again thrive apace with kindly showers to water them. So the crops sown within the confines of a single kingdom—like the rice in the one pot—shall have no uniform character. Howbeit, you have nothing to fear therefrom. Tell me your eleventh dream."

"Methought, sir, I saw sour butter-milk bartered for precious sandal-wood, worth, 100,000 pieces of money. This was my eleventh dream. What shall come of it?"

"This dream too shall not have its fulfillment till the future— in the days when my doctrines is waning. For in day to come many greedy and shameless Brethren shall arise, who for their belly's sake shall preach the very words in which I inveighed against greed! Because they have deserted by reason of their belly and have taken their stand on the side of the heretics, they shall fail to make their preaching lead up to Nirvana. Nay, their only thought, as they preach, shall be by fine words and sweet voices to induce men to give them costly raiment and the like, and to be minded to give such gifts. Others again seated in the highways, at the street-corners, at the doors of kings' palaces, and so forth, shall stoop to preach for money, yea for mere coined kahāpanas, half-kahāpanas, pādas, or māsakas! And as they thus barter away for food or raiment or for kahāpanas and half-kahāpanas my doctrine the worth whereof is Nirvana, they shall be even as those who bartered away for sour butter-milk precious sandal-wood worth 100,000 pieces. Howbeit, you have nothing to fear therefrom. Tell me your twelfth dream."

"Methought, sir, I saw empty pumpkins sinking in the water. What shall come of it?"

"This dream also shall not have its fulfillment till the future, in the days of unrighteous kings, when the world is perverted. For in those days shall kings show favour not to the scions of the nobility, but to the low-born only; and these latter shall become great lords, whilst the nobles sink into poverty. Alike in the royal presence, in the palace gates, in the council chamber, and in the courts of justice, the words of the low-born alone (whom the empty pumpkins typify) shall be established, as though they had sunk down till they rested on the bottom. So too in the assemblies of the Brotherhood, in the greater and lesser conclaves, and in enquiries regarding bowls, robes, lodging, and the like,—the counsel only of the wicked and the vile shall be considered to have saving power, not that of the modest Brethren. Thus everywhere it shall be as when the empty pumpkins sank. Howbeit, you have nothing to fear therefrom. Tell me your thirteenth dream."

Hereupon the king said, "Methought, sir, I saw huge blocks of solid rock. as big as houses", floating like ships upon the waters. What shall come of it?"

'This dream also shall not have its fulfillment before such times as those of which I have spoken. For in those days unrighteous kings shall show honour to the low-born, who shall become great lords, whilst the nobles sink into poverty. Not to the nobles, but to the upstarts alone shall respect be paid. In the royal presence, in the council chamber, or in the courts of justice, the words of the nobles learned in the law (and it is they whom the solid rocks typify) shall drift idly by, and not sink deep into the hearts of men; when they speak, the upstart shall merely laugh them to scorn, saying, 'What is this these fellows are saying?' So too in the assemblies of the Brethren, as afore said, men shall not deem worthy of respect the excellent among the Brethren; the words of such shall not sink deep, but drift idly by,—even as when the rocks floated upon the waters. Howbeit, you have nothing to fear therefrom. Tell me your fourteenth dream."

"Methought, sir, I saw tiny frogs, no bigger than minute flowerets, swiftly pursuing huge black snakes, chopping them up like so many lotus-stalks and gobbling them up. What shall come of this?"

"This dream too shall not have its fulfilment till those days to come such as those of which I have spoken, when the world is decaying. For then shall men's passions be so strong, and their lusts so hot, that they shall be the thralls of the very youngest of their wives for the time being, at whose sole disposal shall be slaves and hired servants, oxen, buffaloes and all cattle, gold and silver, and everything that is in the house. Should the poor husband ask where the money (say) or a robe is, at once he shall be told that it is where it is, that he should mind his own business, and not be so inquisitive as to what is, or is not, in *her* house. And therewithal in diverse ways the wives with abuse and goading taunts shall establish their dominion over their husbands, as over slaves and bond-servants. Thus shall it be like as when the tiny frogs, no bigger than minute flowerets, gobbled up the big black snakes.

Howbeit, you have nothing to fear therefrom. Tell me your fifteenth dream."

"Methought, sir, I saw a village crow, in which dwelt the whole of the Ten Vices, escorted by a retinue of those birds which, because of their golden sheen, are called Royal Golden Mallards. What shall come of it?"

"This dream too shall not have its fulfilment till the future, till the reign of weakling kings. In days to come kings shall arise who shall know nothing about elephants or other arts, and shall be cowards in the field. Fearing to be deposed and cast from their royal estate, they shall raise to power not their peers but their footmen, bath attendants, barbers, and such like. Thus, shut out from royal favour and unable to support themselves, the nobles shall be reduced to dancing attendance on the upstarts, as when the crow had Royal Golden Mallards for a retinue. Howbeit, you have nothing to fear therefrom. Tell me your sixteenth dream."

"Heretofore, sir, it always used to be panthers that preyed on goats; but methought I saw goats chasing panthers and devouring them- munch, munch, munch! — whilst at bare sight of the goats afar off, terror-stricken wolves fled quaking with fear and hid themselves in their fastnesses in the thicket. Such was my dream. What shall come of it?"

"This dream too shall not have its fulfilment till the future, till the reign of unrighteous kings. In those days the low-born shall be raised to lordship and be made royal favourites, whilst the nobles shall sink into obscurity and distress. Gaining influence in the courts of law because of their favour with the king, these upstarts shall claim perforce the ancestral estates, the raiment, and all the property of the old nobility. And when these latter plead their rights before the courts, then shall the king's minions have them cudgeled and bastinadoed and taken by the throat and cast out with words of scorn, such as: 'Know your place, fools! What? Do you dispute with us? The king shall know of your insolence, and we will have your hands and feet chopped off and other correctives applied!' Hereupon the terrified nobles shall affirm that their own belongings really belong to the overbearing upstarts, and will tell the favourites to accept them. And they shall hie them home and there cower in an agony of fear Likewise, evil Brethren shall harry at pleasure good and worthy Brethren, till these latter, finding none to help them shall flee to the jungle. And this oppression of the nobles and of the good Brethren by the low-born and by the evil Brethren, shall be like the scaring of wolves by goats Howbeit, you have nothing to fear therefrom. For this dream too has reference to future times only. It was not truth, it was not love for you, that prompted the brahmins to prophesy as they did. No, it was greed of gain, and the insight that is bred of covetousness, that shaped all their self-seeking utterances"

Thus did the Master expound the import of these sixteen great dreams, adding,— "You, sire, are not the first to have these dreams: they were dreamed by kings of bygone days also; and, then as now, the brahmins found in them a pretext for sacrifices; whereupon, at the instance of the wise and good, the Bodhisatta was consulted, and the dreams were expounded by them of old time in just the same manner as they have now been expounded."

THE CONVERTED MISER

Once upon a time when Brahmadatta was reigning in Benares, there was a gildmaster, Illisa by name, who was worth eighty crores, and had all the defects which fall to the lot of man. He was lame and crook-backed and had a squint; he was an unconverted infidel, and a miser, never giving of his store to others, nor enjoying it himself; his house was like a pool haunted by ogres. Yet, for seven generations, his ancestors had been bountiful, giving freely of their best; but, when he became gildmaster, he broke through the traditions of his house. Burning down the almonry and driving the poor with blows from his gates, he hoarded his wealth.

One day, when returning home from attendance on the

king, he saw a yokel, who had journeyed far and was a-weary, seated on a bench, and filling a mug from a jar of rank spirits, and drinking it off, with a dainty morsel of stinking dried-fish as a relish. At the sight he felt a thirst for spirits, but he thought to himself. "If I drink, others will want to drink with me, and that means a ruinous expense." So he walked about, keeping his thirst under. But, as time wore on, he could do so no longer, he grew as yellow as old cotton; and the veins stood out on his sunken frame. On a day, retiring to his chamber, he lay down hugging his bed. His wife came to him, and rubbed his back, as she asked, "What has gone amiss with my lord?"

(What follows is to be told in the words of the former story.) But, when she in her turn said, "Then I'll only brew liquor enough for you," he said, "If you make the brew in the house there will be many on the watch; and to send out for the spirits and sit and drink it here, is out of the question." So he produced one single penny, and sent a stave to fetch him a jar of spirits from the tavern. When the slave came back he made him go from the town to the riverside and put the jar down in a thicket near the highway. "Now be off" said he and made the slave wait some distance off, while he filled his cup and fell to.

Now the gildmasters father, who for his charity and other good works had been re-born as Sakka in the Realm of gods, was at that moment wondering whether his bounty was still kept up or not, and became aware of the stopping of his bounty, and of his son's behaviour. He saw how his son, breaking through the traditions of his house, had burnt the almonry to the ground, had driven the poor with blows from his gates, and how, in his miserliness, fearing to share with others, that son had stolen away to drink by himself. Moved by the sight, Sakka cried, "I will go to him and make my son see that deeds must have their consequences; I will work his conversion, and make him charitable and worthy of re-birth in the Realm of gods." So he came down to earth, and once more trod the ways of men, putting on the semblance of the gildmaster Illisa, with the latter's lameness, and crook-back. and squint. In this guise, he entered the city of Rājagaha and made his way to the palace-gate, where he bade his coming be announced to the king. "Let him approach," said the king, and he entered and stood with due obeisance before his majesty.

'What brings you here at this unusual hour, Lord gildmaster?" said the king. "I am come, sire, because I have in my house eighty crores of treasure. Deign to have them carried to fill the royal treasury." "Nay, my Lord gildmaster: the treasure within my palace is greater than this." "If you, sire, will not have it, I shall give it away to whom I will" "Do so by all means, gildmaster," said the king. "So be it, sire," said the pretended Illisa, as with due obeisance he departed from the presence to the gildmaster's house. The servants all gathered round him, but not one could tell that it was not their real master. Entering, he stood on the threshold and sent for the porter, to whom he gave orders that if anybody resembling himself should appear and claim to be master of the house they should soundly cudgel such a one and throw him out. Then, mounting the stairs to the upper story, he sat down on a gorgeus couch and sent for Illisa's wife. When she came he said with a smile, "My dear, let us be bountiful."

At these words, wife, children, and servants ail thought, "It's a long time since he was this way minded. It must be through drinking to-day that he is so good-natured and generous." And his wife said to him, "Be as bountiful as you please, my husband." "Send for the crier," said he, "and bid him proclaim by beat of drum all through the city that everyone who wants gold, silver, diamonds, pearls, and the like, is to come to the house of Illisa the gildmaster." His wife did as he bade, and a large crowd soon assembled at the door carrying baskets and sacks. Then Sakka bade the treasure-chambers be thrown open, and cried, "This is my gift to you; take what you will and go your ways." And the crowd seized on the riches there stored, and piled them in heaps on the floor and filled the bags and vessels they had brought, and went off laden with the spoils. Among them *was* a countryman who yoked Illisa's oxen to Illisa's carriage, filled it with the seven things of price, and journeyed out of the city along the highroad. As he went along, he drew near the thicket, and sang the gildmaster's praises in these words: "May you live to be a hundred, my good lord Illisa! What you have done for me this day will enable me to live without doing another stroke of work. Whose were these oxen?" —yours. Whose was this carriage?—yours. Whose the wealth in the carriage?—yours again. It was no father or mother who gave me all this; no, it came solely from you, my lord."

These words filled the gildmaster with fear and trembling. "Why, the fellow is mentioning my name in his talk," said he to himself. "Can the king have been distributing my wealth to the people?" At the bare thought he bounded from the bush, and, recognising his own oxen and cart, seized the oxen by the cord, crying, "Stop, fellow; these oxen and this cart belong to me." Down leaped the man from the cart, angrily exclaiming, "You rascal! Illisa, the gildmaster, is giving away his wealth to all the city. What has come to you?" And he sprang at the gildmaster and struck him on the back like a falling thunderbolt, and went off with the cart. Illisa picked himself up, trembling in every limb, wiped off the mud, and hurrying after his cart, seized hold of it. Again the countryman got down, and seizing Illisa by the hair, doubled him up and thumped him about the head for some time; then taking him by the throat, he flung him back the way he had come, and drove off. Sobered by this rough usage, Illisa hurried off home. There, seeing folk making off with the treasure, he fell to laying hands on here a man and there a man, shrieking, "Hi! what's this? Is the king despoiling me?" And every man he laid hands on knocked him down. Bruised and smarting, he sought to take refuge in his own house, when the porters stopped him with, "Holloa, you rascal! Where might you be going?" And first thrashing him soundly with bamboos, they took their master by the throat and threw him out of doors. "There is none but the king left to see me righted," groaned Illisa, and betook himself to the palace. "Why, oh why, sire," he cried, "have you plundered me like this?"

"Nay, it was not I, my lord gildmaster," said the king. "Did you not yourself come and declare your intention of giving your wealth away, if I would not accept it? And did you not then send the crier round and carry out your threat?" "Oh sire, indeed it was not I that came to you on such an errand. Your majesty knows how near and close I am, and how I never give away so much as the tiniest drop of oil which a blade of grass will take up. May it please your majesty to send for him who has given my substance away, and to question him on the matter."

Then the king sent for Sakka. And so exactly alike were the two that neither the king nor his court could tell which was the real gildmaster. Said the miser Illisa, "Who, and what, sire, is this gildmaster? *I* am the gildmaster."

"Well, really I can't say which is the real Illisa," said the king. "Is there anybody who can distinguish them for certain?" "Yes, sire, my wife." So the wife was sent for and asked which of the two was her husband. And she said Sakka was her husband and went to his side. Then in turn Illisa's children and servants were brought in and asked the same question; and all with one accord declared Sakka was the real gildmaster. Here it flashed across Illisa's mind that he had a wart on his head, hidden among his hair, the existence of which was known only to the barber. So, as a last resource, he asked that his barber might be sent for to identify him. Now at this time the Bodhisatta was his barber. Accordingly, the barber was sent for and asked if he could distinguish the real from the false Illisa. "I could tell, sire," said he, "if I might examine their heads." "Then look at both their heads," said the king. On the instant Sakka caused a wart to rise on his head! After examining the two the Bodhisatta reported that, as both alike had got warts on their heads, he couldn't for the life of him say which was the real man. And therewithal he uttered this stanza:

> Both squint; both halt; both men are hunchbacks too;
> And both have warts alike! I cannot tell
> Which of the two the real Illisa is.

Hearing his last hope thus fail him, the gildmaster fell into a tremble; and such was his intolerable anguish at the loss of his beloved riches, that down he fell in a swoon. Thereupon Sakka put forth his transcendental powers, and, rising in the air, addressed the king thence in these words: "Not Illisa am I, 0 king, but Sakka." Then those around wiped Ililsa's face and dashed water over him. Recovering, he rose to his feet and bowed to the ground before Sakka, King of gods Then said Sakka, "Illisa, mine was the wealth, not thine; I am thy father, and thou art my son. In my lifetime I was bountiful toward the poor and rejoiced in doing good; wherefore, I am advanced to this high estate and am become Sakka. But thou, walking not in my footsteps, art grown a niggard and a very miser; thou hast burnt my almonry to the ground, driven the poor from the gate, and hoarded thy riches. Thou hast no enjoyment thereof thyself, nor has any other human being: but thy store is become like a pool haunted by ogres, whereat no man may slake his thirst. Albeit, if thou wilt rebuild mine almonry and show bounty to the poor, it shall be accounted to thee for righteousness. But, if thou wilt not, then will I strip thee of all that thou hast, and cleave thy head with this thunderbolt of Indra, and thou shall die."

At this threat Illisa, quaking for his life, cried out, "Henceforth I will be bountiful." And Sakka accepted his promise, and, still seated in mid-air, established his son in the Commandments and preached the Truth to him, departing thereafter to his own abode. And Illisa was diligent in almsgiving and other good works, and so assured his rebirth thereafter in heaven.

THE VALIANT DWARF

Once upon a time when Brahmadatia was reigning in Benares the Bodhisatia was born a brahmin in a market-town in the North country, and when he was grown up he studied under a teacher of world-wide fame at Takkasilā. There he learnt the Three Vedas and the Eighteen Branches of knowledge, and completed his education. And he became known as the Sage Little Bowman. Leaving Takkasilā, he came to the Andhra country in search of practical experience. Now, it happened that in this Birth the Bodhisatia was somewhat of a crooked little dwarf, and he thought to himself, "If I make my appearance before any king, he's sure to ask what a dwarf like me is good for; why should I not use a tall broad fellow as my stalking-horse and earn my living in the shadow of his more imposing personality?" So he betook himself to the weavers' quarter, and there espying a huge-weaver named Bhimasena, saluted him, asking the man's name. "Bhimasena is my name," said the weaver. "And what makes a fine big man like you work at so sorry a trade?" "Because I can't get a living any other way." "Weave no more, friend. The whole continent can show no such archer as I am; but kings would scorn me because I am a dwarf. And so you, friend, must be the man to vaunt your prowess with the bow, and the king will take you into his pay and make you ply your calling regularly. Meantime I shall be behind you to perform the duties that are laid upon you, and so shall earn my living in your shadow. In this manner we shall both of us thrive and prosper. Only do as I tell you" "Done with you," said the other.

Accordingly, the Bodhisatta took the weaver with him to Benares, acting as a little page of the bow, and putting the other in the front; and when they were at the gates of the palace, he made him send word of his coming to the king. Being summoned into the royal presence, the pair entered together and bowing stood before the king. "What brings you here?" said the king. "I am a mighty archer," said Bhimasena; "there is no archer like me in the whole continent." "What pay would you want to enter my service?" "A thousand pieces a fortnight, sire." "What is this man of yours?" "He's my little page, sire." 'Very well, enter my service."

So Bhimasena entered the king's service; but it was the Bodhisatta who did all his work for him. Now in those days there was a tiger in a forest in Kāsi which blocked a frequented high-road and had devoured many victims. When this was reported to the king, he sent for Bhimasena and asked whether he could catch the tiger.

"How could I call myself an archer, sire, if I couldn't catch a tiger?" The king gave him largesse and sent him on the errand. And home to the Bodhisatta came Bhimasena with the news. "All right," said the Bodhisatta: "away you go, my friend." "But are you not coming too?" "No, I won't go, but I'll tell you a little plan." "Please do, my friend." "Well, don't you be rash and approach the tiger's lair alone. What you will *do* is to muster a strong band of country-folk to march to the spot with a thousand or two thousand bows; when you know that the tiger is aroused, you bolt into the thicket and lie down flat on your face. The country-folk will beat the tiger to death and as soon as he is quite dead, you bite off a creeper with your teeth, and draw near to the dead tiger, trailing the creeper in your hand. At the sight of the dead body of the brute, you will burst out with—'Who has killed the tiger? I meant to lead it by a creeper, like an ox, to the king, and with this intent had just stepped into the thicket to get a creeper I must know who killed the tiger before I could get back with my creeper.' Then the country-folk will be very frightened and bribe you heavily not to report them to the king; you will be credited with slaying the tiger; and the king too will give you lots of money."

'Very good, said Bhimasena; and off he went and slew the tiger just as the Bodhisatta had told him. Having thus made the road safe for travellers, back he came with a large following to Benares, and said to the king, "I have killed the tiger, sire; the forest is safe for travellers now." Well-pleased, the king loaded him with gifts.

Another day, tidings came that a certain road was infested with a buffalo, and the king sent Bhimasena to kill it. Following the Bodhisatta's directions, he killed the buffalo in the same way as the tiger, and returned to the king, who once more gave him lots of money. He was a great lord now Intoxicated by his new honours, he treated the Bodhisatta with contempt, and scorned to follow his advice, saying, "I can get on without you. Do you think there's no man but yourself?" This and many other harsh things did he say to the Bodhisatta.

Now, a few days later, a hostile king marched upon Benares and beleaguered it, sending a message to the king summoning him either to surrender his kingdom or to do battle. And the king of Benares ordered Bhimasena out to fight him. So Bhimasena was armed cap-a-pie in soldierly fashion and mounted on a war-elephant sheathed in complete armour. And the Bodhisatta, who was seriously alarmed that Bhimasena might get killed, armed himself cap-a-pie also and seated himself modestly behind Bhimasena. Surrounded by a host, the elephant passed out of the gates of the city and arrived in the forefront of the battle. At the first notes of the martial drum Bhimasena fell a-quaking with fear. "If you fall off now, you'll get killed," said Bodhisatta, and accordingly fastened a cord round him. which he held tight, to prevent him from failing off the elephant. But the sight of the field of battle proved too much for Bhimasena, and the fear of death was so strong on him; that he fouled the elephant's back. "Ah," said the Bodhisatta. "the present does not tally with the past. Then you affected the warrior; now your prowess is confined to befouling the elephant you ride on" And so saying, he uttered this stanza:

You vaunted your prowess, and loud was your boast
You swore you would vanquish the foe!
But is it consistent, when faced with their host,
To vent your emotion, sir, so?

When the Bodhisatta had ended these taunts, he said. "But don't you be afraid, my friend. Am I not here to protect you?" Then he made Bhimasena get off the elephant and bade him wash himself and go home. "And now to win renown this day," said the Bodhisatta, raising his battle-cry as he dashed into the fight. Breaking through the king's camp, he dragged the king out and took him alive to Benares. In great joy at his prowess, his royal master loaded him with honours, and from that day forward all India was loud with the fame of the Sage Little Bowman. To Bhimasena he gave largesse, and sent him back to his own home; whilst he himself excelled in charity and all good works, and at his death passed away to fare according to his deserts.

THE STOLEN JEWELS

Once upon a time when Brahmadatta was reigning in Benares, the Bodhisatta, having perfected his education, became one of the king's ministers. One day the king with a large following went into his pleasaunce, and, after walking about the woods, felt a desire to disport himself in the water. So he went down into the royal tank and sent for his harem. The women of the harem, removing the jewels from their heads and necks and so forth, laid them aside with their upper garments in boxes under the charge of female slaves, and then went down into the water. Now, as the queen was taking off her jewels and ornaments, and laying them with her upper robe on a box, she was watched by a female monkey, which was hidden in the branches of a tree near by. Conceiving a longing to wear the queen's pearl necklace, this monkey watched for the slave in charge to be off her guard. At first the girl kept looking all about her in order to keep the jewels safe; but as time wore on, she began to nod. As soon as the monkey saw this, quick as the wind she jumped down, and quick as the wind she was up the tree again, with the pearls round her own neck. Then, for fear the other monkeys should see it, she hid the string of pearls in a hole in the tree and sat on guard over her spoils as demurely as though nothing had happened. By and by the slave awoke, and, terrified at finding the jewels gone, saw nothing else to do but to scream out, "A man has run off with the queen's pearl necklace." Up ran the guards from every side, and hearing this story told it to the king. "Catch the thief," said his majesty; and away went the guards searching high and low for the thief in the pleasaunce. Hearing the din, a poor superstitious rustic took to his heels in alarm. "There he goes," cried the guards, catching sight of the runaway; and they followed him up till they caught him and with blows demanded what he meant by stealing such precious jewels.

Thought he, "If I deny the charge, I shall die with the beating I shall get from these ruffians. I'd better say I took it." So he confessed to the theft and was hauled off a prisoner to the king. "Did you take those precious jewels?" asked the king.

"Yes, your majesty." "Where are they now?" "Please your majesty, I'm a poor man; I've never in my life owned anything, even a bed or a chair, of any value,—much less a jewel. It was the gildmaster who made me take that valuable necklace; and I took it and gave it to him. He knows all about it."

Then the king sent for the gildmaster, and asked whether the rustic had passed the necklace on to him. "Yes, sire," was the answer. "Where is it then?" "I gave it to your majesty's family priest." Then the priest was sent for, and interrogated in the same way. And he said he had given it to the chief musician, who in his turn said he had given it to a courtesan as a present. But she, being brought before the king, utterly denied ever having received it.

Whilst the five were thus being questioned, the sun set. "It's too late now," said the king; "we will look into this to-morrow." So he handed the five over to his ministers and went back into the city. Hereupon the Bodhisatta fell a-thinking. "These jewels," thought he, "were lost inside the grounds, whilst the rustic was outside. There was a strong guard at the gates, and it was impossible for anyone inside to get away with the necklace. I do not see how anyone, whether inside or out, could have managed to secure it. The truth is this poor wretched fellow must have said he gave it to the gildmaster merely in order to save his own skin; and the gildmaster must have said he gave it to the priest, in the hope that he would get off if he could mix the priest up in the matter. Further, the priest must have said he gave it to the chief musician, because he thought the latter would make the time pass merrily in prison; whilst the chief musician's object in implicating the courtesan, was simply to solace himself with her company during imprisonment. Not one of the whole five has anything to do with the theft. On the other hand, the grounds swarm with monkeys, and the necklace must have got into the hands of one of the female monkeys."

When he had arrived at this conclusion, the Bodhisatta went to the king with the request that the suspects might be handed over to him and that he might be allowed to examine personally into the matter. "By all means, my wise friend.' said the king; "examine into it."

Then the Bodhisatta sent for his servants and told them where to lodge the five prisoners, saying, "Keep strict watch over them; listen to everything they say, and report it all to me." And his servants did as he bade them. As the prisoners sat together, the gildmaster said to the rustic, "Tell me, you wretch, where you and I ever met before this day: tell me when you gave me that necklace." 'Worshipful sir," said the other, "it has never been mine to own aught so valuable even as a stool or bedstead that wasn't rickety. I thought that with your help I should get out of this trouble, and that's why I said what I did. Be not angry with me, my lord." Said the priest in his turn to the gildmaster, "How then came you to pass on to me what this fellow had never given to you?" "I only said so because I thought that if you and I, both high officers of state, stand together, we can soon put the matter right." "Brahmin," now said the chief musician to the priest, "when, pray, did you give the jewel to me?" "I only said I did," answered the priest, "because I thought you would help to make the time pass more agreeably." Lastly the courtesan said. "Oh, you wretch of a musician, you know you never visited me, nor I you, so when could you have given me the necklace, as you say?" "Why be angry, my dear?" said the musician; "we five have got to keep house together for a bit; so let us put a cheerful face on it and be happy together."

This conversation being reported to the Bodhisatta by his agents, he felt convinced the five were all innocent of the robbery, and that a female monkey had taken the necklace. 'And I must find a means to make her drop it," said he to himself. So he had a number of bead necklaces made. Next he had a number of monkeys caught and turned loose again with strings of beads on their necks, wrists and ankles Meantime, the guilty monkey kept sitting in the trees watching her treasure. Then the Bodhisatta ordered a number of men to observe every monkey in the grounds carefully, till they saw one wearing

the missing pearl necklace, and then frighten her into dropping
it.

Tricked out in their new splendour, the other monkeys
strutted about till they came to the real thief, to whom they
said, "See our necklaces." Jealousy overcoming her prudence,
she exclaimed, "They're only beads!" putting on her own
necklace of real pearls. This was at once seen by the watchers,
who promptly made her drop the necklace. which they picked
up and brought to the Bodhisatta. He took it to the King, saying,
"Here, sire, is the necklace. The five prisoners are innocent; it
was a female monkey in the pleasaunce that took it." "How
came you find that out?" asked the king; "and how did you
manage to get possession of it again?" Then the Bodhisatta
told the whole story, and the king thanked the Bodhisatta,
saying, "You are the right man in the right place." And he
uttered this stanza in praise of the Bodhisatta:
> For war men crave the hero's might,
> For counsel sage sobriety,
> Boon comrades for their jollity,
> But judgment when in parlous plight.

Over and above these words of praise and gratitude, the
king showered treasures upon the Bodhisatta like a storm-
cloud pouring rain from the heavens. After following the
Bodhisatta's counsel through a long life spent in charity and
good works, the king passed away to fare thereafter according
to his deserts.

THE TOO-CLEVER MERCHANT

Once upon a time when Brahmadatta was reigning in
Benares, the Bodhisatta was born into a merchant's family and
on name-day was named 'Wise.' When he grew up he entered
into partnership with another merchant named Wisest,' and
traded with him. And these two took five hundred waggons of
merchandise from Benares to the country-districts, where they
disposed of their wares returning afterwards with the proceeds
to the city. When the time for dividing came, Wisest said, "I

must have a double share" "Why so?" asked Wise. "Because while you are only Wise, I am Wisest. And Wise ought to have only one share to Wisest's two." "But we both had an equal interest in the stock-in-trade and in the oxen and waggons. Why should you have two shares?" "Because I am Wisest." And so they talked away till they fell to quarrelling.

"Ah!" thought Wisest, "I have a plan." And he made his father hide in a hollow tree, enjoining the old man to say when the two came, "Wisest should have a double portion." This arranged, *he* went to the Bodhisatta and proposed to him to refer the claim for a double share to the competent decision of the tree divinity. Then he made his appeal in these words: "Lord, decide our cause!" Hereupon the father, who was hidden in the tree, in a changed voice asked them to state the case. The cheat addressed the tree as follows: "Lord, here stands Wise, and here stand I Wisest. We have been partners in trade. Declare what share each should receive."

"Wise should receive one share, and Wisest two," was the response.

Hearing this decision, the Bodhisatta resolved to find out whether it was indeed a tree divinity or not. So he filled the hollow trunk with straw and set it on fire. And Wisest's father was half roasted by the rising flames and clambered up by clutching hold of a bough. Falling to the ground, he uttered this stanza:

Wise rightly, Wisest wrongly got his name;
Through Wisest, I'm nigh roasted in the flame.

Then the two merchants made an equal division and each took half, and at their deaths passed away to fare according to their deserts.

THE LOQUACIOUS BRAHMIN

Once upon a time when Brahmadatta was reigning in Benares, the Bodhisatta was one of the king's courtiers. And the king's family priest of those days was so talkative and longwinded that, when he once started, no one else could get a word in. So the king cast about for someone to cut the priest short, and looked high and low for such an one. *Now* at that time there was a cripple in Benares who was a wonderful marksman with stones, and the boys used to put him on a little cart and draw him to the gates of Benares, where there is large branching banyan tree covered with leaves. There they would gather round and give him half-pence, saying 'Make an elephant,' or 'Make a horse.' And the cripple would throw stone after stone till he had cut the foliage into the shapes asked for. And the ground was covered with fallen leaves.

On his way to his pleasaunce the king came to the spot, and all the boys scampered off in fear of the king, leaving the cripple there helpless. At the sight of the litter of leaves the king asked, as he rode by in his chariot, who had cut the leaves off. And he was told that the cripple had done it. Thinking that here might be a way to stop the priest's mouth, the king asked where the cripple was, and was shown him sitting at the foot of the tree. Then the king had him brought to him and, motioning his retinue to stand apart, said to the cripple, "I have a very talkative priest. Do you think you could stop his talking?"

"Yes, sire,—if I had a peashooter full of dry goat's dung," said the cripple. Then the king had him taken to the palace and set with a peashooter full of dry goat's dung behind a curtain with a slit in it, facing the priest's seat. When the brahmin came to wait upon the king and was seated on the seat prepared for him, his majesty started a conversation. And the priest forthwith monopolized the conversation, and no one else could get a word in. Hereon the cripple shot the pellets of goat's dung one by one, like flies, through the slit in the curtain right into the priest's gullet. And the Brahmin swallowed the pellets down as they came, like so much oil, till all had disappeared. When the whole peashooter-full of pellets was lodged in the priest's stomach, they swelled to the size of half a peck; and the king, knowing they were all gone, addressed the brahmin in these words: "Reverend sir, so talkative are you, that you have swallowed down a peashooter-full of goat's dung without noticing it. That's about as much as you will be able to take at a sitting. Now go home and take a dose of panick seed and water by way of emetic, and put yourself right again."

From that day the pnest kept his mouth shut and sat as silent during conversation as though his lips were sealed.

"Well, my ears are indebted to the cripple for this relief," said the king, and bestowed on him four villages, one in the North, one in the South, one in the West, and one in the East, producing a hundred thousand a year.

The Bodhisatta drew near to the king and said, 'In this world, sire, skill should be cultivated by the wise. Mere skill in aiming has brought this cripple all this prosperity." So saying he uttered this stanza:

Prize skill, and note the marksman lame;
—Four villages reward his aim.

THE THREE FISHES

Once upon a time when Brahmadatta was reigning in Benares, there lived in the river of Benares three fishes, named Very thoughtful, Thoughtless, and Duly-thoughtful. And they came down stream from the wild country to where men dwelt. Hereupon Duly-thoughtful said to the other two, "This is a dangerous and perilous neighbourhood, where fishermen catch fish with nets, basket-traps, and such like tackle. Let us be off to the wild country again." But so lazy were the other two fishes, and so greedy, that they kept putting off their going from day to day, until they had let three months slip by. Now fishermen cast their nets into the river; and Very-thoughtful and Thoughtless were swimming on ahead in quest of food when in their folly they blindly rushed into the net. Duly-thoughtful, who was behind, observed the net, and saw the fate of the other two.

"I must save these lazy fools from death," thought he.

So first he dodged round the net, and splashed in the water in front of it like a fish that has broken through and gone up stream; and then doubling back, he splashed about behind it, like a fish that has broken through and gone down stream. Seeing this, the fishermen thought the fish had broken the net and all got away: so they pulled it in by one corner end the two fishes escaped from the net into the open water again. In this way they owed their lives to Duly-thoughtful.

THE LUCKY SNEEZE

Once upon a time when Brahmadatta was reigning in Benares, he had in his service a brahmin who professed to tell whether swords were lucky or not, and all came to pass as in the Introductory Story. And the king called in the surgeons and had him fitted with a false tip to his nose which was cunningly painted for all the world like a real nose; and then the brahmin resumed his duties again about the king. Now Brahmadatta had no son, only a daughter and a nephew, whom he had brought up under his own eye. And when these two grew up, they fell in love with one another. So the king sent for his councillors and said to them. "My nephew is heir to the throne. If I give him my daughter to wife, he shall be anointed king."

But, on second thoughts, he decided that as in any case his nephew was like a son, he had better marry him to a foreign princess, and give his daughter to a prince of another royal house. For, he thought, this plan would give him more grandchildren and vest in his line the sceptres of two several kingdoms. And, after consulting with his councillors, he resolved to separate the two, and they were accordingly made to dwell apart from one another. Now they were sixteen years old and very much in love, and the young prince thought of nothing but how to carry off his cousin from her father's palace. At last the plan struck him of sending for a wise woman, to whom he gave a pocketful of money.

"And what am I to do for this?" said she.

"There is nothing you can't do, tell me how you can get

my uncle to let his daughter out of the palace."

And she promised to help him, and said that she would tell the king that his daughter was under the influence of witchcraft, but that, as the demon had possessed her so long that he was of his guard, she would take the princess one day in a carriage to the cemetery with a strong escort under arms, and there in a magic circle lay the princess on a bed with a dead man under it, and with a hundred and eight douches of scented water wash the demon out of her. "And when on this pretext I bring the princess to the cemetery," continued the wise woman, "mind that you just reach the cemetery before us in your carriage with an armed escort, taking some ground pepper with you. Arrived at the cemetery, you will leave your carriage at the entrance, and despatch your men to the cemetery grove, while you will yourself go to the top of the mound and lie down as though dead. Then I will come and set up a bed over you on which I will lay the princess. Then will come the time when you must sniff at the pepper till you sneeze two or three times, and when you sneeze we will leave the princess and take to our heels. Thereon you and the princess must bathe all over, and you must take her home with you." "Capital," said the prince; "a most excellent device."

So away went the wise woman to the king, and he fell in with her idea, as did the princess when it was explained to her. When the day came, the old woman told the princess their errand, and said to the guards on the road in order to frighten them, "Listen, Under the bed that I shall set up, there will be a dead man; and that dead man will sneeze. And mark well that, so soon as he has sneezed, he will come out from under the bed and seize on the first person he finds. So be prepared, all of you."

Now the prince had already got to the place and got under the bed as had been arranged.

Next the crone led off the princess and laid her upon the bed, whispering to her not to be afraid. At once the prince sniffed at the pepper and fell a-sneezing. And scarce had he begun to sneeze before the wise woman left the princess and with a loud scream was off, quicker than any of them. Not a man stood his ground;—one and all they threw away their arms and bolted for dear life. Hereon the prince came forth and bore off the princess to his home, as had been before arranged. And the old woman made her way to the king and told him what had happened.

'Well," thought the king, "I always intended her for him, and they've grown up together like ghee in rice-porridge." So he didn't fly into a passion, but in course of time made his nephew king of the land, with his daughter as queen-consort.

Now the new king kept on in his service the brahmin who professed to tell the temper of swords, and one day as he stood in the sun, the false tip to the brahmin's nose got loose and fell off. And there he stood, hanging his head for very shame. "Never mind, never mind," laughed the king. "Sneezing is good for some, but bad for others. One sneeze lost you your nose; whilst I have to thank a sneeze for both my throne and queen." So saying he uttered this stanza:

Our diverse fates this moral show.
What brings one weal, may work another woe.

So spake the king, and after a life spent in charity and other good works, he passed away to fare according to his deserts.

THE HYPOCRITICAL JACKAL

Once upon a time when Brahmadatta was reigning in Benares, the Bodhisatta was born a rat, perfect in wisdom, and as big as a young boar. He had his dwelling in the forest and many hundreds of other rats owned his sway.

Now there was a roving jackal who espied this troop of rats and fell to scheming how to beguile and eat them. And he took up his stand near their home with his face to the sun, snuffing up the wind, and standing on one leg. Seeing this when out on his road in quest of food, the Bodhisatta conceived the jackal to be a saintly being, and went up and asked his name.

"'Godly' is my name," said the jackal. 'Why do you stand only on one leg?" "Because if I stood on all four at once, the earth could not bear my weight. That is why I stand on one leg only." "And why do you keep your month open?" "To take the air. I live on air; it is my only food." "And why do you face the sun?" "To worship him." 'What, uprightness!' thought the Bodhisatta, and thence forward he made a point of going, attended by the other rats, to pay his respects morning and evening to the saintly jackal. And when the rats were leaving, the jackal seized and devoured the hinder-most one of them, wiped his lips, and looked as though nothing had happened. In consequence of this the rats grew fewer and fewer, till they noticed the gaps in their ranks, and wondering why this was so, asked the Bodhisatta the reason. He could not make it out, but suspecting the jackal, resolved to put him to the test. So next day he let the other rats go out first and himself brought up the rear. The jackal made a spring on the Bodhisatta who, seeing him coming, faced round and cried: "So this is your saintliness, you hypocrite and rascal!" And he repeated the following stanza:

Where saintliness is but a cloak
Whereby to cozen guileless folk
And screen a villain's treachery,
—The cat-like nature there we see.

So saying, the king of the rats sprang at the jackal's throat and bit his windpipe asunder just under the jaw, so that he died. Back trooped the other rats and gobbled up the body of the jackal with a 'crunch, crunch, crunch';—that is to say, the foremost of them did, for they say there was none left for the last-comers. And ever after the rats lived happily in peace and quiet.

THE GOLDEN GOOSE

Once upon a time when Brahmadata was reigning in
Benares, the Bodhisatta was born a brahmin, and growing up
was married to a bride of his own rank, who bore him three
daughters named Nandā, Nandavati and Sundarinanda. The
Bodhisatta dying, they were taken in by neighbours and friends,
whilst he was born again into the world as a golden goose
endowed with consciousness of its former existences. Growing
up, the bird viewed his own magnificent size and golden
plumage, and remembered that previously he had been a human
being. Discovering that his wife and daughters were living on
the charity of others, the goose bethought him of his plumage
like hammered and beaten gold and how by giving them a
golden feather at a time he could enable his wife and daughters
to live in comfort. So away he flew to where they dwelt and
alighted on the top of the central beam of the roof. Seeing the
Bodhisatta, the wife and girls asked where he had come from;
and he told them that he was their father who had died and
been born a golden goose, and that he had come to visit them
and put an end to their miserable necessity of working for hire.
"You shall have my feathers," said he, "one by one, and they
will sell for enough to keep you all in ease and comfort." So
saying, he gave them one of his feathers and departed. And
from time to time he returned to give them another feather, and
with the proceeds of their sale these brahmin-women grew
prosperous and quite well-to-do. But one day the mother said
to her daughters "There's no trusting animals, my children.
Who's to say your father might not go away one of these days
and never come back again? Let us use our time and pluck him
clean next time he comes so as to make sure of all his feathers."
Thinking this would pain him, the daughters refused. The mother
in her greed called the golden goose to her one day when he
came, and then took him with both hands and plucked him.
Now the Bodhisatta's feathers had this properly that if they
were plucked out against his wish, they ceased to be golden
and became like a crane's feathers. And now the poor bird,
though he stretched his wings, could not fly, and the woman
flung him into a barrel and gave him food there. As time went

on his feathers grew again (though they were plain white ones now), and he flew away to his own abode and never came back again.

THE GRATEFUL MOUSE

Once upon a time when Brahmadatta was reigning in Benares, the Bodhisatta was born a stone-cutter, and growing up became expert in working stones. Now in the Kāsi country there dwelt a very rich merchant who had amassed forty crores in gold. And when his wife died, so strong was her love of money that she was re-born a mouse and dwelt over the treasure. And one by one the whole family died, including the merchant himself. Likewise the village became deserted and forlorn. At the time of our story the Bodhisatta was quarrying and shaping stones on the site of this deserted village; and the mouse used often to see him as she ran about to find food. At last she fell in love with him, and, bethinking her how the secret of all her vast wealth would die with her, she conceived the idea of enjoying it with him. So one day she came to the Bodhisatta with a coin in her mouth. Seeing this, he spoke to her kindly, and said, "Mother, what has brought you here with this coin?" "It is for you to lay out for yourself, and to buy meat with for me as well, my son." Nowise loth, he took the money and spent a half penny of it on meat which he brought to the mouse, who departed and ate to her heart's content. And this went on, the mouse giving the Bodhisatta a coin every day, and he in return supplying her with meat. But it fell out one day that the mouse was caught by a cat.

"Don't kill me," said the mouse.

"Why not?" said cat. I'm as hungry as can be, and really must kill you to allay the pangs."

"First, tell me whether you're always hungry, or only hungry to-day."

"Oh every day finds me hungry again."

"Well then. if this be so, I will find you always in meat:
only let me go."

"Mind you do then," said the cat, and let the mouse go.

As a consequence of this the mouse had to divide the
supplies of meat she got from the Bodisatta into two portions
and gave one half to the cat, keeping the other for herself.

Now, as luck would have it, the same mouse was caught
another day by a second cat and had to purchase her release
on the same terms. So now the daily food was divided into
three portions. And when a third cat caught the mouse and a
like arrangement had to be made, the supply was divided into
four portions. And later a fourth cat caught her, and the food
had to be divided among five, so that the mouse, reduced to
such commons, grew so thin as to be nothing but skin and
bone. Remarking how emaciated his friend was getting, the
Bodhisatta asked the reason. Then the mouse told him all that
had befallen her.

"Why didn't you tell me all this before?" said the
Bodhisatta. "Cheer up, I'll help you out of your troubles." So he
took a block of the purest crystal and scooped out a cavity in
it and made the mouse get inside. "Now stop there," said he,
"and don't fail to fiercely threaten and revile all who come
near."

So the mouse crept into the crystal cell and waited. Up
came one of the cats and demanded his meat. "Away, vile
grimalkin," said the mouse; "why should I supply you? Go
home and eat your kitten!" Infuriated at these words, and never
suspecting the mouse to be inside the crystal, the cat sprang
at the mouse to eat her up, and so furious was its spring that
it broke the walls of its chest and its eyes started from its
head. So that cat died and its carcass tumbled down out of
sight. And the like fate in turn befell all four cats. And ever
after the grateful mouse brought the Bodhisatta two or three
coins instead of one as before, and by degrees she thus gave

him the whole of the hoard. In unbroken friendship the two lived together, till their lives ended and they passed away to fare according to their deserts.

THE TREACHEROUS CHAMELEON

Once upon a time when Brahmadatta was reigning in Benares, the Bodhisatta was born a lizard. When he grew up he dwelt in a big burrow in the river bank with a following of many hundreds of other lizards. Now the Bodhisatta had a son, a young lizard, who was great friends with a chameleon, whom he used to clip and embrace. This intimacy being reported to the lizard king, he sent for his young son and said that such friendship was misplaced, for chameleons were low creatures, and that if the intimacy was persisted in, calamity would befall the whole of the tribe of lizards. And he enjoined his son to have no more to do with the chameleon. But the son continued in his intimacy. Again and again did the Bhodisatta speak with his son, but finding his words of no avail, and foreseeing danger to the lizards from the chameleon, he had an outlet cut on one side of their burrow, so that there might be a means of escape in time of need.

Now as time went on, the young lizard grew to a great size, whilst the chameleon never grew any bigger. And as these mountaineous embraces of the young giant grew painful indeed, the chameleon foresaw that they would be the death of him if they went on a few days longer, and he resolved to combine with a hunter to destroy the whole tribe of lizards.

One day in the summer the ants came out after a thunderstorm, and the lizards darted hither and thither catching them and eating them. Now there came into the forest a lizard trapper with spade and dogs to dig out lizards; and the chameleon thought what a haul he would put in the trapper's way. So he went up to the man, and, lying down before him, asked why he was about in the forest. "To catch lizards," was the reply. "Well, I know where there's a burrow of hundreds of them," said the chameleon; "bring fire and brushwood and follow me." And he brought the trapper to where the lizards dwelt. "Now," said the chameleon, "Put your fuel in there and smoke the lizards out. Meantime let your dogs be all round and take a big stick in your hand. Then as the lizards dash out, strike them down and make a pile of the slain." So saying, the treacherous chameleon withdrew to a spot near by, where he lay down, with his head up, saying to himself,— "This day I shall see the back of my enemy."

The trapper set to work to smoke the lizards out; and fear for their lives drove them helter-skelter from their burrow. As they came out, the trapper knocked them on the head, and if he missed them, they fell a prey to his dogs. And so there was great slaughter among the lizards. Realizing that this was the chameleon's doing, the Bodhisatta cried, "One should never make friends of the wicked, for such bring sorrow in their train. A single wicked chameleon has proved the bane of all these lazards." So saying, he escaped by the outlet he had provided, uttering the stanza:

Bad company can never end in good.
Through friendship with one sole chameleon
The tribe of lizards met their end.

THE CUNNING JACKAL

Once upon a time when Brahmadatta was reigning in Benares, the Bodhisatta was born a jackal, and dwelt in a charnel-grove with a great following of jackals of whom he was king. And at that time there was a festival held at Rājagaha, and a very wet festival it was, with everybody drinking hard. Now a parcel of rogues got hold of victual and drank in abundance, and putting on their best clothes sang and made merry over their fare. By midnight the meat was all gone, though the liquor still held out. Then on one asking for more meat and being told there was none left said the fellow, "Victuals never lack while I am about. I'm off to the charnel-grove, kill a jackal prowling about, to eat the corpses, and bring back some meat." So saying he snatched up a club and made his way out of the city by the sewer to the place, where he lay down, club in hand, feigning to be dead. Just then, followed by the other jackals, the Bodhisatta came up and marked the pretended corpse. Suspecting the fraud, he determined to sift the matter. So he went round to the lee side and knew by the scent that the man was not really dead. Resolving to make the man look foolish before leaving him, the Bodhisatta stole near and took hold of the club with his teeth and tugged at it. The rascal did not leave go: not perceiving the Bodhisatta's approach, he took a tighter grip. Hereon the Bodhisatta stepped back a pace or two and said, "My good man, if you had been dead, you would not have tightened your grip on your club when I was tugging at it, and so have betrayed yourself." So saying, he uttered this stanza:

Thy tightening grip upon thy club doth show
Thy rank imposture-thou'rt no corpse, I trow.

Finding that he was discovered, the rogue sprang to his feet and flung his club at the Bodhisatta, but missed his aim, "Be off, you brute," said he, "I've missed you this time." Turning round, the Bodhisatta said, "True you have missed me, but be assured you will not miss the torments of the Great Hell and the sixteen Lesser Hells."

Empty-handed, the rogue left the cemetery and, after bathing in a ditch went back into the city by the way he had come.

THE FOOLHARDY JACKAL

Once upon a time when Brahmadatta was reigning in Benares, the Bodhisatta was a maned lion and dwelt at Gold Den in the Himalayas. Bounding forth one day from his lair, he looked North and West, South and East, and roared aloud as he went in quest of prey. Slaying a large buffalo, he devoured the prime of the carcass, after which he went to a pool and having drunk his fill of crystal water turned to go towards his den. Now a hungry jackal, suddenly meeting the lion, and being unable to make his escape, threw himself at the lion's feet. Being asked what he wanted, the jackal replied, "Lord, let me be your servant." "Very well," said the lion; "serve me and you shall feed on prime meat." So saying, he went with the jackal following to Gold Den. Thenceforth the lion's leavings fell to the jackal, and he grew fat.

Lying one day in his den, the lion told the jackal to scan the valleys from the mountain top, to see whether there were any elephants or horses or buffaloes about, or any other animals of which he, the jackal, was fond. If any such were in sight, the jackal was to report and say with due obeisance, "Shine forth in thy might, Lord." Then the lion promised to kill and eat, giving a part to the jackal. So the jackal used to climb the heights, and whenever he espied below beasts to his taste, he would report it to the lion, and falling at his feet, say, "Shine forth in thy might, Lord." Hereon the lion would nimbly bound forth and slay the beast, even if it were a rutting elephant, and share the prime of the carcass with the jackal. Glutted with his meal, the jackal would then retire to his den and sleep.

Now as time went on, the jackal grew bigger and bigger till he grew haughty. "Have not I too four legs?" he asked himself. "Why am I a pensioner day by day on other's bounty? Henceforth I will kill elephants and other beasts, for my own eating. The lion, king of beasts, only kills them because of the formula, "Shine forth in thy might Lord.' I'll make the lion call out to me, 'Shine forth in thy might, jackal,'—and then I'll kill an elephant for myself." Accordingly he went to the lion, and pointing out that he had long lived on what the lion had killed, told his desire to eat an elephant of his own killing, ending with a request to the lion to let him, the jackal, couch in the lion's corner in Gold Den whilst the lion was to climb the mountain to look out for an elephant. The quarry found, he asked that the lion should come to him in the den and say, "Shine forth in thy might, jackal." He begged the lion not to grudge him this much. Said the lion, "Jackal. only lions can kill elephants, nor has the world ever seen a jackal able to cope with them. Give up this fancy, and continue to feed on what I kill." But say what the lion could, the jackal would not give way, and still pressed his request. So at last the lion gave way,

and bidding the jackal couch in the den, climbed the peak and
thence espied an elephant in rut. Returning to the mouth of the
cave, he said, "Shine forth in thy might, jackal." Then from
Gold Den the jackal nimbly bounded forth, looked around him
on all four sides, and, thrice raising its howl, sprang at the
elephant, meaning to fasten on its head. But missing his aim,
he alighted at the elephant's feet. The infuriated brute raised
its right foot and crushed the jackal's head, trampling the bones
into powder. Then pounding the carcass into a mass, and
dunging upon it, the elephant dashed trumpeting into the forest.
Seeing all this, the Bodhisatta observed, "Now shine forth in
thy might, jackal," and uttered this stanza:

Your mangled corpse, your brains mashed into clay.
Prove how you've shone forth in your might to-day.

Thus spake the Bodhisatta, and living to a good old age he
passed away in the fulness of time to fare according to his
deserts.

THE FOOLISH CROWS

Once upon a time Brahmadatta was reigning in Benares,
the Bodhisatta was a sea-spirit. Now a crow with his mate
came down in quest of food to the sea-shore where, just before,
certain persons has been offering to the Nāgas a sacrifice of
milk, and rice, and fish, and meat and strong drink and the like.
Up came the crow and with his mate ate freely of the elements
of the sacrifice, and drank a great deal of the spirits. So they
both got very drunk. Then they wanted to disport themselves
in the sea, and were trying to swim on the surf, when a wave
swept the hen-crow out sea and a fish came and gobbled her
up.

"Oh, my poor wife is dead," cried the crow, bursting into
tears and lamentations. Then a crowd of crows were drawn by
his wailing to the spot to learn what ailed him. And when he
told them how his wife had been carried out to sea, they all
began with one voice to lament. Suddenly the thought struck
them that they were stronger than the sea and that all they

had to do was to empty it out and rescue their comrade! So
they set to work with their bills to empty the sea out by mouth-
fuls, betaking themselves to dry land to rest so soon as their
throats were sore with the salt water. And so they toiled away
till their mouths and jaws were dry and inflamed and their
eyes bloodshot, and they were ready to drop for weariness.
Then in despair they turned to one another and said that it was
in vain they laboured to empty the sea, for no sooner had they
got rid of the water in one place than more flowed in, and there
was all their work to do over again; they would never succeed
in bailing the water out sea. And so saying, they uttered this
stanza:

Our jaws are tired, our mouths are sore;
The sea refilleth evermore.

Then all the crows fell to praising the beauty of her beak
and eyes, her complexion, figure and sweet voice, saying that
it was her excellence that had provoked the sea to steal her
from them. But as they talked this nonsense, the sea-spirit
made a bogey appear from the sea and so put them all to flight.
In this wise they were saved.

THE GREEDY JACKAL CAUGHT

Once upon a time when Brahmadatta was reigning in
Benares, the Bodhisatta was re-born into life as a jackal and
dwelt in the forest by the river side. Now an old elephant died
by the banks of the Ganges, and the jackal, finding the carcass,
congratulated himself on lighting upon such a store of meat.
First he bit the trunk, but that was like biting a plough-handle.
"There's no eating here, "said the jackal and took a bite at a
tusk. But that was like biting bones. Then he tried an ear, but
that was like chewing the rim of a winnowing-basket. So he
fell to on the stomach, but found it as tough as a grain basket.
The feet were no better, for they were like a mortar. Next he
tried the tail, but that was like the pestle. "That won't do
either," said the jackal; and having failed elsewhere to find a
toothsome part, he tried the rear and found that like eating a
soft cake. "At last " said he, "I've found the right place," and

ate his way right into the belly, where he made a plenteous meal off the kidneys, heart and the rest, quenching his thirst with the blood. And when night came on, he lay down inside. As he lay there, the thought came into the jackal's mind, "this carcass is both meat and house to me and wherefore should I leave it?" So there he stopped, and dwelt in the elephant's inwards, eating away. Time wore on till the summer sun and the summer winds dried and shrank the elephant's hide, until the entrance by which the jackal had got in was closed and the interior was in utter darkness. Thus the jackal was, as it were, cut off from the world and confined in the interspace between the worlds. After the hide, the flesh dried up and the blood was exhausted. In a frenzy of despair, he rushed to and fro beating against his prison walls in the fruitless endeavour to escape. But as he bobbed up and down inside like a ball of rice in a boiling saucepan, soon a tempest broke and the downpour moistened the shell of the carcass and restored it to its former state, till light shone like a star through the way by which the jackal, had got in. "Saved! Saved!" cried the jackal, and backing into the elephant's head made a rush head-first at the outlet. He managed to get through, it is true, but only by leaving all his hair on the way. And first he ran, then he halted, and then sat down and surveyed his hairless body, now smooth as a palm-stem. "Ah!" he exclaimed, "this misfortune has befallen me because of my greed and my greed alone. Henceforth I will not be greedy nor ever again into the carcass of an elephant." And his terror found expression in this stanza:

Once bitten, twice shy. Ah, great was my fear!
Of elephants' inwards henceforth I'll steer clear.

And with these words the jackal neither made off, nor did he ever again so much as look either at that or at any other elephant's carcass. And thenceforth he was never greedy again.

THE RASH MAGICIAN

Once upon a time when Brahmadatta was reigning in Benares, the Bodhisatta was born into the family of a wealthy brahmin. Arriving at years of discretion, he went to study at

Takkasilā, where he received a complete education. In Benares as a teacher he enjoyed world-wide fame and had five hundred young brahmins as pupils. Among these was one named Sanjiva, to whom the Bodhisatta taught the spell for raising the dead to life. But though the young man was taught this, he was not taught the counter charm. Proud of his new power, he went with his fellow-pupils to the forest wood-gathering, and there came on a dead tiger.

"Now see me bring the tiger to life again," said he.

"You can't," said they.

"You look and you will see me do it."

"Well, if you can, do so," said they, and climbed up a tree forthwith.

Then Sanjiva repeated his charm and struck the dead tiger with a potsherd. Up started the tiger and quick as lighting sprang at Sanjiva and bit him on the throat, killing him outright. Dead fell the tiger then and there, and dead fell Sanjiva too at the same spot. So there the two lay dead side by side.

The young brahmins took their wood and went back to their master to whom they told the story. "My dear pupils," said he, "mark herein how by reason of showing favour to the sinful and paying honour where it was not due, he has brought all this calamity upon himself." And so saying he uttered this stanza:

Befriend a villain, aid him in his need,
And, like that tiger which Sanjiva raised
To life, he straight devours you for your pains.

Such was the Bodhisatta's lesson to the young brahmins, and after a life of almsgiving and other goods deeds he passed away to fare according to his deserts.

THE TWO GOOD KINGS

Once upon a time, when Brahmadatta was king of Benares, the Bodhisatta was conceived by his Queen Consort; and the ceremonies proper to her state having been duly done, she was afterwards safely delivered. On his name-day, the name they gave him was Prince Brahmadatta.

In course of time, he grew up, and at sixteen years went to Takksilā for his education; where he mastered all branches of learning, and on his father's death he became king in his stead, and ruled with uprightness and all rectitude, administrating justice with no regard had to his own will or whim. And as he ruled thus justly, his ministers on their part were also just; thus, while all things were justly done, there was none who brought a false suit into court. Presently all the bustle of suitors ceased within the precincts of the palace; all day long the ministers might sit on the bench, and go away without seeing a single suitor. The courts were deserted.

Then the Bodhisatta thought to himself, "Because of my just government not one suitor comes to try issue in court; the old hubbub is quiet; the courts of law are deserted. Now I must search whether I have any fault in me; which if I find, I will eschew it, and live a good life hereafter." From that time he tried continually to find some one who would tell him of a fault; but of all who were about him at court he could not find one such; nothing could he hear but good of himself. "Perhaps," thought he, "they are all so much afraid of me that they say no ill of me but only good," and so he went about to try those who were outside his walls. But with these it was just the same. Then he made inquisition of the citizens at large, and outside the city questioned those who belonged to the suburbs at the four city gates. Still there was none who had any fault to find; nothing but praises could he hear. Lastly, with intent to try the countryside, he entrusted all government to his ministers, and mounted in his carriage, and taking only the driver with him, left the city in disguise. All the country he traversed, even to the frontier; but not a fault-finder could he light upon; all he could hear was only his own praises. So back he turned from the marches, and set his face homewards again by the high-road.

Now it fortuned that at this very time Mallika, the king of Kosala, had done the very same thing. He too was a just king, and he had been searching for his faults; but amongst those about him there was none who had any fault to find; and hearing nothing but praise, he had been making enquiry throughout all the country, and had but then arrived at that same spot.

These two met, in a place where the carriage-road was deeply sunk between two banks, and there was no room for one carriage to pass another.

"Get your carriage out of the way!" said king Mallika's driver to the driver of the king of Benares.

"No, no, driver," said he, "out of the way with yours! Know that in this carriage sits the great monarch Brahmadatta, lord of the kingdom of Benares!"

"Not, so, driver!" replied the other, "in this carriage sits the great king Mallika, lord of the realm of Kosala! It is for you to make way, and to give place to the carriage of our king!"

"Why, here's a king too," thought the driver of the king of Benares. "What in the world is to be done ?" Then a thought struck him; he would enquire what should be the age of the two kings, so that the younger should give way to the elder. And he made enquiry of the other driver how old his king was; but he learnt that both were of the same age. Thereupon he asked the extent of this king's power, wealth, and glory, and all points touching his caste and clan and his family; discovering that both of them had a country three hundred leagues long, and that they were alike in power, wealth, glory, and the nature of their family and lineage. Then he bethought him that place might be given o the better man; so he requested that the other driver should describe his master's virtues. The man

replied by the first verse of poetry following, in which he set
forth his monarch's faults as though they were so many virtues:

> Rough to the rough, king Mallika the mild with mild ness
> sways,
> Masters the good by goodness, and the bad with badness
> pays
> Give place, give place, O driver! such are this monarch's
> ways!

"Oh," said the man of the king of Benares, "is that all you
have to say about king's virtues?" "Yes," said the other.—"If
these are his virtues, what must his vice be!" "Vices be it,
then," quoth he, "if you will, but let us hear what your king's
virtues may be like!" "Listen then," rejoined the first, and repeated the second verse:

> He conquers wrath by mildness, the bad with goodness
> sways,
> By gifts the miser vanquishes and lies with truth repays.
> Give place, give place, O driver! such are this monarch's
> ways!

At these words both king Mallika and his driver descended
from their carriage, and loosened the horses, and moved it out
of the way, to give place to the king of Benares. Then the king
of Benares gave good admonition to king Mallika, saying, "Thus
and thus must you do"; after which he returned to Benares,
and there gave alms and did good all his life, till at the last he
went to swell the hosts of heaven. And king Mallika look the
lesson to heart; and after traversing the length and breadth of
the land, and lighting upon none who had any fault to find in
him, returned to his own city; where he gave alms all his life
and did good, till at the end he too attained to heaven.

THE GRATEFUL ELEPHANT

Once upon a time, when Brahmadatta was king of Benares,
there was a village of carpenters not far from the city, in which
five hundred carpenters lived. They would go up the river in a

vessel, and enter the forest, where they would shape beams and planks for house-building, and put together the framework of one-storey houses or two-storey houses numbering all the pieces from the mainpost onwards; these then they brought down to the river bank, and put them all aboard; then rowing down stream again, they would build houses to orders as it was required of them; after which, when they received their wage, they went back again for more materials for the building, and in this way they made their livelihood.

Once it befell that in a place where they were at work in shaping timbers, a certain Elephant trod upon a splinter of acacia wood, which pierced his foot, and caused it to swell up and fester, and he was in great pain. In his agony, he caught the sound of these carpenters cutting wood. "There are some carpenters who will cure me," thought he; and limping on three feet, he presented himself before them and lay down close by. The carpenters, noticing his swollen foot, went up and looked; there was a splinter sticking in it. With a sharp tool they made incision about the splinter, and tying a string to it, pulled it right out. Then they lanced the gathering, and washed it with warm water, and doctored it properly; and in a very short time the wound was healed.

Grateful for this cure, the Elephant thought; "My life has been saved by the help of these carpenters; now I must make myself useful to them." So ever after that, he used to pull up trees for them, or when they were chopping he would roll up the logs or bring them their adzes and any tools they might want, holding everything in his trunk like grim death. And the carpenters, when it was time to feed him, used to bring him each a portion of food, so that he had five hundred portions in all.

Now this Elephant had a young one, white all over, a magnificent high-bred creature. The Elephant reflected that he was now old, and he had better bring his young one to serve the carpenters, and himself be left free to go. So without a word to the carpenters, he went off into the wood, and brought his son to them, saying, "The young Elephant is a son of mine. You saved my life, and I give him to you as a fee for your leechcraft; from henceforth he shall work for you." So he explained to the young Elephant that it was his duty to do the work which he had been used to do himself, and then went away into the forest, leaving him with the carpenters. So after that time the young Elephant did all their work, faithfully and obediently; and they fed him, as they had fed the other, with five hundred portions for a meal.

His work once done, the Elephant would go play about in the river, and then return again. The carpenters' children used to pull him by the trunk, and play all sorts of pranks with-him in water and out. Now noble creatures, be they elephants, horses, or men, never dung or stale in the water. So this Elephant did nothing of the kind when he was in the water, but waited until he came out upon the bank.

One day, rain had fallen up river; and by the flood a half-dry cake of his dung was carried into the river. This floated down to the Benares landing place, where it stuck fast in a bush. Just then the king's elephant keepers had brought down five hundred elephants to give them a bath. But the creatures scented this soil of a noble animal, and not one would enter the water; up went their tails, and off they all ran. The keepers told this to the elephant trainers; who replied, "There must be something in the water, then." So orders were given to cleanse the water; and there in the bushes this lump was seen. "That's what the matter is!" cried the men. So they brought a jar, and filled it with water; next powdering the stuff into it, they sprinkled the water over the elephants, whose bodies then became sweet. At once they went down into the river and bathed.

When the trainers made their report to the king, they advised him to secure the Elephant for his own use and profit.

The king accordingly embarked upon a raft, and rowed up stream until he arrived at the place where the carpenters had settled. The young Elephant, hearing the sound of drums as he was playing in the water, came out and presented himself before the carpenters, who one and all came forth to do honour to the king's coming, and said to him, "Sire, if woodwork is wanted, what need to come here? Why not send and have it brought to you?"

"No, no, good friends", "the king answered, "tis not for wood that I come but for this elephant here."

"He is yours, Sire!"— But the Elephant refused to budge.

"What do you want me to do, gossip Elephant?" asked the king.

"Order the carpenters to be paid for what they have spent on me, Sire."

"Willingly, friend." And the king ordered a hundred thousand pieces of money to be laid by his tail, and trunk, and by each of his four feet. But this was not enough for the Elephant; go he would not. So to each of the carpenters was given a pair of clothes, and to each of their wives robes to dress in, nor did he omit to give enough whereby his playmates, the children, should be brought up; then with a last look upon the carpenters, and the women, and the children, he departed in company with the king.

To his capital city the king brought him; and city and stable were decked out with all magnificence. He led the Elephant round the city in solemn procession, and thence into his stable, which was fitted up with splendour and pomp. There he solemnly sprinkled the Elephant, and appointed him for his own riding; like a comrade he treated him, and gave him the half of his kingdom, taking as much care of him as he did of himself. After the coming of this Elephant, the king won supremacy over all India.

In course of time the Bodhisatta was conceived by the

Queen consort; and when her time was near come to be delivered, the king died. Now if the Elephant learnt news of the
king's death, he was sure to break his heart; so he was waited
upon as before, and not a word said. But the next neighbour,
the king of kosala, heard of the king's death. "Surely the land
is at my mercy," thought he; and marched with a mighty host
to the city, and beleaguered it. Straight the gates were closed,
and a message was sent to the king of kosala: "Our Queen is
near the time of her delivery; and the astrologers have declared
that in seven days she shall bear a son. If she bears a son, we
will not yield the kingdom, but on the seventh day we will give
you battle. For so long we pray you wait!" And to this the king
agreed.

In seven days the Queen bore a son. On his name-day they
call him Prince Winheart, because, said they, he was born to
win the hearts of the people.

On the very same day that he was born, the townsfolk
began to do battle with the king of Kosala. But as they had no
leader, little by little the army gave way, great though it was.
The courtiers told this news to the Queen, adding, "Since our
army loses ground in this way, we fear defeat. But the state
Elephant, our king's bosom friend, has never been told that the
king is dead and a son born to him, and that the king of Kosala
is here to give us battle. Shall we tell him?"

"Yes, do so, said the Queen. So she dressed up her son,
and laid him in a fine linen cloth; after which she with all the
court came down from the palace and entered the Elephant's
stable. There she laid the babe at the Elephant's feet, saying,
"Master, your comrade is dead, but we feared to tell it you lest
you might break your heart. This is your comrade's son; the
king of Kosala has run a leaguer about the city, and is making
war upon your son; the army is losing ground; either kill your
son yourself, or else win the kingdom back for him!"

At once the Elephant stroked the child with his trunk, and
lifted him upon his own head; then making moan and lamen-

tation he took him down and laid him in his mother's arms, and with the words—"I will master the king of Kosala!" he went forth hastily.

Then the courtiers put his armour and caparison upon him, and unlocked the city gate and escorted him thither. The Elephant emerging trumpeted, and frightened all the host so that they ran away, and broke up the camp; then seizing the king of Kosala by his topknot, he carried him to the young prince, at whose feet he let him fall. Some rose to kill him, but them the Elephant stayed; and he let the captive king go with this advice: "Be careful for the future, and be not presumptuous by reasons that our Prince is young."

After that, the power over all India fell into the Bodhisatta's own hand, and not a foe was able to rise up against him. The Bodhisatta was consecrated at the age of seven years, as king Winheart; just was his reign, and when he came to life's end he attained to heaven.

THE PET ELEPHANT

Once upon a time, while Brahmadatta was king of Benares, the Bodhisatta was born of a Brahmin family. On growing up he left his worldly home and took to the religious life, and in time became the leader of a company of five hundred anchorites, who all lived together in the region of Himalaya.

Amongst the anchorites was a headstrong and unteachable person named Indasamānagotta. He had a pet elephant. The Bodhisatta sent for him when he found this out, and asked if he really did keep a young elephant? "Yes," the man said, "he had an elephant which had lost its dam." "Well," the Bodhisatta said, "when elephants grow up they kill even those who foster them; so you had better not keep it any longer." "But I can't live without him, my Teacher!" was the reply. "Oh, well," said the Bodhisatta, "you'll live to repent it."

Howbeit he still reared the creature, and by and by it grew

to an immense size.

It happened once that the anchorites had all gone far afield to gather roots and fruits in the forest, and they were absent for several days. At the first breath of the south wind this elephant fell in a frenzy. "Destruction to this hut!" thought he, "I'll smash the water-jar! I'll overturn the stone bench ! I'll tear up the pallet ! I'll kill the hermit, and then off I'll go!" So he sped into the judge, and waited watching for their return.

His master came first, laden with food for his pet. As soon as he saw him, he hastened up, thinking all was well. Out rushed the elephant from the thicket, and seizing him in his trunk, dashed him to the ground, then with a blow on the head crushed the life out of him; and madly trumpeting he scampered into the forest.

The other anchorites brought this news to the Bodhisatta. Said he, "We should have no dealings with the bad"; and then he repeated these two verses:

Friendship with evil let the good eschew,
The good, who know what duty bids them do:
They will work mischief, be it soon or late,
Even as the elephant his master slew.
But if a kindred spirit thus shalt see,
In virtue, wisdom, learning like to thee,
Choose such an one to be thy own true friend;
Good friends and blessing go in company.

In this way the Bodhisatta showed his band of anchorites that it is well to be docile and not obstinate. Then he performed Indasamānagotta's obsequies, and cultivating the Excellences, came at last into Brahma's heaven.

THE MONGOOSE AND THE SNAKE

Once upon a time, when Brahmadatta was king of Benares, the Bodhisatta was born in a certain village as one of a brahmin family. When he came of age, he was educated at Takkasilā;

then, renouncing the world he became a recluse, cultivated the Faculties and the Attainments, and dwelt in the region of Himalaya, living upon wild roots and fruits which he picked up in his goings to and fro.

At the end of his cloistered walk lived a Mongoose in an ant-heap; and not far off, a Snake lived in a hollow tree. These two, Snake and Mongoose, were perpetually quarrelling. The Bodhisatta preached to them the misery of quarrels and the blessing of cultivating friendship, and reconciled the two together, saying, "You ought to cease your quarrelling and live together as one."

When the Serpent was abroad, the Mongoose at the end of the walk lay with his head out of the hole in his ant-hill, and mouth open, and thus fell asleep, heavily drawing his breath in and out. The Bodhisatta saw him sleeping there, and asking him, "Why, what are you afraid of?" repeated the first stanza:

Creature, your egg-born enemy a faithful friend is made:
Why sleep you there with teeth all bare? Of what are you afraid?

"Father," said the Mongoose, "never despise a former enemy, but always suspect him": and he repeated the second stanza:

Never despise an enemy nor ever trust a friend:
A fear that springs from unfeared things uproots and makes an end.

"Fear not," replied the Bodhisatta. "I have persuaded the Snake to do you no harm; distrust him no more." With this advice, he proceeded to cultivate the four Excellences, and became destined for Brahma's heaven. And the others too passed away to fare hereafter according to their deeds.

THE JACKAL BETRAYED BY HIS HOWL

Once upon a time, when Brahmadatta was reigning in Benares, the Bodhisatta was born as a young lion, and was the king of many lions. With a suite of lions he dwelt in Silver Cave. Near by was a Jackal, living in another cave.

One day, after a shower of rain, all the lions were together at the entrance of their leader's cave, roaring loudly and gamboling about as lions do. As they were thus roaring and playing, the jackal too lifted up his voice. "Here's this jackal, giving tongue along with us!" said the lions; they felt ashamed, and were silent. When they all fell silent, the Bodhisatta's cub asked him this question. "Father, all these lions that were roaring and playing about have fallen silent for very shame on hearing yon creature. What creature is it that betrays itself thus by its voice?" And he repeated the first stanza:

Who is it with a mighty cry makes Daddara resound?
Who is it, Lord of Beasts? And why has he no wel-come
found?

At his son's words the old lion repeated the second stanza:
The jackal, of all beasts most vile, 'tis he that makes that
sound:
The lions loathe his baseness, while they sit in   silence
round.

THE PENNY-WISE MONKEY

Once upon a time, when Brahmadatta was reigning in Benares, he had a councillor who was his right-hand man and gave him advice in things spiritual and temporal. There was a rising on the frontier, and the troops there stationed sent the king a letter. The king started, rainy season though it was, and formed a camp in his park. The Bodhisatta stood before the king. At that moment the people had steamed some peas for the horses, and poured them out into a trough. One of the monkeys that lived in the park jumped down from a tree, filled his mouth and hands with the peas, then up again, and sitting down in the tree he began to eat. As he ate, one pea fell from his hand upon the ground. Down dropped at once all the peas from his hands and mouth, and down from the tree he came, to hunt for the lost pea. But that pea he could not find; so he climbed up his tree again, and sat still, very glum, looking like some one who had lost a thousand in some lawsuit.

The king observed how the monkey had done, and pointed it out to the Bodhisatta. "Friend, what do you think of that?" he asked. To which the Bodhisatta made answer: "King, this is what fools of little wit are wont to do; they spend a pound to win a penny"; and he went on to repeat the first stanza:
A foolish monkey, living in the trees,
O king, when both his hands were full of peas,
Has thrown them all away to look for one:
There is no wisdom, Sire, in such as these.

Then the Bodhisatta approached the king, and addressing him again, repeated the second stanza:
Such are we, O mighty monarch, such all those that greedy
be;
Losing much to gain a little, like the monkey and the pea.

On hearing this address the king turned and went straight back to Benares. And the outlaws hearing that the king had set forth from his capital to make mincemeat of his enemies hurried away from the borders.

THE INCOMPARABLE ARCHER

Once upon a time, when Brahmadatta was king of Benares, the Bodhisatta was conceived as the son of the Queen Consort. She was safely delivered; and on his name-day they gave him the name of Asadisa-Kumāra, Prince Peerless. About the time he was able to walk, the Queen conceived one who was also to be a good being. She was safely delivered, and on the name-day they called the babe Brahmadatta-Kumāra, or Prince Heaven-sent.

When Prince Peerless was sixteen he went to Takkasilā for his education. There at the feet of a world-famed teacher he learnt the Three Vedas and Eighteen Accomplishments; in the science of archery he was peerless; then he returned to Benares.

When the king was on his deathbed he commanded that Prince Peerless should be king in his stead, and Prince Brahamadatta the viceroy. Then he died; after which the king-ship was offered to Peerless, who refused, saying that he cared not for it. So they consecrated Brahmadatta to be king by sprinkling him. Peerless cared nothing for glory, and wanted nothing.

While the younger brother ruled, Peerless lived in all royal state. The slave came and slandered him to his brother; "Prince Peerless wants to be king!" said they. Brahmadatta believed them, and allowed himself to be deceived; he sent some men to take Peerless prisoner.

One of Prince Peerless' attendants told him what was afoot. He waxed angry with his brother, and went away into another country. When he arrived there, he sent in word to the king that an archer was come, and awaited him. "What wages does he ask?" the king enquired. "A hundred thousand a year." "Good," said the king; "let him enter."

Peerless came into the presence, and stood waiting. "Are you the archer?" asked the king. "Yes, Sire." "Very well, I take you into my service." After that peerless remained in the service of this king. But the old archers were annoyed at the wage which was given him; "Too much," they grumbled.

One day it so happened that the king went out into his park. There, at foot of a mango tree, where a screen had been put up before a certain stone seat of ceremony, he reclined upon a magnificent couch. He happened to look up, and there right at the treetop he saw a cluster of mango fruit.

"It is too high to climb for," thought he; so summoning his archers he asked them whether they could cut off you cluster with an arrow, and bring it down for him. "Oh," said they, "that is not much for us to do. But your majesty has seen our skill often enough. The newcomer is so much better paid than we, that perhaps you might make him bring down the fruit."

Then the king sent for Peerless, and asked him if he could do it . "Oh yes, your Majesty, if I may choose my position." "What position do you want?" "The place where your couch stands." The king had a couch removed, and gave place.

Peerless had no bow in his hand; he used to carry it underneath his body-cloth; so he must needs have a screen. The king ordered a screen to be bought and spread for him and our archer went in. He doffed the white cloth which he wore over all, and put on a red cloth next his skin; then he fastened his girdle, and donned a red waistcloth. From a bag he took out a sword in pieces, which he put together and girt on his left side. Next he put on a mailcoat of gold, fastened his bow-case over his back, and took out his great ramshorn bow, made in several pieces, which he fitted together, fixed the bow-string, red as coral; put a turban upon his head; twirling the arrow with his nails, he threw open the screen and came out, looking like a Nāga prince just emerging from the riven ground. He went to the place of shooting, arrow set to bow, and then put this question to the king. "Your Majesty," said he, "am I to bring this fruit down with an upward shot, or by dropping the arrow upon it?"

"My son," said the king," I have often seen a mark brought down by the upward shot, but never one taken in the fall. You had better make the shaft fall on it."

"Your Majesty," said the archer, "this arrow will fly high. Up to the heaven of the Four Great kings it will fly, and then return of itself. You must please be patient till it returns." The king promised. Then the archer said again, "Your Majesty, this arrow in its upshot will pierce the stalk exactly in the middle; and when it comes down, it will not swerve a hairsbreadth either way, but hit the same spot to a nicety, and bring down the cluster with it." Then he sped the arrow forth swiftly. As the arrow went up it pierced the exact center of the mango stalk. By the time the archer knew his arrow had reached the place of the Four Great kings, he let fly another arrow with greater speed than the first. This struck the feather of the first

arrow, and turned it back; then itself went up as far as the
heaven of the Thirty-three gods. There the deities caught and
kept it.

The sound of the falling arrow as it cleft the air was as the
sound of a thunderbolt. "What is that noise?" asked every man.
"That is the arrow falling," our archer replied. The bystanders
were all frightened to death, for fear the arrow should fall on
them; but Peerless comforted them. "Fear nothing," said he,
"and I will see that it does not fall on the earth." Down came
the arrow, not a hairbreadth out either way, but neatly cut
through the stalk of the mango cluster. The archer caught the
arrow in one hand and the fruit in the other, so that they should
not fall upon the ground. "We never saw such a thing before!"
cried the onlookers, at this marvel. How they praised the great
man! how they cheered and clapped and snapped their fingers,
thousands of kerchiefs waving in the air ! In their joy and delight the courtiers gave presents to Peerless amounting to ten
millions of money. And the king too showered gifts and honours
upon him like rain.

While the Bodhisatta was receiving such glory and honour
at the hands of this king, seven kings, who knew that there
was no Prince Peerless in Benares drew a leaguer around the
city, and summoned its king to fight or yield. The king was
frightened out of his life. "Where is my brother?" he asked. "He
is in the service of a neighbouring king," was the reply. "If my
dear brother does not come, said he, "I am a dead man. Go, fall
at his feet in my name, appease him, bring him hither!" His
messengers came and did their errand. Peerless took leave of
his master, and returned to Benares. He comforted his brother
and bade him fear nothing; then scratched a message upon an
arrow to this effect: "I, Prince Peerless, am returned. I mean to
kill you all with one arrow which I will shoot at you. Let those
who care for life make their escape." This he shot so that it fell
upon the very middle of a golden dish, from which the seven
kings were eating together. When they read the writing they
all fled, half-dead with fright.

Thus did our Prince put to flight seven kings, without shedding even so much blood as a little fly might drink; then looking upon his younger brother, he renounced his lusts and forsook the world, cultivated the Faculties and the Attainments, and at his life's end came to Brahma's heaven.

THE MAGIC TREASURES

Once upon a time, when Brahmadatta was reigning in Benares, four brahmins brothers, of the land of Kāsi, left the world and became hermits; they built themselves four huts in a row in the highlands of the Himalaya, and there they lived.

The eldest brother died, and was born as Sakka. Knowing who he had been, he used to visit the others every seven or eight days, and lend them a helping hand.

One day, he visited the eldest of the anchorites, and after the usual greeting, took his seat to one side. "Well, Sir, how can I serve you?" he enquired. The hermit, who was suffering from jaundice, replied, "Fire is what I want." Sakka gave him a razor-axe. (A razor-axe is called so because it serves as razor or as axe according as you fit it into the handle.) "Why," said the hermit, "who is there to get me firewood with this?" "If you want a fire, Sir," replied Sakka, "all you have to do to strike your hand upon the axe and say—'Fetch wood and make a fire!' The axe will fetch the wood and make you the fire."

After giving him this razor-axe he next visited the second brother, and asked him the same question—"How can I serve you, Sir?" Now there was an elephant track by his hut and the creatures annoyed him. So he told Sakka that he was annoyed by elephants, and wanted them to be driven away. Sakka gave him a drum. "If you beat upon this side, Sir," he explained, "your enemies will run away; but if you strike the other, they will become your firm friends, and will encompass you with an army in fourfold array." Then he handed him the drum.

Lastly he made a visit to the youngest, and asked as before

how he could serve him. He too had jaundice, and what he said was—"Please give me some curds." Sakka gave him a milk-bowl, with these words: "Turn this over if you want anything, and a great river will pour out it, and will flood the whole place, and it will be able even to win a kingdom for you." With these words he departed.

After this the axe used to make fire for the eldest brother, the second used to beat upon one side of his drum and drive the elephants away, and the youngest had his curds to eat.

About this time a wild boar, that lived in a ruined village, hit upon a gem possessed of magic power. Picking up the gem in his mouth, he rose in the air by its magic. From afar he could see an isle in mid-ocean, and there he resolved to live. So descending he choose a pleasant spot beneath a fig tree, and there he made his abode.

One day he fell asleep under the tree, with the jewel lay-ing in front of him. Now a certain man from the Kāsi country, who had been turned out of doors by his parents as a ne'er-do-well, had made his way to a seaport, where he embarked on shipboard as a sailors' drudge. In midsea the ship was wrecked, and he floated upon a plank to this island. As the wandered in search of fruit, he espied our boar fast asleep. Quietly he crept up, seized the gem, and found himself by magic rising through the air! He alighted on the fig tree, and pondered. "The magic of this gem," thought he, "has taught you boar to be a sky-walker; that's how he got here, I suppose. Well! I must kill him and make a meal of him first; and then I'll be off." So he snapt off a twig, dropping it upon the boar's head. The boar woke up, and seeing no gem, ran trembling up and down. The man up in the tree laughed. The boar looked up, and seeing him ran his head against the tree, and killed himself.

The man came down, lit a fire, cooked the boar and made a meal. Then he rose up in the sky, and set out on his journey.

As he passed over the Himalaya, he saw the hermits'

settlement. So he descended, and spent two or three days in the eldest brother's hut, entertaining and entertained, and he found out the virtue of the axe. He made up his mind to get it for himself. So he showed our hermit the virtue of his gem and offered to exchange it for the axe. The hermit longed to be able to pass through mid-air, and stuck the bargain. The man took the axe, and departed; but before he had gone very far, he struck upon it and said—"Axe! Smash that hermit's skull and bring that gem to me!" Off flew the axe, clove the hermit's skull, and brought the gem back.

Then the man hid the axe away, and paid a visit to the second brother. With him the visitor stayed a few days, and soon discovered the power of his drum. Then he exchanged his gem for the drum, as before, and as before made the axe cleave the owner's skull. After this he went on to the youngest of the three hermits, found out the power of the milk-bowl, gave his jewel in exchange for it, and as before sent his axe to cleave the man's skull. Thus he was now owner of jewel, axe, drum, and milk-bowl, all four.

He now rose up and passed through the air. Stopping near by Benares, he wrote a letter which he sent by a messenger's hands, that the king must either fight him or yield. On receipt of this message the king sallied forth to "seize the scoundrel." But he beat on one side of his drum, and was promptly surrounded by an army in fourfold array. When he saw that the king had deployed his forces, he then overturned the milk-bowl, and a great river poured forth; multitudes were drowned in the river of curds. Next he struck upon his axe. "Fetch me the king's head!" cried he; away went the axe, and came back and dropt the head at his feet. Not a man could raise hand against him.

So encompassed by a mighty host, he entered the city, and caused himself to be anointed king under the title of king Dadhi-vāhana, or Carried-on-the-Curds, and ruled righteously.

One day, as the king was amusing himself by casting a

net into the river, he caught mango fruit, fit for the gods, which
had floated down from lake Kannamunda. When the net was
hauled out, the mango was found, and shown to the king. It
was a huge fruit, as big as a basin, round, and golden in colour.
The king asked what the fruit was: Mango, said the foresters.
He ate it, and had the stone planted in his park, and watered
with milk-water.

The tree sprouted up, and in three years it bore fruit. Great
was the worship paid to this tree: milk-water was poured about
it; perfumed garlands with five sprays were hung upon it;
wreaths were festooned about it; a lamp was kept burning,
and fed with scented oil; and all round it was a screen of cloth.
The fruit was sweet, and had the colour of fine gold. King
Dadhi-vāhana, before sending presents of these mangoes to
other kings, used to prick with a thorn that place in the stone
where the sprout would come from, for fear of their growing the
like by planting it. When they ate the fruit, they used to plant
the stone; but they could not get it to take root. They enquired
the reason, and learnt how the matter was.

One king asked his gardener whether he could spoil the
flavour of this fruit, and turn it bitter on the tree. Yes, the man
said he could; so his king gave him a thousand pieces and sent
him on his errand.

So soon as he had arrived in Benares, the man sent a
message to the king that a gardener has come. The king admitted him to the presence. After the man had saluted him the
king asked, "You are a gardener?" "Yes, Sire", said the man,
and began to sound his own praises. "Very well," said the
king, "you may go and assist my park-keeper." So after that
these both used to look after the royal grounds.

The newcomer managed to make the park look more beautiful by forcing flowers and fruit out of their season. This pleased
the king, so that he dismissed the former keeper and gave the
park into sole charge of the new one. No sooner had this man
got the park into his own hands than he planted the nimbs and

creepers about the choice mango tree. By and by the nimbs sprouted up. Above and below, root with root, and branch with branch, these were all entangled with the mango tree. Thus this tree, with its sweet fruit, grew bitter as the bitter-leaved nimb by the company of this noxious and sour plant. As soon as the gardener knew that the fruit had gone bitter, he took to his heels.

King Dadhi-vāhana went a walking in his pleasaunce, and took a bit of the mango fruit. The juice in his mouth tasted like nasty nimb; swallow it he could not, so he coughed and spat it out. Now at that time the Bodhisatta was his temporal and spiritual counselor. The king turned to him. "Wise Sir, this tree is as carefully cared for as ever, and yet its fruit has gone bitter. What's the meaning of it?" and asking this question, he repeated the first stanza:

Sweet was once the mango's savour, sweet its scent, its
                                              colour gold:

What has caused this bitter flavour? for we tend it as of
                                              old.

The Bodhisatta explained the reason in the second stanza:

Round about the trunk entwining, branch with branch,
                                              and root with root,

See the bitter creeper climbing; that is what has spoilt
                                              your fruit;

So you see bad company will make the better follow suit.

On hearing this the Bodhisatta caused all the nimbs and creepers to be removed, and their roots pulled up; the noxious soil was all taken away, and sweet earth put in its place; and the tree was carefully fed with sweet water, milk-water, scented water. Then by absorbing all this sweetness its fruits grew sweet again. The put his former gardener in charge of the park, and after his life was done passed away to fare according to his deserts.

THE ASS IN THE LION'S SKIN

Once upon a time, when Brahmadatta was reigning in Benares, the Bodhisatta was born in a farmer's family, and when he grew up he got a livelihood by tillage.

At the same time there was a Merchant who used to go about hawking goods, which a donkey carried for him. Wherever he went, he used to take his bundle off the ass, and throw a lionskin over him, and then turn him loose in the rice and barley fields. When the watchmen saw this creature, they imagined him to be a lion, and so dared not come near him.

One day this hawker stopped at a certain village, and while he was getting his own breakfast cooked, he turned the ass loose in a barley field with the lionskin on. The watchmen thought it was a lion, and dared not come near, but fled home and gave the alarm. All the villagers armed themselves, and hurried to the field shouting and blowing on conches and beating drums. The ass was frightened out of its wits, and gave a hee-haw! Then the Bodhisatta, seeing that it was a donkey, repeated the first stanza:

Nor lion nor tiger I see,
Not even a panther is he:
But a donkey—the wretched old hack!
With a lionskin over his back!

As soon as the villages learnt that it was only an ass, they cudgeled him tell they broke his bones, and then went off with the lionskin. When the Merchant appeared, and found that his ass has come to grief, he repeated the second stanza:

The donkey, if he had been wise,
Might long the green barley have eaten;
A lionskin was his disguise:—
But he gave a hee-haw, and got beaten!

As he was in the act of uttering these words, the ass expired. The merchant left him, and went his way.

THE PRIEST IN HORSE-TRAPPINGS

Once upon a time, when king Brahmadatta was reigning in Benares, the Bodhisatta was born of his chief queen. He came of age, and his father passed away; and then he became king and ruled in righteousness.

The Bodhisatta had a family priest named Ruhaka and this Ruhaka had an old Brahmin woman to wife.

The king gave the Brahmin a horse accoutred with all its trappings, and he mounted the horse and went to wait upon the king. As he rode along on the back of his richly caparisoned steed, the people on this side and that were loud in its praise: "See that fine horse!" they cried; "What a beauty!"

When he came home again, he went into his mansion and told his wife, "Good wife," said he, "our horse is passing fine! Right and left the people are all speaking of it."

Now his wife was no better than she should be, and full of deceit; so she made reply to him thus.

"Ah, husband, you do not know wherein lies the beauty of this horse. It is all in his fine trappings. Now if you would make yourself fine like the horse, put his trappings on yourself and go down into the street, prancing along horse-fashion. You will see the king, and he will praise you, and all the people will praise you."

This fool of a brahmin listened to it all, did not know what she purposed. So he believed her, and did as she had said. All that saw him laughed aloud: "There goes a fine professor!" said they all. And the king cried shame on him. "Why, my Teacher," said he, "has you bile gone wrong? Are you crazy?" At this the Brahmin thought that he must have behaved amiss, and he was ashamed. So he was wroth with his wife, and made haste home, saying to himself, "The woman has shamed me before the king and all his army: I will chastise her and turn her out of doors!"

But the crafty woman found out that he had come home in anger, she stole a march on him, and departed by a side door, and made her way to the palace, where she stayed four or five days. When the king heard of it, he sent for his priest, and said to him.

"My Teacher, all womankind are full of faults; you ought to forgive this lady"; and with intent to make him forgive he uttered the first stanza:

Even a broken bowstring can be mended and made whole:
Forgive your wife, and cherish not this anger in your soul.
Hearing this, Ruhaka uttered the second:

While there is bark and workmen too
'Tis easy to buy bowstrings new.
Another wife I will procure;
I've had enough of this one, sure.

So saying, he sent her way away, and took him another bahmin woman to wife.

INGRATITUDE PUNISHED

Once upon time, when king Brahmadatta reigned over Benares, the Bodhisatta was born as his chief Queen's son. On his name-day, they called him Prince Paduma, the Lotus Prince. After him came six younger brothers. One after another these seven came of age and married and settled down, living as the king's companions.

One day the king looked out into the palace courts, and as he looked he saw these men with a great following on the way to wait upon himself. He conceived the suspicion that they meant to slay him, and seize his kingdom. So he sent for them and after this fashion bespake them.

"My sons, you may not dwell in this town. So go else-where, and when I die you shall return and take the kingdom which belongs to our family."

They agreed to their father's words; and went home weep-ing and wailing. "It matters not where we go!" they cried; and taking their wives with them, they left the city, and journeyed along the road. By and by they came to a wood, where they could get no food or drink. And being unable to bear the pangs of hunger, they determined to save their lives at the women's cost. They seized the youngest brother's wife, and slew her; they cut up her body into thirteen parts, and ate it. But the Bodhisatta and his wife set aside one portion, and ate the other between them.

Thus they did six days, and slew and ate six of the women; and each day the Bodhisatta set one portion aside, so that he had six portions saved. On the seventh day the others would have taken the Bodhisatta's wife to kill her, but instead he gave them the six portions which he had kept. "Eat these," said he; "to-morrow I will manage." They all did eat the flesh; and when the time came that they fell asleep, the Bodhisatta and his wife made off together.

When they had gone a little space, the woman said, "Hus-band, I can go no further." So the Bodhisatta took her upon his shoulders, and at sunrise he came out of the wood. When the sun was risen, said she—"Husband, I am thirsty!"

"There is no water, dear wife!" said he.

But she bagged him again and again, until he struck his right knee with his sword, and said.

"Water there is none; but sit you down and drink the blood here from my knee." And so she did.

By and by they came to the mighty Ganges. They drank, they bathed, they ate all manner of fruits, and rested in a pleasant spot. And there by a bend of the river they made a hermit's hut and took up their abode in it.

Now it happened that a robber in the regions of upper Ganges had been guilty of high treason. His hands and feet, and his nose and ears had been cut off, and he was laid in a canoe, and left to drift down the great river. To this place he floated, groaning aloud with pain. The Bodhisatta heard his piteous wailing.

"While I live," said he, "no poor creature shall-perish for me!" and to the river bank he went, and saved the man. He brought him to the hut, and with astringent lotions and oint-ments he tended his wounds.

But his wife said to herself, "Here is a nice lazy fellow he has fetched out of the Gangas, to look after!" and she went about spitting for disgust at the fellow.

Now when the man's wounds were growing together, the Bodhisatta had him to dwell there in the hut alongwith his wife, and he brought fruits of all kinds from the forest to feed both him and the women. And as they thus dwelt together, the woman fell in love with the fellow, and committed sin.

Then she desired to kill the Bodhisatta, and said to him, "Husband, as I sat on your shoulder when I came out from the forest, I saw you hill, and I vowed that if ever you and I should be saved, and came to no harm, I would make offering to the holy spirit of the hill. Now this spirit haunts me: and I desire to pay my offering!"

"Very good," said the Bodhisatta, not knowing her guile. He prepared an offering, and delivering to her the vessel of offering, he climbed the hill-top. Then his wife said to him,

"Husband, not the hill-spirit, but you are my chief of gods ! Then in your honour first of all I will offer wild flowers, and walk revently round you, keeping you on the right, and salute you and after that I will make my offering to the mountain spirit." So saying, she placed him facing a precipice, and pretended to salute him by offering flowers and walking around him. Thus getting behind him, she smote him on the back, and hurled him down the precipice. Then she cried in her joy, "I have seen the back of my enemy!" and she came down from the mountain, and went into the presence of her paramour.

Now the Bodhisatta tumbled down the cliff; but he stuck fast in a clump of leaves on the top of a fig-tree where there were no thorns. Yet he could not get down the hill, so there he sat among the branches, eating the figs. It happened that a huge lizard king used to climb the hill from the foot of it, and would eat the fruit of this fig-tree. That day he saw the Bodhisatta and took to flight. On the next day, he came and ate some fruit on one side of it. Again and again he came, till at last he struck up a friendship with the Bodhisatta.

"How did you get to this place?" he asked; and the Bodhisatta told him how.

"Well, don't be afraid," said the lizard; and taking him on his own back he descended the hill and brought him out of the forest. There he set him upon the high-road, and showed him what way he should go, and himself returned to the forest.

The other proceeded to a certain village, and dwelt there till he heard of his father's death. Upon this he made his way to Benares. There he inherited the kingdom which belonged to his family, and took the name of king Lotus; the ten rules of righteousness for kings he did not transgress, and he ruled uprightly. He built six Halls of Bounty, one at each of the four gates, one in the midst of the city, and one before the palace; and every day he distributed in gifts six hundred thousand pieces of money.

Now the wicked wife took her paramour upon her shoulders and came forth out of the forest; and she went a-begging among the people, and collected rice and gruel to support him withal. If she was asked what the man was to her, she would reply, "His mother was sister to my father, he is my cousin; to him they gave me. Even if he were doomed to death I would take my own husband upon my shoulders, and care for him, and beg food for his living!"

"What a devoted wife!" said all the people. And thenceforth they gave her more food than ever. Some of them also offered advice, saying, "Do not live in this way. King Lotus is lord of Benares; he has set all India in a stir by his bounty. It will delight him to see you; so delighted will he be, that he will give you rich gifts. Put your husband in this basket and make your way to him." So saying, they persuaded her, and gave her a basket of osiers.

The wicked woman placed her paramour in the basket, and taking it up she repaired to Benares, and lived on what she got at the Halls of Bounty. Now the Bodhisatta used to ride an alms-hall upon the back of a splendid elephant richly dight; and after giving alms to eight or ten people, he would set out again for home. Then the wicked woman placed her paramour in the basket, and taking it up, she stood where the king was to pass. The king saw her. "Who is this?" he asked. "A devoted wife," was the answer. He sent for her, and recognized who she was. He caused the man to be put down from the basket, and asked her, "What is this man to you?"—"He is the son of my father's sister, given me by my family, my own husband," she answered.

"Ah, what a devoted wife!" cried they all: for they knew not the ins and outs of it; and they praised the wicked woman.

"What—is the scoundrel your cousin? did your family give him to you?" asked the king; "your husband, is he?"

She did not recognize the king: and "Yes, my lord!" said she, as bold as you like.

"And is this the king of Benares' son? Are you not the wife

of prince Lotus, the daughter of such and such a king, your name so and so? Did not you drink the blood from my knee? Did you not fall in love with this rascal, and throw me down a precipice? Ah, you thought that I was dead, and here you are with death written upon your own forehead—and here am I, alive!" Then he turned to his courtiers. "Do you remember what I told you, when you questioned me? My six younger brothers slew their six wives and ate them; but I kept my wife unhurt, and brought her to Ganges' bank. Where I dwelt in a hermit's hut: I hauled a condemned criminal out of the river, and supported him; this woman fell in love with him, and threw me down a precipice, but I saved my life by showing kindness. This is no other than the wicked woman who threw me off the crag: this, and no other, is the condemned wretch!" And then he uttered the following verses:

'Tis|—no other, and this quean is she;
The handless knave, no other, there you see;
Quoth she—"This is the husband of my youth."
Women deserve to die; they have no truth.
With a great club beat out the scoundrel's life
Who lies in wait to steal his neighbour's wife
Then take the faithful harlot by and by,
And shear off nose and ears before she die.

But although the Bodhisatta could not swallow his anger, and ordained this punishment for them, he did not do accordingly; but he smothered his wrath, and had the basket fixed upon her head so fast that she could not take it off; the villain he had placed in the same, and they were driven out of his kingdom.

THE GOBLIN CITY

Once upon a time there was in the island of Ceylon a goblin town called Sirisavatthu, peopled by she-goblins. When a ship is wrecked, these adorn and deck themselves and taking rice and gruel, with trains of slaves, and their children on their hip, they come up to the merchants. In order to make them imagine that theirs is a city of human beings, they make them see here and there men ploughing and tending kine, herds of cattle, dogs, and the like. Then approaching the merchants they invite them to partake of the gruel, rice, and other food which they bring. The merchants, all unaware, eat of what is offered. When they have been eaten and drunken, and are taking their rest, the goblins address them thus: "Where do you live? Where do you come from? Whither are you going, and what errand brought you here?" "We were shipwrecked here," they replied. "Very good, noble sirs," the others make answer; "tis three years ago since our own husbands went on board ship; they must have perished. You are merchants too; we will be your wives." Thus they lead them astray by their women's wiles, and tricks, and dalliance, until they get them into the goblin city; then, if they have any others already caught, they bind these with magic chains, and cast them into the house of torment. And if they find no shipwrecked men in the place where they dwell, they scour the coast so far as the river Kalyāni on one side and the island of Nāgadipa on the other. This is their way.

Now it happened once that five hundred shipwrecked traders were cast ashore near the city of these she-goblins. The goblins came up to them and enticed them, till they brought them to their city; those whom they had caught before, they bound with magic chains and cast them into the house of torment. Then the chief goblin took the chief man, and the others took the rest, till five hundred had the five hundred traders; and they made the men their husbands. Their in the night time, when her man was asleep, the chief she-goblin rose up, and made her way to the house of death, slew some of the men and ate them. The others did the same. When the eldest goblin returned from eating men's flesh, her body was cold. The eldest merchant embraced her, and perceived that she was a goblin. "All the five hundred of them must be goblins!" he thought to himself: "we must make our escape!"

So in the early morning, when he went to wash his face he bespake the other merchants in these words. "These are goblins, and not human beings! As soon as other shipwrecked men can be found, they will make them their husbands, and will eat us; come—let us escape!"

Two hundred and fifty of them replied, "We cannot leave them; go ye, if ye will, but we will not flee away."

Then the chief trader with two hundred and fifty, who were ready to obey him, fled away in fear of the goblins.

Now at that time, the Bodhisatta had come into the world as a flying horse, white all over, and beaked like a crow, with hair like munja grass, possessed of supernatural power, able to fly through the air. From Himalaya he flew through the air until he came to Ceylon. There he passed over the ponds and tanks of Ceylon, and ate the paddy that grew wild there. As he passed on thus, he thrice uttered human speech filled with mercy, saying— "Who wants to go home? Who wants to go home?" The traders heard his saying, and cried—"We are going home master!" joining their hands, and raising them respectfully to their foreheads. "Then climb up on my back," said the Bodhisatta. Thereafter some of them climbed up, some remained standing with a respectful salute. Then the Bodhisatta took up even those who stood still saluting him, and conveyed all of them, even two hundred and fifty, to their own country, and set down each in his own place; then he went to his place of dwelling.

And the she-goblins, when other men came to that place, slew those two hundred and fifty who were left, and devoured them.

THE TELL-TALE PARROT

Once upon a time, when Brahmadatta was king of Benares, the Bodhisatta came into the world as a young parrot. His name was Rādha, and his youngest brother was named Potthapāda. While they were yet quite young, both of them were caught by a fowler and handed over to a brahmin in Benares. The brahmin cared for them as if they were his children. But the brahmin's wife was a wicked woman; there was no watching her.

The husband had to go away on business, and addressed his young parrots thus. "Little dears, I am going away on business. Keep watch on your mother in season and out of season; observe whether or not any man visits her." So off he went, leaving his wife in charge of the young parrots.

As soon as he was gone, the woman began to do wrong; night and day the visitors came and went—there was no end to them. Potthapāda, observing this, said to Rādha—"Our master gave this woman into our charge, and here she is doing wickedness. I will speak to her."

"Don't" said Rādha. But the other would not listen. "Mother," said he, "why do you commit sin?"

How she longed to kill him! But making as though she would fondle him, she called him to her.

"Little one, you are my son! I will never do it again! Here then, the dear!" So he came out; then she seized him crying:

"What! You preach to me! You don't know your measure!" and she wrung his neck, and threw him into the oven.

The Brahmin returned. When he had rested, he asked the Bodhisatta: "Well, my dear, what about your mother—does she do wrong, or no?" and as he asked the question, he repeated the first couplet:

I come, my son, the journey done, and now I am at home again:
Come tell me; is your mother true? Does she make love to other men?

Rādha answered, "Father dear, the wise speak not of things which do not conduce to blessing, whether they have happened or not"; and he explained this by repeating the second couplet:

> For what he said he now lies dead, burnt up beneath
> the ashes there:
> It is not well the truth to tell, lest Potthapāda's fate I
> share.

Thus did the Bodhisatta hold forth to the brahmin; and he went on—"This is no place for me to live in either"; then bidding the Brahmin farewell, he flew away to the woods.

THE CHOICE OF A HUSBAND

Once upon a time, when Brahmadatta ruled in Benares, the Bodhisatta was born as a brahmin's son. He came of age, and received his education at Takkasilā; then on returning he became a famous teacher.

Now there was a Brahmin who had four daughters. These four were wooed by four persons as told above. The brahmin could not decide to whom to give them. "I will enquire of the teacher," he thought, "and then he shall hand them to whom they should be given." So he came into the teacher's presence, and repeated the first couplet:

> One is good, and one is noble; one has beauty, one has
> years.
> Answer me this question, brahmin; of the four, which best
> appears?

Hearing this, the teacher replied, "Even though there be beauty and the like qualities, a man is to be despised if he fail in virtue. Therefore the former is not the measure of a man; those that I like are the virtuous." And in explanation of this matter, he repeated the second couplet:

> Good is beauty: to the aged show respect, for this is right:
> Good is noble birth; but virtue—virtue, that is my delight.

When the Brahmin heard this, he gave all his daughters to

the virtuous wooer.

THE FOOLHARDY CROW

Once upon a time, while Brahmadatta reigned as king in Benares, the Bodhisatta became a marsh crow, and dwelt by a certain pool. His name was Viraka, the Strong.

There arose a famine in Kāsi. Men could not spare food for the crows, nor make offering to globins and nāgas. One by one the crows left the famine-stricken land, and betook them to the woods.

A certain crow named Savitthaka, who lived at Benares, took with him his lady crow and went to the place where Viraka lived, making his abode beside the same pool.

One day, this crow was seeking food about the pool. He saw how Viraka went down into it, and make a meal off some fish; and afterwards came up out of the water again, and stood drying his features. "Under the wing of that crow," thought he, "plenty of fish are to be got. I will become his servant." So he drew near.

"What is it, Sir?" asked Viraka.

"I want to be your servant, my lord!" was the reply.

Viraka agreed, and from that time the other served him. And from that time, Viraka used to eat enough fish to keep him alive, and the rest he gave to Savitthaka as soon as he had caught them; and when Savitthaka had eaten enough to keep him alive, he gave what was over to his wife.

After a while pride came into his heart. "This crow", said he, "is black and so am I : in eyes and beak and feet, too, there is no difference between us. I don't want his fish; I will catch my own!" So he told Viraka that for the future he intended to go down to the water and catch fish himself. Then Viraka said,

"Good friend, you do not belong to a tribe of such crows as are born to go into water and catch fish. Don't destroy yourself!"

But in spite of this attempt to dissuade him, Savitthaka did not take the warning to heart. Down he went to the pool, down into the water; but he could not make his way through the weeds, and come out again—there he was entangled in the weeds with only the tip of his break appearing above the water. So not being able to breathe he perished there beneath the water.

His mate noticed that he did not return, and went to Viraka to ask news of him. "My lord," she asked, "Savitthaka is not to be seen: where is he?" And as he asked him this, she repeated the first stanza:

O have you seen Savitthaka, O Viraka, have you seen
My sweet-voiced mate whose neck is like the peacock in
its sheen?

When Viraka heard it, he replied, "Yes, I know where he is gone," and recited the second stanza:

He was not born to dive beneath the wave,
But what he could not do he needs must try;
So the poor bird has found a watery grave,
Entangled in the weeds, and left to die.

When the lady-crow heard it, weeping, she returned to Benares.

THE WOODPECKER, TORTOISE AND ANTELOPE

Once upon a time, when Brahmadatta was king of Benares, the Bodhisatta became an antelope, and lived within a forest in a thickest near a certain lake. Not far from the same lake, sat a woodpecker perched at the top of a tree; and in the lake dwelt a tortoise. And the three became friends, and lived together in amity.

A hunter, wandering about in the wood, observed the

Bodhisatta's footprint at the going down into the water; and he
set a trap of leather, strong, like an iron chain, and went his
way. In the first watch of the night the Bodhisatta went down
to drink, and got caught in the noose; whereat he cried the cry
of capture. Thereupon the woodpecker flew down from her tree-
top, and the tortoise came out of the water, and consulted
what was to be done.

Said the woodpecker to the tortoise, "Friend, you have
teeth—bite this snare through; I will go and see to it that the
hunter keeps away; and if we both do our best, our friend will
not lose his life." To make this clear he uttered the first stanza:

Come, tortoise, tear the leathern snare, and bite it through
and through,
And of the hunter I'll take care, and keep him off from you.

The tortoise began to gnaw the leather throng; the woodpecker made his way to the hunter's dwelling. At dawn of day
the hunter went out, knife in hand. As soon as the bird saw
him start, he uttered a cry, flapped his wings, and struck him
in the face as he left the front door. "Some bird of ill omen has
struck me!" thought the hunter; he turned back, and lay down
for a little while. Then he rose up again, and took his knife. The
bird reasoned within himself, "The first time he went out by
the front door, so now he will leave by the back": and he sat
down behind the house. The hunter, too, reasoned in the same
way: "When I went out by the front door, I saw a bad omen,
now I will go out by the back!" and so he did. But the bird
cried out again struck by a bird of ill omen, the hunter exclaimed, "This creature will not let me go!" and turning back
he lay down until sunrise, and when the sun was risen, he took
his knife and started.

The woodpecker made all haste back to his friends. "Here
comes the hunter!" he cried. By this time the tortoise had
gnawed through all the thongs but one tough thong: his teeth
seemed as through they would fall out, and his mouth was all
smeared with blood. The Bodhisatta saw the young hunter

coming on like lightning, knife in hand; he burst the thong, and fled into the woods. The Woodpecker perched upon his tree-top. But the Tortoise was so weak, that he lay where he was. The hunter threw him into a bag, and tied it to a tree.

The Bodhisatta observed that the tortoise was taken, and determined to save his friends life. So he let the hunter see him, and made as though he were weak. The hunter saw him, and thinking him to be weak, seized his knife and set out in pursuit. The Bodhisatta, keeping just out of his reach, led him into the forest; and when he saw that they had come far away, gave him the slip and returned swift as the wind by another way. He lifted the bag with his horns, threw it upon the ground, ripped it open and let the tortoise out. And the woodpecker came down from the tree.

Then the Bodhisatta thus addressed them both: "My life has been saved by you, and you have done a friend's part to me. Now the hunter will come and take you; so do you, friend woodpecker, migrate elsewhere with your brood, and you friend tortoise, dive into the water." They did so.

The Master, as the All-enlightened One, uttered the second stanza:
The tortoise went into the pond, the deer into the wood.

The hunter returned, and saw none of them. He found his bag torn: picked it up, and went home sorrowful. And the three friends lived all their life long in unbroken amity, and then passed away to fare according to their deeds.

THE CROCODILE AND THE MONKEY

Once upon a time, while Brahmadatta was king of Benares, the Bodhisatta came to life at the foot of Himalaya as a monkey. He grew strong and sturdy, big of frame, well-to-do, and lived by a curve of the river Ganges in a forest haunt.

Now at that time there was a crocodile dwelling in the

Ganges. The crocodile's mate saw the great frame of the monkey, and she conceived a longing for his heart to eat. So she said to her lord: "Sir, I desire to eat the heart of that great king of the monkeys!"

"Good wife," said the crocodile, "we live in the water and he lives on dry land; how can we catch him?"

"By hook or by crook," she replied, "caught he must be. If I don't get him, I shall die."

"All right," answered the crocodile, consoling her, "don't trouble yourself. I have a plan; I will give you his heart to eat."

So when the Bodhisatta was sitting on the bank of the Ganges, after taking a drink of water, the crocodile drew near, and said:

"Sir Monkey, why do you live on bad fruits in this old familiar place? On the other side of the Ganges there is no end to the mango trees and bread-fruit trees, with fruit sweet as honey! Is it not better to cross over and have all kinds of wild fruit to eat?"

"Lord Crocodile," the monkey made answer, "deep and wide is the Ganges: how shall I get across?"

"If you will go, I will mount you on my back, and carry you over."

The Monkey trusted him, and agreed. "Come here, then," said the other, "up on my back with you!" and up the monkey climbed. But when the crocodile had swum a little way, he plunged the monkey under the water.

"Good friend, you are letting me sink!" cried the monkey. "What is that for?"

Said the crocodile, "You think I am carrying you out of

pure good nature? Not a bit of it! My wife has a longing for your heart, and I want to give it her to eat!"

"Friend," said the monkey, "it is nice of you to tell me. Why, if our heart were inside us when we go jumping among the tree-tops, it would be all knocked to pieces!"

"Well, where do you keep them?" asked the other.

The Bodhisatta pointed out a fig-tree with clusters of ripe fruit, standing not far off. "See," said he, "there are our hearts hanging on yon fig-tree."

"If you will show me your heart," said the crocodile, "then I won't kill you."

"Take me to the tree, then, and I will point it out to you hanging upon it."

The crocodile brought him to the place. The monkey leapt off his back, and climbing up the fig-tree sat upon it. "O silly crocodile!" said he, "you thought that there were creatures that kept their hearts in a tree-top! You are a fool, and I have out-witted you! You may keep your fruit to yourself. Your body is great, but you have no sense." And then to explain this idea he uttered the following stanzas:

Rose-apple, bread-fruit, mangoes too across the water there
I see;
Enough of them, I want them not; my fig is good enough
for me!
Great is your body, verify, but how much smaller is your
wit!
Now go your ways, Sir crocodile, for I have had the best
of it.

The crocodile, feeling as sad and miserable as if he had lost a thousand pieces of money, went back sorrowing to the place where he lived.

THE BRAHMIN AND THE ACROBAT

Once upon a time, while Brahmadatta was reigning in Benares, the Bodhisatta was born as one of a family of poor acrobats, that lived by begging. So when he grew up, he was needy and squalid, and by begging he lived.

There was at the time, in a certain village of Kāsi a brahmin whose wife was bad and wicked, and did wrong. And it befell that the husband went abroad one day upon some matter, and her lover watching his time went to visit the house. After she had received him, he said, "I will eat a bit before I go." So she made ready the food, and served up rice hot with sauce and curry, and gave it him, bidding him eat: she herself stood at the door, watching the brahmin's coming. And while the lover was eating, the Bodhisatta stood waiting for a morsel.

At that moment the Brahmin set his face for home. And his wife saw him drawing nigh, and ran in quickly— "Up, my man is coming!" and she made her lover go down into the store-room. The husband came in; she gave him a seat, and water for washing the hands; and upon the cold rice that was left by the other she turned out some hot rice,.and set it before him. He put his hand into the rice, and felt that it was hot above and cold below. "This must be some one else's leaving," thought he; and so he asked the woman about it in the words of the first stanza:

Hot at top, and cold at bottom, not alike it seems to be:
I would ask you for the reason: come, my lady answer me!

Again and again he asked, but she, fearing lest her deed should be discovered, held her peace. Then a thought came into our tumbler's mind. "The man down in the store-room must be a lover, and this is the master of the house: the wife says nothing, for fear that her deed be made manifest. Soho! I will declare the whole matter, and show the brahmin that a man is hidden in his larder." And he told him the whole matter: how that when he had gone out from his house, another had come in, and had done evil; how he had eaten the first rice, and the wife had stood by the door to watch the road; and how the other man had been hidden in the storeroom. And in so saying, he repeated the second stanza:

I am a tumbler, Sir: I came on begging here intent;
He that you seek is hiding in the store-room, where he
went!

By his top-knot he haled the man out of the store-room, and bade him take care not to do the like again; and then he went away. The brahmin rebuked and beat them both, and gave them such a lesson that they were not likely to do the same again. Afterwards he passed away to fare according to his deserts.

THE TORTOISE AND THE GEESE

Once upon a time when Brahmadatta was king of Benares, and the Bodhisatta, being born to one of the king's court, grew up, and became the king's adviser in all things human and divine. But this king was very talkative; and when he talked there was no chance for any other to get in a word. And the Bodhisatta, wishing to put a stop to his much talking, kept watching for an opportunity.

Now there dwelt a tortoise in a certain pond in the region of Himalaya. Two young wild geese, searching for food, struck up an acquaintance with him; and by and by they grew close friends together. One day these two said to him: "Friend tortoise, we have a lovely home in Himalaya, on a plateau of Mount Cittakūta in a cave of gold! Will you come with us?"

"Why," said he, "how can I get there?"
"Oh, we will take you, if only you can keep your mouth shut, and say not a word to anybody."

"Yes, I can do that," said he; "take me along!"

So they made the tortoise hold a stick between his teeth; and themselves taking hold of the two ends, they sprang up into the air.

The village children saw this, and exclaimed—"There are two geese carrying a tortoise by a stick!"

(By this time the geese flying swiftly had arrived at the space above the palace of the king at Benares.) The tortoise wanted to cry out—"Well, and if my friends do carry me, what is that to you, you caitiffs?"—and he let go the stick from between his teeth, and falling into the open country he split in two. What an uproar there was! "A tortoise has fallen in the courtyard, and broken in two!" they cried. The king, with the Bodhisatta, and all his court, came up to the place, and seeing the tortoise asked the Bodhisatta a question. "Wise Sir, what made this creature fall?"

"Now's my time?" thought he. "For a long while I have been wishing to admonish the king, and I have gone about seeking my opportunity. No doubt the truth is this: the tortoise and the geese became friendly; the geese must have meant to carry him to Himalaya, and so made him hold a stick between his teeth, and then lifted him into the air; then he must have heard some remark, and wanted to reply; and not being able to keep his mouth shut he must have let himself go; and so he must have fallen from the sky and thus come by his death." So thought he; and addressed the king: "O king, they that have too much tongue, that set no limit to their speaking, ever come to such misfortune as this"; and he uttered the following verses:

The tortoise needs must speak aloud,
Although between his teeth
A stick he bit: yet, spite of it,
He spoke—and fell beneath.

And now, O mighty master, mark it well.
See thus speak wisely, see thou speak in season.
To death the tortoise fell:
He talked too much: that was the reason.

"He is speaking of me!" the king thought to himself; and asked the Bodhisatta if it was so.

"Be it you, O great king, or be it another," replied he, "Whosoever talks beyond measure comes by some misery of this kind"; and so he made the thing manifest. And thence forward the king abstained from talking, and became a man of few words.

THE STOLEN PLOUGHSHARES

One upon a time, while Brahmadatta was king of Benares, the Bodhisatta came into this world as the son of one in the king's court. When he grew up he was made a Lord Justice.

At that time, two traders one from a village and one of the town, were friends together. The villager deposited with the townsman five hundred ploughshares. The other sold these, and kept the price, and in the place where they were he scattered mouse dung. By and by came the villager, and asked for his ploughshare. "The mice have eaten them up!" said the cheat, and pointed out the mouse dung to him.

"Well, well, so be it," replied the other: "what can be done with things which the mice have eaten?"

Now at the time of bathing he took the other trader's son, and set him in a friend's house, in an inner chamber, bidding them not suffer him to go out any whither. And having washed himself he went to his friend's house.

"Where is my son?" asked the cheat.

"Dear friend," he replied, "I took him with me and left him on the river-side; and when I was gone down into the water, there came an osprey, and seized your son in his extended claws, and flew up into the air. I beat the water, shouted, struggled—but could not make him let go."

"Lies!" cried the rouge. "No osprey could carry off a boy!"

"Let be, dear friend: if things happen that should not, how

can I help it? Your son has been carried off by an osprey, as I say."

The other reviled him. "Ah, you scoundrel! You murderer! Now I will go to the judge, and have you dragged before him!" And he departed. The villager said, "As you please," and went to the court of justice. The rogue addressed the Bodhisatta thus:

"My lord, this fellow took my son with him to bathe, and when I asked where he was, he answered, that an osprey had carried him off. Judge my cause!"

"Tell the truth," said the Bodhisatta, asking the other.

"Indeed, my lord," he answered, "I took him with me, and a hawk has carried him off."

"But where in the world are there ospreys which carry off boys?"

"My lord," he answered, "I have a question to ask you. If ospreys cannot carry off boys into the air, can mice eat iron ploughshares?"

"What do you mean by that?"

"My lord, I deposited in this man's house five hundred ploughshares. The man told me that the mice had devoured them, and showed me the droppings of the mice that had done it. My lord, if mice eat ploughshares, then ospreys carry off boys; but if mice cannot do this, neither will hawks carry the boy off. This man says the mice ate my ploughshares. Give sentence whether they are eaten or no. Judge my cause!"

"He must have meant," thought the Bodhisatta, "to fight the trickster with his own weapons.—Well devised!" said he, and then he uttered these two verses:

Well planned indeed! The biter bit,

The trickster tricked—a pretty hit!
If mice can eat a ploughshare, why,
Ospreys away with boys can fly!

A rogue out-rogued with tit for tat!
Give back the plough, and after that
Perhaps the man who lost the plough
May give your son back to you now!

Thus he that had lost his son received him again, and he received his ploughshare that had lost it; and afterwards both passed away to fare according to their deeds.

THE HERO'S TASKS

Once upon a time reigned at Benares a king named Yasapāni, the Glorious. His chief captain was named Kālaka, or Blackie. At the time the Bodhisatta was his family priest, and had the name of Dhammaddhaja, the Banner of the Faith. There was also a man Chattapāni, maker of ornaments to the king. The king was a good king. But his chief captain swallowed bribes in the judging of causes; he was a backbiter; he took bribes, and defrauded the rightful owners.

On a day, one who has lost his suit was departing from the court, weeping and stretching out his arms, when he fell in with the Bodhisatta as he was going to pay his service to the king. Falling at his feet, the man cried out, telling how he had been worsted in his cause: "Although such as you, my lord, instruct the king in the things of this world and the next, the Commander-in-chief takes bribes, and defrauds rightful owners!"

The Bodhisatta pitied him, "Come, my good fellow", said he, "I will judge your cause for you!" and he proceeded to the court-house. A great company gathered together. The Bodhisatta reversed the sentence, and gave judgment for him that had the right. The spectators applauded. The sound was great. The king heard, it and asked—"What sound is this I hear?"

"My lord king," they answered, "it is a cause wrongly judged that has been judged aright by the wise Dhammaddhaja; that is why there is this shout of applause."

The king was pleased and sent for the Bodhisatta. "They tell me," he began, "that you have judged a cause?"

"Yes, great king, I have judged that which Kālaka did not judge aright."

"Be you judge from this day," said the king; "it will be a joy for my ear, and prosperity for the world!" He was unwilling, but the king begged him—"In mercy to all creatures, sit you in judgment!" and so the king won his consent.

From that time Kālaka received no presents; and losing his gains he spoke calumny of the Bodhisatta before the king, saying, "O mighty king, the wise Dhammaddhaja covets your kingdom!" But the king would not believe; and bade him say not so.

"If you do not believe me," said Kālaka, "look out of the window at the time of his coming. Then you will see that he has got the whole city into his own hands."

The king saw the crowd of those that were about him in his judgment hall. "There is his retinue," thought he. He gave way. "What are we to do, Captain?" he asked.

"My lord, he must be put to death."

"How can we put him to death without having found him out in some great wickedness?"

"There is a way," said the other.

"What way?"

"Tell him to do what is impossible, and if he cannot, put him to death for that."

"But what is impossible to him?"

"My lord king," replied he, "it takes two years or twice two for a garden with good soil to bear fruit, being planted and tended. Send for him, and say—"We want a garden to disport ourselves in to-morrow. Make us a garden!' This he will not be able to do; and we will slay him for that fault."

The king addressed himself to the Bodhisatta. "Wise Sir, we have sported long enough in our old garden; now we crave to sport in a new. We shall sport to-morrow. Make us a garden! If you cannot make it, you must die."

The Bodhisatta reasoned, "It must be that Kālaka has, set the king against me, because he gets no present.—If I can, he said to the king, "O mighty king, I will see to it." And he went home. After a good meal he lay upon his bed, thinking. Sakka's palace grew hot. Sakka reflecting perceived the Bodhisatta's difficulty. He made haste to him, entered his chamber, and asked him—"Wise Sir, what think you on?"—poised he while in mid-air.

"Who are you?" asked the Bodhisatta.

"I am Sakka."

"The king bids me make a garden: that is what I am thinking upon."

"Wise Sir, do not trouble: I will make you a garden like the groves of Nandana and Cittlalatā! In what place shall I make it?"

"In such and such place," he told him. Sakka made it, and returned to the city of the gods.

Next day, the Bodhisatta beheld the garden there in very truth, and sought the king's presence. "O king, the garden is ready: go to your sport!"

The king came to the place, and beheld a garden girt with
a fence of eighteen cubits, vermilion tinted, having gates and
ponds, beautiful with all manner of trees, laden heavy with
flowers and fruit! "The sage has done my bidding," said he to
Kālaka: "now what are we do?"

"O mighty king!" replied he, "if he can make a garden in
one night can he not seize upon your kingdom?"

"Well, what are we to do?"

"We will make him perform another impossible thing."

"What is that?" asked the king.

"We will bid him make a lake possessed of the seven precious jewels!"

The king agreed, and thus addressed the Bodhisatta.

"Teacher, you have made a park. Make now a lake to match
it, with the seven precious jewels. If you cannot make it, you
shall not live!"

"Very good, great king," answered the Bodhisatta, "I will
make it if I can."

Then Sakka made a lake of great splendour, having an
hundred landing-places, a thousand inlents, covered over with
lotus plants of five different colours, like the lake in Nandana.

Next day, the Bodhisatta beheld this also, and told the king:
"See, the lake is made!" And the king saw it, and asked of
Kālaka what was to be done.

"Bid him, my lord, make a house to suit it," said he.

"Make a house, Teacher," said the king to the Bodhisatta,
"all of ivory, to suit with the park and the lake: if you do not

make it, you must die!"

Then Sakka made him a house likewise. The Bodhisatta
beheld it next day, and told the king. When the king had seen
it he asked Kālaka again, what was to do. Kālaka told him to bid
the Bodhisatta make a jewel to suit the house. The king said to
him, "Wise Sir, make a jewel to suit with this ivory house; I will
go about looking at it by the light of the jewel: if you cannot
make one, you must die!" Then Sakka made him a jewel too.
Next day the Bodhisatta beheld it, and told the king. When the
king had seen it, he again asked Kālaka what was to be done.

"Mighty king!" answered he, "I think there is some divinity who does each thing that the Brahmin Dhammaddhaja
wishes. Now bid him make something which even a divinity
cannot make. Not even a deity can make with all four virtues;
therefore bid him make a keeper with these four." So the king
said, "Teacher, you have made a park, a lake, and a palace, and
a jewel to give light. Now make me a keeper with four virtues,
to watch the park; if you cannot, you must die."

"So be it," answered he, "if it is possible, I will see to it."
He went home, had a good meal, and lay down. When he awoke
in the morning, he sat upon his bed, and thought thus. "What
the great king Sakka can make by his power, that he has made.
He cannot make a park-keeper with four virtues. This being so,
it is better to die forlorn in the woods, than to die at the hand
of other men." So saying no word to any man, he went down
from his dwelling and passed out of the city by the chief gate,
and entered the woods where he sat him down beneath a tree
and reflected upon the religion of the good. Sakka perceived it;
and in the fashion of a forester he approached the Bodhisatta
saying:

"Brahmin, you are young and tender: why sit you here in
this wood, as though you had never seen pain before?" As he
asked it, he repeated the first stanza:

You look as though your life must happy be;
Yet to the wild woods you would homeless go,

Like some poor wretch whose life was misery,
And pine beneath this tree in lonely woe.

To this the Bodhisatta made answer in the second stanza:

I look as though my life must happy be;
Yet to the wild woods I would homeless go,
Like some poor wretch whose life was misery,
And pine beneath this tree in lonely woe.
Pondering the truth that all the saints do know.

Then Sakka said, "If so, then why, Brahmin, are you sitting here?"

"The king," he made answer, "requires a park-keeper with four good qualities; such an one cannot be found; so I thought— Why perish by the hand of man? I will off to the woods, and die a lonely death. So here I came, and here I sit."

Then the other replied, "Brahmin, I am Sakka, king of the gods. By me was your park made, and those other things. A park-keeper possessed of four virtues cannot be made; but in your country there is one Chattapāni, who makes ornaments for the head, and he is such a man. If a park-keeper is wanted, go and make this workman the keeper." With these words Sakka departed to his city divine, after consoling him and bidding him fear no more.

The Bodhisatta went home, and having broken his fast, he repaired to the palace gates, and there in that spot he saw Chattapāni. He took him by the hand, and asked him—"Is it true, as I hear, Chattapāni, that you are endowed with the four virtues?"

"Who told you so?" asked the other.

"Sakka, king of the gods."

"Why did he tell you?" He recounted all, and told the

reason. The other said,

"Yes, I am endowed with the four virtues." The Bodhisatta taking him by the hand led him into the king's presence. "Here, mighty monarch, is Chattapāni, endowed with four virtues. If there is need of a keeper for the park, make him keeper."

"Is it true, as I hear," the king asked him, "that you have four virtues?"

"Yes, mighty king."

"What are they?" he asked.

I envy not, and drink no wine;
No strong desire, no wrath is mine,
said he.

"Chattapāni," cried the king," did you say you have no envy?"

"Yes, O king, I have no envy."

"What experience was it that made you to be without envy?"

"Listen, my lord!" said he; and then he told him why he felt no envy in the following lines:

A chaplain once in bonds I threw—
Which thing a woman made man do;
He built me up in holy lore;
Since when I never envied more.

Then the king said, "Dear Chattapāni, what has made you to abstain from strong drink?" And the other answered in the following verse:
Once I was drunken, and I ate
My own son's flesh upon my plate;

Then, touched with sorrow and with pain,
Swore never to touch drink again.

Then the king said, "But what has made you to be indifferent without love?" The man explained it in these words:

King Kitavāsa was my name;
A mighty king was I;
My boy a Buddha's basin broke
And so he had to die.

Said the king then, "What was it, good friend, that made you to be without anger?" And the other made the matter clear in these lines:
As Araka, for seven years
I practiced charity;
And then for seven ages dwelt
In Brahma's heaven on high.

When Chattapāni had thus explained his four attributes, the king made a sign to his attendants. And in an instant all the court, priests and laymen and all, rose up, and cried out upon Kālaka—"Fie, bribe-swallowing thief and scoundrel! You couldn't get your bribes, and so you would murder the wise man by speaking ill of him!" They seized him by hand and foot, and bundled him out of the palace; and catching up whatever they could get hold of, this a stone, and this a staff, they broke his head and did him to death: and dragging him by the feet they cast him upon a dunghill.

Thenceforward the king ruled in righteousness, until he passed away according to his deserts.

DEFEATING THE KING OF DEATH

Once upon a time reigned at Benares a wicked and unjust king named Mahā-pingala, the Great Yellow King, who did sinfully after his own will and pleasure. With taxes and fines, and many mutilations and robberies, he crushed the folk as it were sugarcane in a mill; he was cruel, fierce, ferocious. For other people he had not a grain of pity; at home he was harsh and implacable towards his wives, his sons and daughters, to his brahmin courtiers and the householders of the country. He was like a speck of dust that falls in the eye, like gravel in the broth, like a thorn sticking in the heel.

Now the Bodhisatta was a son of king Mahā-pingala. After this king had reigned for a long time, he died. When he died all the citizens of Benares were overjoyed and laughed a great laugh; they burnt his body with a thousand cartloads of logs, and quenched the place of burning with thousands of jars of water, and consecrated the Bodhisatta to be king: they caused a drum of rejoicing to beat about the streets, for joy that they had got them a righteous king. They raised flags and banners, and decked out the city; at every door was set a pavilion, and scattering parched corn and flowers, they sat them down upon the decorated platforms under fine canopies, and did eat and drink. The Bodhisatta himself sat upon a fine divan on a great raised dais, in great magnificence, with a white parasol stretched above him. The courtiers and householders, the citizens and the doorkeepers stood around their king.

But one doorkeeper, standing not far from the king, was sighing and sobbing. "Good Porter," said the Bodhisatta, observing him, "all the people are making merry for joy that my father is dead, but you stand weeping. Come, was my father good and kind to you? And with the question he uttered the first stanza:
> The Yellow King was cruel to all men;
> Now he is dead, all freely breathe again
> Was he, the yellow-eyed, so very dear?
> Or, Porter, why do you stand weeping here?

The man heard and answered: "I am not weeping for sorrow that Pingala is dead. My head would be glad enough. For King Pingala, every time he came down from the palace, or went up into it, would give me eight blows over the head with his fist, like the blows of a blacksmith's hammer. So when he goes down to the other world, he will deal eight blows on the head of Yama, the gatekeeper of hell, as though he were striking me. Then the people will cry—He is too cruel for us, and will send him up again. And I fear he will come and deal fisticuffs on my head again, and that is why I weep." To explain the matter he uttered the second stanza:

The Yellow King was anything but dear:
It is his coming back again I fear.
What if he beat the king of Death, and then
The king of Death should send him back again?

Then said the Bodhisatta. "That king has been burnt with a thousand cartloads of wood; the place of his burning has been soaked with water from thousands of pitchers, and the ground has been dug up all round; beings that have gone to the other world, otherwise than by re-birth, do not return to the same bodily shape as they had before; do not be afraid!" and to comfort him, he repeated the following stanza:

Thousands of loads of wood have burnt him quite,
Thousands of pitchers quenched what still did burn;
The earth is dug about to left and right—
Fear not—the king will never more return.

After that, the porter took comfort. And the Bodhisatta ruled in righteousness; and after giving gifts and doing other good acts, he passed away to fare according to his deserts.

THE JACKAL'S SPELL

Once upon a time, Brahmadatta was king of Benares and the Bodhisatta was this family priest, and he had mastered the three Vedas and the eighteen branches of knowledge. He knew the spell entitled 'Of subduing the world.' (Now this spell is one which involves religious meditation.)

One day, the Bodhisatta thought that he would recite this spell; so he sat down in a place apart upon a flat stone, and there went through his reciting of it. It is said that this spell could be taught to no one without use of a special rite; for which reason he recited it in the place just described. It so happened that jackal lying in a hole heard the spell at the time that he was reciting it, and got it by heart. We are told that this jackal in a previous existence had been some Brahmin who had learnt the charm 'Of subduing the World.'

The Bodhisatta ended his recitation, and rose up, saying— "Surely I have that spell by heart now." Then the jackal arose out of his hole, and cried—"Ho, Brahmin! I have learnt the spell better than you know it yourself!" and off he ran. The Bodhisatta set off in chase, and followed some way crying—"You jackal will do a great mischief—catch him, catch him!" But the jackal got clear off into the forest.

The Jackal found a she-jackal, and gave her a little nip upon the body. "What is it, master?" she asked. "Do you know me," he asked, "or do you not?" "I do not know you." He repeated the spell, and thus had under his orders several hundreds of jackals, and gathered round him all the elephants and horses, lions and tigers, swine and deer, and all other four-footed creatures; and their king he became, under the title of Sabbadātha, or Alltusk, and a she-jackal, he made his consort. On the back of two elephants stood a lion, and on the lion's back sat Sabbadātha, the jackal king, along with his consort the she-jackal; and great honour was paid to them.

Now the jackal was tempted by his great honour, and became puffed up with pride, and he resolved to capture the kingdom of Benares. So with all the four-footed creatures in his train, he came to a place near to Benares. His host covered twelve leagues of ground. From his position there he sent a message to the king, "Give up your kingdom, or fight for it." The citizens of Benares, smitten with terror, shut close their gates and stayed within.

Then the Bodhisatta drew near the king, and said to him, "Fear not, mighty king! Leave me the task of fighting with the jackal king, Sabbadātha. Except only me, no one is able to fight with him at all." Thus he gavē heart to the king and the citizens. "I will ask him at once,"—he went on, "what he will do in order to take the city." So he mounted the tower over one of the gates, and cried out—"Sabbadātha, what will you do to get possession of this realm?"

"I will cause the lions to roar, and with the roaring I will frighten the multitude: thus will I take it!"

"Oh, that's it," thought the Bodhisatta, and down he came from the tower. He made proclamation by beat of drum that all the dwellers in the great city of Benares, over all its twelve leagues must stop up their ears with flour. The multitude heard the command; they stopped up their own ears with flour, so that they could not hear each other speak:—nay, they even did the same to all their animals down to the cats.

Then the Bodhisatta went up a second time into the tower, and cried out "Sabbadātha!"

"What is it, Brahmin?" quoth he.

"How will you take this realm?" he asked.

"I will cause the lions to roar, and I will frighten the people and destroy them; thus will I take it!" he said.

"You will not be able to make the lions roar; these noble lions, with their tawny paws and shaggy manes; will never do the bidding of an old jackal like you!"

The jackal, stubborn with pride, answered, "Not only will the other lions obey me, but I'll make this one, upon whose back I sit, roar alone!"

"Very well," said the Bodhisatta, "do it if you can."

So he tapped with his foot on the lion which he sat upon, to roar. And the lion resting his mouth upon the Elephant's temple, roared thrice, without any manner of doubt. The elephants were terified, and dropped the jackal down at their feet; they trampled upon his head and crushed it to a atoms. Then and there Sabbadātha perished. And the elephants, hearing the roar of the lion, were frightened to death, and wounding one another, they all perished there. The rest of the creatures, deer and swine, down to the hares and cats, perished then and there, all except the lions; and these ran off and took to the woods. There was a heap of carcasses covering the ground for twelve leagues.

The Bodhisatta came down from the tower, and had the gates of the city thrown open. By beat of drum he caused proclamation to be made throughout the city: "Let all the people take the flour from out of their ears, and they that desire meat let them take!" the people all ate what meat they could fresh, and the rest they dried and preserved.

It was at this time, according to tradition, that people first began to dry meat.

THE JUDAS-TREE

Once upon a time Brahmadatta the king of Benares had four sons. One day they sent for the charioteer, and said to him,

"We want to see a Judas-tree; show us one!"

"Very well, I will," the charioteer replied. But he did not show it them all together. He took the eldest at once to the forest in the chariot, and showed him the tree at the time when the buds were just sprouting from the stem. To the second he showed it when the leaves were green, to the third at the time of blossoming, and to the fourth when it was bearing fruit.

After this it happened that the four brothers were sitting together, and some one asked, "What sort of a tree is the Judas-tree?" Then the first brother answered,
Like a burnt stump!"
And the second cried, "Like a banyan-tree!"

And the third—"Like a piece of meat!"
And the fourth said, "Like the acacia!"

They were vexed at each other's answers, and ran to find their father, "My lord," they asked, "what sort of a tree is the Judas-tree?"

What is that you say?" he asked. They told him the manner of their answers. Said the king,

"All four of you have seen the tree. Only when the charioteer showed you the tree, you did not ask him 'What is the tree like at such a time?' or 'at such another time?' You made no distinctions, and that is the reason of your mistake." And he repeated the first stanza:
    All have seen the Judas-tree—
    What is your perplexity?
    No one asked the charioteer
    What its form the livelong year!

THE JUDGMENTS OF KING MIRROR-FACE

Once upon a time, brethren, when Janasandha was reigning in Benares, the Bodhisatta came to life as the son of his chief queen. His face was resplendent, wearing a look of a auspicious beauty, like a golden mirror well polished. On the day of his naming they called him Ādāsa mukha, Prince Mirror-face.

Within the space of seven years his father caused him to be taught the three Vedas, and all the duties of this world; and then he died, when the lad was seven years old. The courtiers performed the king's obsequies with great pomp, and made the offerings for the dead; and on the seventh day they gathered together in the palace court, and talked together. The prince was very young, they thought, and he could not be made king.

Before they made him king, they would test him. So they prepared a court of justice, and set a divan. Then they came into the prince's presence, and said they, "You must come, my lord, to the law-court." To this the prince agreed; and with a great company he repaired thither, and sat upon the dais.

Now at the time when the king sat down for judgment, the courtier had dressed up a monkey, in the garb of a man who is skilled in the lore, which tells what are good sites for a building. They made him go upon two feet, and brought him into the judgment hall.

"My lord," said they, " In the time of the king your father this man was one who divined by magic as to desirable sites, and well did he know his art. Down in the earth as deep as seven cubits he can see a fault. By his help there was a place chosen for the king's house; let the king provide for him, and give him a post."

The prince scanned him from head to foot. "This is no man, but a monkey," he thought; and monkeys can destroy what other have made, but of themselves can neither make anything nor carry out such a thing." And so he repeated the first stanza to his court:

It is not a clever builder but an ape with a wrinkled face
He can destroy what others make; that is the way of his race.

"It must be so, my lord!" said the courtiers, and took him away. But after a day or two they dressed this same creature in grand clothes, and brought him again to the judgment hall. "In the king your father's time, my lord, this was a judge who dealt justice. Him should you take to help you in the awarding of justice."

The prince looked at him. Thought he, "A man with mind and reason is not so hairy as all that. This witless ape cannot dispense justice"; and he repeated the second stanza:

There's no wit in this hairy creature; he breeds no confidence;

He knows naught, as my father taught: the animal has no sense!

"So it must be, my lord!" said the courtiers, and led him away. Yet once again did they dress up the very same monkey, and bring him to the hall of judgment, "Sire," said they, "In the time of the king your father this man did his duty to father and mother, and paid respect to old age in his family. Him you should keep with you."

Again the prince looked at him, and thought—"Monkeys are fickle of mind; such a thing they cannot do." And then he repeated the third stanza:
One king Dasaratha has taught me; no help such a creature would send
To father or mother, to sister or brother, or any who call him friend!

"So must it be, my lord!" answered they, and took him away again. And they said amongst themselves." 'Tis a wise prince; he will be able to rule"; and they made the Bodhisatta king; and throughout the city by beat of drum they made proclamation, saying, "The edicts of king Mirror-face!"

Form that time the Bodhisatta reigned righteously; and his wisdom was noised abroad throughout all India. To show forth the matter of this wisdom of his, these fourteen problems were brought to him to decide:
An ox, a lad, a horse, a basket-knight,
A squire, alight-o'-love, and a young dame,
A snake, a deer, a partridge, and a sprite,
A snake, ascetics, a young priest I name.

This happened, as we shall now explain. When the Bodhisatta was inaugurated king, a certain servant of king Janasandha, named Gāmani-canda, thus considered within himself: "This kingdom is glorious if it be governed by aid of those who are of an age with the king. Now I am old, and I cannot wait upon a young prince: So I will get me a living by farming in the country" So he departed form the city a distance of three leagues, and abode in a certain village. But he had no oxen for farming. And so, after rain had fallen, he begged the loan of two oxen from a friend; all day long he ploughed with them; and then he gave them grass to eat, and went to the owner's house to give them back again. At the moment it happened that the owner sat at meal with his wife; and the oxen entered the house, quite at home. As they entered, the master was raising his plate, and the wife putting hers down. Seeing that they did not invite him to share the meal, Gāmani-canda departed without formally making over the oxen. During the night, thieves broke into the crow- pen, and stole the oxen away.

Early on the morrow, the owner of these oxen entered the crow-shed, but cattle there were none; he perceived that they had been stolen away by thieves. "I'll make Gāmani pay for it!" thought he, and to Gāmani he went.

"I say, return me my oxen!" cried he.
"Are not they in their stall?"
"Now did you return them to me?"

"No, I didn't"

"Here's the king's officer: come along!"

Now this people have a custom that they pick up bit of stone or potsherd, and say—"Here's the king's officer: come long!" If any man refuses to go, he is punished. So when Gāmani heard the word "officer," he went along.

So they went together towards the king's court. On the way, they came to a village where dwelt a friend of Gāmani's. Said he to the other.

"I say, I'm very hungry. Wait here till I go in and get me something to eat!" and he entered his friend's house.

But his friend was not at home. The wife said,

"Sir, there is nothing cooked. Wait but a moment; I will cook at once and set before you."

"She climbed a ladder to the grain store, and in her haste she fell to the ground. And as she was seven months gone with child, a miscarriage followed.

At that moment, in came the husband, and saw what had happened. "You have struck my wife," cried he, "and brought her labour upon her untimely! Here's a king's officer for you— come along!" and he carried him off. After this they went on, the two of them, with Gāmani between.

As they went, there was a horse at a village gate; and the groom could not stop it, but it ran along with them. The horsekeeper called out to Gāmani—

"Uncle Candagāmani, hit the horse with something, and head him back!" Gāmani picked up the stone, and threw it at the horse. The stone struck his foot, and broke it like the stalk of a castor-oil plant. Then the man cried,

"Oh, you've broken my horse's leg! Here's a king's officer for you!" and he laid hold of him.

Gāmani was thus three men's prisoner. As they led him along, he thought: "These people will denounce me to the king; I can't pay for the oxen; much less the fine for causing an untimely birth; and then where shall I get the price of the horse? I were better dead." So, as they went along, he saw a wood near by the road, and in it a hill with a precipice on one side of it. In the shadow of it were two basket-makers, father and son, weaving a mat. Said Gāmani,

"I say, I want to retire for a moment: wait here, while I go aside"; and with these words he climbed the hill, and threw himself down the precipice. He fell upon the back of the elder basket-maker, and killed him on the spot. Gāmani got up, and stood still.

"Ah, you villain! You've murdered my father!" cried the younger basket-maker; "here's the king's officer!" He seized Gāmani's hands, and came out of the thicket.

"What's this?" asked the others.

"The villain has murdered my father!"

So on they went, the four of them, with Gamani in the middle.

They came to the gate of another village. The headman was there, who hailed Gāmani: "Uncle Canda, whither away?"

"To see the king," says Gāmani.

"Oh indeed, to see the king. I want to send him a message; will you take it?"

"Yes, that I will."

"Well—I am usually handsome, rich, honoured, and healthy; but now I am miserable and have the jaundice too. Ask the king why this is. He is a wise man, so they say; he will tell you, and you can bring me his message again."

To this the other agreed.

At another village a light-o-love called out to him—"Whither bound, Uncle Canda?"

"To see the king," says he.

"They say the king is a wise man; take him a message from me " says the woman. "Aforetime I used to make great gains; now I don't get the worth of a betel-nut, and nobody courts me. Ask the king how this may be, and then you can tell me."

At a third village, there was young woman who told Gāmani,

"I can live neither with my husband nor with my own family. Ask the king how this is, and then tell me."

A little further on there was a snake living in an ant-hill near the road. He saw Gāmani, and called out,

"Whither away, Canda?"

"To see the king."

"The king is wise; take him a message from me. When I go out to get my food, I leave this ant-hill faint and famishing, and yet I fill the entrance hole with my body, and I get out with difficulty, myself along. But When I come in again, I feel satisfied, and fat, yet I pass quickly through the hole without touching the sides. How is this? ask the king, and bring me his answer."

And further on a deer saw him, and said—"I can't eat grass anywhere but underneath this tree. Ask the king the reason." And again a partridge said, "When I sit at the foot of this ant heap, and utter my note, I can make it prettily; but nowhere else. Ask the king why." And again, a tree spirit saw him, and said,

"Whither away, Canda?"

"To the king."

"The king's a wise man, they say. In former times I was highly honoured; now I don't receive so much as a handful of twigs. Ask the king what the reason is."

And further on again he was seen by a naga king, who spoke to him thus: "The king is said to be a wise man; then ask him this question. Heretofore the water in this pool has been clear as crystal. Why is it that now it has become turbid, with scum all over it?"

Further on, not fair from a town, certain ascetics who dwelt in a park saw him, and said, in the same way, "They say the king is wise. Of yore there were in this park sweet fruits in plenty, now they have grown tasteless and dry. Ask him what the reason is." Further on again, he was accosted by some brahmin students who were in hall at the gate of a town. They said to him,

"Where are you going, Canda, eh?"

"To the king," says Canda.

"Then take a message for us. Till now, whatever passage we learnt was bright and clear; now it does not stay with us, it is not understood, but all is darkness,—it is like water in a leaky jar. Ask the king what the reason is."

Gāmani-canda came before the king with his fourteen questions. When the king saw him, he recognised him, "This is my father's servant, who used to dandle me in his arms. Where has he been living all this time?" And "Canda," said he, "Where have you been living all this time? We have seen nothing of you for a long while; what brings you here?"

"Oh, my lord, when my lord the late king went to heaven, I departed into the country and kept myself by farming. Then this man summoned me for a suit regarding his cattle, and here he has brought me."

"If you had not been brought here, you would have never come; but I'm glad that you were brought anyhow. Now I can see you. Where is that man?"

"Here, my lord."

"Is it you that summoned our friend Canda?"

"Yes, my lord."

"Why?"

"He refuses to give back my pair of oxen!"

"Is this so, Canda?"

"Hear my story too, my lord!" said Canda; and told him the whole. When he had heard the tale, the king accosted the owner of the oxen. "Did you see the oxen," said he, "entering the stall?"

"No, my lord," the man replied.

"Why, man did you never hear my name? They call me king Mirror-face. Speak out honestly."

"I saw them my lord!" said he.

"Now, Canda," said the king, "you failed to return the oxen, and therefore you are his debtor for them. But this man in saying that he had not seen them, told a direct lie. Therefore you with your own hands shall pluck his eyes out, and you shall yourself pay him twenty-four pieces of money as the price of the oxen." Then they led the owner of the oxen out of doors.

"If I lose my eyes, what do I care for the money?" thought he. And he fell at Gāmani's feet, and besought him—"O master Canda, keep those twenty-four pieces, and take these too!" and he gave him other pieces, and ran away.

The second man said, "My lord, this fellow struck my wife, and made her miscarry." "Is this true, Canda?" asked the king. Canda begged for a hearing, and told the whole story.

"Did you really strike her, and cause her to miscarry?" asked the king.

"No my lord! I did no such thing."

"Now, can you"—to the other—"can you heal the miscarriage which he has caused?"

"No my lord, I cannot."

"Now, what do you want to do?"

"I ought to have a son, my lord."

"Now then, Canda—you take the man's wife to your house; and when a son shall be born to you, hand him over to the husband."

Then this man also fell at Canda's feet, crying, "Don't break up my home, master!" threw down some money, and made off.

The third man then accused Canda, of laming his horse's foot. Canda as before told what had happened. Then the king asked the owner.

"Did you really bid Canda strike the house, and turn him back?"

"No, my lord, I did not." But on being pressed, he admitted that he had said so.

"This man," said the king, "has told a direct lie, in saying that he did not tell you to head back the horse. You may tear out his tongue; and then pay him a thousand pieces for the horse's price, which I will give you." But the fellow even gave him another sum of money, and departed.

Then the basket-maker's son said,

"This fellow is a murderer, and he killed my father!"

"It is so, Canda?" asked the king. "Hear me, my lord," said Canda, and told him about it.

"Now, what do you want?" asked the king.

"My lord, I must have my father."

"Canda," said the king, "this man must have a father. But you cannot bring him back from the dead. Then take his mother to your house, and do you be a father to him."

"Oh, master!" cried the man, "don't break up my dead father's home!" He gave Gāmani a sum of money, and hurried away.

Thus Gāmani won his suit, and in great delight he said to the king.

"My lord, I have several questions for you from several persons; may I tell you them?"

"Say on," said the king.

So Gāmani told them all in reverse order, beginning with the young brahmins. The king answered them in turn. To the first question, he answered; "In the place where they lived there used to be a crowing cock that knew the time. When they heard his crow, they used to rise up, and repeat their texts, until the sun rose, and thus they did not forget what they learnt. But now there is a cock that crows out of season; he crows at dead of night, or in broad day. When he crows in the depth of night, up they rise, but they are too sleepy to repeat the text. When he crows in broad day, they rise up, but they have not the chance to repeat their texts. Thus it is, that whatever they learn, they soon forget."

To the second question, he answered: "Formerly these men used to do all the duties of the ascetic, and the induced the mystic trance. Now they have neglected the ascetic's duties, and they do what they ought not to do; the fruits which grow in the park they give to their attendants; they live in a sinful way, exchanging their alms. This is why this fruit does not grow sweet. If they once more with one consent do their duty as ascetics, again the fruit will grow sweet for them. Those hermits know not the wisdom of kings; tell them to live the ascetic life."

He heard the third question, and answered, "Those nâga chiefs quarrel one with another, and that is why the water becomes turbid. If they make friends as before, the water will be clear again." After hearing the fourth, "The tree-spirit," said he, "used formerly to protect men passing through the wood, and therefore it received many offerings. Now it gives them no protection, and so it receives no offerings. If it protects them as before, it will receive choice offerings again. It knows not that there are kings in the world. Tell it, then, to guard the men who go up into that wood." And on hearing the fifth, "Under the ant-hill where the partridge finds himself able to utter a pleasant cry is a crock of treasure; dig it up and get it." To the sixth he answered, "On the tree under which the deer found he could eat grass, is a great honeycomb. He craves the grass on which this honey has dropped, and so he can eat no other. You get the honeycomb, send the best of it to me, and eat the rest yourself." Then on hearing the seventh, "Under the snake's ant-heap lies a large treasure-crock, and there he lives guarding it. So when he goes out, from greed for this treasure his body sticks fast; but after he has fed, his desire for the treasure prevents his body from sticking and he goes in quickly and easily. Dig up the treasure, and keep it." Then he replied to the eighth question, "Between the villages where dwell the young woman's husband and her parents lives a lover of hers in a certain house. She remembers him, and her desire is toward him; therefore she cannot stay in her husband's house, but says she will go and see her parents, and on the way she stays a few days with her lover. When she has been at home a few days, again she remembers him, and saying she will return to her husband, she goes again to her lover. Go, tell her there are kings in the land; say she must dwell with her husband, and if she will not, let her have a care, the king will cause her to be seized, and she shall die." He heard the ninth, and to this he said, "The woman used formerly to take a price from the hand of one, and not to go with a another until she was off with him, and that is how she used to receive much. Now she has changed her manner, and without leave of the first she goes with the last, so that she receives nothing, and none seek after her. If she keeps to her old custom, it will be as it was before. Tell her that she should keep to that."

On hearing the tenth, he replied, "That village headman used once to deal justice indifferently, so that men were pleased and delighted with him; and in their delight they gave him many a present. This is what made him handsome, rich, and honoured. Now he loves to take bribes, and his judgment is not fair; so he is poor and miserable, and jaundiced. If he judges once again with righteousness, he will be again as he was before. He knows not that there are kings in the land. Tell him that he must us justice in giving judgment.

And Gāmani-canda told all these message, as they were told to him. And the king having resolved all these questions by his wisdom, like Buddha omniscient, gave rich presents to Gāmani-canda; and the village where Canda dwelt he gave to him, as a brahmin's gift, and let him go. Canda went out of the city, and told the king's answer to the brahmin youths, and the ascetics, to the naga and to the tree-spirit; he took the treasure from the place where the partridge sat, and from the tree beneath which the deer did eat, he took the honeycomb, and sent honey to the king; he broke into the snake's ant-hill, gathered the treasure out of it; and to the young woman, and the light-o'-love, and the village headman he said even as the king had told him. Then he returned to his own village, and dwelt there so long as he lived, and afterward passed away to fare according to his deserts. And king Mirror-face also gave alms, and wrought goodness, and finally after his death attained to heaven.

THE CRAB AND THE ELEPHANT

Once upon a time, when Brahmadatta was king of Benares, there was a great lake in Himalaya, wherein was a great golden crab. Because he lived there, the place was known as the Crab Tarn. The crab was very large, as big and round as a threshing floor; it would catch elephants, and kill and eat them; and from fear of it the elephants dared not go down and browse there.

Now the Bodhisatta was conceived by the mate of an elephant, the leader of a herd, living near by this Crab Tarn. The mother, in order to be safe till her delivery, sought another place

on a mountain, and there she delivered a son; who in due time
grew to years of wisdom, and was great and mighty, and pros-
pered, and he was like a purple mountain of collyrium.

He chose another elephant for his mate, and he resolved to
catch this crab. So with his mate and his mother, he sought out
the elephant herd, and finding his father, proposed to go and
catch the crab.

"You will not be able to do that, my son," said he.

But he begged the father again and again to give him
leave, until at last he said, "Well, you may try."

So the young elephant collected all the elephants beside
the Crab Tarn, and led them close by the lake. "Does the crab
catch them when they go down, or while they are feeding, or
when they come up again?"

They replied, "When the beasts come up again."

"Well then," said he, "do you all go down to the lake and
eat whatever you see, and come up first; I will follow last behind
you." And so they did. Then the crab, seeing the Bodhisatta
coming up last, caught his feet tight in his claw, like a smith
who seizes a lump of iron in a huge pair of tongs. The Bodhisatta's
mate did not leave him, but stood there close by him. The
Bodhisatta pulled at the crab, but could not make him budge.
Then the crab pulled, and drew him towards himself. In deadly
fear the elephant roared the cry of capture; hearing which all
the other elephants, in deadly terror, ran off trumpeting, and
dropping excrement. Even his mate could not stand, but began
to make off. Then to tell her how he was held a prisoner, he
uttered the first stanza, hoping to stay her from her flight:

Gold-clawed creature with projecting eyes,
Tarn-bred, hairless, clad in bony shell,
He has caught me! Hear my woeful cries!
Mate! don't leave me—for you love me well!

Then his mate turned round, and repeated the second stanza to his comfort:

Leave you? never! never will I go—
Noble husband, with your years threescore.
All four quarters of the earth can show
None so dear as you have been of yore.

In this way she encouraged him; and saying, "Noble sir, now I will talk to the crab a while to make him let you go," she addressed the crab in the third stanza:

Of all the crabs that in the sea,
Ganges, or Nerbudda be,
You are best and chief, I know:
Hear me—let my husband go!

As she spoke thus, the crab's fancy was smitten with the sound of the female voice, and forgetting all fear he loosed his claws from the elephant's leg, and suspected nothing of what he would do when he was set free. Then the elephant lifted his foot, and stepped upon the crab's back; and at once his eyes started out. The elephant shouted the joy-cry. Up ran the other elephants all, pulled the crab along and set him upon the ground, and trampled him to mincemeat. His two claws broken from his body lay apart. And this Crab Tarn, being near the Ganges, when there was a flood in the Ganges, was filled with Ganges water; when the water subsided it ran from the lake into the Ganges. Then these two claws were lifted and floated along the Ganges. One of them reached the sea, the other was found by the ten royal brothers while playing in the water, and they took it and made of it the little drum called Ānaka. The Titans found that which reached the sea, and made it into the drum called Ālambara. These afterwards being worsted in battle with Sakka, ran off and left it behind. Then Sakka caused it to be kept for his own use; and it is of this they say, "There is thunder like the Ālambara cloud!"

THE OWL AS KING

Once upon a time, the people who lived in the first cycle of the world gathered, and took for their king a certain man, handsome, auspicious, commanding, and altogether perfect. The quadrupeds also gathered, and chose for king the Lion; and the fish in the ocean chose them a fish called Ānanda. Then all the birds in the Himalayas assembled upon a flat rock, crying:

"Among men there is a king, and among the beasts, and the fish have one too; but amongst us birds king there is none. We should not live in anarchy; we too should choose a king. Fix on some one fit to be set in the king's place!"

They searched about for such a bird, and chose the owl; "Here is the bird we like," said they. And a bird made proclamation three times to all that there would be a vote taken on this matter. After patiently hearing this announcement twice, on the third time up rose a crow, and cried out:

"Stay now! If that is what he looks like when he is being consecrated king, what will he look like when he is angry? If he only looks at us in anger, we shall be scattered like sesame seeds thrown on a hot plate. I don't want to make this fellow king!" and enlarging upon this he uttered the first stanza:
The owl is king, you say, o'er all bird-kind
With your permission, may I speak my mind?

The birds repeated the second, granting him leave to speak:
You have our leave, Sir, so it be good and right:
For other birds are young, and wise, and bright.

Thus permitted, he repeated the third:
I like not (with all deference be it said)
To have the Owl anointed as our Head.
Look at his face! if this good humour be,
What will he do when he looks angrily?

Then he flew up into the air, cawing out "I don't like it! I

don't like it!" The owl rose and pursued him. Thenceforward
those two nursed enmity one towards another. And the birds
chose a golden mallard for their king, and dispersed.

THE ELEPHANT-TRAINER'S LUCK

Once upon a time, when Brahmadatta reigned in Benares,
the Bodhisatta was born into a brahmin family in the realm of
Kāsi. On growing up, he was educated at Takkasilā, and lived
among his family; but when his parents died, much distressed
he retired to the life of a recluse in the Himalaya, and there he
cultivated the Attainments.

A long time passed, and he came down to inhabited parts
for salt and savouring, and took up his quarters in the gardens
of the king of Benares. Next day, on his begging rounds, he
came to the door of an elephant-trainer. This man took a fancy
to his ways and manners, fed him, and gave him lodging in his
own grounds, waiting upon him continually.

Now it happened just then that a man whose business it
was to gather firewood failed to get back to town from the
woods in time. He lay down for the night in the temple, placing
a bundle of sticks under his head for a pillow. At this temple
there were a number of cocks quite free, which had perched
close by on a tree. Towards morning, one of them, who was
roosting high, let fall a dropping on the back of a bird below.
"Who dropt that on me?" cried this one. "I did," cried the first.
"And why?" "Didn't think," said the other; and then did it
again. Hereupon they both began to abuse each other, crying—
"What power have you? what power have you?" At last the
lower one said, "Anybody who kills me, and eats my flesh roasted
on the coals, gets a thousand pieces of money in the morning!"
And the one above answered—"Pooh, pooh, don't boast about
a little thing like that! Anybody who eats my fleshy parts will
become king; if he eats my outside, he'll become commander-in-
chief or chief queen, according as he's man or woman; if he eats
the flesh by my bones, he'll get the post of royal treasurer, if he
be a householder; or, if a holy man, will become the king's

favourite!"

The stick-picker heard all this, and pondered. "Now if I become king, there'll be no need of a thousand pieces of money. Quietly he climbed the tree, caught the top-most cock and killed him: he fastened him in a fold of his dress, saying to himself—"Now I'll be king!" As soon as the gates were opened, in he walked. He plucked the fowl, and cleaned it, and gave it to his wife, bidding her make the meat nice for eating. She got ready the meat with some rice, and set it before him, bidding her lord eat.

"Good wife," said he, "there's great virtue in this meat. By eating it I shall become king, and you my queen!" So they took the meat and rice down to the Ganges bank, intending to bathe before eating it. Then, putting meat and rice down upon the bank, in they went to bathe.

Just then a breeze stirred up the water, which washed away the meat. Down the river if floated, till if came in sight of an elephant-trainer, a great personage, who was giving his elephant a bath lower down. "What have we here?" said he, and picked it up. "It's fowl and rice, my lord," was the reply. He bade wrap it up, and seal it, and sent it home to his wife, with a message not to open it till he returned.

The stick-picker also ran off, with his belly puffed out with sand and water which he had swallowed.

Now a certain ascetic, who had divine vision, the family priest of the elephant-trainer, was thinking to himself, "My patron friend does not leave his post with the elephants. When will he attain promotion?" As he thus pondered, he saw this man by his divine insight, and perceived what was a-doing. He went on before, and sat in the patron's house.

When the master returned, he greeted him respectfully and sat down on one side. Then sending for the parcel, he ordered food and water to be brought for the ascetic. The ascetic took the rice which was offered; but not the meat, and said, "I will divide this meat." The master gave him leave. Then separating the meat into portions, he gave to the elephant-trainer the fleshly parts, the outside to his wife, and took the flesh about the bones for his own share. After the meal was over, he said, "On the third day from this you will become king. Take care what you do!" and away he went.

On the third day a neighbouring king came and belea-guered Benares. The king told his elephant-trainer to dress in the royal robes, bidding him go mount his elephant and fight. He himself put on a disguise, and mingled with the ranks; swift came an arrow, and pierced him, so that he perished then and there. The trainer learning that the king was dead, sent for a great quantity of money, and beat the drum proclaiming, "Let those who want money, advance, and fight!" the warrior host in a twinkling slew the hostile king.

After the king's obsequies the courtiers deliberated who was to be made king. Said they, "While our king was yet alive, he put his royal robes upon the elephant-trainer. This very man has fought and won the kingdom. To him the kingdom shall be given!" And they consecrated him king, and his wife they made the chief queen. The Bodhisatta became his confidant.

THE WISHING-CUP

Once upon a time, when Brahmadatta was reigning in Benares, the Bodhisatta was born as a rich merchant's son; and after his father's death, took his place. In his house was buried a treasure of four hundred million. He had an only son. The Bodhisatta gave alms and did good until he died, and then he came to life again as Sakka, king of the gods. His son proceeded to make a pavilion across the road, and sat down with many friends round him, to drink. He paid a thousand pieces to run-ners and tumblers, singers and dancers, and passed his time in drinking, gluttony, and debauchery; he wandered about, asking only for song, music and dancing, devoted to his boon-compan-ions, sunk in sloth. So in short time he squandered all his treasure, of four hundred millions, all his property, goods, and furniture, and got so poor and miserable that he had to go about clad in rags.

Sakka, as he meditated, became aware how poor he was. Overcome with love for his son, he gave him a Wishing Cup, with these words: "Son, take care not to break this cup. So long as you keep it, your wealth will never come to an end. So take good care of it!" and then he returned to heaven.

After that the man did nothing but drink out of it. One day, he was drunk, and threw the cup into the air, catching it as it fell. But once he missed it. Down it fell upon the earth, and smashed! Then he got poor again, and went about in rags, begging, bowl in hand, till at last he lay down by a wall, and died.

THE JACKAL AND THE CROW

Once upon a time, when Brahmadatta was king of Benares, the Bodhisatta became a tree-spirit in a certain rose-apple grove. A crow perched upon a branch of his tree, and began to eat the fruit. Then came a jackal, and looked up and spied the crow. Thought he, "If I flatter this creature, perhaps I shall get some of the fruit to eat!" So in flattery he repeated the first stanza:
Who is it sits in a rose-apple tree—
Sweet singer! Whose voice trickles gently to me?
Like a young peacock she coos with soft grace,
And ever sits still in her place.

The crow, in his praise, responded with the second:
He that is noble in breeding and birth
Can praise others' breeding, knows what they are worth.
Like a young tiger thou seemest to be:
Come, eat what I give, Sir, to thee!

With these words she shook the branch and made some fruit drop. Then the spirit of the tree, beholding these two eating, after flattering each other, repeated the third stanza:

Liars, foregather, I very well know.
Here, for example, a carrion Crow,
And corpse-eating Jackal, with puerile clatter
Proceed one another to flatter!

After repeating this stanza, the tree-spirit, assuming a fearful shape, scared them both away.

THE WOLF'S SABBATH

Once upon a time, when Brahmadatta reigned king in Benares, the Bodhisatta came to life as Sakka, king of the gods. At that time a wolf lived on a rock by the Ganges bank. The winter floods came up and surrounded the rock. There he lay upon the rock, with no food and no way of getting it. The water rose and rose, and the wolf pondered: "No food here, and no way to get it. Here I lie, with nothing to do. I may as well keep a Sabbath fast." Thus resolved to keep a sabbath, as he lay he solemnly resolved to keep the religious precepts. Sakka in his meditations perceived the wolf's weak resolve. Thought he, "I'll plague that wolf"; and taking the shape of a wild goat, he stood near, and let the wolf see him.

"I'll keep Sabbath another day!" thought the wolf, as he spied him; up he got, and leapt at the creature. But the goat jumped about so that the wolf could not catch him. When our wolf saw that he could not catch him, he came to a standstill, and went back, thinking to himself as he lay down again, "Well, my sabbath is not broken after all."

Then Sakka, by his divine power, hovered above in the air; said he:

"What have such as you, all unstable, to do with keeping a sabbath? You didn't know that I was Sakka, and wanted a meal of goat's flesh!" and thus plaguing and rebuking him, he returned to the world of the gods.

THE KING AND THE FRUIT-GIRL

Once upon a time when Brahmadatta was king at Benares,

the Bodhisatta was his minister and his temporal and spiritual adviser.

Now one day the king stood at an open window looking into the palace court. And at this very moment the daughter of a fruiterer, a beautiful girl in the flower of her youth, stood with a basket of jujubes on her head crying, "Jujubes, ripe jujubes, who'll buy my jujubes?" But she did not venture into the royal court.

And the king no sooner heard her voice than he fell in love with her, and when he learned that she was unmarried he sent for her and raised her to the dignity of chief queen, and bestowed great honour upon her. Now she was dear and pleasing in the king's eyes. And one day the king sat eating jujubes in a golden dish. And the queen Sujātā, when she saw the king eating jujubes, asked him, saying, "My lord, what in the world are you eating?" And she uttered the first stanza:

What is this egg-shaped fruit, my lord, so pretty and red of hue,

In a gold dish set before thee? Pray tell me, where they grew.

And the king was wroth and said, "O daughter of a greengrocer, dealer in ripe jujubes, do you not recognise the jujubes, the special fruit of your family?" And he repeated two stanzas:

Bare-headed and meanly clad, my queen, thus once didst feel no shame,

To fill thy lap with the jujube fruit, and now thou dost ask its name;

Thou art eaten up with pride, my queen, thou findest no pleasure in life,

Begone and gather thy jujubes again. Thou shall be no longer my wife.

Then the Bodhisatta thought, "No one, except myself, will be able to reconcile this pair. I will appease the king's anger and prevent him from turning her out of doors." Then he repeated the fourth stanza:

These are the sins of a woman, my lord, promoted to high
                                                            estate
Forgive her and cease from thine anger, O king, for
'twas thou didst make her great.

So the king at his word put up with the offence of the
queen and restored her to her former position. And thenceforth
they lived amicably together.

THE WOODPECKER AND THE LION

Once upon a time when Brahmadatta was reigning in
Benares, the Bodhisatta came to life as a woodpecker in the
Himalaya country.

Now a certain lion, while devouring his prey, had a bone
stick in his throat. His throat swelled up so that he could not
take any food and severe pains set in. Then this woodpecker,
while intent on seeking its own food, as it was perched on a
bough, saw the lion and asked him, saying, "Friend, what ails
you?" He told him what was the matter, and the bird said, "I
would take the bone out of your throat, friend, but I dare not put
my head into your mouth, for fear you should eat me up."

"Do not be afraid, friend; I will not eat you up. Only save
my life."

"All right," said the bird, and ordered the lion to lie down
upon his side. Then it thought: "Who knows what this fellow
will be about?" And to prevent his closing his mouth, it fixed
a stick between his upper and lower jaw, and then entering into
the lion's mouth, it struck, the end of the bone with its beak.
The bone fell out and disappeared. And then the woodpecker
came out of the lion's mouth, and with a blow from its beak
knocked out the stick, and hoping off sat on the top of a bough.

The lion recovered from his sickness and one day was
devouring a wild buffalo which he had killed. Thought the

woodpecker: "I will now put him to the test," and perching on a bough above the lion's head, it fell to conversing with him and uttered the first stanza:

> Kindness as much as in us lay,
> To thee my lord, we once did show:
> On us in turn, we humbly pray,
> Do thou a trifling boon bestow.

On hearing this the lion repeated the second stanza:

> To trust thy head to a lion's jaw,
> A creature red in tooth and claw,
> To dare such a deed and be living still,
> Is token enough of my good will.

The woodpecker on hearing this uttered two more stanzas:

> From the base ingrate hope not to obtain
> The due requital of good service done:
> From bitter thought and angry word refrain,
> But haste the presence of the wretch to shun,

With these words the woodpecker flew away.

THE HARE'S SELF-SACRIFICE

Once upon a time when Brahmadatta was reigning in Benares, the Bodhisatta came to life as a young hare and lived in a wood. On one side of this wood was the foot of a mountain, on another side a river, and on the third side a border-village. The hare had three friends—a monkey, a jackal and an otter. These four wise creatures lived together and each of them got his food on his own hunting-ground, and in the evening they again came together. The hare in his wisdom by way of admonition preached the Truth to his three companions, teaching that alms are to be given, the moral law to be observed, and holy days to be kept. They accepted his admonition and went each to his own part of the jungle and dwelt there.

And so in the course of time the Bodhisatta one day observing the sky, and looking at the moon knew that the next day
would be a fast-day, and addressing his three companions he
said, "To-morrow is a fast-day. Let all three of you take upon you
the moral precepts, and observe the holy day. To one that
stands fast in moral practice, almsgiving brings a great reward.
Therefore feed any beggars that come to you by giving them
food from your own table." They readily assented, and abode
each in his own place of dwelling.

On the morrow quite early in the morning, the otter sallied
forth to seek his prey and went down to the bank of the Ganges.
Now it came to pass that a fisherman had landed seven red fish,
and stringing them together on a withe, he had taken and
buried them in the sand on the river's bank. And then he dropped
down the stream, catching more fish. The otter scenting the
buried fish, dug up the sand till he came upon them, and pull-
ing them out cried thrice, "Does anyone own these fish?" And
not seeing any owner he took hold of the withe with his teeth
and laid the fish in the jungle where he dwelt, intending to eat
them at a fitting time. And then he lay down, thinking how
virtuous he was! The jackal too sallied forth in quest of food and
found in the jut of a field-watcher two spits, a lizard and a pot
of milk curd. And after thrice crying aloud, "To whom do these
belong?" and not finding an owner, he put on his neck the rope
for lifting the pot, and grasping the spits and the lizard with his
teeth, he brought and laid them in his own lair, thinking, "In
due season I will devour them," and so lay down, reflecting how
virtuous he had been.

The monkey also entered the clump of trees, and gathering
a bunch of mangoes laid them up in his part of the jungle,
meaning to eat them in due season, and then lay down, thinking how virtuous he was. But the Bodhisatta in due time came
out, intending to browse on the kusa-grass, and as he lay in the
jungle, the thought occurred to him, "It is impossible for me to
offer grass to any beggars that may chance to appear, and I have
no sesame, rice, and such like. If any beggar shall appeal to me,
I shall have to give him my own flesh to eat." At this splendid

display of virtue, Sakka's white marble throne manifested signs of heat. Sakka on reflection discovered the cause and resolved to put this royal hare to the test. First of all he went and stood by the otter's dwelling-place, disguised as a brahmin, and being asked why he stood there, he replied, "Wise Sir, if I could get something to eat, after keeping the fast, I would perform all my ascetic duties." The otter replied, "Very well, I will give you some food," and as he conversed with him he repeated the first stanza:

> Seven red fish I safely brought to land from Ganges flood.
> O brahmin, eat thy fill, I pray, and stay within this wood.

The brahmin said, "Let be till to-morrow. I will see to it by and by." Next he went to the jackal, and when asked by him why he stood there, he made the same answer. The jackal, too, readily promised him some food, and in talking with him repeated the second stanza:

> A lizard and a jar of curds, the keeper's evening meal,
> Two spits of roasted flesh withal I wrongfully did steal:
> Such as I have I give to thee: O brahmin, eat, I pray,
> If thou shouldst deign within this wood a while with us to
> stay.

Said the brahmin, "Let be till to-morrow. I will see to it by and by." Then he went to the monkey, and when asked what he meant by standing there, he answered just as before. The monkey readily offered him some food, and in conversing with him gave utterance to the third stanza:

> An icy stream, a mango ripe, and pleasant greenwood
> shade,
> 'Tis thine to enjoy, if thou canst dwell content in forest
> glade.

Said the brahmin, "Let be till to-morrow. I will see it by any by." And he went to the wise hare, and on being asked by him why he stood there, he made the same reply. The Bodhisatta on hearing what he wanted was highly delighted, and said, "Brahmin, you have done well in coming to me for food. This day will I grant you a boon that I have never granted before but you shall not break the moral law by taking animal life. Go, friend, and when you have piled together logs of wood, and kindled a fire, come and let me know, and I will sacrifice myself by falling into the midst of the flames, and when body is roasted, you shall eat my flesh and fulfill all your ascetic duties." And in thus addressing him the hare uttered the fourth stanza:

> Nor sesame, nor beans, nor rice have I as food to give,
> But roast with fire my flesh I yield, if thou with us wouldst
> live.

Sakka, on hearing what he said, by his miraculous power caused a heap of burning coals to appear, and came and told the Bodhisatta. Rising from his bed of kusa-grass and coming to the place, he thrice shook himself that if there were any insects within his coat, they might escape death. Then offering his whole body as a free gift he sprang up, and like a royal swan, alighting on a cluster of lotuses, in an ecstasy of joy he fell on the heap of live coals. But the flame failed even to heat the pores of the hair on the body of the Bodhisatta, and it was as if he had entered a region of frost. Then he addressed Sakka in these words: "Brahmin, the fire you have kindled is icy-cold: it fails to heat even the pores of the hair on my body. What is the meaning of this?" "Wise Sir," he replied, "I am no brahmin. I am Sakka, and I have come to put your virtue to the test." The Bodhisatta said, "If not only thou, Sakka, but all the inhabitants of the world were to try me in this matter of almsgiving, they would not find in me any unwillingness to give," and with this the Bodhisatta uttered a cry of exultation like a lion roaring. Then said Sakka to the Bodhisatta, "O wise hare, be thy virtue known throughout a whole aeon." And squeezing the mountain, with the essence thus extracted, he daubed the sign of a hare on the orb of the moon. And after depositing the hare on a bed of young kusa-grass, in the same wooded part of the jungle, Sakka returned to his own place in heaven. And these four wise creatures dwelt happily and harmoniously together, fulfilling the moral law and observing holy days, till they departed to fare according to their deeds.

UNASKED-FOR ADVICE

Once upon a time when Brahmadatta was reigning in
Benares, the Bodhisatta came to life as a young singila bird.
And when he grew to be a big bird, he settled in the Himalaya
country and built him a nest to his fancy, that was proof against
the rain. Then a certain monkey in the rainy season, when the
rain fell without intermission, sat near the Bodhisatta, his teeth
chattering by reason of the severe cold. The Bodhisatta, seeing
him thus distressed, fell to talking with him, and uttered the
first stanza:

> Monkey, in feet and hands and face
> So like the human form,
> Why buildest thus no dwelling-place,
> To hide thee from the storm?

The monkey, on hearing this replied with a second stanza:

> In feet and hands and face, O bird,
> Though close to man allied.
> Wisdom, chief boon on him conferred,
> To me has been denied.

The Bodhisatta, on hearing this, repeated yet two more
couplets:

> He that inconstancy betrays, a light and fickle mind,
> Unstable proved in all his ways, no happiness may find.

> Monkey, in virtue to excel, do thou thy utmost strive,
> And safe-from wintry blast to dwell, go, hut of leaves
> contrive.

Thought the monkey, "This creature, though dwelling in a
place that is sheltered from the rain despises me. I will not
suffer him to rest quietly in the nest." Accordingly, in his eager-
ness to catch the Bodhisatta, he made a spring upon him. But
the Bodhisatta, he made a spring upon him. But the Bodhisatta

flew up into the air, and winged his way elsewhere. And the monkey, after smashing up and destroying his nest, betook himself off.

THE FLIGHT OF THE BEASTS

Once upon a time when Brahmadatta was reigning in Benares, the Bodhisatta came to life as a young lion. And when fully grown he lived in a wood. At this time there was near the Western Ocean a grove of palms mixed with vilva trees. A certain hare lived here beneath a palm sapling, at the foot of a vilva tree. One day this hare after feeding came and lay down beneath the young palm tree. And the thought struck him: "If this earth should be destroyed, what would become of me?" And at this very moment a ripe vilva fruit fell on a palm leaf. At the sound of it, the hare thought: This solid earth is collapsing, and starting up he fled, without so much as looking behind him. Another hare saw him scampering off, as if frightened to death, and asked the cause of his panic flight. "Pray, don't ask me," he said. The other hare cried, "Pray, Sir what is it?" and kept running after him. Then the hare stopped a moment and without looking back said, "The earth here is breaking up." And at this the second hare ran after the other. And so first one and then another hare caught sight of him running, and joined in the chase till one hundred thousand hares all took o flight together. They were seen by a deer, a boar, an elk, a buffalo, a wild ox, a rhinoceros, a tiger, a lion and an elephant. And when they asked what it meant and were told that the earth was breaking up, they too took to flight. So by degrees this host of animals extended to the length of a full league.

When the Bodhisatta saw this headlong flight of the animals, and heard the cause of it was that the earth was coming to an end, he thought: "The earth is nowhere coming to the end. Surely it must be some sound, which was misunderstood by them. And if I don't make a great effort, they will all perish. I will save their lives." So with the speed of a lion he got before them to the foot of a mountain, and lion-like roared three times. They were terribly frightened at the lion, and stopping in their flight stood all huddled together. The lion went in amongst them and asked why they were running away.

"The earth is collapsing," they answered

"Who saw it collapsing?" he said.

"The elephants know all about it", they replied.

He asked the elephants. "We don't know," they said, "the lions know." But the lions said, "We don't know, the tigers know." The tigers said, "The rhinoceroses know." The rhino ceroses said, "The wild oxen know." The wild oxen, "the buffaloes." The buffaloes, "the elks." The elks, the boars." The boars, "the deer." The deer said, "We don't know, the hares know." When the hares were questioned, they pointed to one particular hare and said, "this one told us."

So the Bodhisatta asked, "Is it true, Sir, that the earth is breaking up?"

"Yes, Sir, I saw it," said the hare.

"Where," he asked, "were you living, when you saw it?"

"Near the ocean, Sir, in a grove of palms mixed with vilva trees. For as I was lying beneath the shade of a palm sapling at the foot of a vilva tree, me thought, 'If this earth should break up, where shall I go?' And at that very moment I heard the sound of the breaking up of the earth and I fled."

Thought the lion: "A ripe vilva fruit evidently must have fallen on a palm leaf and made a 'thud,' and this hare jumped to the conclusion that the earth was coming to an end, and ran away. I will find out the exact truth, about it." So he reassured the herd of animals, and said, "I will take the hare and go and find out exactly whether the earth is coming to an end or not, in the place pointed out by him. Until I return, you do stay here." Then placing the hare on his back, he sprang forward with the speed of lion, and putting the hare down in the palm grove, he said, "Come show us the place you meant."

"I dare not, my lord," said the hare.

"Come, don't be afraid," said the lion.

The hare, not venturing to go near the vilva tree, stood afar off and cried, "Yonder, Sir, is the place of dreadful sound," and so saying, he repeated the first stanza:
From the spot where I did dwell
Issued forth a fearful 'thud';
What it was I could not tell,
Nor what caused it understood.

After hearing what the hare said, the lion went to the foot of the vilva tree, and saw the spot where the hare had been lying beneath the shade of the palm tree, and the ripe vilva fruit that fell on the palm leaf, and having carefully ascertained that the earth had not broken up, he placed the hare on his back and with the speed of a lion soon came again to the herd of beasts.

Then he told them the whole story, and said, "Don't be afraid." And having thus reassured the herd of beasts, he let them go. Verify, if it had not been for the Bodhisatta at that time, all the beasts would have rushed into the sea and perished. It was all owing to the Bodhisatta that they escaped death.

THE CONCEITED MENDICANT

Once upon a time the Bodhisatta was born in a merchant family and plied his trade. At that time a certain religious mendicant, clad in a leather garment, in going his rounds for alms, came to the rams' fighting ground, and on seeing a ram falling back before him, he fancied it did this as a mark of respect, and did not himself retire. "In the whole world," he thought, "this ram alone recognizes my merits," and raising his joined hands in respectful salutation he stood and repeated the first stanza:

The kindly beast obeisance makes before
The high-caste brahmin versed in holy lore.
Good honest creature thou,
Famous above all other beasts, I vow!

At this moment the wise merchant sitting in his stores, to restrain the mendicant, uttered the second stanza:
Brahmin, be not so rash this beast to trust,
Else will he haste to lay thee in the dust,
For this the ram falls back,
To gain an impetus for his attack.

While this wise merchant was still speaking, the ram came on at full speed, and striking the mendicant on the thigh, knocked him down. He has maddened with the pain and lay groaning. The Master, to explain the incident, gave utterance to the third stanza:
With broken leg and bowl for alms upset,
His damaged fortune he will sore regret.
Let him not weep with outstretched arms in vain,
Haste to rescue, ere the priest is slain,

Then the mendicant repeated the fourth stanza:
Thus all that honour to the unworthy pay,
Share the same fate that I have met to-day;
Prone in the dust by butting ram laid low
To foolish confidence my death I owe.

Thus lamenting he there and then came by his death.

THE IMPERMANENCE OF WORLDLY JOYS

Once upon a time when Brahmadatta was reigning in Benares, the Bodhisatta was born into a brahmin family. And when he grew up, he studied all the arts at Takkasilā and then returned to his parents. In this birth the Great Being became a holy young student. Then his parents told him they would look out a wife for him.

"I have no desire for a married life," said the Bodhisatta. "When you are dead, I will adopt the religious life of an ascetic."

And being greatly importuned by them, he had a golden image made, and said, "If you can find me a maiden like unto this, I will take her to wife." His parents sent forth some emissaries with a large escort, and bade them place the golden image in a covered carriage and go and search through the plains of India, till they found just such a young brahmin girl, when they were to give this golden image in exchange, and bring the girl back with them. Now at this time a certain holy man passing from the Brahma world was born again in the form of a young girl in a town in the kingdom of Kāsi, in the house of a brahmin worth eighty crores, and the name given her was Sammillabhāsini. At the age of sixteen she was a fair and gracious maiden, like an Apsara, endued with all the marks of female beauty. And since no thought of evil was ever suggested to her by the power of sinful passion, she was perfectly pure. So the men took the golden image and wandered about till they reached this village. The inhabitants on seeing the image asked, "Why is Sammillabhāsini, the daughter of such and such a brahmin, placed there?" The messengers on hearing this found the brahmin family and chose Sammillabhāsini for the young man's bride. She sent a message to her parents, saying, "When you are dead, I shall adopt the religious life; I have no desire for the marriage state." They said, "What art thou thinking of, maiden?" And accepting the golden image they sent off their daughter with a great retinue. The marriage ceremony took place against the wishes of both the Bodhisatta and Sammillabhāsini. Though sharing the same room and the same bed they did not regard one another with the eye of passion, but dwelt together like holy men or two female saints.

By and by the father and mother of the Bodhisatta died. He performed their funeral rites and calling to him Sammilla-bhāsini, said to her, "My dear, my family property amounts to eighty crores, and yours too is worth another eighty crores. Take all this and enter upon household life. I shall become an ascetic."

"Sir," she answered, "if you become an ascetic, I will become one too. I cannot forsake you."

"Come then," he said. So spending all their wealth in almsgiving and throwing up their worldly fortune as it were a lump of phlegm, they journeyed into the Himalaya country and both of them adopted the ascetic life. There after living for a long time on wild fruits and roots, they at length came down from the Himalayas to procure salt and vinegar, and gradually found their way to Benares, and dwelt in the royal grounds. And while they were living there, this young and delicate female ascetic, from eating insipid rice of a mixed quality, was attacked by dysentery and not being able to get any healing remedies, she grew very weak. The Bodhisatta at the time for going his rounds o beg for alms, took hold of her and carried her to the gate of the city and there laid her on a bench in a certain hall, and himself went into the city for alms. He had scarce gone out when she expired. The people, beholding the great beauty of this female ascetic, thronged about her, weeping and lamenting. The Bodhisatta after going his round of begging returned, and hearing of her death he said, "That which has the quality of dissolution is dissolved. All impermanent existences are of this kind." With these words he sat down on the bench whereon she lay and eating the mixture of food he rinsed out his mouth. The people that stood by gathered round him and said,

"Reverend Sir, what was this female ascetic to you?"

"When I was layman," he replied, "she was my wife."

"Holy Sir," they said, "while we weep and lament and cannot control our feelings, why do you not weep?"

The Bodhisatta said, "While she was alive, she belonged to me in some sort. Nothing belongs to her that is gone to another world: she has passed into the power of others. Wherefore should I weep?" And teaching the people the Truth, he recited these stanzas:
Why should I shed tears for thee,

Fair Sammillabhāsini?
Passed to death's majority
Thou art henceforth lost to me.

Wherefore should frail man lament
What to him is only lent?
He too draws his mortal breath
Forfeith every hour to death.
Be he standing, sitting still,
Moving, resting, what he will,
In the twinkling of an eye,
In a moment death is nigh.

Life I count a thing unstable,
Loss of friends inevitable.
Cherish all that are alive,
Sorrow not shouldst thou survive.

Thus did the Great Being teach the Truth, illustrating by these four stanzas the impermanence of things. The people performed funeral rites over the female ascetic. And the Bodhisatta returned to the Himalayas, and entering on the higher knowledge arising from mystic meditation was destined to birth in the Brahma- world.

THE TESTING OF VIRTUE

This was a story told by the Master when at Jetavana, about a brahmin who was ever proving his virtue. Two similar stories have been told before. In this case the Bodhisatta was the family priest of the king of Benares.

In testing his virtue he for three days took a coin from the royal treasurer's board. They informed against him as a thief, and when brought before the king, he said:
Power on earth beyond compare,
Thus virtue owns wondrous charm:
Putting on a virtuous air
The deadly snake escapes all harm.

After thus praising virtue in the first stanza, he gained the king's consent and adopted the ascetic life. Now a hawk seized a piece of meat in a butcher's shop and darted up into the air. The other birds surrounded him and struck at him with feet, claws and beaks. Unable to bear the pain he dropped the piece of meat. Another bird seized it. It too in like manner being hard pressed let the meat fall. Then another bird pounced on it, and whosoever got the meat was pursued by the rest, and whosoever let it go was left in peace. The Bodhisatta on seeing this thought, "These desires of ours are like pieces of meat. To those that grasp at them is sorrow, and to those that let them go is peace." And he repeated the second stanza:

While the bird had aught to eat,
Ospreys pecked at him full sore,
When perforce he dropped the meat,
Then they pecked at him no more.

The ascetic going forth from the city, in the course of his journey came to a village, and at evening lay down in a certain man's house. Now a female slave there named Pingalā made an assignation with a man, saying, "You are to come at such and such an hour." After she had bathed the feet of her master and his family, when they had lain down, she sat on the threshold, looking out for the coming of her lover, and passed the first and the middle watch, repeating to herself, "Now he will be coming," but at daybreak, losing hope, she said, "He will not come now," and lay down and fell asleep. The Bodhisatta seeing this happen said," this woman sat ever so long in the hope that her lover would come, but now that she knows he will not come, in her despair, she slumbers peacefully." And with the thought that while hope in the passions bring sorrow, despair brings peace, he uttered the third stanza:

The fruit of hope fulfilled is bliss;
How differs loss of hope from this?
Though dull despair her hope destroys,
Lo! Pingalā calm sleep enjoys.

Next day going forth from that village he entered into a forest, and beholding a hermit seated on the ground and indulging in meditation he thought, "Both in this world and in the next there is no happiness beyond the bliss of meditation." And he repeated the fourth stanza:

In this world and in worlds to be
Naught can surpass ecstatic joy:
To holy calm a devotee,
Himself unharmed, will none annoy.

Then he went into the forest and adopted the ascetic life of a Rishi and developed the higher knowledge born of meditation, and became destined to birth in the Brahma-world.

A KING'S LIFE SAVED BY SPELLS

Once upon a time when Brahmadatta reigned in Benares, the Bodhisatta was far-famed teacher at Takkasilā and trained many young princes and sons of brahmins in the arts. Now the son of the king of Benares, when he was sixteen years old came to him and after he had acquired the three Vedas and all the liberal arts and was perfect in them, he took leave of his master. The teacher regarding him by his gift of prognostication thought, "There is danger coming to this man through his son. By my magic power I will deliver him from it." And composing four stanzas he gave them to the young prince and spoke as follows: "My son, after you are seated on the throne, when your son is sixteen years old, utter the first stanza while eating your rice; repeat the second stanza at the time of the great levee; the third, as you are ascending to the palace roof, standing at the head of the stairs, and the fourth, when entering the royal chamber, as you stand on the threshold."

The prince readily assented to this and saluting his teacher went away. And after acting as viceroy, on his father's death he ascended the throne. His son, when he was sixteen years of age, on the king's going forth to take his pleasure in the garden, observing his father's majesty and power was filled with a desire to kill him and seize upon his kingdom, and spoke to his attendants about it. They said, "True, Sir, what is the good of obtaining power, when one is old? You must by some means or other kill the king and possess yourself of his kingdom." The prince

said, "I will kill him by putting poison in his food." So he took
some poison and sat down to eat his evening meal with his
father. The king, when the rice was just served in the bowl,
spoke the first stanza:

> With sense so nice, the husks from rice
> Rats keen are to discriminate:
> They cared not much the husks to touch,
> But grain by grain the rice they ate.

"I am discovered," thought the prince, and not daring to
administer the poison in the bowl of rice, he rose up and bowing to the king went away. He told the story to his attendants
and said, "To-day I am found out. How now shall I kill him?"
From this day forth they lay concealed in the garden, and consulting together in whispers said, "There is still one expedient.
When it is time to attend the great levee, gird on your sword,
and taking your stand amongst the councilors, when you see
the king off his guard, you must strike him a blow with your
sword and kill him." Thus they arranged it. The prince readily
agreed, and at the time of the great levee, he girt on his sword
and moving about from place to place looked out for an opportunity to strike the king. At this moment the king uttered the
second stanza:

> The secret counsel taken in the wood
> By me is understood:
> The village plot soft whispered in the ear
> That too I hear.

Thought the prince, "My father knows that I am his enemy," and ran away and told his attendants. After the laps of
seven or eight days they said, "Prince, your father is ignorant
of your feeling towards him. You only fancy this in your own
mind. Put him to death." So one day he took his sword and stood
at the top of the stairs in the royal closet. The king standing at
the head of the staircase spoke the third stanza:

> A monkey once did cruel measures take
> His tender offspring impotent to make.

Thought the prince, "My father wants to seize me," and in his terror he fled away and told his attendants he had been threatened by his father. After the lapse of a fortnight they said, "Prince, if the king knew this, he would not have put up with it so long a time. Your imagination suggests this to you. Put him to death." So one day he took his sword and entering the royal chamber of the upper floor of the palace he lay down beneath the couch, intending to slay the king, as soon as he came. At the close of the evening meal, the king sent his retinue away, wishing to lie down, and entering the royal chamber, as he stood on the threshold, he uttered the fourth stanza:

Thy cautious creeping ways
Like one-eyed goat in mustard field that strays,
And who thou art that lurkest here below,
This too I know.

Thought the prince, "My father has found me out. Now he will put me to death." And seized with fear he came out from beneath the couch, and throwing down his sword at the king's feet and saying, "Pardon me, my lord," he lay groveling before him. The king said, "You thought, no one knows what I am about." And after rebuking him he ordered him to be bound in chains and put into the prison house, and set a guard over him. Then the king meditated on the virtues of the Bodhisatta. And by and by he died. When they had celebrated his funeral rites, they took the young prince out of prison and set him on the throne.

THE HERON'S REVENGE

This story was told by the Master at Jātavana, concerning a heron that lived in the house of the king of Kosala. She carried messages, they say, for the king, and had two young ones. The king sent this bird with a letter to some other king. When she was gone away, the boys in the royal family squeezed the young birds to death in their hands. The mother bird came back and missing her young ones, asked who had killed her offspring. They said, "So and so." And at this time there was a fierce and savage tiger kept in the palace, fastened by a strong chain. Now these boys came to see the tiger and the heron went with them, thinking, "Even as my young ones were killed by them, just so will I deal with these boys," and she took hold of them and threw them down at the foot of the tiger. The tiger with a growl crunched them up. The bird said, "Now is the wish of my heart fulfilled," and flying up into the air made straight for the Himalayas. On hearing what had happened there started a discussion in the Hall of Truth, saying. "Sirs, a heron, it is said, in the king's palace threw down before a tiger the boys who killed her young ones, and when she had thus brought about their death, she made off". The Master came and inquired what it was the brethren were discussing and said, "Not now only, brethren, but formerly also did she bring about the death of those who killed her young ones." And herewith he related a legend of the past.

Once upon a time the Bodhisatta at Benares ruled his kingdom with justice and equity. A certain heron in his house carried messages for him. And so on just as before. But the special point here is that in this case the bird, having let the tiger kill the boys, thought, "I can no longer remain here. I will take my departure, but though I am going away I will not leave without telling the king, but as soon as I have told him I will be off." And so she drew nigh and saluted the king, and standing a little way off said, "My lord, it was through your carelessness that the boys killed my young ones, and under the influence of passion I in revenge caused their death. Now I can no longer live here." And uttering the first stanza she said:

> Long I held this house as mine,
> Honour great I did receive,
> It is due to act of thine
> I am now compelled to leave.

The king on hearing this repeated the second stanza:

> Should one to retaliate,
> Wrong with equal wrong repay,
> Then his anger should abate;

So, good heron, prithee stay.

Hearing this the bird spoke the third stanza:
Wronged can with wrong-doer ne'er
As of old be made at one:
Nought, O king can keep me here,
Lo! From henceforth I am gone.

The king, on hearing this, spoke the fourth stanza:
Should they wise, not foolish be,
With the wronged wrong-doer may
Live in peace and harmony:
So, good heron, prithee, stay.

The bird said, "As things are, I cannot stay, my lord," and saluting the king she flew up into the air and made straight for the Himalayas.

THE LION AND THE BULL

Once upon a time when Brahmadatta was reigning in Benares, the Bodhisatta was born as his son, and after acquiring all the arts at Takkasilā, on his father's death, he ruled his kingdom righteously.

At that time a certain neatherd, who was tending cattle in their sheds in the forest, came home and inadvertently left behind him a cow that was in calf. Between the cow and a lioness sprang up a firm friendship. The two animals became fast friends and went about together. So after a time the cow brought forth a calf and the lioness a cub. These two young creatures also by force of family ties became fast friends and wandered about together. Then a certain forester, after observing their affection, took such wares as are produced in the forest and went to Benares and presented them to the king. And when the king asked him, "Friend, have you seen any unusual marvel in the forest?" he made answer, "I saw nothing else that was wonderful, my lord, but I did see a lion and a bull wandering about together, very friendly one towards another."

"Should a third animal appear," said the king, "there will certainly be mischief. Come and tell me, if you see the pair joined by a third animal."

"Certainly my lord," he answered.

Now when the forester had left for Benares, a jackal ministered to the lion and the bull. When he returned to the forest and saw this he said, "I will tell the king that a third animal has appeared," and departed for the city. Now the jackal thought, "There is no meat that I have not eaten except the flesh of lions and bulls. By setting these two at variance, I will get their flesh to eat." And he said, "This is the way he speaks of you," and thus dividing them one from another, he soon brought about a quarrel and reduced them to a dying condition.

But the forester came and told the king, "My lord a third animal has turned up." "What is it?" said the king. "A jackal, my lord." Said the king, "he will cause them to quarrel, and will bring about their death. We shall find them dead when we arrive." And so saying, he mounted upon his chariot and traveling on the road pointed out by the forester, he arrived just as the two animals had by their quarrel destroyed one another. The jackal highly delighted was eating, now the flesh of the lion, now that of the bull. The king when he saw that they were both dead, stood just as he was upon his chariot and addressing his charioteer gave utterance to these verses:
Nought in common had this pair,
Neither wives nor food did share;
Yet behold how slanderous word,
Keen as any two-edged sword,

Did devise with cunning art
Friends of old to keep apart,
Thus did bull and lion fall
Prey to meanest beast of all:

So will all bed-fellows be
With this pair in misery,

If they lend a willing ear
To the slanderer's whispered sneer.

But they thrive exceeding well,
E'en as those in heaven that dwell,
Who to slander ne'er attend—
Slander parting friend from fried.
The king spoke these verses, and bidding them gather together the mane, skin, claws, and teeth of the lion, returned straight to his own city.

THE QUAIL'S FRIENDS

Once upon a time when Brahmadatta was reigning in Benares, the Bodhisatta came to life as a young elephant, and growing up a fine comely beast, he became the leader of the herd, with a following of eighty thousand elephants, and dwelt in the Himalayas. At that time a quail laid her eggs in the feeding ground of the elephants. When the eggs were ready to be hatched, the young birds broke the shells and came out. Before their wings had grown, and when they were still unable to fly, the Great Being with his following of eighty thousand elephants, in ranging about for food, came to this spot. On seeing them the quail thought, "This royal elephant will trample on my young ones and kill them. Lo! I will implore his righteous protection for the defence of my brood." Then she raised her two wings and standing before him repeated the first stanza:

Elephant of sixty years,
Forest lord amongst thy peers,
I am but a puny bird,
Thou a leader of the herd;
With my wings I homage pay,
Spare my little ones, I pray.

The Great Being said, "O quail, be not troubled. I will protect thy offspring." And standing over the young birds, while the equity thousand elephants passed by, he thus addressed the quail; "Behind us comes a solitary rogue elephant. He will not do our bidding. When he comes, do thou entreat him too,

and so insure the safety of thy offspring." And with these words
he made off. And the quail went forth to meet the other elephant, and with the both wings uplifted, making respectful
salutation, she spoke the second stanza:

Roaming over hill and dale
Cherishing thy lonely way,
Thee, O forest king, I hail,
And with wings my homage pay.
I am but a wretched quail,
Spare my tender brood to slay.

On hearing her words, the elephant spoke the third stanza:
I will slay thy young ones, quail;
What can thy poor help avail?
My left foot can crush with ease
Many thousand birds like these.

And so saying, with his foot he crushed the young birds to
atoms, and staling over them washed them away in a flood of
water, and went off loudly trumpeting. The quail sat down on
a bough of a tree and said, "Then be off with you and trumpet
away. You shall very soon see what I will do. You little know
what a difference there is between strength of body and strength
of mind. Well! I will teach you this lesson." And thus threatening him she repeated the fourth stanza:

Power abused is not all gain,
Power is often folly's bane.
Beast that didst my young ones kill,
I will work thee mischief still.

And so saying, shortly afterwards she did a good turn to a
crow and when the crow, who was highly pleased, asked, "What
can I do for you?" the quail said, "There is nothing else, Sir, to
be done, but I shall expect you to strike with your beak and to
peck out the eyes of this rogue elephant." The crow, readily
assented, and the quail then did a service to a blue fly, and
when the fly asked, "What can I do for you?" she said, "When
the eyes of this rogue elephant have been put out by the crow,
then I want you to let fall a nit upon them." The fly agreed, and

then the quail did a kindness to a frog, and when the frog asked what it was to do, she said, "When this rogue elephant becomes blind, and shall be searching for water to drink, then take your stand and utter a croak on the top of a mountain, and when he has climbed to the top, come down and croak again at the bottom of the precipice. This much I shall look for at your hands." After hearing what the quail said, the frog readily assented. So one day the crow with its beak pecked out both the eyes of the elephant, and the fly dropped its eggs upon them, and the elephant being eaten up with maggots was maddened by the pain, and overcome with thirst wandered about seeking for water to drink. At this moment the frog standing on the top of a mountain uttered a croak. Thought the elephant, "There must be water there," and climbed up the mountain. Then the frog descended, and standing at the bottom croaked again. The elephant thought, "There will be water there," and moved forward towards the precipice, and rolling over fell to the bottom of the mountain and was killed. When the quail knew that the elephant was dead, she said, "I have seen the back of mine enemy," and in a high state of delight strutted over his body, and passed away to fare according to her deeds.

QUEEN SUSSONDI

Once upon a time king Tamba reigned in Benares, and his queen-consort named Sussondi was a woman of surpassing beauty. At the time the Bodhisatta came to life as a young Garuda. Now the Naga island was then known as Seruma island, and the Bodhisatta lived on this island in the abode of the Garudas. And he went to Benares, disguised as a youth, and played at dice with king Tamba. Remarking his beauty they said to Sussondi, "Such and such a youth plays a dice with our king." She longed to see him, and one day she adorned herself and repaired to the dice-chamber. There taking her stand amongst the attendants, she fixed her gaze on the youth. He too gazed on the queen, and the pair fell in love with one another. The Garuda king by an act of supernatural power stirred up a storm in the city. The people, through fear of the house falling, fled out of the palace. By his power he caused it to be dark, and

carrying off the queen with him in the air, he made his way to
his own abode in Naga island. But no one knew of the coming
or going of Sussondi. The Garuda took his pleasure with her,
and still came to play at dice with the king. Now the king had
a minstrel named Sagga, and not knowing where the queen had
gone, the king addressed the minstrel and said, "Go now and
explore every land and sea, and discover what has become of
the queen." And so saying he bade him begone.

He took what was necessary for his journey, and beginning
the search from the city gate, at last came to Bharukaccha. At
that time certain merchants of Bharukaccha were setting sail
for the Golden Land. He approached them and said, "I am a
minstrel. If you remit my passage money, I will act as your
minstrel. Take me with you." They agreed to do so, and putting
him on board weighed anchor. When the ship was fairly off,
they called him and bade him make music for them. He said, "I
would make music, but if I do, the fish will be so excited that
your vessel will be wrecked." "If a mere mortal," they said
"make music, there will be no excitement on the part of the fish.
Play to us." "Then do not be angry with me," he said, and
tuning his lute and keeping perfect harmony between the words
of his song and the accompaniment of the lute string, he made
music for them. The fish were maddened at the sound and
splashed about. And a certain sea monster leaping up fell upon
the ship and broke it in two. Sagga lying on a plank was carried
along by the wind till he reached a banyan tree in the Naga
island, where the Garuda king lived. Now queen Sussondi,
whenever the Garuda king went to play at dice, came down
from her place of abode, and as she as wandering on the edge
of the shore, she saw and recognized the minstrel Sagga, and
asked him how he got there. He told her the whole story. And
she comforted him and said, "Do not be afraid," and embracing
him in her arms, she carried him to her abode and laid him on
a couch. And when he was greatly revived, she fed him with
heavenly food, bathed him in heavenly scented-water, arrayed
him in heavenly raiment, and adorned him with flowers of heavenly perfume, and made him recline upon a heavenly couch.
Thus did she watch over him, and whenever the Garuda king

returned, she hid her lover, and so soon as the king was gone, under the influence of passion she took her pleasure with him. At the end of a month and a half from that time some merchants, who dwelt at Benares, landed at the foot of the banyan tree in this island, to get fire-wood and water. The minstrel went on board ship with them, and on reaching Benares, as soon as he saw the king, while he was playing at dice, Sagga took his lute, and making music recited the first stanza:

> I scent the fragrance of the timira grove,
> I hear the moaning of the weary sea:
> Tamba, I am tormented with my love,
> For fair Sussondi dwells afar from me.

On hearing this the Garuda king uttered the second stanza:

> How didst thou cross the stormy main,
> And Seruma in safety gain?
> How didst thus, Sagga, tell me, pray,
> To fair Sussondi win thy way?

Then Sagga repeated three stanzas:

> With trading-folk from Bharukaccha land
> My ship was wrecked by monsters of the sea
> I on a plank did safely gain the strand,
>
> When an anointed queen with gentle hand
> Upbore me tenderly upon her knee,
> As though to her a true son I might be.
>
> She food and raiment brought, and as I lay
> With love-lorn eyes hung o'er my couch all day.
> Know, Tamba, well; this word is sooth I say.

The Garuda, while the minstrel thus spake, was filled with regrets and said: "Though I dwelt in the abode of the Garudas, I failed to guard her safely. What is this wicked woman to me?" So he brought her back and presented her to the king and departed. And thenceforth he came not there any more.

THE BETRAYER BETRAYED

Once upon a time in the reign of Brahmadatta, king of Benares, the Bodhisatta was re-born as Sakka. At that time a certain young brahmin of Benares acquired all the liberal arts at Takkasila, and having attained to proficiency in archery, he was known as the clever Little Archer. Then his master thought, "This youth has acquired skill equal to my own," and he gave him his daughter to wife. He took her and wishing to return to Benares he set out on the road. Half way on his journey, an elephant laid waste a certain place, and no man dared to ascend to that spot. The clever Little Archer, though the people tried to stop him, took his wife and climbed up to the entrance of the forest. Then when he was in the midst of the wood, the elephant rose up to attack him. The Archer wounded him in the forehead with an arrow, which piercing him through and through came out at the back of his head, and the elephant fell down dead on the spot. The clever Archer after making this place secure, went on further to another wood. And there fifty robbers were infesting the road. Up to this spot too, though men tried to stop him, he climbed till he found the regular place, where the robbers killed the deer, roasted and ate the venison, close to the road. The robbers, seeing him approach with his gaily attired wife, made a great effort to capture him. The robber chief, being skilled in reading a man's character, just gave one look at him, and recognising him as a distinguished hero, did not suffer them to rise up against him, though he was single-handed. The clever Archer sent his wife to these robbers, saying, "Go and bid them give us a spit of meat, and bring it to me." So she went and said, "Give me a spit of meat." The robber chief said, "He is a noble fellow," and bade them give it her. The robbers said, "What! is he to eat our roast meat?" And they gave her a piece of raw meat. The Archer, having a good opinion of himself, was wroth with the robbers for offering him raw meat. The robbers said, "What! is he the only man, and are we merely women?" And thus threatening him, they rose up against him. The archer wounded and struck to the ground fifty robbers save one with the same number of arrows. He had no arrow left to wound the robber chief. There had been full fifty arrows in his quiver. With one of them he had wounded the elephant, and with the rest the fifty robbers save one. So he knocked down the robber chief, and sitting on his chest bade his wife bring him his sword in her hand to cut off his head. At that very moment she conceived a passion for the robber chief and placed the hilt of the sword in his hand and the sheath in that of her husband. The robber grasping the hilt drew out the sword, and cut off the head of the Archer. After slaying her husband he took the woman with him, and as they journeyed together he enquired of her origin. "I am the daughter," she said, "of a world-famed professor at Takkasila."

"How did he get you for his wife?" he said.

"My father," she said, was so pleased at his having acquired from him an art equal to his own, that he gave me to him to wife. And because I fell in love with you, I let you kill my lawful husband."

Thought the robber chief, "This woman now has killed her lawful husband. As soon as she sees some other man, she will treat me too after the same sort. I must get rid of her."

And as he went on his way, he saw their path cut off by what was usually a poor little shallow stream, but which was now flooded, and he said, "My dear, there is a savage crocodile in this river. What are we to do?"

"My lord," she said, "take all the ornaments I wear, and make them into a bundle in your upper robe, and carry them to the further side of the river, and then come back and take me across."

"Very well," he said, and took all her adornments, and going down to the stream, like one in great haste, he gained the other bank, and left her and fled.

On seeing this she cried, "My lord, you go as if you were leaving me. Why do you do this? Come back and take me with

you." And addressing him she uttered the first stanza:
   Since thou hast gained the other side,
   With all my goods in bundle tied,
   Return as quickly as may be
   And carry me across with thee.

The robber, on hearing her, as he stood on the further bank,
repeated the second stanza:
   Thy fancy, lady, ever roves
   From well-tried faith to lighter loves,
   Me too thou wouldst ere long betray,
   Should I not hence flee far away.

But when the robber said, "I will go further hence: you stop
where you are," he screamed aloud, and he fled with all her
adornments. Such was the fate that overtook the poor fool
through excess of passion. And being quite helpless she drew
nigh to a clump of cassia plants and sat there weeping. At that
moment Sakka, looking down upon the world, saw her smitten
with desire and weeping for the loss of both husband and lover.
And thinking he would go and rebuke her and put her to
shame, he took him Matali and Pancasikha, and went and stood
on the bank of the river and said, "Matali, you do become a fish,
Pancasikha, you change into a bird, and I will become a jackal.
And taking a piece of meat in my mouth, I will go and place
myself in front of this woman, and when you see me there, you
Matali, are to leap up out of the water, and fall before me, and
when I shall drop the piece of meat I have taken in my mouth,
and shall spring up to seize the fish, at that moment, you
Pancasikha, are to pounce upon the piece of meat, and to fly up
into the air, and you, Matali, are to fall into the water."

Thus did Sakka instruct them And they said, "Good my
lord." Matali was changed into a fish, Pancasikha into a bird,
and Sakka became a jackal. And taking a piece of meat in his
mouth, he went and placed himself in front of the woman. The
fish leaping up out of the water fell before the jackal. The jackal
dropping the piece of meat he held in his mouth, sprang up to
catch the fish. The fish jumped up and fell into the water and

the bird seized the piece of meat and flew up into the air. The jackal thus lost both fish and meat and sat sulkily looking towards the clump of cassia. The woman seeing this said, "Through being too covetous, he got neither flesh nor fish," and, as if she saw the point of the trick, she laughed heartily.

The jackal, on hearing this, uttered the third stanza:
Who makes the cassia thicket ring
With laughter, though none dance or sing,
Or clap their hands, good time to keep?
Fair one, laugh not, when thou shouldst weep.

On hearing this, she repeated the fourth stanza:
O silly jackal, thou must wish
Thou hadst not lost both flesh and fish.
Poor fool! Well mayst thou grieve to see
What comes of thy stupidity.

Then the jackal repeated the fifth stanza:
Another's faults are plainly seen,
'Tis hard to see one's own, I ween.
Methinks thou too must count the cost,
When spouse and lover both are lost.
On hearing his words she spoke this stanza:
King jackal, 'tis just as you say,
So I will hie me far away,
And seek another wedded love
And strive a faithful wife to prove.

Then Sakka, king of heaven, hearing the words of this vicious and unchaste woman, repeated the final stanza:
He that would steal a pot of clay
Would steal brass one any day;
And thou who wast thy husband's bane
Wilt be as bad or worse again.

Thus did Sakka put her to shame and brought her to repent and then returned to his own abode.

THE CAT AND THE COCK

Once upon a time when Brahmadatta was king in Benares, the Bodhisatta was born as a cock and lived in the forest with a retinue of many hundred cocks. Not far away lived a she cat: and she deceived by devices the other cocks except the Bodhisatta and ate them: but the Bodhisatta did not fall into her power. She thought, "This cock is very crafty, but he knows not that I am crafty and skillful in device: it is good that I cajole him, saying, 'I will be your wife,' and so eat him when he comes into my power." She went to the root of the tree where he perched, and praying him in a speech preceded by praise of his beauty, she spoke the first stanza:

Bird with wings that flash so gaily crest that droops so
                                                   gracefully,
I will be your wife for nothing, leave that bough and come
                                                      to me.

The Bodhisatta hearing her thought, "She has eaten all my relatives: now she wishes to cajole me and eat me: I will get rid of her." So he spoke the second stanza:

Lady fair and winning, you have four feet, I have only two:
Beasts and birds should never marry: for some other hus
                                                  band sue.

Then she thought, "He is exceedingly crafty; by some device or other I will deceive him and eat him"; so she spoke the third stanza:

I will bring thee youth and beauty, pleasant speech and
                                                   courtesy:
Honoured wife or simple slave-girl, at thy pleasure deal
                                                   with me.

Then the Bodhisatta thought, "It is best to revile her and drive her away," so he spoke the fourth stanza:

Thou hast drunk my kindred's blood, and robbed and slain
                                              them cruelly:
"Honoured wife!" there is no honour in thy heart when
                                              wooing me.

She was driven away and did not endure to look at him again.

THE LANGUAGE OF ANIMALS

Once upon a time when a king named Senaka was reigning in Benares, the Bodhisatta was Sakka. The king Senaka was friendly with a certain naga-king. This naga-king, they say, left the naga-world and ranged the earth seeking food. The village boys seeing him said, "This is a snake," and struck him with clods and other things. The king, going to amuse himself in his garden, saw them and being told they were beating a snake, said, "Don't let them beat him, drive them away"; and this was done. So the naga-king got his life, and when he went back to the naga-world, he took many jewels and coming at midnight to the king's bed-chamber he gave them to him, saying, "I got my life through you": so he made friendship with the king and came again and again to see him. He appointed one of his naga-girls, insatiate to pleasures, to be near the king and protect him: and he gave the king a charm, saying, "If ever you do not see her, repeat this charm." One day the king went to the garden with the naga girl and was amusing himself in the lotus-tank. The naga girl seeing a water-snake quitted her human shape and made off with him. The king not seeing the girl said, "where is she gone?" and repeated the spell; then he saw her in her misconduct and struck her with a piece of bamboo. She went in anger to the naga-world, and when she was asked, "Why have you come?" she said, "Your friend struck me on the back because I did not do his bidding," showing the mark of the blow. The naga-king, not knowing the truth, called four naga youths and sent them with orders to enter Senaka's bed-chamber and destroy him like chaff by the breath of their nostrils. They entered the chamber at the royal bed-time. As they came in, the king was saying to the queen: "Lady, do you know where the naga girl has gone?" "King, I do not." "To-day when we were bathing in the tank, she quitted her shape, and misconducted herself with a water-snake: I said, 'Don't do that,' and struck her with a piece of bamboo to give her a lesson: and now I fear she may have gone one to the naga-world and told some

lie to my friend, destroying his good-will to me." The young
nagas hearing this turned back at once to the naga world and
told their king. He being moved went instantly to the king's
chamber, told him all and was forgiven: then he said, "In this
way I make amends," and gave the king a charm giving knowledge of all sounds: "This, O king, is a priceless spell: if you give
anyone this spell you will at once enter the fire and die." The
king said, "It is well," and accepted it. From that time he understood the voice even of ants. One day he was sitting on the
dais eating solid food with honey and molasses and a drop of
honey, a drop of molasses and a morsel of cake fell on the
ground. An ant seeing this comes crying, "The king's honey-jar
is broken on the dais, his molasses-cart and cake cart are upset;
come, and eat honey and molasses and cake". The king hearing
the cry laughed. The queen being near him thought. "What has
the king seen that he laughs?" When the king had eaten his
solid food and bathed and sat down cross-legged, a fly said to
his wife, "Come, lady, let us enjoy love." She said, "Excuse me
for a little, husband: they will soon be bringing perfumes to the
king; as he perfumes himself some powder will fall at his feet:
I will stay there and become fragrant, then we will enjoy ourselves lying on the king's back." The king hearing the voice
laughed again. The queen thought again, "What has he seen
that he laughs?" Again when the king was eating his supper,
a lump of rice fell on the ground. The ants cried, " A wagon of
rice has broken in the king's palace, and there is none to eat it."
The king hearing this laughed again. The queen took a golden
spoon and helping him reflected, "Is it at the sight of me that
the king laugh?' She went to the bed-chamber with the king
and at bed-time she asked, "Why did you laugh, my king?" He
said, "What have you to do with why I laugh" but being asked
again and again he told her. Then she said," Give me your spell
of knowledge." He said, "It cannot be given": but though re-
pulsed she pressed him again.

The king said, "If I give you this spell, I shall die." "Even
though you die, give it me." The king, being in the power of
womankind, saying, "Very well," consented and went to the
park in a chariot, saying, "I shall enter the fire after giving away

this spell." At that moment, Sakka, king of gods, looked down
on the earth and seeing this case said, "This foolish king, knowing that he will enter the fire through womankind, is on his
way; I will give him his life": So he took Suja, daughter of the
Asuras, and went to Benares. He became a he-goat and made
her a she-goat, and resolving that the people should not see
them, he stood before the king's chariot. The king and the Sindh
horses yoked in the chariot saw him, but none else saw him. For
the sake of starting talk he was as if making love with the she-
goat. One of the Sindh horses yoked in the chariot seeing him
said, "Friend goat, we have heard before, but not seen, that
goats are stupid and shameless; but you are doing, with all of
us looking on, this thing that should be done in secret and in
a private place, and are not ashamed: what we have heard
before agrees with this that we see": and so he spoke the first
stanza:

"Goats are stupid," say the sages, and the words are surely
true:

    This one knows not he's parading what in secret he should
do.

The goat hearing him spoke two stanzas:

Truly you're a stupid fool, you donkey! let me make it plain,
With a bit your mouth is wrenched, you head is twisted
with the rein.
When you're loosed, you don't escape, sir, that's a stupid
habit too:
And that Senaka you carry, he's more stupid still than you.

The king understood the talk of both animals, and hearing
it he quickly sent away the chariot. The horse hearing the
goat's talk spoke the fourth stanza:

Well, Sir king of goats, you fully know my great stupidity:
But how Senaka is stupid, prithee do explain to me.

The goat explaining this spoke the fifth stanza:

He who his own special treasure on his wife will throw
away,

Cannot keep her faithful ever and his life he must betray.

The king hearing his words said, "King of goats, you will surely act for my advantage: tell me now what is right for me to do." Then the goat said, "King, to all animals no one is dearer than self; it is not good to destroy oneself and abandon the honour one has gained for the sake of anything that is dear": so he spoke the sixth stanza:

A king, like thee, may have conceived desire
And yet renounced it if his life's the cost:
Life is the chief thing: what can man seek higher?
If life's secured, desires need ne'er be crossed.

So the Bodhisatta exhorted the king. The king, delighted, asked, "King of goats, whence come you?" "I am Sakka, O king, come to save you from death out of pity for you." "King of gods, I promised to give her the charm: what am I to do now?" "There is no need for the ruin of both of you: you say, 'It is the way of the craft', and have her beaten with some blows: by this means she will not get it." The king said, "Very well," and agreed. The Bodhisatta after exhortation to the king went to his own place. The king went to the garden, had the queen summoned and then said, "Lady, will you have the charm?" "Yes, lord." "Then go through the usual custom." "What custom?" "A hundred stripes on the back, but you must not make a sound." She consented through greed for the charm. The king made his slaves take whips and beat her on both sides. She endured two or three stripes and then cried, "I don't want the charm." The king said, "You would have killed me to get the charm," and so flogging the skin off her back he sent her away. After that she could not bear to talk of it again.

THE THEFT OF A SMELL

Once upon a time when Brahmadatta was reigning in Benares, the Bodhisatta was born in a Brahmin family of a village in Kasi: when he grew up he learned the arts at Takkasila, and afterwards became an ascetic and lived near a lotus-pool. One day he went down into the pool and stood smelling a lotus

in full flower. A goddess who was in a hollow in a truck of a tree
alarming him spoke the first stanza:
> You were never given that flower you smell, though its
> > only a single bloom;
> 'Tis a species of larceny, reverend sir, you are stealing its
> > perfume.

Then the Bodhisatta spoke the second stanza:
> I neither take nor break the flower: from afar I smell the
> > bloom.
> I cannot tell on what pretence you say I steal perfume.

At the same moment a man was digging in the pool for
lotus-fibres and breaking the lotus-plants. The Bodhisatta seeing him said, " You call a man thief if he smells the flower from
afar: Why do you not speak to that other man?" So in talk with
her he spoke the third stanza:
> A man who digs the lotus-roots and breaks the stalks I see:
> Why don't you call the conduct of that man disorderly?

The goddess, explaining why she did not speak to him,
spoke the fourth and fifth stanzas:
> Disgusting like a nurse's dress are men disorderly:
> I have no speech with men like him, but I deign to speak
> > to thee,
> When a man is free from evil stains and seeks for purity,
> A sin like a hair-tip shows on him like a dark cloud in the
> > sky.

So alarmed by her the Bodhisatta in emotion spoke the
sixth stanza:
> Surely, fairy, you know me well, to pity me you deign;
> If you see me do the like offence, pray speak to me again.

Then the goddess spoke to him the seventh stanza:
> I am not here to serve you, no hireling folk are we:
> Find, Brother, for yourself the path to reach felicity.

So exhorting him she entered her own abode. The
Bodhisatta entered on high meditation and was born in the

Brahma-world.

THE LION IN BAD COMPANY

Once upon a time when Brahmadatta was reigning in Benares the Bodhisatta was a lion and living with a lioness had two children, a son and a daughter. The son's name was Manoja. When he grew up he took a young lioness to wife: and so they became five. Manoja killed wild buffaloes and other animals, and so got flesh to feed his parents, sister and wife. One day in his hunting ground he saw a jackal called Giriya, unable to run away and lying on his belly. "How now, friend?" he said. "I wish to wait on you, my lord." "Well do so." So he took the jackal to his den. The Bodhisatta seeing him said, "Dear Manoja, jackals are wicked and sinners, and give wrong advice; don't bring this one near you": but could not hinder him. Then one day the jackal wished to eat horseflesh, and said to Manoja, "Sir except horseflesh there is nothing we have not eaten; let us take a horse." "But where are there horses, friend?" "At Benares by the river bank." He took this advice and went with him there when the horse bathe in the river; he took one horse, and throwing it on his back he came with speed to the mouth of his den. His father eating the horseflesh said, "Dear, horses are kings' property. Kings have many stratagems, they have skilful archers to shoot; lions who eat horseflesh don't live long, henceforward don't take horses." The lion not following his father's advice went on taking them. The king, hearing that a lion was taking the horse, had a bathing-tank for horses made inside the town: but the lion still came and took them. The king had a stable made, and had fodder and water given them inside it. The lion came over the wall and took the horses even from the stable. The king had an archer called who shot like lightning, and asked if he could shoot a lion. He said he could and making a tower near the wall where the lion came he waited there. The lion came and, posting the jackal in a cemetery outside, sprang into the town to take horses. The archer thinking "His speed is very great when he comes," did not shoot him, but when he was going away after taking a horse, hampered by the heavy weight, he hit him with a sharp arrow in the hind quarters. The arrow came out at his front quarters and flew in the air. The lion yelled, "I am shot". The archer after shooting him twanged his bow like thunder. The jackal hearing the noise of lion and bow said to himself, "My comrade is shot and must be killed, there is no friendship with the dead, I will now go to my old home in the wood," and so he spoke to himself in two stanzas:

The bow is bent, the bowstring sounds amain;
Manoja, king of beasts, my friend, is slain,
Alas, I seek the woods as best I may:
Such friends are naught; others must be my stay.

The lion with a rush came and threw the horse at the den's mouth, falling dead himself. His kinsfolk came out and saw him blood-stained, blood flowing from his wounds, dead from following the wicked; and his father, mother sister and wife seeing him spoke four stanzas in order:

His fortune is not prosperous whom wicked folk entice;
Look at Manoja lying there, through Giriya's advice.
No joy have mothers in a son whose comrades are not good:
Look at Manoja lying there all covered with his blood.
And even so fares still the man, in low estate he lies,
Who follows not the counsel of the true friend and the
                                                    wise.
This, or worse than this, his fate
Who is high, but trusts the low:
See, 'tis thus from kingly state
He has fallen to the bow.

THE OTTERS AND THE JACKAL

Once upon a time when Brahmadatta was reigning in Benares, the Bodhisatta was a tree-spirit by a river-bank. A jackal, named Mayavi, had taken a wife and lived in a place by that river-bank. One day his mate said to him, "Husband, a longing has come upon me: I desire to eat a fresh rohita fish." He said, "Be easy, I will bring it you," and going by the river he wrapt his feet in creepers, and went along the bank. At the moment, two otters, Gambhiracari and Anutiracari, were standing on the bank looking for fish. Gambhiracari saw a great rohita fish, and entering the water with a bound he took it by the tail. The fish was strong and went away dragging him. He called to the other, "This great fish will be enough for both of us, come and aid me," speaking the first stanza:

Friend Anutiracari rush to my aid, I pray:
I've caught a great fish: but by force he's carrying me away.
Hearing him, the other spoke the second stanza.
Gambhiracari, luck to you! Your grip be firm and stout,
And as a roc would lift a snake, I'll lift the fellow out.

Then the two together took out the rohita fish, laid him on the ground and killed him: but saying each to the other, "You divide him," they quarreled and could not divide him: and so sat down, leaving him. At the moment the jackal came to the spot. Seeing him, they both saluted him and said, "Lord of the grey grass-colour, this fish was taken by both of us together: a dispute arose because we could not divide him: do you make an equal division and part it," speaking the third stanza:

A strife arose between us, mark! O thou of grassy hue,
Let out contention, honoured sir, be settled fair by you.

The jackal hearing them, said, declaring his own strength:

I've arbitrated many a case and done it peacefully:
Let out contention, honoured sirs, be settled fair by me.
Having spoken that stanza, and making the division, he spoke this stanza:
Tail, Anutiracari: Gambhiracari, head:
The middle to the arbiter will properly be paid.

So having divided the fish, he said, "You eat head and tail without quarrelling," and seizing the middle portion in his mouth he ran away before their eyes. They sat downcast, as if they had lost a thousand pieces, and spoke the sixth stanza:

But for our strife, it would have long sufficed us with
                                                  out fail;
But now the jackal takes the fish, and leaves us head
and tail.

The jackal was pleased and thinking "Now I will give my wife rohita fish to eat," he went to her. She saw him coming and saluting him spoke a stanza:

> Even as a king is glad to join a kingdom to his rule,
> So I am glad to see my lord to-day with his mouth full.

Then she asked him about the means of attainment, speaking a stanza:

> How being of the land, have you from water caught a fish?
> How did you do the feat, my lord? pray answer to my wish.

The jackal, explaining the means to her, spoke the next stanza:

> By strife it is their weakness comes, by strife their means
> decay:
> By strife the others lost their prize: Mayavi, eat the prey.

THE BRAHMIN AND THE SNAKE

Once upon a time a king called Janaka was reigning in Benares. At that time the Bodhisatta was born in a brahmin family, and they called his name young Senaka. When he grew up he learned all the arts of Takkasila, and returning to Benares saw the king. The king set him in the place of minister and gave him great glory. He taught the king things temporal and spiritual. Being a pleasant preacher of the law he established the king in the five precepts, in alms giving in keeping the fasts, in the ten ways of right action, and so established him in the path of virtue. Throughout the kingdom it was as it were the time of the appearing of the Buddhas. On the fortnightly fast the king, the viceroys and others would all assemble and decorate the place of meeting. The Bodhisatta taught the law in a decorated room in the middle of a deer-skin-couch with the power of a Buddha, and his word was like the preaching of Buddhas. Then a certain old brahmin begging for money-alms got a thousand pieces, left them in a brahmin family and went to seek alms again. When he had gone, that family spent all his pieces. He came back and would have his pieces brought him. The brahmin, being unable to give them to him, gave him his daughter to wife. The other brahmin took her and made his dwelling in a brahmin village not far from Benares. Because of her youth his wife was unsatisfied in desires and sinned with another young brahmin. There are sixteen things that cannot be satisfied; and what are these sixteen? The sea is not satisfied with all rivers, nor the fire with fuel, nor a king with his kingdom, nor a fool with sins, nor a woman with three things, intercourse, adornment and child-bearing, nor a brahmin with sacred texts, nor a sage with ecstatic meditation, nor a novice with honour, nor one free from desires with penance, nor the energetic man with energy, nor the talker with talk, nor the politic man with the council, nor the believer with serving the church, nor the liberal man with giving away, nor the learned with hearing the law, nor the four congregations with seeing the Buddha. So this brahmin woman, being unsatisfied with intercourse, wished to put her husband away and do her sin with boldness. So one day in her evil purpose she lay down. When he said, "How is it, wife?" she answered, "Brahmin, I cannot do the work of your house, get me a maid." "Wife, I have no money, what shall I give to get her?" "Seek for money by begging for alms and so get her." "Then, wife, get ready something for my journey." She filled a skin-bag with baked meal and unbaked meal, and gave them to him. The brahmin, going through villages, towns and cities, got seven hundred pieces, and thinking, "This money is enough to buy slaves, male and female," he was returning to his village: at a certain place convenient for water he opened his sack, and eating some meal he went down to drink water without tying the mouth. Then a black snake in a hollow tree, smelling the meal, entered the bag and lay down in a coil eating the meal. The brahmin came, and without looking inside fastened the sack and putting it on his shoulder went his way. Then a spirit living in a tree, sitting in a hollow of the trunk, said to him on the way, "Brahmin, if you stop on the way you will die, if you go home to-day your wife will die," and vanished. He looked, but not seeing the spirit was afraid and troubled with the fear of death, and so came to the gate of Benares weeping and lamenting. It was the fast on the fifteenth day, the day of the Bodhisatta's preaching, seated on the decorated seat of the law, and a multitude with perfumes and flowers and the like in their hands came in troops to hear the preaching. The brahmin said, "Where are ye going?" and was told, "O brahmin, today wise Senaka preaches the law with sweet voice and the charm of a Buddha: do you not know?" He thought, "They say he is a wise preacher, and I am troubled with the fear of death: wise men are able to take away even great sorrow: it is right for me too to go there and hear the law." So he went with them, and when the assembly and the king among them had sat down round about the Bodhisatta, he stood at the outside, not far from the seat of the law, with his mealsack on his shoulder, afraid with the fear of death. The Bodhisatta preached as if he were bringing down the heavenly Ganges or showering ambrosia. The multitude became well pleased, and making applause listened to the preaching. Wise men have far sight. At that moment the Bodhisatta, opening his eyes gracious with the five graces, surveyed the assembly on every side and, seeing that brahmin, thought, "This great assembly has become well pleased and listens to the law, making applause, but that one brahmin is ill-pleased and weeps: there must be some sorrow within him to cause his tears: as if touching rust with acid, or making a drop of water roll from a lotus leaf, I will teach him the law, making him free from sorrow and well pleased in mind." So he called him, "Brahmin, I am wise Senaka, now will I make thee free from sorrow, speak boldly," and so talking with him he spoke the first stanza:

Thou art confused in thought, disturbed in sense,
Tears streaming from thine eyes are evidence;
What hast thou lost, or what dost wish to gain
By coming hither? Give me answer plain.

Then the brahmin, declaring his cause of sorrow, spoke the second stanza:

If I go home my wife it is must die,
If I go not, the yakkha said, 'tis I;
That is the thought that pierces cruelly:
Explain the matter, Senaka, to me.

The Bodhisatta, hearing the brahmin's words, spread the net of knowledge as if throwing a net in the sea, thinking,

"There are many causes of death to beings in this world: some die sunk in the sea, or seized therein by ravenous fish, some falling in the Ganges, or seized by crocodiles, some falling from a tree or pierced by a thorn, some struck by weapons of diverse kinds, some by eating poison or hanging or falling from a precipice or by extreme cold or attacked by diseases of diverse kinds, so they die: now among so many causes of death from which cause shall this brahmin die if he stays on the road to-day, or his wife if he goes home?" As he considered, he saw the sack on the brahmin's shoulder and thought, "There must be a snake who has gone into that sack, and entering he must have gone in from the smell of the meal when the brahmin at his breakfast had eaten some meal and gone to drink water without fastening the sack's mouth: the brahmin coming back after drinking water must have gone on after fastening and taking up the sack without seeing that the snake had entered: if he stays on the road, he will say at evening when he rests, 'I will eat some meal,' and opening the sack will put in his hand: then the snake will bite him in the hand and destroy his life: this will be the cause of his death if he stays on the road: but if he goes home the sack will come into his wife's hand: she will say, "I will took at the ware within,' and opening the sack put in her hand, then the snake will bite her and destroy her life, and this will be the cause of her death if he goes home to-day." This he knew by his knowledge of expedient. Then this came into his mind, "The snake must be a black snake, brave and fearless; when the sack strikes against the brahmin's broadside, he shows no motion or quivering; he shows no sign of his being there amidst such an assembly: therefore he must be a black snake, brave and fearless": from his knowledge of expedients he knew this as if he was seeing with a divine eye. So as if he had been a man who had stood by and seen the snake enter the sack, deciding by his knowledge of expedients, the Bodhisatta answering the brahmin's question in the royal assembly spoke the third stanza:

First with many a doubt I deal,
Now my tongue the truth, declares:
Brahmin, in your bag of meal
A snake has entered unawares.

So saying he asked, "O brahmin, is there any meal in that sack of yours?" "There is, O sage." "Did you eat some meal to-day at your breakfast time?" "Yes, O sage." "Where were you sitting?" "In a wood, at the root of a tree." "When you ate the meal, and went to drink water, did you fasten the sack's mouth or not?" "I did not, O sage." "When you drank water and came back, did you look in before fastening the sack?" "I fastened it without looking in, O sage." "O brahmin, when you went to drink water, I think a snake entered the sack owing to the smell of the meal without your knowledge: such is the case: therefore put down your sack, set it in the midst of the assembly and opening the mouth, stand back and taking a stick beat the sack with it: then when you see a black snake coming out with its hood spread and hissing, you will have no doubt": so he spoke the fourth stanza:

Take a stick and beat the sack,
Dumb and double-tongued is he;
Cease your mind with doubts to rack
Ope the sack, the snake you'll see.

The brahmin, hearing the Great Being's words, did so, though alarmed and frightened. The snake came out of the sack when his hood was struck with the stick, and stood looking at the crowd.

When the question had been so answered by the Bodhisatta a certain snake-charmer made a mouth-band for the snake, caught him and let him loose in the forest. The brahmin, coming up to the king, saluted him and made obeisance, and praising him spoke half a stanza:

Well won is Janaka the king's great gain,
That he wise Senaka doth see.

After praising the king, he took seven hundred pieces from the bag and praising the Bodhisatta, he spoke a stanza and a half wishing to give a delight:

Art thou the All-seer, queller of what is vain?
Doth wisdom dream belong to thee?
These seven hundred pieces, see,

Take them all, I give them thee:
'Tis to thee I owe my life,
And the welfare of my wife.

Hearing this, the Bodhisatta spoke the eighth stanza:
For reciting poetry
Wise men can't accept a wage:
Rather let us give to thee,
Ere thou take the homeward stage.

So saying, the Bodhisatta made a full thousand pieces to be given to the brahmin, and asked him, "By whom were you sent to beg for money?" "By my wife, O sage." "Is your wife old or young?" "Young, O sage." "Then she is doing sin with another, and sent you away thinking to do so in security: if you take these pieces home, she will give to her lover the pieces won by your labour: therefore you should not go home straight, but only after leaving the pieces outside the town at the root of a tree or somewhere": so he sent him away. He, coming near the village, left his pieces at the root of a tree, and came home in the evening. His wife at that moment was seated with her lover. The brahmin stood at the door and said, "Wife." She recognised his voice and putting out the light opened the door: when the brahmin came in, she took the other and put him at the door: then coming back and not seeing anything in the sack she asked, "Brahmin, what alms have you got on your journey?" "A thousand pieces." "Where is it?" "It is left at such and such a place: never mind, we will get it to-morrow." She went and told her lover. He went and took it as if it were his own treasures. Next day the brahmin went and not seeing the pieces came to the Bodhisatta who said, "What is the matter, brahmin?" "I don't see the pieces, O sage." "Did you tell your wife?" "Yes, O sage." Knowing that the wife had told her lover, the Bodhisatta asked, "Brahmin, is there a brahmin who is a friend of your wife's?" "Yes, O sage," Then the Great Being caused seven days' expenses to be given him and said, "Go, do you two invite and entertain the first day fourteen brahmins, seven for yourself and seven for your wife: from next day onwards take one less each day, till on the seventh day you invite, one brahmin and your wife one: then if you notice that the brah nin your wife asks on the seventh day has come every time, tell me." The brahmin did so, and told the Bodhisatta, "O sage, I have observed the brahmin who is always our guest." The Bodhisatta sent men with him to bring that other brahmin, and asked him, "Did you take a thousand pieces belonging to this brahmin from the root of such and such a tree?" "I did not, O sage." "You do not know that I am the wise Senaka; I will make you fetch those pieces." He was afraid and confessed, saying, "I took them." "What did you do?" "I put them in such and such a place, O sage." The Bodhisatta asked the first brahmin, "Brahmin, will you keep your wife or take another?" "Let me keep her, O sage." The Bodhisatta sent men to fetch the pieces and the wife, and gave the brahmin the pieces from the thief's hand; he punished the other, removing him from the city, punished also the wife, and gave great honour to the brahmin, making him dwell near himself.

THE BRAHMIN'S REVENGE ON THE MONKEYS

Once upon a time when Brahmadatta was king in Benares, the Bodhisatta was born as a monkey, and lived in the king's garden with a retinue of five hundred monkeys. Devadatta was also born as a monkey, and lived there also with a retinue of five hundred monkeys. Then one day when the king's family priest had gone to the garden, bathed and adorned himself, one tricky monkey going ahead of him sat above the gateway arch of the garden, and let excrement fall on the priest's head as he went out. When the priest looked up, he let it fall again in his mouth. The priest turned back, saying, in threat to the monkeys, "Very well, I shall know how to deal with you," and went away after washing. They told the Bodhisatta that he had been angry and threatened the monkeys, He made announcement to the thousand monkeys, "It is not well to dwell near the habitation of the angry; let the whole troop of monkeys flee and go elsewhere." A disobedient monkey took his own retinue and did not flee, saying, "I will see about it afterwards." The Bodhisatta took his own retinue and went to the forest. One day a female slave pounding rice had put some rice out in the sun and a goat was eating it: getting a blow with a torch and running away on fire, he was rubbing himself on the wall of a grass-hut near an elephant-stable; in it the elephants' backs were burnt, and the elephant doctors were attending the elephants. The family priest was always going about watching for an opportunity of catching the monkeys. He was sitting in attendance on the king, and the king said, "Sir, many of our elephants have been injured, and the elephant doctors do not know how to cure them; do you know any remedy?" "I do, great king." "What is it?" "Monkey's fat, great king." "How shall we get it?" "There are many monkeys in the garden." The king said, "Kill monkeys in the garden and get their fat." The archers went and killed five hundred monkeys with arrows. One old monkey fled although wounded by an arrow, and though he did not fall on the spot, fell when he came to the Bodhisatta's place of abode. The monkeys said, "He has died when he reached our place of abode," and told the Bodhisatta that he was dead from a wound he had got. He came and sat down among the assembly of monkeys, and spoke these stanzas by way of exhorting the monkeys with the exhortation of the wise, which is "Men dwelling near their enemies perish in this way."

> Let not the wise man dwell where dwells his foe:
> One night, two nights, so near will bring him woe.
> A fool's a foe to all who trust his word:
> One monkey brought distress on all the herd.
> A foolish chief, wise in his own conceit,
> Comes ever, like this monkey, to defeat.
> A strong fool is not good to guard the herd,
> Curse to his kindred, like the decoy-bird.
> One strong and wise is good the herd to guard,
> Like Indra to the God's his kin's reward.
> Who virtue, wisdom, learning, doth posses,
> His deeds himself and other men will bless.
> Therefore virtue, knowledge, learning, and himself let him
> regard,
> Either be a lonely Saint or o'er the flock keep watch and
> ward.

So the Bodhisatta, becoming king of monkeys, explained

the way of learning the Discipline.

THE MONKEYS HEROIC SELF-SACRIFICE

Once upon a time when Brahmadatta was reigning in Benares, the Bodhisatta was born as a monkey. When he grew up and attained stature and stoutness, he was strong and vigorous, and lived in the Himalaya with a retinue of eighty thousand monkeys. Near the Ganges bank there was a mango tree (others say it was a banyan), with branches and forks, having a deep shade and thick leaves, like a mountain-top. Its sweet fruits, of divine fragrance and flavour, were as large as water-pots: from one branch the fruits fell on the ground, from one into the Ganges water, from two into the main trunk of the tree. The Bodhisatta, while eating the fruit with a troop of monkeys, thought, "Someday danger will come upon us owing to the fruit of this tree falling on the water"; and so, not to leave one fruit on the branch which grew over the water, he made them eat or throw down the flowers at their season from the time they were of the size of a chick-pea. But notwithstanding, one ripe fruit, unseen by the eighty thousand monkeys hidden by an ant's nest, fell into the river, and stuck in the net above the king of Benares who was bathing for amusement with a net above him and another below. When the king had amused himself all day and was going away in the evening, the fisherman, who were drawing the net, saw the fruit and not knowing what it was, showed it to the king. The king asked, "What is this fruit?" "We do not know, sire." "Who will know?" "The foresters, sire." He had the foresters called, and learning from them that it was a mango, he cut it with a knife, and first making the foresters eat of it, he ate of it himself and had some of it given to his seraglio and his ministers. The flavour of the ripe mango remained pervading the king's whole body. Possessed by desire of the flavour, he asked the foresters where that tree stood, and hearing that it was on a river bank in the Himalaya quarter, he had many rafts joined together and sailed upstream by the route shown by the foresters. The exact account of days is not given. In due course they came to the place, and the foresters said to the king, "Sire, there is the tree." The king stopped the rafts and

went on foot with a great retinue, and having a bed prepared
at the foot of the tree, he lay down after eating the mango fruit
and enjoying the various excellent flavours. At every side they
set a guard and made a fire. When the men had fallen asleep,
the Bodhisatta came at midnight with his retinue. Eighty thousand monkeys moving from branch to branch ate the mangoes.
The king, waking and seeing the herd of monkeys, roused his
men and calling his archers said, "Surround these monkeys that
eat the mangoes so that they may not escape, and shoot them:
to-morrow we will eat mangoes with monkey's flesh." The archers obeyed, saying, "Very well," and surrounding the tree
stood with arrows ready. The monkey's seeing them and fearing
death, as they could not escape, came to the Bodhisatta and
said, "Sire, the archers stand round the tree, saying, 'We will
shoot those vagrant monkeys': what are we to do?" and so stood
shivering. The Bodhisatta said, "Do not fear, I will give you life",
and so comforting the herd of monkeys, he ascended a branch
that rose up straight, went along another branch that stretched
towards the Ganges, and springing from the end of it, he passed
a hundred bow-lengths and lighted on a bush on the bank.
Coming down, he marked the distance, saying, "That will be
the distance I have come": and cutting a bamboo shoot at the
root and stripping it, he said, "So much will be fastened to the
tree, and so much will stay in the air," and so reckoned the two
lengths, forgetting the part fastened on his own waist. Taking
the shoot he fastened one end of it to the tree on the Ganges
bank and the other to his own waist, and then cleared the space
of a hundred bow-lengths with a speed of a cloud torn by the
wind. From not reckoning the part fastened to his waist, he
failed to reach the tree: so seizing a branch firmly with both
hands he gave signal to the troop of monkeys, "Go quickly with
good luck, treading on my back along the bamboo shoot." The
eighty thousand monkeys escaped thus, after saluting the
Bodhisatta and getting his leave. Devadatta was then a monkey
and among that herd: he said, "This is a chance for me to see
the last of my enemy," so climbing up a branch he made a
spring and fell on the Bodhisatta's back. The Bodhisatta's back
broke and great pain came on him. Devadatta having caused
that maddening pain went away: and the Bodhisatta was alone.

The king being awake saw all that was done by the monkey's and the Bodhisatta: and he lay down thinking, "This animal, not reckoning his own life, has caused the safely of his troop." When day broke, being pleased with the Bodhisatta, he thought, "It is not right to destroy this king of the monkeys: I will bring him down by some means and take care of him": So turning the raft down the Ganges and building a platform there, he made the Bodhisatta come down gently, and had him clothed with a yellow robe on his back and washed in Ganges water, made him drink sugared water, and had his body cleansed and anointed with oil refined a thousand times; then he put an oiled skin on a bed and making him lie there, he set himself, on a low seat, and spoke the first stanza:

You made yourself a bridge for them to pass in safety through:
What are you then to them, monkey, and what are they
                                                    to you?

Hearing him, the Bodhisatta instructing the king spoke the other stanzas:

Victorious king, I guard the herd, I am their lord and chief,
When they were filled with fear of tree and stricken sore
                                                    with grief.

I leapt a hundred times the length of bow outstretched
                                                    that lies,
When I had bound a bamboo-shoot firmly around my thighs:
I reached the tree like thunder-cloud sped by the tempest's
                                                    blast;
I lost my strength, but reached a bough: with hands I held
it fast.

And as I hung extended there held fast by shoot and bough,
My monkeys passed across my back and are in safety now.
Therefore I fear no pain of death, bonds do not give me
                                                    pain,
The happiness of those was won o'er whom I used to reign.

A parable for thee, O king, if thou the truth would'st read:
The happiness of kingdom and of army and of steed

And city must be dear to thee, if thou would'st rule indeed.

The Bodhisatta, thus instructing and teaching the king, died. The king, called his ministers, gave orders that the monkey-king should have obsequies like a king, and he sent to the seraglio, saying, "Come to the cemetery, as retinue for the monkey-king, with red garments, and disheveled hair, and torches in your hands." The ministers made a funeral pile with a hundred waggon loads of timber. Having prepared the Bodhisatta's obsequies in a royal manner, they took his skull, and came to the king. The king caused a shrine to be built at the Bodhisatta's burial-place, torches to be burnt there and offerings of incense and flowers to be made; he had the skull inlaid with gold, and put in front raised on a spearpoint: honouring it with incense and flowers, he put it at the king's gate when he came to Benares, and having the whole city decked out he paid honour to it for seven days. Then taking it as a relic and raising a shrine, he honoured it wit incense and garlands all his life; and established in the Bodhisatta's teaching he did alms and other good deeds, and ruling his kingdom righteously became destined for heaven.

THE ADVENTURES OF THE PRINCE AND HIS BROTHER

Once upon a time when Brahmadatta was reigning in Benares, the Bodhisatta was born as the son of his chief queen. When he grew up, he learned all the arts at Takkasila, and acquired a spell for the understanding of all animals' cries. After listening duly to his teacher, he returned to Benares. His father appointed him viceroy: but though he did so, he became anxious to kill him and would not even see him.

A she-jackal with two cubs entered the city at night by a sewer, when men were retired to rest. In the Bodhisatta's palace, near his bedroom, there was a chamber, where a single traveller, who had taken his shoes off and put them by his feet on the floor, was lying down, not yet asleep, on a plank. The jackal-cubs were hungry and gave a cry. Their mother said in the speech of jackals, "Do not make a noise, dears: there is a man in that chamber who has taken his shoes off and laid them on the floor; he is lying on a plank, but is not asleep yet: when he falls asleep, I will take his shoes and give you food." By the power of the spell the Bodhisatta understood her call, and leaving his bedroom he opened a window and said, "Who is there?" "I, your majesty, a traveller." "Where are your shoes?" "On the floor." "Lift them and hang them up." Hearing this the jackal was angry with the Bodhisatta. One day she entered the city again by the same way. That day a drunken man went down to drink in a lotus-tank: falling in, he sank and was drowned. He possessed the two garments he was wearing, a thousand pieces in his under-garment, and a ring on his finger. The jackal-cubs cried out for hunger, and the mother said, "Be quiet, dears: there is a dead man in this lotus-tank, he had such and such property: he is lying dead on the tank-stair, I will give you his flesh to eat." The Bodhisatta, hearing her, opened the window and said, "Who is in the chamber?" One rose and said, "I." "Go and take the clothes, the thousand pieces and the ring from the man who is lying dead in yonder lotus-tank, and make the body sink so that it cannot rise out of the water." The man did so. The jackal was angry again: "The other day you prevented my children eating the shoes; to-day you prevent them eating the dead man. Very well: on the third day from this a hostile king will come and encompass the city, your father will send you to battle, they will cut off your head: I will drink your throat's blood and satisfy my enmity: you make yourself an enemy of mine and I will see to it"; so she cried abusing the Bodhisatta. Then she took her cubs and went away. On the third day the hostile king came and encompassed the city. The king said to the Bodhisatta. "Go, dear son, and fight him." "O king, I have seen a vision: I cannot go, for I fear I shall lose my life." "What is your life or death to me? Go." The Great Being obeyed: taking his men he avoided the gate where the hostile king was posted, and went out by another, which he had opened. As he went the whole city became as it were deserted, for all men went out with him. He encamped in a certain open space and waited. The king thought, "My viceroy has emptied the city and fled with all my forces; the enemy is lying all round the city: I am but a dead man." To save his life he took his chief queen, his family priest, and a single attendant named Parantapa: with them he fled in disguise by night and entered a wood. Hearing of his flight, the Bodhisatta entered the city, defeated the hostile king in battle and took the kingdom. His father made a hut of leaves on a river bank and lived there on wild fruits. He and the family priest used to go looking for wild fruits: the servant Parantapa stayed with the queen in the hut. She was with child by the king: but owing to being constantly with Parantapa, she sinned with him. One day she said to him, "If the king knows, neither you nor I would live: kill him." "In what way?" "He makes you carry his sword and bathing-dress when he goes to bathe: take him off his guard at the bathing-place, cut off his head and chop his body to pieces with the sword and then bury him in the ground." He agreed. One day the priest had gone out for wild fruits: he had climbed a tree near the king's bathing-place and was gathering the fruit. The king wished to bathe, and came to the water-side with Parantapa carrying his sword and bathing-dress. As he was going to bathe, Parantapa, meaning to kill him when off his guard, seized him by the neck and raised the sword. The king cried out in fear of death. The priest heard the cry and saw from above that Parantapa was murdering him: but he was in great terror and slipping down from his branch in the tree, he hid in a thicket. Parantapa heard the noise he made as he slipped down, and after killing and burying the king he thought, "There was a noise of slipping from a branch thereabouts; who is there?" But seeing no man he bathed and went away. Then the priest came out of his hiding-place; knowing that the king had been cut in pieces and buried in a pit, he bathed and in fear of his life he pretended to be blind when he came back to the hut. Parantapa saw him and asked what had happened to him. He feigned not to know him and said, "O king, I am come back with my eyes lost: I was standing by an ant-hill in a wood full of serpents, and the breath of some venomous serpent must have fallen on me." Parantapa thought the priest was addressing him as king in ignorance, and to put his mind at rest he said, "Brahmin, never mind, I will take care of you," and so comforted him and gave him plenty of wild fruits. From that time it was Parantapa who gathered the fruits. The queen bore a son. As he was growing up, she said to

Parantapa one day at early morning when seated comfortably, "Some one saw you when you were killing the king?" "No one saw me: but I heard the noise of something slipping from a bough: whether it was man or beast I cannot tell: but whenever fear comes on me it must be from the cause of the boughs creaking," and so in conversation with her he spoke the first stanza:

Terror and fear fall on me even now,
For then a man or beast did shake a bough.

They thought the priest was asleep, but he was awake and heard their talk. One day, when Parantapa had gone for wild fruits, the priest remembered his brahmin-wife and spoke the second stanza in lamentation:

My true wife's home is near at hand: my love will make me be
Pale like Parantapa and thin, at quivering of a tree.

The queen asked what he was saying. He said, "I was only thinking": but one day again he spoke the third stanza:

My dear wife's in Benares: her absence wears me now
To pallor like Parantapa's at shaking of a bough.

Again one day he spoke a fourth stanza:

Her black eye's glow, her speech and smiles in thought do bring me now.
To pallor like Parantapa's at shaking of a bough.

In time the young prince grew up and reached the age of sixteen. Then the brahmin made him take a stick, and going with him to the bathing-place opened his eyes and looked. "Are you not blind, brahmin?" said the prince. "I am not, but by this means I have saved my life: do you know who is your father?" "Yes." "That man is not your father: your father was king of Benares: that man is a servant of your house, he sinned with your mother and in this spot killed and buried your father"; and so saying he pulled up the bones and showed them to him. The prince grew very angry, and asked, "What am I to do?" "Do to that man what he did to your father here," and showing him the whole matter he taught him in a few days how to handle a sword. Then one day the prince took sword and bathing-dress and said, "Father, let us go and bathe." Parantapa consented and went with him. When he went down into the water, the prince took his top-knot in the left hand and the sword in the right, and said, "At this spot you took my father by the top-knot and killed him as he cried out: even so will I do to you." Parantapa wailed in fear of death and spoke two stanzas:

Surely that sound has come to you and told you what
befell:
Surely the man who bent the bough has come the tale
to tell.

The foolish thought that once I had has reached your knowledge now:
That day a witness, man or beast, was there and shook
the bough.

Then the prince spoke the last stanza:
'Twas thus you slew my father with trait'rous word, untrue;
You hid his body in the boughs: now fear has come to you.

So saying, he slew him on the spot, buried him and covered the place with branches: then washing the sword and bathing, he went back to the hut of leaves. He told the priest how he had killed Parantapa: he censured his mother, and saying, "What shall we do now?" the three went back to Benares. The Bodhisatta made the young prince viceroy and doing charity and other good works passed fully through the path to heaven.

THE PANTHER AND THE GOAT

The Master told his tale while dwelling in Jetavana, concerning a certain she-goat. At one time the Elder Moggallana lived in a dwelling with one door, in mountain enclosure, surrounded by hills. His covered walk was close by the door. Some goatherds thought the enclosure would be a good place for their goats, so they drove them in and lived there at their pleasure. One day they came in the evening, took all the goats,

and went away: but one she-goat had wandered far, and not
seeing the goats departing, she was left behind. As she was
going after them, a panther saw her, and thinking to eat her
stood by the door of the enclosure. She looked all round, and
saw the panther. "He is there because he wishes to kill and eat
me," she thought; "if I turn and run, my life is lost: I must play
the man, and so she tossed her horns and sprang straight at him
with all her might. She escaped his grip, though he was quivering with the thought of catching her: then running at full
speed she came up with the other goats. The Elder observed
how all the animals had behaved: next day he went and told the
Buddha, "So, lord, this she-goat performed a feat by her readi-
ness in device, and escaped from the panther." The Master
answered, "Moggallana, the panther failed to catch her this
time, but once before he killed her though she cried out, and ate
her." Then at Moggallana's request, he told an old tale.

Once upon a time the Bodhisatta was born in a certain
village of the Magadha kingdom, in a wealthy family. When he
grew up, he renounced desires and adopted the religious life,
reaching the perfection of meditation. After dwelling long in
the Hamalaya, he came to Rajagaha for salt and vinegar, and
dwelt in a hut of leaves, which he made in a mountain enclosure. Just as in the introductory story, the goatherds drove their
goals thither: and in the same way, one day as a single she –
goat was going out later than the rest, a panther waited by the
door, thinking to eat her. When she saw him, she thought, "My
life is forfeit: by some means I must get him into pleasant and
kindly talk, and so soften his heart and save my life." Beginning
a friendly talk with him from some distance, she approached
and spoke the first stanza:
> How fares it with you, uncle? And is it well with you?
> My mother sends her kind regards: and I'm your friend so
> true.

Hearing her, the panther thought, "this baggage would
beguile me by calling me 'uncle': she does not know how hard
I am", and so spoke the second stanza:
> You've trod upon my tail, miss goat, and done me injury:

And think you by saying 'Uncle' that you can go scot-free?

When she heard him, she said, "O uncle, don't talk in the way," and spoke the third stanza:
I face you as I came, good Sir, you face me as you sit:
Your tail is all behind you: how could I tread on it?
He answered, "What do you say, she-goat? Is there any place where my tail might not be?" and so he spoke the fourth stanza:
As far as four great continents with seas and mountains
                                                                                    spread,
My tail extends: how could you fail on such a tail to tread?

The she-goat, when she heard this, thought, "This wicked one is not attracted by soft words: I will answer him as an enemy," and so she spoke the fifth stanza:
Your villain's tail is long, I know, for I had warning fair:
Parents and brothers told me so: but I flew through the air.

Then he said, "I know you came through the air: but as you came, you spoilt my food by your way of coming," and so he spoke the sixth stanza:
The sight of you, miss goat, on high, the air a flying through
Frightened a herd of deer: and so my food was spoilt by
                                                                                    you.

Hearing this, the goat in fear of death could bring no other excuse, but cried out, "Uncle, do not commit such cruelty, spare my life." But though she cried out, the other seized her by the shoulder, killed her and ate her.

The ascetic saw the whole matter of the two animals.

THE GRATEFUL PARROT

Once upon a time many myriads of parrots lived in the Himalaya country on the bank of the Ganges in a grove of fig-tree. A king of the parrots there, when the fruit of the tree in which he dwell had come to an end, ate whatever was left, whether shoot or leaf or bark or rind, and drank of water from the Ganges, and being very happy and contented he kept where he was. Owing to his happy and contented state the abode of Sakka was shaken. Sakka reflecting on the cause saw the parrot, and to test his virtue, by his supernatural power he withered up the tree, which became a mere stump perforated with holes, and stood to be buffeted by every blast of wind, and from the holes dust came out. The parrot king ate this dust and drank the water of the Ganges, and going nowhere else sat perched on the top of the fig-stump, racking nought of wind and sun.

Sakka noticed how very contented the parrot was, and said, "After hearing him speak of the virtue of friendship, I will come and give him his choice of a boon, and cause the fig-tree to bear ambrosial fruit." So he took the form of a royal goose, and preceded by Suja in the shape of an Asura nymph, he went to the grove of fig-trees, and perching on the bough of a tree close by, he entered into conversation with the parrot and spoke the first stanza:

Where fruitful tree abound,
A flock of hungry birds is found:
But should the trees all withered be,
Away at once the birds will flee.

And after these words, to drive the parrot thence, he spoke the second stanza:

Haste thee, Sir Redbeak, to be gone;
Why dost thou sit and dream alone?
Come tell me, prithee, bird of spring,
To this dead stump why dost thou cling?

Then the parrot said, "O goose, from a feeling of gratitude, I forsake not this tree," and he repeated two stanzas:

They who have been close friends from youth,
Mindful of goodness and of truth,
In life and death, in weal and woe
The claims of friendship ne'er forego.

I too would fain be kind and good

To one that long my friend has stood:
I wish to live, but have no heart
From this old tree, though dead, to part.

Sakka on hearing what he said was delighted, and praising him wished to offer him a choice, and uttered two stanzas:
I know thy friendship and thy grateful love,
Virtues that wise men surely must approve.

I offer thee whate'er thou wilt for choice;
Parrot what boon would most thy heart rejoice?

On hearing this, the king parrot making his choice spoke the seventh stanza:
If thou, O goose, what most I crave wouldst give,
Grant that the tree I love, again may live.
Let it once more with its old vigour shoot,
Gather fresh sweetness and bear goodly fruit.

Then Sakka, granting the boon, spoke the eighth stanza:

Lo! friend, a fruitful and right noble tree,
Well fitted for thy dwelling-place to be.
Let it once more with its old vigour shoot,
Gather fresh sweetness and bear goodly fruit.

With these words Sakka quitted his present form, and manifesting the supernatural power of himself and Suja, he took up water from the Ganges in his hand and dashed it against the fig-tree stump. Straightway the tree rose up rich in branch and stem and with honey-sweet fruit, and stood a charming sight, like unto the bare Jewel-Mount. The parrot king on seeing it was highly pleased, and singing the praises of Sakka he spoke the ninth stanza:
May Sakka and all loved by Sakka blessed be,
As I to-day am blest this goodly sight to see!

Sakka, after granting the parrot his choice, and causing the fig-tree to bear ambrosial fruit, returned with Sujata to his own abode.

THE GOBLIN'S GIFT

Once upon a time in the reign of Brahmadatta, king of
Benares, his queen-consort after falling into sin was questioned
by the king, and taking an oath she said, "If I have sinned
against you, I shall become a female Yakkha with a face like a
horse." After her death she became a horse-faced Yakkha and
dwelt in a rock-cave in a vast forest at the foot of a mountain,
and used to catch and devour the men that frequented the road
leading from the East to the Western border. After serving
Vessavana three years, it is said, she got leave to eat people in
a certain space, thirty leagues long by five leagues broad. Now
one day a rich, wealthy, handsome brahmin, accompanied by a
large suite, ascended that road. The Yakkha, on seeing him, with
a loud neigh rushed upon him, and his attendants all fled. With
the speed of the wind she seized brahmin and threw him on her
back, and in entering the cave, through coming into contact
with the man, under the influence of passion she conceived an
affection for him, and instead of devouring him she made him
her husband, and they lived harmoniously together. And thenceforth the Yakkha whenever she captured men, also took their
clothes and rice and oil and the like, and serving him with
various dainty food she herself would eat man's flesh. And
whenever she went away, for fear of his escaping, she closed
the mouth of the cave with a huge stone before leaving. And
while they were thus living amicably together, the Bodhisatta
passing from his former existence was conceived in the womb
of the Yakkha by the brahmin. After ten-months she gave birth
to a son, and filled with love for the brahmin and her child, she
fed them both. By and by when the boy was grown up, she put
him also inside the cave with his father, and closed the door.
Now one day the Bodhisatta knowing she had gone away removed the stone and let his father out. And when she asked on
her return who had removed the stone, he said, "I did, mother:
we cannot sit in darkness." And through love for her child she
did not say another word. Now one day the Bodhisatta asked his
father, saying, "Dear father, your mouth is different from my

mother's: what is the reason?" "My son, your mother is a Yakkha and lives on man's flesh, but you and I are men." "If so, why do we live here? Come, we will go to the haunts of men." "My dear boy, if we shall try to escape, your mother will kill us both." The Bodhisatta reassured his father and said, "Do not be afraid, dear father; that you shall return to the haunts of men shall be my charge." And next day when his mother had gone away, he took his father and fled. When the Yakkha returned and missed them, she rushed forward with the swiftness of the wind and caught them and said, "O brahmin, why do you run away? Is there anything that you want here?" "My dear," he said, "do not be angry with me. Your son carried me off with him." And without another word, owing to her love for her child, she comforted them and making for her place of abode she brought them back after a flight of some days. The Bodhisatta thought, "My mother must have a limited sphere of action. Suppose I were to ask her the limits of space over which her authority extends. Then I will escape by going beyond this." So one day sitting respectfully near his mother he said, "My dear, that which belongs to a mother comes to the children; tell me now what is the boundary of our ground." She told him all the landmarks, mountains and such like in all directions, and pointed out to her son the space, thirty leagues long and five leagues broad, and said, "Consider it to be so much my son." After the lapse of two or three days, when his mother had gone to the forest, he put his father on his shoulder and rushing on with the swiftness of the wind, by the hint given him by his mother, he reached the bank of the river that was the limit. The mother too, when on her return she missed them, pursued after them. The Bodhisatta carried his father into the middle of the river, and she came and stood on the river bank, and when she saw that they had passed beyond the limits of her sphere, she stopped where she was and cried, "My dear child, come here with your father. What is my offence? In what respect do not things go well with you? Come back, my lord." Thus did she beseech her child and husband. So the brahmin crossed the river. She prayed to her child also, and said, "Dear son, do not act after this sort: come back again." "Mother, we are men: you are a Yakkha. We cannot always abide with you." "And will you not return?" "No, mother." "Then if you refuse to return—as it is painful to live in the world of men, and they who know not any craft cannot live—I am skilled in the lore of a wishing-jewel: by its power, one can follow after the lapse of twelve years in the steps of those that have gone away. This will prove a livelihood to you. Take, my child, this invaluable charm." And though overcome by such great sorrow, through love of her child, she gave him the charm. The Bodhisatta, still standing in the river, folded his hands tortoise-wise and took the charm. and saluting his mother cried, "Goodbye, mother." The Yakkha said, "If you do not return, my son, I cannot live," and she smote upon her breast, and straightway in sorrow for her son her heart was broken and she fell down dead on the spot. The Bodhisatta, when he knew his mother was dead, called to his father and went and made a funeral pile and burned her body. After extinguishing the flames, he made offerings of various coloured flowers, and with weeping and lamentation returned with his father to Benares.

It was told the king, "A youth skilled in tracking footsteps is standing at the door." And when the king bade him enter, he came in and saluted the king. "My friend," he said, "do you know any craft?" "My lord, following on the track of one who has stolen any property twelve years ago, I can catch him." "Then enter my service," said the king. "I will serve you for a thousand pieces of money daily." "Very well, friend, you shall serve me." And the king had him paid a thousand pieces of money daily. Now one day the family priest said to the king, "My lord, because this youth does nothing by the power of his art, we do not know whether he has any skill or not: we will now test him." The king readily agreed, and the pair gave notice to the keepers of the various treasures, and taking the most valuable jewels descended from the terrace, and after groping their way three times round the palace, they placed a ladder on the top of the wall and by means of it descended to the outside. Then they entered the Hall of Justice, and after sitting there they returned and again placing the ladder on the wall descended into the harem. Coming to the edge of a tank they thrice marched rightwise round it, and then dropped their treasure in the tank, and climbed back to the terrace. Next day there was a great outcry and men said, "Treasure has been stolen from the palace." The king pretending ignorance summoned the Bodhisatta and said, "Friend, much valuable treasure has been stolen from the palace: we must trace it." "My lord, for one who is able to follow the traces of robbers and recover treasure stolen twelve years ago, there is nothing marvelous in his recovering stolen property after a single day and night. I will recover it; do not be troubled." "Then recover it, friend." "Very well, my lord," he said, and went and saluting his mother's memory he repeated the spell, still standing on the terrace, and said, "My lord, the steps of two thieves are to be seen." And following in the steps of the king and the priest he entered the royal closet, and issuing thence he descended from the terrace, and after thrice making a circuit of the palace he drew near the wall. Standing on it he said, "My lord, starting in this place from the wall I see footsteps in the air: bring me a ladder." And having had a ladder placed for him against the wall, he descended by it, and still following in their track he came to the Hall of Justice. Then returning to the palace he had the ladder planted against the wall, and descending by it he came to the tank. Going thrice rightwise round it he said, "My lord, the thieves went down into this tank," and taking out the treasure, as if he had deposited it there himself, he gave it to the king and said, "My lord, these two thieves are men of distinction: by this way they climbed up into the palace." The people snapped their fingers in a high state of delight, and there was a great waving of cloths. The king thought, "this youth, methinks, by following in their steps knows the place where the thieves put the treasures, but the thieves he cannot catch." Then he said, "You at once brought us the property carried off by the thieves, but will you be able to catch the thieves and bring them to us?" "My lord, the thieves are here: they are not far off." "Who are they?" "Great king, let any one that likes be the thief. From the time you recovered your treasure, why should you want the thieves? Do not ask about that." "Friend, I pay you daily a thousand pieces of money: bring the thieves to me." "Sire, when the treasure is recovered, what need of the thieves?" It is better, friend, for us to catch the thieves than to recover the treasure." "Then, sire, I will not tell you, 'So and so are the thieves,' but I will tell you a thing that happened long ago. If you are wise, you will know what it means." And herewith he told an old tale.

Once upon a time, sire, a certain dancer named Patala lived not far from Benares, in a village on the river's bank. One day he went into Benares with his wife and after gaining money by his singing and dancing, at the end of the fete he procured some rice and strong drink. On his way to his own village he came to the bank of the river, and sat down watching the freshly flowing stream, to drink his strong drink. When he was drunk and unconscious of his weakness, he said, "I will fasten my big lute about my neck and go down into the river." And he took his wife by the hand and went down into the river. The water entered intothe holes of the lute, and then the weight of his lute made him begin to sink. But when his wife saw he was sinking, she let go of him and went up out of the river and stood upon the bank. The dancer Patala now rises and now sinks, and his belly became swollen from swallowing the water. So his wife thought, "My husband will now die: I will beg of him one song, and by singing this in the midst of the people, I shall earn my living." And saying, "My lord, you are sinking in the water: give me just one song, snd I will earn my living by it," she spoke this stanza.

O Patala, by Ganges swept away,
Famous in dance and skilled in roundelay,
Patala, all hail! As thou art borne along,
Sing me, I pray, some little snatch of song.

Then the dancer Patala said, "My dear, how shall I give you a little song? The water that has been the salvation of the people is killing me," and he spoke a stanza:

Where are sprinkled fainting souls in pain,
I straight am killed. My refuge proved my bane.

The Bodhisatta in explanation of this stanza said: "Sire, even as water is the refuge of the people, so also is it with kings. If danger arises from them, who shall avert the danger? This sire, is a secret matter. I have told a story intelligible to the wise:

understand it, sire." "Friend, I understand not a hidden story
like this. Catch the thieves and bring them to me." Then the
Bodhisatta said, "Here then this sire, and understand." And he
told yet another tale.

"My lord, formerly in a village outside the city gates of
Benares, a potter used to fetch clay for his pottery, and constantly getting it in the same place he dug a deep pit inside a
mountain-cave. Now one day while he was getting the clay, an
unseasonable storm-cloud sprang up, and let fall a heavy rain,
and the flood overwhelmed and threw down the side of the pit,
and the man's head was broken by it. Loudly lamenting he
spoke this stanza:
That by which seeds do grow, man to sustain,
Has crushed my head. My refuge proved my bane.

"For even as the mighty earth, sire, which is the refuge of
the people, broke the potter's head, even so when a king, who
like the mighty earth, is the refuge of the whole world, rises up
and plays the thief, who shall avert the danger? Can you, sire,
recognize the thief hidden under the guise of the story?" "Friend,
we do not want any hidden meaning. Say, 'Here is the thief,' and
catch him and hand him over to me."

Still shielding the king and without saying in words, "Thou
art the thief," he told yet another story.

In this very city, sire, a certain man's house was on fire. He
ordered another man to go into the house and bring out his
property. When this man had entered the house and was
bringing out his goods, the door was shut. Blinded with smoke
and unable to find his way out and tormented by the rising
flame, he remained inside lamenting, and spoke this stanza:
That which destroys the cold, and parches grain,
Consumes my limbs. My refuge proves my bane.

"A man, O king, who like fire was the refuge of the people,
stole the bundle of jewels. Do not ask me about the thief."
"Friend, just bring me the thief." Without telling the king that

he was a thief, he told yet another story.

Once, sire, in this very city a man ate to excess and was unable to digest his food. Maddened with pain and lamenting he spoke this stanza:

Food on which countless brahmins life sustain
Killed me outright. My refuge proved my bane.

"One, who like rice, sire, was the refuge of the people, stole the property. When that is recovered, why ask about the thief?" "Friend, if you can, bring me the thief." To make the king comprehend, he told yet another story.

Formerly, sire, in this very city a wind arose and broke a certain man's limbs. Lamenting he spoke this stanza:

Wind that in June wise men by prayer would gain,
My limbs doth break. My refuge proved my bane.

"Thus, sire, did danger arise from his refuge. Understand this story." "Friend, bring me the thief." To make the king understand he told him yet another story.

"Once upon a time, sire, on the side of the Himalayas grew a tree with forked branches, the dwelling-place of countless birds. Two of its boughs rubbed against one another. Hence arose smoke, and sparks of fire were let fall. On seeing this the chief bird uttered this stanza:

Flame issues from the tree where we have lain:
Scatter ye birds. Our refuge proves our bane.

"For just as, sire, the tree is the refuge of birds, so is the king the refuge of his people. Should he play the thief, who shall avert the danger? Take note of this, sire." "Friend, only bring me the thief." Then he told the king yet another story.

In a village of Benares, sire, on the western side of a gentleman's house was a river full of savage crocodiles, and in this family was an only son, who on the death of his father watched over his mother. His mother against his will brought home a gentleman's daughter as his wife. At first she showed affection for her mother-in-law, but afterwards when blest with numerous sons and daughters of her own, she wished to get rid of her. Her own mother also lived in the same house. In her husband's presence she found all manner of fault with her mother-in-law, to prejudice him against her, saying, "I cannot possibly support your mother: you must kill her." And when he answered, "Murder is a serious matter: how am I to kill her?" she said, "When she has fallen asleep, we will take her, bed and all, and throw her into the crocodile river. Then the crocodiles will make an end of her." "And where is your mother?" he said. "She sleeps in the same room as your mother." "Then go and set a mark on the bed on which she lies, by fastening a rope on it." She did so, and said, "I have put a mark on it." The husband said, "Excuse me a moment; let the people go to bed first." And he lays down pretending to go to sleep, and then went and fastened the rope on his mother-in-law's bed. Then he woke his wife, and they went together and lifting her up, bed and all, threw her into the river. And the crocodiles there killed and ate her. Next day she found out what had happened to her own mother, and said, "My lord, my mother is dead, now let us kill yours." "Very well then," he said "we will make a funeral pile in the cemetery, and cast her into the fire and kill her." So the man and his wife took her while she was asleep to the cemetery, and deposited her there. Then the husband said to his wife, "Have you brought any fire?" "I have forgotten it, my lord." "Then go and fetch it." "I dare not go, my lord, and if you go, I dare not stay here: we will go together." When they were gone, the old woman was awakened by the cold wind, and finding it was a cemetery, she thought, "They wish to kill me; they are gone to fetch fire. They do not know how strong I am." And she stretched a corpse on the bed and covered it over with a cloth, and ran away and hid herself in a mountain-cave in that same place. The husband and wife brought the fire and taking the corpse to be the old woman they burned it and went away. A certain robber had left his bundle in this mountain cave and coming back to fetch it he saw the old woman and thought, "This must be a Yakkha: my bundle is possessed by goblins," and he fetched a devil-doctor. The doctor uttered a spell and

entered the cave. Then she said to him, "I am no Yakkha; come, we will enjoy this treasure together." "How is this to be believed?" "Place your tongue on my tongue." He did so, and she bit a piece off his tongue and let it drop to the ground. The devil-doctor thought. "This is certainly a Yakkha; come, he cried aloud and fled away, with the blood dripping from his tongue. Next day the old woman put on a clean undergarment and took the bundle of all sorts of jewels and went home. The daughter-in-law on seeing her asked, "Where, mother, did you get this?" "My dear, all that are burned on a wooden pile in this cemetery receive the same." "My dear mother, can I too get this?" "If you become like me, you will." So without saying a word to her husband, in her desire for a lot of ornaments to wear, she went there and burned herself. Her husband next day missed her and said, "My dear mother, at this time of day is not your daughter-in-law coming/" Then she reproached him saying, "Fie! You bad man, how do the dead come back?" And she uttered this stanza:

A maiden fair, with wreath upon her head,
Fragrant with sandal oil, by me was led
A happy bride within my home to reign:
She drove me forth. My refuge proved my bane.

"As the daughter-in-law, sire, is to the mother-in-law, so is the king a refuge to his people. If danger arises thence, what can one do? take note of this, sire." "Friend, I do not understand the things you tell me; only bring me the thief." He thought, "I will shield the king," and he told yet another story.

Of old, sire, in this very city a man in answer to his prayer had a son. At his birth the father was full of joy and gladness at the thought of having got a son, and cherished him. When the boy was grown up, he wedded him to a wife, and by and by he himself grew old and could not undertake any work. So his son said, "You cannot do any work: you must go from hence," and he drove him out of the house. With great difficulty he kept himself alive on alms, and lamenting he uttered this stanza:

He for whose birth I longed, nor longed in vain,
Drives me from home. My refuge proved my bane.

"Just as an aged father, sire, ought to be cared for by an able-bodied son, so too ought all the people to be protected by the king, and this danger now present has arisen from the king, who is the guardian of all men. Know, sire, from this fact that the thief is so and so." "I do not understand this, be it fact or no fact: either bring me the thief, or you yourself must be the thief." Thus did the king again and again question the youth. So he said to him, "Would you, sire, really like the thief to be caught?" "Yes, friend." "Then I will proclaim it in the midst of the assembly, So and So is the thief," "Do so, friend." On hearing his words he thought, "This king does not allow me to shield him: I will now catch the thief." And when the people had gathered together, he addressed them and spoke these stanzas:

Let town and country folk assembled all give ear
Lo! water is ablaze. From safety cometh fear.

The plundered realm may well of king and priest complain:
Henceforth protect yourselves. Your refuge proves your
bane.

When they heard what he said, the people thought, "The king, though he ought to have protected others, threw the blame on another. After he had with his own hands placed his treasure in the tank, he went about looking for the thief. That he may not in future go on playing the part of a thief, we will kill this wicked king." So they rose up with sticks and clubs in their hands, and then and there beat the king and the priest till they died. But they sprinkled the Bodhisatta with the ceremonial sprinkling and set him on the throne.

THE WISE GOAT AND THE JACKAL

Once upon a time in the reign of Brahmadatta, king of Benares, many hundreds of wild goats dwelt in a mountain-cave in a wooden district on the slopes of the Himalayas. Not far from their place of abode a jackal named Putimamsa with his wife Veni lived in a cave. One day as he was ranging about with his wife, he spied those goats and thought, "I must find some means to eat the flesh of these goats," and by some device he killed a single goat. Both he and his wife by feeding on goat's flesh waxed strong and gross of body. Gradually the goats were destroyed. Amongst them was a wise she-goat named Melamata. The jackal though skilful in devices could not kill her, and taking counsel with his wife he said, "My dear, all the goats have died out. We must devise how to eat this she-goat. Now here is my plan. You are to go by yourself, and become friendly with her, and when confidence has sprung up between you, I will lie down and pretend to be dead. Then you are to draw nigh to the goat and say, 'My dear, my husband is dead and I am desolate; except you I have no relative: come, let us weep and lament, and bury his body.' And with these words come and bring her with you. Then I will spring up and kill her by a bite in the neck." She readily agreed and after making friends with the goat, when confidence was established, she addressed her in the words suggested by her husband. The goat replied, "My dear all my kinfolk have been eaten by your husband. I am afraid; I cannot come." "Do not be afraid, what harm can the dead do you?" "Your husband is cruelly minded; I am afraid." But afterwards being repeatedly importuned the goat thought, "He certainly must be dead," and consented to go with her. But on her way there she thought, "Who knows what will happen?" and being suspicious she made the she-jackal go in front, keeping a sharp look-out for the jackal. He heard the sound of their steps and thought, "Here comes the goat," and put up his head and rolling his eyes looked about him. The goat on seeing him do this said, "This wicked wretch wants to take me in and kill me: he lies there making a pretence of being dead," and she turned about and fled. When the she-jackal asked why she ran away, the goat gave the reason and spoke the first stanza:

Why thus does Putimamsa stare?
His look misliketh me:
Of such a friend one should beware
And far away should flee.

With these words she turned about and made straight for her own abode. And the she-jackal failing to stop her was enraged with her, and went to her husband and sat down lamenting. Then the jackal rebuking her spoke the second stanza:

Veni, my wife, has lost her wit,
She boasts of friends that she has made;
Left in the lurch she can but sit
And grieve, by Mela's art betrayed.

On hearing this the she-jackal spoke the third stanza:
You too, my lord, were hardly wise,
And, witless creature, raised your head,
Staring about with open eyes,
Though feigning to be dead.

But the she-jackal comforted Putimamsa and said, "My lord do not vex yourself, I will find a way to bring her here again, and when she comes, be on your guard and catch her." Then she sought the goat and said, "My friend, your coming proved of service to us; for as soon as you appeared, my lord recovered consciousness, and he is now alive. Come and have friendly speech with him," and so saying she spoke the fifth stanza:
Our former friendship, goat, once more revive,
And come with well-filled bowl to us, I pray,
My lord I took for dead is still alive,
With kindly greeting visit him to-day.

The goat thought, "This wicked wretch wants to take me in. I must not act like an open foe; I will find means to deceive her," and she spoke the sixth stanza:
Our former friendship to revive,
A well-filled bowl I gladly give:
With a big escort I shall come:
To feast us well, go hasten home.

Then the she-jackal enquired about her followers, and spoke the seventh stanza:
What kind of escort will you bring,
That I am bid to feast you well?
The names of all remembering
To us, I pray you, truly tell.

The goat spoke the eighth stanza and said:

Hounds Grey and Tan, and Four-eyed too,
With Jambuk form my escort true:
Go hurry home, and quick prepare:
For all abundance of good fare.

"Each of these," she added, "is accompanied by five hundred dogs: so I shall appear with a guard of two thousand dogs. If they should not find food, they will kill and eat you and your mate." On hearing this the she-jackal was so frightened that she thought, "I have had quite enough of her coming to us; I will find means to stop her from coming," and she spoke the ninth stanza:

Don't leave your house, or else I fear
Your goods will all soon disappear:
I'll take your greeting to my lord;
Don't stir: nay, not another wore!

With these words she ran in great haste, as for her life, and taking her lord with her, fled away. And they never durst come back to the spot.

THE UNGRATEFUL SON

Once upon a time, when Brahmadatta was king of Benares, there was in a family of a certain village of Kasi an only son named Vasitthaka. This man supported his parents, and after his mother's death, he supported his father as has been described in the introduction. But there is this difference. When the woman said, "Look there! that is your father's doing! I am constantly begging him not to do this and that, and he only gets angry!" She went on, "My lord, your father is fierce and brash, for ever picking quarrels. A decrepit old man like that, tormented with disease, is bound to die soon; and I can't live in the same house with him. He will die of himself before many days are out; well, take him to a cemetery, and dig a pit, throw him in and break his head with the spade; and when he is dead, shovel the earth upon him, and leave him there." At last, by dint of this dinning in his ears, said he, "Wife, to kill a man is a serious matter: how can I do it?" "I will tell you of a way", quoth she—"Say on, then."—"Well, my lord, at break of day, go to the place where your father sleeps; tell him very loud, that all may hear, that a debtor of his is in a certain village, that you went and he would not pay you, and that if he dies the man will never pay at all; and say that you will both drive there together in the morning. Then at the appointed time get up, and put the animals to the cart and take him in it to the cemetery. When you get there, bury him in a pit, make a noise as if you had been robbed, wound and wash your head, and return." "Yes, that plan will do," said Vasitthaka. He agreed to her proposal, and got the cart ready for the journey.

Now the man had a son, a lad of seven years, but wise and clever. The lad overhead what his mother said. "My mother," thought he, "is a wicked woman, and is trying to persuade father to murder his father. I will prevent my father from doing this murder." He ran quickly, and lay down beside his grandsire. Vasitthaka, at the time suggested by the wife prepared the cart. "Come, father, let us get that debt!" said he, and placed his father in the cart. But the boy got in first of all. Vasitthaka could not prevent him, so he took him to the cemetery with them. Then, placing his father and his son together in a place apart, with the cart, he got down, took spade and basket, and in a spot where he was hidden from them began to dig a square hole. The boy got down, and followed him, and as though ignorant what was afoot, opened a conversation by repeating the first stanza:

No bulbs are here, no herbs for cooking meat,
No catmint, nor no other plant to eat.
Then father, why this pit, if need be none,
Devine in Death's acre mid the woods alone?

Then his father answered by repeating the second stanza:
Thy grandsire, son, is very weak and old,
Opprest by pain from ailments manifold:
Him will I bury in a pit to-day;
In such a life I could not wish him stay.

Hearing this, the boy answered by repeating a half stanza:
Thou hast done sinfully in wishing this

And for the deed, a cruel deed it is.

With these words, he caught the spade from his father's hands, and at no great distance began to dig another pit.

His father approaching asked why he dug that pit; to whom he made reply by finishing the third stanza:
I too, when thou art aged, father mine,
Will treat my father as thou treatest thine;
Following the custom of the family
Deep in a pit I too will bury thee.
To this the father replied by repeating the fourth stanza:
What a harsh saying for a boy to say,
And to upbraid a father in this way!
To think that my own son should rail at me,
And to his truest friend unkind should be!

When the father had thus spoken, the wise lad recited three stanzas, one by way of answer, and two as a solemn utterance:
I am not harsh, my father, nor unkind,
Nay, I regard thee with a friendly mind:
But this thou dost, this act of sin, thy son
Will have no strength to undo again, once done.
Whoso, Vasittha, hurts with ill intent
His mother or his father, innocent,
He, when the body is dissolved, shall be
In hell for his next life undoubtedly.
Whoso, with meal and drink, Vasittha, shall
His mother or his father feed withal,
He, when the body is dissolved, shall be
In heaven for his next life undoubtedly.

The father, after hearing his son thus discourse, repeated the eighth stanza:
Thou art no heartless ingrate, son, I see,
But kindly-hearted, O my son, to me;
'Twas is obedience to thy mother's word
I thought to do this horrid deed abhorred.

Said the lad, when he heard this, "Father, women, when a wrong is done and they are not rebuked, again and again commit sin. You must bend my mother, that she may never again do such a deed as this." And he repeated the ninth stanza:
That wife of yours, that ill-conditioned dame,
My mother, she that brought me forth—that same,
Let us from out our dwelling far expel,
Last she work other woe on thee as well.

Hearing the words of his wise son, well pleased was Vasitthaka, and saying, "Let us go, my son!" he seated himself in the cart with son and father and set off.

Now the woman too, this sinner, was happy at heart; for thought she, this ill-luck is out of the house now. She plastered the place with wet cowdung, and cooked a mess of rice porridge. But as she sat watching the road by which they would return, she espied them coming. "There he is, back with old ill-luck again!" thought she, much in anger. "Fie, good-for-nothing!" cried she, "what, bring back the ill-luck you took away with you!" Vasitthaka said not a word, but unyoked the cart. Then said he, "Wretch, what is that you say?" He gave her a sound drubbing, and bundled her head over heels out of doors, bidding her never darken his door again. Then he bathed his father and his son, and took a bath himself, and the three ate the rice porridge. The sinful woman dwelt for a few days in another house.

Then the son said to his father: "Father, for all this my mother does not understand. Now let us try to vex her. You give out that in such and such a village lives a niece of yours, who will attend upon your father and your son and you; so you will go and fetch her. Then take flowers and perfumes, set off with your cart, and ride about country all day, returning in the evening." And so he did. The women in the neighbour's family told his wife this— "Have you heard," said they, "that your husband has gone to get another wife in such a place?" "Ah, then I am undone!" quoth she, "and there is no place for me left!" But she would enquire of her son; so quickly she came to

him, and fell at his feet, crying— "Save thee I have no other
refuge! Henceforward I will tend your father and grandsire as
I would tend a beauteous shrine! Give me entrance into this
house once more!" "Yes, mother," replied the lad, "If you do no
more as you did, I will; be in earnest!" and at his father's coming
he repeated the tenth stanza:

That wife of yours, that ill-conditioned dame,
My mother, she that brought me forth,—that same,—

Like tamed elephant, in full control,
Let her return again, that sinful soul.

So said he to his father, and then went and summoned his
mother. She being reconciled to her husband and the father,
was thenceforward tamed, and endued with righteousness, and
watched over her husband and his father and her son; and
these two, steadfastly following their son's advice, gave alms
and did good deeds, and became destined hosts of heaven.

THE TEN SLAVE- BRETHREN

Once upon a time, a king named Mahakamsa reigned in
Uttarapatha, in the Kamsa district, in the city of Asitanjana. He
had two sons, Kamsa and Upakamsa, and one daughter named
Devagabbha. On her birthday the Brahmins skilled in omens
foretold of her: "A son born of this girl will one day destroy the
country and the lineage of Kamsa. The king was too fond of the
girl to put her to death; but leaving her brothers to settle it,
lived his days out, and then died. When he died Kamsa became
king, and Upakamsa was viceroy. They thought that there would
be an outcry were they to put their sister to death, so resolved
to give her in marriage to none, but to keep her husbandless,
and watch; and they built a single round-tower, for her to live
in.

Now she had a serving-woman named Nandagopa, and the
woman's husband, Andhakavenhu, was the servant who watched
her. At that time a king named Mahasagara reigned in Upper
Madhura, and he had two sons, Sagara and Upasagara. At their

father's death, Sagara became king, and Upsagara was viceroy. This lad was Upakamsa's friend brought up together with him and trained by the same teacher. But he intrigued in his brother's zenana, and being detected, ran away to Upakamsa in the Kamsa estate. Upakamsa introduced him to king Kamsa, and the king had him in great honour.

Upasagara while waiting upon the king observed the tower where dwelt Devagabbha; and on asking who lived there, heard the story, and fell in love with the girl. And Devagabbha one day saw him as he went with Upakamsa to wait upon the king. She asked who that was and being told by Nandagopa that is was Upasagara, son of the great king Sagara, she too fell in love with him. Upasagara gave a present to Nandagopa, saying, "Sister, you can arrange a meeting for me with Devagabbha." "Easy enough," quoth Nandagopa, and told the girl about it. She being already in love with him, agreed at once. One night Nandagopa arranged a tryst, and brought Upasagara up into the tower; and there he stayed with Devagabbha. And by their constant intercourse, Devagabbha conceived. By and by when the affair became known, the two brothers questioned Nandagopa. She made them promise her pardon, and then told the ins and outs of the matter. When they heard the story they thought," We cannot put our sister to death. If she bears a daughter, we will spare the babe also; if a son will kill him." And they gave Devagabbha to Upasagara to wife.

When her full time was come, she gave birth to a daughter. The brothers on hearing this were delighted, and gave her the name of the Lady Anjana. And they allotted to them a village for their estate, named Govaddhamana. Upasagara took Devagabbha and lived with her at the village of Govaddhamana.

Devagabbha was again with child, and that very day Nandagopa conceived also. When their time was come, they brought forth on the same day, Devagabbha a son and Nandagopa a daughter. But Devagabbha, in fear that her son might be put to death, sent him secretly to Nandagopa, and received Nandagopa's daughter in return. They told the brothers of the birth. "Son or daughter?" they asked. "Daughter," was the reply. "Then see that it is reared," said the brothers. In the same way Devagabbha bore ten sons and Nandagopa ten daughters. The sons lived with Nandagopa and the daughters with Devagabbha, and not a soul knew the secret.

The eldest son of Devagabbha was named Vasudeva, the second Baladeva, the third Candadeva, the fourth Suriyadeva, the fifth Aggideva, the sixth Varunadeva, the seventh Ajjuna, the eight Pajjuna, the ninth Ghatapandita, the tenth Amkura. They were well known as the sons of Andhakavenhu the servitor the Ten Slave-Brethren.

In course of time they grew big, and being very strong, and withal fierce and ferocious, they went about plundering, they even went so far as to plunder a present being conveyed to the king. The people came crowding in the king's court yard, complaining. "Andhakavenhu's sons, the Ten Brethern, are plundering the land!" So the king summoned Andakavenhu, and rebuked him for permitting his sons to plunder. In the same way complaint was made three or four times, and the king threatened him. He being in fear of his life craved the boon of safety from the king, and told the secret, that how these were no sons of his, but of Upasagara. The king was alarmed. "How can we get hold of them?" he asked his courtiers. They replied," Sire, they are wrestlers. Let us hold a wrestling match in the city, and when they enter the ring we will catch them and put them to death." So they sent for two wrestlers, Canura and Mutthika, and caused proclamation to be made throughout the city by beat of drum, that on the seventh day there would be a wrestling match.

The wrestling ring was prepared in front of the king's gate; there was an enclosure for the games, the ring was decked out gaily, the flags of victory were ready tied. The whole city was in a whirl; line over line rose the seats, tier above tier, Canura and Mutthika went down into the ring, and strutted about jumping, shouting, clapping their hands. The Ten Brethren came too. On their way they plundered the washermen's street, and

clad themselves in robes of bright colours, and stealing perfume
from the perfumers' shops, and wreaths of flowers from the
florists, with their bodies all anointed, garlands upon their heads,
earrings in their ears, they strutted into the ring, jumping,
shouting, clapping their hands.

At the moment, Canura was walking about clapping his
hands. Baladeva, seeing him, thought, "I won't touch yon fellow
with my hand!" so catching up a think strap from the elephant
stable, jumping and shouting he threw it round Canura's belly,
and joining the ends together, brought them tight, then lifting
him up, swung him round over his head, and dashing him on
the ground rolled him outside the arena. When Canura was
dead, the king sent for Mutthika. Up got Mutthika, jumping,
shouting, clapping his hands. Baladeva smote him, and crushed
in his eyes; and as he cried out—"I'm no wrestler! I'm no
wrestler!" Baladeva tied his hands together, saying, "Wrestler
or no wrestler, it is all one to me," and dashing him down on the
ground killed him and threw him outside the arena.

Mutthika in his death-throes, uttered a prayer—"May I
become a goblin, and devour him!" And he became a goblin, in
a forest called by the name of Kalamattiya. The king said, "Take
away the Ten Slave-Brethren." At that moment, Vasudeva threw
a wheel, which lopped off the heads of the two brothers. The
crowd, terrified, fell at his feet, and besought him to be their
protector.

Thus the Ten Brethren, having slain their two uncles,
assumed the sovereignty of the city of Asitanjana, and brought
their parents thither.

They now set out, intending to conquer all India. In a while
they arrived at the city of Ayojjha, the seat of king Kalasena.
This they encompassed about, and destroyed the jungle around
it, breached the wall and took the king prisoner, and took the
sovereignty of the place into their hands. Thence they proceeded
to Dvaravati. Now this city had on one side the sea and on one
the mountains. They say that the place was goblin-haunted. A

goblin would be stationed on the watch, who seeing his enemies, in the shape of an ass would bray as the ass brays. At once, by goblin magic the whole city used to rise in the air, and deposit itself on an island in the midst of the sea; when the foe was gone, it would come back and settle in its own place again. This time, as usual, no sooner the ass saw those Ten Brethren coming, than he brayed with the bray of an ass. Up arose the city in the air, and settled upon the island. No city could they see, and turned back; then back came the city to its own place again. They returned—again the ass did as before. The sovereignty of the city of Dvaravati they could not take.

So they visited Kanhadipayana, and said: "Sir, we have failed to capture the kingdom of Dvaravati; tell us how to do it." He said: "In a ditch, in such a place, is an ass walking about. He brays when he sees an enemy, and immediately the city arises in the air. You must clasp hold of his feet, and that is the way to accomplish your end." Then they took leave of the ascetic; and went all ten of them to the ass, and falling at his feet, said, "Sir, we have no help but thee! When we come to take the city, do not bray!" The ass replied," I cannot help braying. But if you come first, and four of you bring great iron ploughs, and at the four gates of the city dig great iron posts into the ground, and when the city begins to rise, if you will fix on the post a chain of iron fastened to the plough, the city will not be able to rise." They thanked him; and he did not utter a sound while they got ploughs, and fixed the posts in the ground at the four gates of the city, and stood waiting. Then the ass brayed, the city began to rise but those who stood at the four gates with the four ploughs, having fixed to the posts iron chains which were fastened to the ploughs, the city could not rise. Thereupon the Ten Brethren entered the city, killed the king, and took his kingdom.

Thus they conquered all India, and in three and sixty thousand cities they slew by the wheel all the kings of them, and lived at Dvaravati, dividing the kingdom into ten shares. But they had forgotten their sister, the Lady Anjana. So "Let us make eleven shares of it," said they. But Amkura answered,

"Give her my share, and I will take to some business for a living; only you must remit my taxes each in your own country." They consented, and gave his share to his sister; and with her they dwelt in Dvaravati, nine kings, while Amkura embarked in trade.

In come of time, they were all increased with sons and with daughters; and after a long time had gone by, their parents died. At that period, they say that a man's life was twenty thousand years.

Then died one dearly beloved son of the great King Vasudeva. The king, half dead with grief, neglected everything, and lay lamenting, and clutching the frame of his bed. Then Ghatapandita thought to himself, "Except me, no one else is able to soothe my brother's grief; I will find some means of soothing his grief for him." So assuming the appearance of madness, he paced through the whole city, gazing up at the sky, and crying out, "Give me a hare! Give me a hare!" All the city was excited: "Ghatapandita has gone mad!" they said. Just then a courtier named Rohineyya, went into the presence of King Vasudeva, and opened a conversation with him by reciting the first stanza:

Black Kanha rise! why close the eyes to sleep? why Lying there?
Thine own born brother—see, the winds away his wit, do bear,
Away his wisdom! Ghata raves, thou of the long black hair!

Up rose the king, and quickly came down from his chamber; and proceeding to Ghatapandita, he got fast hold of him with both hands; and speaking to him, uttered the third stanza:

In maniac fashion, why do you pace Dvaraka all through,
And cry, "Hare, hare!" Say, who is there has taken a hare from you?

To these words of the king, he only answered by repeating the same cry over and over again. But the king recited two more stanzas:

Be it of gold, or made of jewels fine,

Or brass, or silver, as you may incline,
Shell, stone, or coral, I declare
I'll make a hare.
And many other hares there be,
that range the woodland wide,
They shall be brought,
I'll have them caught: say, which do you decide?

On hearing the king's words, the wise man replied by
repeating the sixth stanza:
I crave no hare of earthly kind, but that within the moon:
O bring him down, O Kesava! I ask no other boon!

"Undoubtedly my brother has gone mad, "thought the king,
when he heard this. In great grief, he repeated the seventh
stanza:
In sooth, my brother, you will die, if you make such a prayer,
And ask for what no man may pray, the moon's celestial
hare.

Ghatapandita, on hearing the king's answer, stood stock
still, and said: "My brother, you know that if a man prays for the
hare in the moon, and cannot get it, he will die; then why do
you mourn for your dead son?

If, Kanha, this you know, and can console another's woe,
Why are you mourning still the son who died so long ago?"

Then he went on, standing there in the street—"And I
brother, pray only for what exists, but you are mourning for
what does not exist." Then he instructed him by repeating two
more stanzas:
My son is born, let him not die! Nor man nor deity
Can have that boon; then wherefore pray for what can
never be?
Nor mystic charm, nor magic roots, nor herbs, nor money
spent,
Can bring to life again that ghost whom, Kanha, you
lament.

The king, on hearing this, answered, "Your reminder was good, dear one. You did it to take away my trouble." Then in praise of Ghatapandita he repeated four stanzas:

Men had I, wise and excellent to give me good advice:
But how hath Ghatapandita opened this day mine eyes!
Blazing was I, as when a man pours oil upon a fire;
Thou didst bring water, and didst quench the pain of my
                                                    desire.
Grief for my son, a cruel shaft was lodged within my heart;
Thou hast consoled me for my grief, and taken out the
                                                    dart.
That dart extracted, free from pain, tranquil, and calm I
                                                    keep;
Hearing, O youth, thy words of truth, no more I grieve nor
                                                    weep.

In this manner was Vasudeva consoled by Prince Ghata.

After the laps of a long time, during which he ruled his kingdom, the sons of the ten brethren thought: "They say that Kanhadipayana is possessed for the divine eye. Let us put him to the test." So they procured a young lad, and dressed him up, and by binding a pillow about his belly, made it appear as though he were with child. Then they brought him into his presence, and asked him, "To what, sir, will this girl give birth?" The ascetic perceived that the time has come for the destruction of the royal brothers; then, looking to see what the term of his own life should be, he perceived that he must die that very day. Then he said, "Young sirs, what is this man to you?" "Answer us," they replied persistently. He answered, "This man on the seventh day from now will bring forth a knot of acacia wood. With that he will destroy the line of Vasudeva, even though ye should take the piece of wood and burn it, and cast the ashes into the river." "Ah, false ascetic!" said they, "a man can never bring forth a child!" and they did the rope and string business, and killed him at once. The kings sent for the young men, and asked them why they had killed the ascetic. When they heard all, they were frightened. They set a guard upon the man; and when on the seventh day, he voided from his belly a knot of acacia wood, they burnt it, and cast the ashes into the river. The ashes floated down the river, and struck on one side by a postern gate; from thence sprung an eraka plant.

One day the kings proposed that they should go and disport themselves in the water. So to this postern gate they came; and they caused a great pavilion to be made, and in that gorgeous pavilion they ate and drank. Then in sport they began to catch hold of hand and foot, and dividing into two parts, they became very quarrelsome. At last one of them, finding nothing better for a club, picked a leaf from the eraka plant, which even as he plucked it became a club of acacia wood in his hand. With this he beat many people. Then the others plucked also, and the things as they took them became clubs, and with them they cudgeled one another until they were killed. As these were destroying each other, four only—Vasudeva, Baladeva, the lady Anjana their sister, and the family priest—mounted a chariot and fled away; the rest perished, every one.

Now these four, fleeing away in the chariot, came to the forest of Kalamattika. There Mutthika the Wrestler had been born, having become according to his prayer a goblin. When he perceived the coming of Baladeva, he created a village in that spot; and taking the semblance of wrestler, he went jumping about, and shouting, "Who's for a fight?" snapping his fingers the while. Baladeva, as soon as he saw him, said, "Brother, I'll try a fall with this fellow." Vasudeva tried and tried his best to prevent him; but down he got from the chariot, and went up to him, snapping his fingers. The other just seized him in the hollow of his hand, and gobbled him up like a radish-bulb. Vasudeva perceiving that he was dead, went on all night long with his sister and the priest, and at sunrise arrived at a frontier village. He lay down in the shelter of a bush, and sent his sister and the priest into the village, with others to cook some food and bring it to him. A huntsman (his name was Jara, or Old Age) noticed the bush shaking. "A pig, sure enough," thought he; he threw a spear, and pierced his feet. "Who has wounded me?" cried out Vasudeva. The huntsman, finding that he had wounded a man, set off running in terror. The king, recovering his wits, got up, and called the huntsman—"Uncle, come here, don't be afraid!" When he came—"Who are you?" asked Vasudeva. "My name is Jara, my lord." "Ah," thought the king, "whom Old Age wounds will die, so the ancients used to say. Without doubt I must die to-day." Then he said, "Fear not, Uncle; come bind up my wound." The mouth of the wound bound up, the king let him go. Great pains came upon him; he could not eat the food that the others brought. Then addressing himself to the others, Vasudeva said: "This day I am to die. You are delicate creatures, and will never be able to earn anything else for a living; so learn this science from me." So saying, he taught them a science, and let them go; and then died immediately.

Thus excepting the lady Anjana, they perished every one, tis said.

RAMA AND SITA

Once upon a time, at Benares, a great king named Dasaratha renounced the ways of evil, and reigned in righteousness. Of his sixteen thousand wives, the eldest and queen-consort bore him two sons; the elder son was named Ramapandita, or Rama the Wise, the second was named Prince Lakkhana, or Lucky.

In course of time, the queen-consort died. At her death the king was for a long time crushed by sorrow, but urged by his courtiers he performed her obsequies, and set another in her place as queen-consort. She was dear to the king and beloved. In time she also conceived, and all due attention having been given her, she brought forth a son, and they named him Prince Bharata.

The king loved his son much, and said to the queen, "Lady, I offer you a boon: choose." She accepted the offer, but put it off for the time. When the lad was seven years old, she went to the king, and said to him, "My lord, you promised a boon for my son. Will you give it to me now?" "Choose, lady," said he. "My lord," quoth she, "give my son the kingdom." The king snapt his fingers at her; "Out, vile jade!" said he angrily, " my other two

sons shine like blazing fires; would you kill them, and ask the
kingdom for a son of your?" She fled in terror to her magnificent
chamber, and on other days again and again asked the king the
same. The king would not give her this gift. He thought within
himself: "Women are ungrateful and treacherous. This woman
might use a forged letter or a treacherous bribe to get my sons
murdered." So he sent for his sons, and told them all about it,
saying: "My sons, if you live here some mischief may befall you.
Go to some neighbouring kingdom, or to the woodland, and
when my body is burnt, then return and inherit the kingdom
which belongs to your family." Then he summoned soothsayers,
and asked them the limits of his own life. They told him he
would live yet twelve years longer. Then he said, "Now my sons,
after twelve years you must return, and uplift the umbrella of
royalty." They promised, and after taking leave of their father,
went forth from the palace weeping.

These three departed amidst a great company of people.
They sent the people back, and proceeded until at last they
came to Himalaya. There in the spot well-watered, and
convenient for the getting of wild fruits, they built a hermitage,
and there lived, feeding upon the wild fruits.

Lakkhana-pandita said to Rama-pandita, "You are in place
of a father to me; remain then in the hermitage, and I will bring
fruits, and feed you." He agreed. Thenceforward Rama-pandita
stayed where he was; Lakkhana-pandita brought the fruits and
fed him.

Thus they lived there, feeding upon the wild fruit; but King
Dasaratha pined after his sons, and died in the ninth year. When
his obsequies were performed, the queen gave orders that the
umbrella should be raised over her son, Prince Bharata. But the
courtiers said, "The lords of the umbrella are dwelling in the
forest, and they would not allow it." Said Prince Bharata, "I will
fetch back my brother Rama-pandita from the forest, and raise
the royal umbrella over him." Taking the five emblems of royalty,
he proceeded with a complete host of the four arms to their
dwelling-place. Not far away he caused camp to be pitched,

and then with a few courtiers he visited the hermitage, at the
time when Lakkhana-pandita was away in the woods. At the
door of the hermitage sat Rama-pandita, undismayed and at
ease, like figure of fine gold firmly set. The prince approached
him with a greeting, and standing on one side, told him of all
that had happened in the kingdom, and falling at his feet along
with the courtiers, burst into weeping. Rama-pandita neither
sorrowed nor wept; he showed no change of feeling. When
Bharata had finished weeping, and sat down, towards evening
Lakkhana-pandita returned with wild fruits. Rama-pandita
thought— "He is young: all-comprehensive wisdom like mine is
not his. If he is told on a sudden that our father is dead, the pain
will be greater than he can bear, and who knows but his heart
may break. I will find a device to persuade him to go down in
to the water, and then tell him the news." Then pointing out to
him a place in front where there was water, he said, "You have
been out too long: let this be your penance-go into that water,
and stand there." Then he repeated a half-stanza:
Let Lakkhana into that pond descend.

One word sufficed, into the water he went, and stood there.
Then he told him the news by repeating the other half-stanza:
Bharata says king Dasaratha's life is at an end.

When he heard the news of his father's death, he fainted.
Again he repeated it, again he fainted, and when even a third
time he fainted away, the courtiers raised him and brought him
out of the water, and set him upon dry ground. When he had
been comforted, they all sat weeping and wailing together.
Then prince Bharata thought: "My brother Prince Lakkhana
cannot restrain his grief to hear of our father's death; but Rama-
pandita neither wails nor weeps. I wonder what can the reason
be that he grieves not? I will ask." Then he repeated the second
stanza asking the question:
Say by what power thou grievest not, Rama, when grief
                                            should be?

Though it is said thy sire is dead grief overwhelms not
                                                    thee!

Then Rama-pandita explained the reason of his not grieving by saying,

When man can never keep a thing, though loudly he may
cry,
Why should a wise intelligence torment itself thereby?
The young in years, the older grown, the fool, and eke the
wise,
For rich, for poor one end is sure: each man among them
dies.
As sure as for the ripened fruit there comes the fear of fall,
So surely comes the fear of death to mortals one and all.
Who in the morning light are seen by evening oft are gone,
And seen at evening time, is gone by morning many a one.
If to a fool infatuate a blessing could accrue
When he torments himself with tears, the wise this same
would do.
By this tormenting of himself he waxes thin and pale;
This cannot bring the dead to life, and nothing tears avail.
Even as a blazing house may be put out with water, so
The strong, the wise, the intelligent, who well the scrip
tures know,
Scatter their grief like cotton when the stormy winds do
blow.
One mortal dies—to kindred ties born is another straight:
Each creature's bliss dependent is on ties associate.
The strong man therefore, skilled in sacred text,
Keen-contemplating this world and the next,
Knowing their nature, not by any grief,
However great, in mind and heart is vext.
So to my kindred I will give, them will I keep and feed,
All that remain I will maintain: such is the wise man's
deed.

In these stanzas he explained the Impermanence of things.

When the company heard this discourse of Rama-pandita, illustrating the doctrine of impermanence, they lost all their grief.

"Brother," said Rama, "take Lakkhanna with you and administer the kingdom your selve." "No, my lord, you take it." "Brother, my father commanded me to receive the kingdom at the end of twelve years. If I go now, I shall not carry out his bidding. After three more years I will come." "Who will carry on the government all that time?" "You do it." "I will not." "Then until I come, these slippers shall do it, " said Rama, and doffing his slippers of straw he gave them to his brother. So these persons took the slippers, and bidding the wise man farewell, went to Benares with their great crowd of followers.

For three years the slippers ruled the kingdom. The courtiers placed these straw slippers upon the royal throne, when they judged a cause. If the cause were decided wrongly, the slippers beat upon each other, and at that sign it was examined again; when the decision was right, the slippers lay quiet.

When the three years were over, the wise man came out of the forest, and came to Benares, and entered the park. The princes hearing of his arrival proceeded with a great company to the park, and making Sita the queen-consort, gave to them both the ceremonial sprinkling. The sprinkling thus performed, the Great Being, standing in a magnificent chariot, and surrounded by a vast company, entered the city, making a solemn circuit rightwise; then mounting to the great terrace of his splendid palace Sucandaka, he reigned there in righteousness for sixteen thousand years, and then went to swell the hosts of heaven.

THE WICKED STEP-MOTHER

Once upon a time, When Brahmadatta was king of Benares, the Bodhisatta was born as the son of his chief queen; and because his all-blessed countenance was like a lotus full-blown, Paduma-Kumara they named him, which is to say, the Lotus Prince. When he grew up he was educated in all arts and accomplishments. Then his mother departed this life; the king took another consort, and appointed his son viceroy

After this the king, being about to set forth to quell a rising on the frontier, said to his consort, "Do you lady, stay here, while I go forth to quell the frontier insurrection." But she replied, "No, my lord, here I will not remain, but I will go with you." Then he showed her the danger which lay on the field of battle, adding to it this: "Stay then here without vexation until my return, and I will give charge to Prince Paduma, that he be careful in all that should be done for you, and then I will go." So thus he did, and departed.

When he had scattered his enemies, and pacified the country, he returned, and pitched his camp without the city. The Bodhisatta learning of his father's return adorned the city, and setting a watch over the royal palace, went forth alone to meet his father. The queen observing the beauty of his appearance, became enamoured of him. In taking leave of her, the Bodhisatta said, "Can I do anything for you, mother?" "Mother, do you call me?" quoth she. She rose up and seized his hands, saying, "Lie on my couch!" "Why?" he asked. "Just until the king comes," she said, "let us both enjoy the bliss of love!" "Mother, my mother you are, and you have a husband living. Such a thing I have never before seen, that a woman, a matron, should break the moral law in the way of fleshly lust. How can I do such a deed with you?" Twice and thrice she besought him, and when he would not, said she, "Then you refuse to do as I ask?" — "Indeed I do refuse." — "Then I will speak to the king, and cause you to be beheaded." "Do as you will," answered the Great Being; and having shamed her he left her. Then in fear she thought: "If he tells the king first, there is no life for me! I must get speech of him first myself." Accordingly leaving her food untouched she donned a soiled robe, and made nail-scratches upon her body; giving orders to her attendants, that when the king should ask of the queen's whereabouts, he should be told she was ill, she lay down making a pretence of illness.

Now the king made solemn procession about the city rightwise, and went up into his dwelling. When he saw her not, he asked, "Where is the queen?" "She is ill," they said. He entered the state chamber, and asked her, "What is amiss with

you, lady?" She made as though she heard nothing. Twice and
yet thrice he asked, and then she answered, "O great king, why
do you ask? Be silent: woman that have a husband must be even
as I am." "Who has annoyed you?" said he. "Tell me quickly, and
I will have him beheaded."—"Whom did you leave behind you
in this city, when you went away?"—"Prince Paduma." "And
he, "she went on, "came into my room, and I said, "My son, do
not so, I am your mother': but say what I would, he cried, 'None
is king here but me, and I will take you to my dwelling, and
enjoy your love'; then he seized me by the hair of my head, and
plucked it out again and again, and as I would not yield to his
will, he wounded and beat me, and departed." The king made
no investigation, but furious as a serpent, commanded his men,
"Go and bind Prince Paduma, and bring him to me!" They went
to his house, swarming as it were through the city, and bound
him and beat him, bound his hands fast behind his back, put
about his neck the garland of red flowers, making him a
condemned criminal, and led him thither, beating him the while.
It was clear to him that this was the queen's doing, and as he
went along he cried out, "Ho fellows, I am not one that has
offended against the king! I am innocent." All the city was a-
bubble with the news: "They say the king is going to execute
Prince Paduma at the bidding of a woman!" They flocked
together, they fell at the prince's feet, lamenting with a great
voice, "You have not deserved this, my lord!"

    At last they brought him before the king. At sight of him,
the king could not restrain what was in his heart, and cried out,
"This fellow is no king, but he plays the king finely! My son he
is, yet he has insulted the queen. Away with him, down with
him over the thieves' cliff, make an end of him!" But the prince
said to his father, "No such crime lies at my door, father. Do not
kill me on a woman's word." The king would not listen to him.
Then all those of the royal seraglio, in number sixteen thousand,
raised a great lamentation, saying, "Dear Paduma, mighty Prince,
the dealing you have never deserved!" And all the warrior
chiefs and great magnates of the land, and all the attendant
courtiers cried, "My lord! the prince is a man of goodness and
virtuous life, observes the traditions of his race, heir to the

kingdom! Do not slay him at a woman's word, without a hearing!
A king's duty it is to act with all circumspection." So saying,
they repeated seven stanzas;

No king should punish an offence, and hear no pleas at all,
Not thoroughly sifting it himself in all points, great and
small.
The warrior chief who punishes a fault before he tries,
Is like a man born blind, who eats his food all bones and
flies.
Who punishes the guiltless, and lets go the guilty, knows
No more than one who blind upon a ragged highway goes.
He who all this examines well, in things both great and
small,
And so administers, deserves to be the head of all.
He that would set himself on high must not all-gentle be
Nor all-server: but both these things pracitse in company.
Contempt the all-gentle wins, and he that's all-severe has
wrath:
So of the pair be well aware, and keep a middle path.
Much can the angry man, O king, and much the knave can
say:
And therefore for a woman's sake thy son thou must not
slay.

But for all they could say in many ways the courtiers could
not win him to do their bidding. The Bodhisatta also, for all his
beseeching, could not persuade him to listen: nay, the king,
blind fool, said—"Away! down with him over the thieves' cliff !"
repeating the eighth stanza:

One side the whole world stands, my queen on the other
all alone;
Yet her! cleave to : cast him down the cliff, and get you
gone!

At these words, not one among the sixteen thousand
women could remain unmoved, while all the populace stretched
out their hands, and tore their hair, with lamentations. The king
said, "Let these but try to prevent the throwing of this fellow
over the cliff !" and amidst his followers, though the crowd

wailed around, he caused the prince to be seized, and cost down the precipice over heels head-first.

Then owing to the magic power due to his practice of friendliness the deity of the hill comforted the prince, saying, "Fear not, Paduma !" and in both hands he caught him, pressed him to his heart, sent a divine thrill through him, set him in the abode of the nagas of the eight ranges, within the hood of the naga-king. The king received the Bodhisatta into the abode of the nagas, and gave him the half of his own glory and State. There for one year he dwelt. Then he said, "I would go back to the ways of men." "Whither?" they asked. "To Himalaya, where I will become an ascetic." The naga-king gave his consent; taking him, he conveyed him to the place where men go to and fro, and gave him the requisites of an ascetic, and went back to his own place.

So he proceeded to Himalaya, became a hermit-sage, and cultivated the faculty of ecstatic bliss; there he abode, feeding upon fruits and roots of the woodland.

Now a certain wood-ranger, who dwelt in Benares, came to that place, and recognized the Great Being. "Are you not," he asked, "the great Prince Paduma, my lord?" "Yes sir," he replied. The other saluted him, and there for some days he remained. Then he returned to Benares; and said to the king, "Your son, my lord, has embraced the religious life in the region of Himalaya, and lives in a hut of leaves. I have been staying with him, and thence I come." "Have you seen him with your own eyes?" asked the king. "Yes, my lord." The king with a great host went thither, and on the outskirts of the forest he pitched his camp; then with his courtiers around him, went to salute the Great Being, who sat at the door of his hut of leaves, in all the glory of his golden form, and sat on one side; the courtiers also greeted him, and spoke pleasantly to him, and sat on one side. The Bodhisatta on his part invited the king to share his wild fruits, and talked pleasantly with him. Then said the king, "My son, by me you were cast down a deep precipice, and how is it you are yet alive?" Asking which, he repeated the ninth stanza:

As into hell-mouth, you were cast over a beetling hill,
No succour—many palm trees deep: how are you living
Still?

These are the remaining stanzas, and of the five, taken
alternately, three were spoken by the Bodhisatta, and two by
the king.

A naga mighty, full of force, born on that mountain land,
Caught me within his coils; and so here safe from death
I stand.
Lo! I will take you back, O prince, to my own home again:
And there — What is the wood to you? —with blessing
you shall reign.
As who a hook has swallowed, and draws it forth all blood,
Drawn forth, is happy: so I see in me this bliss and good.
Why speak you thus about a hook, why speak you thus of
gore,
Why speak about the drawing out? Come tell me, I implore.
Lust is the hook: fine elephants and horse by blood I show;
These by renouncing I have drawn; this, chieftain, you
must know.

"Thus, O great king, to be king is nothing to me; but do you
see to it, that you break not the Ten Royal Virtues, but forsake
evil-doing, and rule in righteousness." In those words the Great
Being admonished the king. He with weeping and wailing
departed, and on the way to his city he asked his courtiers, "On
whose account was it that I made a breach with a son so
virtuous?" they replied, "The queen's." Her the king caused to
be seized, and cast headlong over the thieves' cliff, and entering
his city ruled in righteousness.

THE LOST CHARM

Once upon a time, when Brahmadatta was king of Benares,
the family of his household priest was destroyed by malarial
fever. One son only broke through the wall and escaped. He
came to Takkasila, and under a world-renowned teacher learnt
the Vedas and the other arts. Then he bade his teacher farewell,

and departed, with the intent to travel in different regions; and on his travels he arrived at a frontier village. Near to this was a great village of low-caste Candalas. Then the Bodhisatta abode in this village, a learned sage. A charm he knew which could make fruit to be gathered out of due season. Early of a morning he would take his carrying pole, forth from that village he would go, until he reached a mango tree which grew in the forest; and standing seven foot off, he would recite that charm, and throw a handful of water so as to strike on that tree. In a twinkling down fall the sere leaves, sprout forth the new, flowers blow and flowers fall, the mango fruits swell out: but one moment—they are ripe, they are sweet and luscious, they grow like fruit divine, they drop from the tree! The Great Being chooses and eats such as he will, then fills the baskets hung from his pole, goes home and sells the fruit, and so finds a living for wife and child.

Now the young brahmin saw the Great Being offer ripe mangoes for sale out of season. "Without doubt," thought he, "It must be by virtue of some charm that these are grown. This man can teach me a charm which has no price." He watched to see the manner in which the Great Being procured his fruit, and found it out exactly. Then he went to the Great Being's house at the time when he was not yet returned from the forest, and making as though he knew nothing, asked the wise man's wife, "Where is the Teacher?" Quoth she, "Gone to the woods." He stood waiting until he saw him come, then went to him, and taking the pole and baskets from him, carried them into the house and there set them. The Great Being looked at him, and said to his wife, "Lady this youth has come to get the charm; but no charm will stay with him, for no goodman is he." But the youth was thinking, "I will get the charm by being my teacher's servant"; and so from that time he did all that was to be done in the house; brought wood, pounded the rice, did the cooking, brought all that was needed for washing the face, washed the feet.

One day when the Great Being said to him, "My son, bring me a stool to support my feet," the youth, seeing no other way, kept the Great Teacher's feet on his own thigh all night. When at a later season the Great Being's wife brought forth a son, he did all the service that has to be done at a childbirth. The wife said one day to the Great Being: — "Husband, this lad, well-born though he is, for the charm's sake performs menial service for us. Let him have the charm, whether it stays with him or no." To this he agreed. He taught him the charm, and spoke after this fashion: "My son, 'tis a priceless charm; and you will get great gain and honour thereby. But when the king, or his great minister, shall ask you who was your teacher, do not conceal my name; for if you are ashamed that a low-caste man taught you the charm, and say your teacher was a great magnate of the brahmins, you will have no fruit of the charm." "Why should I hide your name?" quoth the lad. "Whenever I am asked, I shall say it is you." Then he saluted his teacher, and from the low caste village he departed pondering on the charm, and in due time came to Benares. There he sold mangoes, and gained much wealth.

Now on a day the keeper of the park presented to the king a mango which he had bought from him. The king, having eaten it, asked whence he procured so fine a fruit. "My lord" was the answer, "there is a young man who brings mangoes out of season, and sells them: from him I procured it." "Tell him", says the king. "from henceforth to bring the mangoes hither tome." This the man did; and from that time the young man took his mangoes to the king's household. The king, inviting him to enter his service, he became a servant of the king; and gaining great wealth, by degrees he grew into the king's confidence.

One day the king asked him, and said: — "Young man, where do you get these mangoes out of season, so sweet and fragrant and of fine colour? Does some naga or garula give them to you, or a god, or is this the power of magic?" "No one gives them to me, O mighty king!" replied the young man, "but I have a priceless charm, and this is the power of the charm." "Well then we should like to see the power of the charm one of these days." "By all means, lord, I will show it, " quoth he. Next day the king went with him into the park, and asked to be shown this charm. The young man was willing, and approaching a mango tree, stood at a distance of seven foot from it, and repeated the charm, throwing water against the tree. On the instant the mango tree had fruit in the manner above described: a shower of mangoes fell, a very storm; the company showed great delight, waving their kerchiefs; the king ate of the fruit, and gave him a great reward, and said, "Young man, who taught you this charm so marvellous?" Now thought the young man, "If I say a low-caste candala taught me, I shall be put to shame, and they will flout at me; I know the charm by heart and now I can never lose it; well, I will say it was a world-renowned teacher." So he lied, and said, "I learnt it at Takkasila, from a teacher renowned the wide world over." As he said the words, denying his teacher, that very instant the charm was gone. But the king, greatly pleased, returned with him into the city.

On another day the king desired mangoes to eat; and going into the park, and taking his seat upon a stone bench, which was used on state occasions, he bade the youth get him mangoes. The youth, willing enough, went up to a mango tree, and standing at a distance of seven foot from the tree, set about repeating the charm; but the charm would not come. Then he knew that he had lost it, and stood there ashamed. But the king thought, "Formerly this fellow gave me mangoes even in the midst of a crowd, and like heavy shower rained the fruit down. Now there he stands like a stock: What can the reason be?" Which he enquired by repeating the first stanza:

Young student, when I asked it you of late,
You brought me mango fruit both small and great:
Now no fruit, Brahmin, on the tree appears,
Though the same charm you still reiterate.

When he heard this, the young man thought to himself, if he should say this day no fruit was to be had, the king would be wroth; wherefore he thought to deceive him with a lie, and repeated the second stanza:

The hour and moment suit not: so wait I
Fit junction of the planets in the sky.
The due conjunction and the moment come,

Then will I bring you mangoes plenteously.

"What is this," the king wondered, "The fellow said nothing
of planetary conjunctions before!" To resolve which questions,
he repeated two stanzas:

You said no word of times and seasons nor
Of planetary junctions heretofore:
But mangoes, fragrant, delicate I taste,
Of colour fine, you brought in plenteous store.
Aforetime, Brahmin, you produced so well
Fruit on the tree by muttering of your spell:
To-day you cannot, mutter as you may.
What means this conduct, I would have you tell?

Hearing this, the youth thought, "There is no deceiving
the king with lies. If, when the truth is told, he punishes me, let
him punish me: but the truth I will tell," Then he recited two
stanzas:

A low-caste man my teacher was, who taught
Duly and well the charm, and how it wrought :
Saying, "If you are asked my name and birth,
Hide nothing, or the charm will come to nought."
Asked by the Lord of Men, though well I knew,
Yet in deceit I said what was not true :
"A brahmin's spells, "I lying said; and now,
Charm lost, my folly bitterly I rue.

This heard, the king thought within himself, "This sinful
man took no care of such a treasure! When one has a treasure
so priceless, what has birth to do with it? And in anger he
repeated the following stanzas:

Nimb, castor oil, or judas tree, whatever be the tree
Where he who seeks finds honeycombs, 'tis best of trees,
                                                thinks he.
Be it Khattiya, Brahmin, Vessa, he from whom a man learns
                                                right—
Sudda, Candala, Pukkusa—seems chiefest in his sight.
Punish the worthless churl, or even slay,
Hence hale him by the throat without delay,

Who having gained a treasure with great toil,
Throws it with overweening pride away!

The king's men so did, saying, "Go back to your teacher,
and win his forgiveness; then, if you can learn the charm once
more, you may come hither again, but if not, never more may
you set eyes on this country." Thus they banished him.

The man was all forlorn. "There is no refuge for me," he
thought, "except my teacher. To him I will go, and win his
pardon, and learn the charm again." So lamenting he went on
his way to that village. The Great Being perceived him coming,
and pointed him out to his wife, saying, "See, lady, there comes
that scoundrel again, with his charm lost and gone!" The man
approached the Great Being, and greeted him, and sat on one
side. "Why are you here?" asked the other. "O my teacher!" the
man said, "I uttered a lie, and denied my teacher, and I am
utterly ruined and undone!" Then he recited his transgression
in a stanza, asking again for the charms:
Of he who thinks the level ground is lying at his foot,
    Falls in a pool, pit, precipice, trips on a rotten root;
Another treads what seems a cord, a jet-black snake to
                       find;
Another steps into the fire because his eyes are blind:
So I have sinned, and lost my spell; but you, O teacher wise,
Forgive! And let me once again find favour in your eyes!

Then his teacher replied, "What say you, my son? Give but
a sign to the blind, he goes clear of pools and what not; but I
told it to you once, and what do you want here now?" Then he
repeated the following stanzas:
To you in right due manner I did tell,
You in due manner rightly learnt the spell,
Full willingly its nature I explained:
Ne'er had it left you, had you acted well.
Who with much toil, O fool! Hath learnt a spell
Full hard for those who now in this world dwell,
Then, foolish one! A living gained at last,
Throws all away, because he lies will tell,

To such a fool, unwise, of lying fain,
Ungrateful, who cannot himself restrain, —
Spells, quotha! mighty spells we give not him:
Go hence away, and ask me not again!

Thus dismissed by his teacher, the man thought, "What is life to me?" and plunging into the woods, died forlorn.

THE PRINCE'S WOOING AND THE THRONE OF THE BUDDHAS

Once upon a time, in the kingdom of Kalinga, and in the city of Dantapura, regined a king named Kalinga. He had two sons, named Maha Kalinga and Culla-Kalinga, Kalinga the Greater and the Less. Now fortune-tellers had foretold that the eldest son would reign after his father's death; but that the youngest would live as an ascetic, and live by alms, yet his son would be an universal monarch.

Time passed by, and on his father's death the eldest son became king, the youngest viceroy. The youngest ever thinking that a son born of him was to be an universal monarch, grew arrogant on that account. This the king could not brook, so sent a messenger to arrest Kalinga the Less. The man came and said, "Prince, the king wishes to have you arrested, so save your life." The prince showed the courtier charged with this mission his own signet ring, a fine rug, and his sword: these three. Then he said, "By these tokens you shall know my son, and make him king. With these words, he sped away into the forest. There he built him a hut in a pleasant place, and lived as an ascetic upon the bank of a river.

Now in the kingdom of Madda, and in the city of Sagala, a daughter was born to the King of Madda. Of the girl, as of the prince, fortune-tellers foretold that she should live as an ascetic, but her son was to be an universal monarch. The Kings of India, hearing this rumour, came together with one accord, and surrounded the city. The king thought to himself, "Now, if I give my daughter to one, all the other kings will be enraged. I will try to save her." So with wife and daughter he fled disguised away into the forest; and after building him a hut some distance up the river, above the hut of Prince Kalinga, he lived there as an ascetic, eating what he could pick up.

The parents, wishing to save their daughter, left her behind in the hut, and went out to gather wild fruits. While they were gone she gathered flowers of all kinds, and made them into a flower-wreath. Now on the bank of the Ganges there is a mango tree with beautiful flowers, which forms a kind of natural ladder. Upon this she climbed, and playing managed to drop the wreath of flowers into the water.

One day, as Prince Kalinga was coming out of the river after a bath, this flower-wreath caught in his hair.

He looked at it, and said, "Some woman made this, and no full-grown woman but a tender young girl. I must make search for her." So deeply in love he journeyed up the Ganges, until he heard her singing in a sweet voice, as she sat in the mango tree. He approached the foot of the tree, and seeing her, said, "What are you, fair lady?" "I am human, sir," she replied. "Come down, then," quoth he. "Sir, I cannot; I am of the warrior caste." "So am I also, lady: come down!" "No, no, sir, that I cannot do. Saying will not make a warrior; if you are so, tell me the secrets of that caste." Then they repeated to each other these caste secrets. And the princess came down, and they were united one with the other.

When her parents returned she told them about this son of the King of Kalinga, and how he came into the forest, in all detail. They consented to give her to him. While they lived together in happy union, the princess conceived, and after ten months brought forth a son with the signs of good luck and virtue; and they named him Kalinga. He grew up, and learnt all arts and accomplishments from his father and grandfather.

At length his father knew from conjunctions of the stars that his brother was dead. So he called his son, and said, "My son, you must not spend your life in the forest. Your father's brother, Kalinga the Greater, is dead; you must go to Dantapura, and receive your hereditary kingdom." Then he gave him the things he had brought away with him, signet, rug, and sword, saying, "My son, in the city of Dantapura, in such a street, lives a courtier who is my very good servant. Descend into his house and enter his bedchamber, and show him these three things and tell him you are my son. He will place you upon the throne."

The lad bade farewell to his parents and grandparents; by the magic power of his virtue he passed through the air, and descending into the house of that courtier entered his bedchamber. "Who are you?" asked the other. "The son of Kalinga the Less," said he, disclosing the three tokens. The courtier told it to the palace, and all those of the court decorated the city and spread the umbrella of royalty over his head. Then the family priest, who was named Kalinga-bharadvaja, taught him the ten ceremonies, which an universal monarch has to perform, and he fulfilled those duties. Then on the fifteenth day, the fast-day, came to him from Cakkadaha the precious Wheel of Empire, from the Uposatha stock the precious Elephant, from the royal Valaha breed the precious Horse, from Vepulla the precious Jewel; and the precious wife, retinue, and prince made their appearance. Then he achieved sovereignty in the whole terrestrial sphere.

One day, surrounded by a company, which covered six-and-thirty leagues, and mounted upon an elephant all white, tall as a peak of Mount Kelasa, in great pomp and spendour he went to visit his parents. But beyond the circuit around the great bo-tree, the throne of victory of all the Buddhas, which has become the very navel of the earth, beyond this the elephant was unable to pass: again and again the king urged him on, but pass he could not.

Hereupon the king's chaplain, who was traveling with the king, thought to himself, "In the air is no hindrance; why cannot the king make his elephant go on? I will go, and see." Then, descending from the air, he beheld the throne of victory of all

Buddhas, the navel of the earth, that circuit around the great bo-tree. At that time, it is said, for the space of a royal *karisa* was never a blade of grass, not so big as a hare's whisker; it seemed as it were a smooth-spread sand bright like a silver plate; but on all sides were grass, creepers, mighty trees like the lords of the forest, as though standing in reverent wise all about with their faces turned towards the throne of the bo-tree. When the Brahmin beheld this spot of earth, "This, "thought he, "is the place where all the Buddhas have crushed all the desires of the flesh; and beyond this none can pass, no not if he were Sakka himself." Then approaching the king, he told him the quality of the bo-tree circuit, and bade him descend.

Pierced and pierced again by the king, this elephant could not endure the pain, and so died; but the king knew not he was dead, and sat died; and sat there still on his back. Then Kalinga-bharadvaja said, "O great king! Your elephant is dead; pass on to another." By the magical power of the king's virtue, another beast of the Uposatha breed appeared and offered his back. The king sat on his back. At that moment the dead elephant fell upon the earth.

Thereupon the king came down from the air, and beholding the precinct of the bo-tree, and the miracle that was done, he praised Bharadvaja, saying.
To Kalinga-bharadva king Kalinga thus did say:
"All thou know'st and understandest, and thou seest all
always."

Now the brahmin would not accept this praise; but standing in his own humble place, he extolled the Buddhas, and praised them.

The king, hearing the virtues of the Buddhas, was delighted in heart; and he caused all the dwellers in the world to bring fragrant wreaths in plenty, and for seven days he made them do worship at the circuit of the Great Bo-tree.

Having in this manner done worship to the Great Bo-tree,

he visited his parents, and took them back with him again to Dantapura; where he gave alms and did good deeds, until he was born again in the Heaven of the Thirty-Three.

THE FOLLY OF GARRULITY

Once upon a time, when Brahmadatta was king of Benares, his family priest was tawny-brown and had lost all his teeth. His wife committed sin with another Brahmin. This man was just like the other. Then priest tried times and again to restrain his wife, but could not. Then he thought, "This my enemy I cannot kill with my own hands, but I must devise some plan to kill him."

So he came before the king, and said, "O king, your city is the chiefest city of all India, and you are the chiefest king: but chief king though you are, your southern gate is unlucky, and ill put together." "well now, my teacher, what is to be done?" "You must bring good luck into it and set it right." "What is to be done?" "We must pull down the old door, get new and lucky timbers, do sacrifice to the spirits that guard the city, and set up the new on a lucky conjunction of the stars." "So do, then," said the king.

At that time, the Bodhisatta was a young man named Takkariya, who was studying under this man.

Now the priest caused the old gate to be pulled down, and the new was made ready; which done, he went and said to the king. "The gate is ready, my lord: to-morrow is an auspicious conjunction; before the morrow is over, we must do sacrifice and set up the new gate." "Well, my teacher, and what is necessary for the rite?" "My lord, a great gate is possessed and guarded by great divinities. A Brahmin, tawny-brown and toothless, of pure blood on both sides, must be killed; his flesh and blood must be offered in sacrifice, and his body laid beneath, and the gate raised upon it. This will bring luck to you and your city," "Very well, my teacher have such a Brahmin slain, and set up the gate upon him."

The priest was delighted. "To-morrow," said he, "I shall see the back of my enemy!" Full of energy he returned to his home, but could not keep a still tongue in his head, and said quickly to his wife, "Ah, you foul hag, whom will you have now to take your pleasure with? To-morrow I shall kill your leman and make sacrifice of him." "Why will you kill an innocent man?" "The king has commanded me to slay and sacrifice a tawny-brown, and to set up the city gate upon him. Your leman is tawny-brown, and I mean to slay him and sacrifice him." She sent her paramour a message, saying, "They say the king wishes to slay a tawny-brown Brahmin in sacrifice: if you would save your life, flee away in time, and with you all they who are like you." So the man did: the news spread abroad in the city, and all those in the whole city who were tawny-brown fled away.

The priest, nothing aware of his enemy's flight, went early next morning to the king, and said, "My lord, in such a place is a tawny-brown brahmin to be found; have him taken." The king sent some men for him, but they saw none, and returning informed the king that he was fled away. "Search elsewhere," said the king. All over the city they searched, but found none. "Search quickly!" said the king. "My lord," they replied, "except your family priest there is no such other." "A priest," quoth he, "cannot be killed." "What do you say, my lord? According to the priest, if the gate is not set up to-day, the city will be in danger. When the priest explained the matter, he said that if we let this day go by, the auspicious moment will not come again until the end of a year. The city without a gate for a year, what a chance for our enemies! Let us kill some one, and sacrifice by the aid of some other wise brahmin, and sacrifice by the aid of some other wise brahmin, and set up the gate." "But is there another wise brahmin like my teacher?" "There is, my lord, his pupil a young man named Takkariya; make him your family priest and do the lucky ceremony." The king sent for him, and did honour to him, and made him priest, and commanded to do as had been said. The young man went to the gate with a great crowd following. In the king's name they bound and brought the priest. The Great Being caused a pit to be dug in the place where the gate was to be set up, and a tent to be placed over it, and with his teacher entered into the tent. The teacher beholding the pit, and seeing no escape, said to the Great Being, "My aim had succeeded. Fool that I was, I could not keep a still tongue, but hastily told that wicked woman. I have slain myself with my own weapon." Then he recited the first stanza:

I spoke in folly, as a frog might call
Upon a snake i' the forest : so I fall
Into this pit, Takkariya. How true
Words spoken out of season one must rue!

Then the other addressing him, recited this stanza:
The man who out of season speaks, will go
Like this to ruin, lamentation, woe:
Here you should blame yourself, now you must have
This delved pit, my teacher, for your grave.

To these words he added yet this: "O teacher, not thou only, but many another likewise, has come to misery because he set not a watch upon his words." So saying, he told him a story of the past to prove it.

Once upon a time, they say, there lived a courtesan in Benares named Kali, and she had a brother named Tundila. In one day Kali would earn a thousand pieces of money. Now Tundila was a debauchee, a drunkard, a gambler; she gave him money, and whatever he got he wasted. Do what she would to restrain him, restrain him she could not. One day he was beaten at hazard, and lost the very clothes he was clad in. Wrapping about him a rag of loin-cloth, he repaired to his sister's house. But command had been given by her to her serving-maids, that if Tundila should come, they were to give him nothing, but take him by the throat and cast him out. And so they did: he stood by the threshold, and made his moan. Now a certain gild-merchant's son, who used constantly to give Kali a thousand pieces of money, on that day happened to see him, and says he, "Why are you weeping, Tundila?" "Master," said he, "I have been beaten at the dice, and came to my sister; and the serving-maids took me by the throat and cast me out." "Well, stay here," quoth the other, "and I will speak to your sister." He entered the

house, and said, "Your brother stands waiting clad in a rag of
loin-cloth. Why do you not give him something to wear?"
"Indeed," she replied. "I will give nothing. If you are fond of
him, give it yourself." Now in that house of ill-fame the fashion
was this: out of every thousand pieces of money received, five
hundred were for the woman, five hundred were the price of
clothes, perfumes and garlands; the men who visited that house
received garments to clothe themselves in, and stayed the night
there, then on the next day they put off the garments they had
received, and put on those they had brought, and went their
ways. On this occasion the merchant's son put on the garments
provided for him, and gave his own clothes to Tundila. He put
them on, and with loud shouts hastened to the tavern. But Kali
ordered her women that when the young man should depart
next day, they should take away his clothes. Accordingly, when
he came forth, they ran up from this side and that, like so many
robbers, and took the clothes from him, and stript him naked,
saying, "Now, young sir, be off!" Thus they got rid of him. Away
he went naked: the people made sport of him, and he was
ashamed, and lamented, saying, "It is my own doing, because
I could not keep watch over my lips!" To make this clear, the
Great Being recited the third stanza:

> Why ask of Tundila how he should fare
> At Kalika his sister's hands? now see!
> My clothes are gone, naked am I and bare;
> 'Tis very like what happened late to thee.

Another person relates this story. By carelessness of the
goat-herds, two rams fell a-fighting on a pasture at Benares. As
they were hard at it, a certain bird, a fork-tail, thought to himself,
"These two will crack their polls and perish; I must restrain
them." So he tried to restrain them by calling out—"Uncle,
don't fight!" Not a word he got from them: in the midst of the
battle, mounting first on the back, then on the head, he besought
them to stop, but could do nothing. At last he cried "Fight,
then, but kill me first!" and placed himself between the two
heads. They went on butting away at each other. The bird was
crushed as by a pounder, and came to destruction by his own
act. To explain this other tale the Great Being repeated the

fourth stanza:

Between two fighting rams a fork-tail flew,
Though in the fray he had no part nor share.
The two rams' heads did crush him then and there.
He in his fate was very like to you!

Another. There was a tal-tree which the cow-herds set great store by. The people of Benares seeing it sent a certain man up the tree to gather fruit. As he was throwing down the fruit, a black snake issuing forth from an ant-hill began to ascend the tree; they who stood below tried to drive him off striking at him with sticks and other things, but could not. Then they called out to other, "A snake is climbing the tree!" and he in terror uttered a loud cry. Those who stood below seized a stout cloth by the four corners, and bade him fall into the cloth. He let himself drop, and fell in the midst of the cloth between the four of them; swift as the wind he came, and the men could not hold him, but jolled their four heads together and broke them and so died. To explain this story the Great Being recited the fifth stanza:

Four men, to save a fellow from his fate,
Held the four corners of a cloth below.
They all fell dead, each with a broken pate.
These men were very like to you, I trow.

Others again tell this. Some goat-thieves who lived at Benares having stolen a she-goat one night, determined to make a meal in the forest: to prevent her bleating they muffled her snout and tied her up in a bamboo clump. Next day, on their way to kill her, they forgot the chopper. "Now we'll kill the goat and cook her," said they; "bring the chopper here!" But nobody had one. "Without a chopper," said they, "we cannot eat the beast, even if we kill her: let her go! This is due to some merit of hers." So they let her go. Now it happened that a worker in bamboos, who had been there for a bundle of them, left a basket-maker's knife there hidden among the leaves, intending to use it when he came again. But the goat, thinking herself to be free, began playing about under the bamboo clump, and kicking with her hind legs made the knife drop. The thieves heard the sound of the falling knife, and on coming to find out what it was, saw it, to their great delight; then they killed the goat, and ate her flesh. Thus to explain how this she-goat was killed by her own act the Great Being recited the sixth stanza:

A she-goat, in a bamboo thicket bound,
Frisking about, herself a knife had found.
With that same knife cut the creature's throat.
It strikes me you are very like that goat.

After recounting this, he explained, "But they who are moderate of speech, by watching their words have often been freed from the fate of death," and then told a story of fairies.

A hunter, we are told, who lived in Benares, being once in the region of Himalaya, by some means or other captured a brace of supernatural beings, a fairy and her husband; and them he took and presented to the king. The king had never seen such beings before. "Hunter," quoth he, "what kind of creatures are these?" Said the man, "My lord, these can sing with a honey-voice, they dance delightfully: no men are able to dance or sing as they can." The king bestowed a great reward on the hunter, and commanded the fairies to sing and dance. But they thought, "If we are not able to convey the full sense of our song, the song will be a failure, they will abuse and hurt us; and then again, those who speak much speak falsely": so for fear of some falsehood or other they neither sang not danced, for all the king begged them again and again. At last the king grew angry, and said, "Kill these creatures, and cook them, and serve them up to me." This command he delivered in the words of the seventh stanza:

No gods are these nor heaven's musicianers,
Beasts brought by one who fain would fill his purse,
So for my supper let them cook me one,
And one for breakfast by the morrow's sun.

Then the fairy-dame thought to herself, "Now the king is angry; without doubt he will kill us. Now it is time to speak." And immediately she recited a stanza:

A hundred thousand ditties all sung wrong

All are not worth a tithe of one good song.
To sing ill is a crime; and this is why
(Not out of folly) fairy would not try.

The king pleased with the fairy, at once recited a stanza:
She that hath spoken, let her go, that she
The Himalaya hill again may see,
But let them take and kill the other one,
And for to-morrow's breakfast have him done.

But the other fairy thought, "If I hold my tongue, surely the
king will kill me; now is the time to speak"; and then he recited
another stanza:
The kine depend upon the coulds, and men upon the kine,
And I, O king! Depend on thee, one me this wife of mine.
Let one, before he seek the hills, the other's fate divine.

When he had said this, he repeated a couple of stanzas, to
make it clear, that they had been silent not from unwillingness
to obey the king's word, but because they saw that speaking
would be a mistake.
O monarch! Other people, other ways:
'Tis very hard to keep you clear of blame.
The very thing which for the one wins praise,
Another finds reproof for just the same.
Some one there is who each man foolish finds;
Each by imagination different still;
All different, many men and many minds,
No universal law is one man's will.

Quoth the king, "He speaks the truth; 'tis a sapient fairy"
and much pleased he recited the last stanza:
Silent they were, the fairy and his mate:
And he who now did utter speech for fear,
Unhurt, free, happy, let him go his gait.
This is the speech brings good, as oft we hear.

Then the king placed the two fairies in a golden cage, and
sending for the huntsman, made him set them free in the same

place where he had caught them.

The Great Being added, "See, my teacher! In this manner the fairies kept watch on their words, and by speaking at the right time were set free for their well speaking; but you by your ill speaking have come to great misery." Then after showing him this parallel, he comforted him, saying, "Fear not, my teacher; I will save your life." "Is there indeed a way," asked the other, "how you can save me?" He replied, "It is not yet the proper conjunction of the planets." He let the day go by, and in the middle watch of the night brought thither a dead goat. "Go when you will, Brahmin, and live," said he, then let him go and never a soul the wiser. And he did sacrifice with the flesh of the goat, and set up the gate upon it.

THE HAWKS AND THEIR FRIENDS

Once upon a time, when Brahmadatta was king of Benares, certain men of the marches used to make a settlement, wheresoever they could best find much meat, dwelling in the forest, and killing for meat for themselves and their families the game which abounded there. Not far from their village was a large natural lake, and upon its southward shore lived a hawk, on the west a she-hawk; on the north a lion, king of the beasts; on the east an osprey, king of the birds; in the middle dwelt a tortoise on a small island. The hawk asked the she-hawk to become his wife. She asked him' "Have you any friend?" "No, madam," he replied. "We must have some one who can defend us against any danger or trouble that may arise, and you must find some friends." "Whom shall I make friends with?" "Why, with king osprey who lives on the eastern shore, and with the lion on the north, and with the tortoise who dwells in the middle of this lake." He took her advice and did so. Then the two lived together (it should be said that on a little islet in the same lake grew a kadamba tree, surrounded by the water on all sides) in a nest which they made.

Afterwards there were given to them two sons. One day, while the wings of the younglings were yet callow, some of the country folk went foraging through the woods all day and found nothing. Not wishing to return home empty-handed they went down to the lake to catch a fish or a tortoise. They got on the island, and lay down beneath the kadamba tree; and there being tormented by the bites of gnats and mosquitoes, to drive these away, they kindled a fire by rubbing sticks together, and made a smoke. The smoke rising annoyed the birds, and the young ones uttered a cry. "'Tis the cry of birds!" said the country folk. "Up, make up the fire: we cannot lie here hungry, but before we lie down we will have a meal of fowl's flesh." They made the fire blaze, and built it up. But the mother bird hearing the sound, thought, "These men wish to eat our young ones. We made friends to save us from that danger. I will send my mate to the great osprey." Then she said, "Go, my husband, tell the osprey of the danger which threatens our young" repeating this stanza:

> The country churls build fires upon the isle,
> To eat my young ones in a little while:
> O Hawk! to friend and comrade give the word,
> My children's danger tell to every bird!

The cock-bird flew at all speed to the place, and gave a cry to announce his arrival. Leave given, he came near to the osprey, and made his greeting. "Why have you come?" asked the osprey. Then the cock repeated the second stanza:

> O winged fowl! chiefest of birds art thou:
> So, Osprey king, I seek thy shelter now.
> Some country-folk a-hunting now are fain
> To eat my young: be thou my joy again!

"Fear not," said the osprey to the Hawk, and consoling him he repeated the third stanza:

> In season, out of season, wise men make
> Both friends and comrades for protection's sake:
> For thee, O Hawk! I will perform this deed;
> The good must help each other at their need.'

Then he went on to ask, "Have the churts climbed up the tree, my friend?" "They are not climbing yet; they are just piling

wood on the fire." "Then you had better go quickly and comfort
my friend your mate, and say I am coming." He did so. The
osprey went also, and from a place near to the kadamba tree he
watched for the men to climb, sitting upon a tree-top. Just as
one of the boors who was climbing the tree had come near to
the nest, the osprey dived into the lake, and from wings and
beak sprinkled water over the burning brands, so that they
were put out. Down came the men, and made another fire to
cook the bird and its young; when they climbed again, once
more osprey demolished the fire. So whenever a fire was made,
the bird put it out, and midnight came. The bird was much
distressed: the skin under his stomach had become quite thin,
his eyes were blood-shot. Seeing him, the hen-bird said to her
mate. "My lord, the osprey is tired out; go and tell the tortoise,
that he may have a rest."

When he heard this, the bird approaching the osprey,
addressed him in a stanza:
Good help the good: the necessary deed
Thou hast in pity done for us at need.
Our young are safe, thou living: have a care
Of thy own self, nor all thy strength outwear.

On hearing these words, loud as a lion's roar he repeated
the fifth stanza:
While I am keeping guard about this tree,
I care not if I lose my life for thee:
So use the good: thus friend will do for friend:
Yea, even if he perish at the end.

Then the hawk said, "Rest awhile, friend osprey," and then
away to be tortoise, whom he aroused. "What is your errand,
friend?" asked the tortoise.—"Such and such a danger has come
upon us, and the royal osprey has been labouring hard ever
since the first watch, and is very weary; that is why I have come
to you." With these words he repeated the seventh stanza:
Even they who fall through sin or evil deed
May rise if friends will help them in their need.
My young in danger, straight I fly to thee:

O dweller in the lake, come, succour me!

On hearing this the Tortoise repeated another stanza:
The wise man to a man who is his friend,
Both food and goods, even life itself, will lend.
For thee, O Hawk! I will perform this deed:
The good must help each other at their need.

His son, who lay not far off, hearing the words of his father,
thought, "I would not have my father troubled but I will do my
father's part," and therefore he repeated the ninth stanza:
Here at thy ease remain, O father mine,
And I thy son will do this task of thine.
A son should serve a father, so 'tis best;
I'll save the hawk his young ones in the nest.

The father tortoise addressed his son in a stanza:
So do the good, my son, and it is true
That son for father service ought to do.
Yet they may live the hawk's young brood alone,
Perchance, if they see me so fully grown.

With these words the tortoise sent the hawk away, adding,
"Fear not, my friend, but go you before and I will come presently
after." He dived into the water, collected some mud, and went
to the island, quenched the flame, and lay still. Then the
countrymen cried, "Why should we trouble about the young
hawks? Let us roll over this one-eyed tortoise, and kill him! He
will be enough for all." So they plucked some creepers and got
some strings, but when they had made them fast in this place
or that, and torn their clothes to strips for the purposes, they
could not roll the tortoise over. The tortoise lugged them along
with him and plunged in deep water. The men were so eager
to get him that in they fell after; splashed about, and scrambled
out with a bellyful of water. "Just look," said they: "half the
night one osprey kept putting out our fire, and now this tortoise
has made us fall into the water and swallow it, to our great
discomfort. Well, we will light another fire, and at sunrise we
will eat those young hawks." Then they began to make a fire.

The hen-bird feared the noise they were making, and said, "My husband, sooner or later these men will devour our young and depart, you go and tell our friend the lion." At once he went to the lion, who asked him why he came at such an unseasonable hour. The bird told him all from the beginning, and repeated the eleventh stanza:

Mightiest of all the beasts, both beasts and men
Fly to the strongest when beset with fear.
My young ones are in danger; help me then:
Thou art our king, and therefore I am here.

This said, the lion repeated a stanza:
Yes, I will do this service, hawk, for thee:
Come, let us go and slay this gang of foes!
Surely the prudent, he who wisdom knows,
Protector of a friend must try to be.

Having thus spoken, he dismissed him, saying, "Now go, and comfort your young ones." Then he went forward, churning up the crystal water. When the churls perceived him approaching, they were frightened to death: "The osprey," they cried, "put out our firebrands; the tortoise made us lose the clothes we had on: but now we are done for. This lion will destroy us at once." They ran this way and that: when the lion came to the foot of the tree, nothing could he see. Then the Osprey, the hawk, and the tortoise came up, and accosted him. He told them the profitableness of friendship, and said, "From this time forth be careful never to break the bonds of friendship." With the advice he departed: and they also went each to his own place. The hen-hawk looking upon her young, thought—"Ah, through friends have my young been given back to me!" and as she rejoiced, she spoke to her mate, and recited six stanzas declaring the effect of friendship:

Get friends, a houseful of them without fail
Get a great friend: a blessing he'll be found:
Vain strike the arrows on a coat of mail.
And we rejoice, our younglings safe and sound,
Through the kind help of their own friend, who stayed to
Take their parts,

The old birds chirp, the young reply, with notes that charm
the heart.

The wise asks help at friend's or comrade's hand,
Lives happy with his goods and brood of kind:
So I, my mate, and young, together stand,
Because our friend to pity was inclined.

A man needs king and warriors for protection:
And these are his whose friendship is perfection:
Thou cravest happiness: he is famed and strong;

He surely prospers to whom friends belong.

Even by the poor and weak, O Hawk, good friends must
needs be found:
By a friend's kindness we and ours, behold, are safe and
sound.

The bird who wins a hero strong to play a friendly part,
As thou and I are happy, hawk, is happy in his heart.

So she declared the quality of friendship in six stanzas.
And all this company of friends lived all their lives long without
breaking the bond of friendship, and then passed away
according to their deeds.

THE PRINCE WHO COULD NOT LAUGH

Once upon a time, there reigned a king Suruci in Mithila,
This king, having a son born to him, gave him the name of
Suruci-Kumara, or Prince Splendid. When he grew up, he
determined to study at Takkasila; so thither he went, and sat
down in a hall at the city gate. Now the son of the king of
Benares also, whose name was Prince Brahmadatta, went to the
same place, and took his seat on the same bench where Prince
Suruci sat. They entered into converse together, and became
friends, and went both together to the teacher. They paid the
fee, and studied, and ere long their education was complete.

Then they took leave of their teacher, and went on their road together. After traveling thus a short distance, they came to a stop at a place where the road parted. Then they embraced, and in order to keep their friendship alive they made a compact together: "If I have a son and you a daughter, or if you have a son and I a daughter, we will make a match of it between them."

When they were on the throne, a son was born to king Suruci, and to him also the name of Prince Suruci was given. Brahmadatta had a daughter, and her name was Sumedha, the Wise Lady. Prince Suruci in due time grew up, went to Takkasila for his education, and that finished returned. Then his father, wishing to mark out his son for king by ceremonial sprinkling, thought to himself, "My friend the king of Benares has a daughter, so they say: I will make her my son's consort." For this purpose he sent an ambassador with rich gifts.

But before they had yet come, the king of Benares asked his queen this question: "Lady, what is the worse misery for a woman?" "To quarrel with fellow-wives," "Then, my lord, to save our daughter the Princess Sumedha from this misery, we will give her to none by him that will have her and no other." So when the ambassadors came, and named the name of his daughter, he told them, "Good friends, indeed it is true I promised my daughter to my old friend long ago. But we have no wish to cast her into the midst of a crowd of women, and we will give her only to one who will wed her and no other." This message they brought back to the king. But the king was displeased. "Ours is a great kingdom," said he, "the city of Mithila covers seven leagues, the measure of the whole kingdom is three hundred leagues. Such a king should have sixteen thousand women at the least." But prince Suruci, hearing the great beauty of Sumedha, fell in love from hearing of it only. So he sent word to his parents, saying, "I will take her and no other: what do I want with a multitude of women? Let her be brought." They did not thwart his desire, but sent a rich present and a great ambassador to bring her home. Then she was made his queen-consort, and they were both together consecrated by sprinkling.

He became king Suruci, and ruling in justice lived a life of high happiness with his queen. But although she dwelt in his palace for ten thousand years, never son nor daughter she had of him.

Then all the townsfolk gathered together in the palace courtyard, with upbraidings. "What is it?" the king asked. "Fault we have no other to find," said they, "but this, that you have no son to keep up your line. You have but one queen, yet a royal prince should have sixteen thousand at the least. Choose a company of women, my lord: some worthy wife will bring you a son." "Dear friends, what is this you say? I passed my word I would take no other but one, and on those terms I got her. I cannot lie, no host of women for me." So he refused their request, and they departed. But Sumedha heard what was said. "The king refuses to choose him other wives for his truth's sake," thought she; "well, I will find him some one." Playing the part of mother and wife to the king, she chose at her own will a thousand maidens of the warrior caste, a thousand of the courtiers, a thousand daughters of householders, a thousand of all kinds of dancing girls, four thousand in all, and delivered them to him. And all these dwelt in the palace for ten thousand years, and never a son or daughter they brought between them. In this way she three times brought four thousand maidens, but they had neither son nor daughter. Thus she brought him sixteen thousand wives in all. Forty thousand years went, by that is to say, fifty thousand in all, counting the ten thousand he had lived with her alone. Then the townsfolk again gathered together with reproaches. "What is it now?" the king asked. "My lord command your women to pray for a son." The king was not unwilling, and commanded so to pray. Thenceforward praying for a son, they worshipped all manner of deities and offered all kinds of vows; yet no son appeared. Then the king commanded Sumedha to pray for a son. She consented. On the fast of the fifteenth day of the month, she took upon her the eightfold Sabbath vows, and sat meditating upon the virtues in a magnificent room upon a pleasant couch. The others were in the park, vowing to do sacrifice with goats or kine. By the glory of Sumedha's virtue Sakka's dwelling place began to tremble.

Sakka pondered, and understood that Sumedha prayed for a son; well, she should have one. "But I cannot give her this or that son indifferently; I will search for one which shall be suitable." Then he saw a young god called Nalakara, the Basket-weaver. He was a Being endowed with merit, who in a former life lived in Benares, when this befell him. At seed-time as he was on his way to the fields he perceived a Pacceka Buddha. He sent on his hinds, bidding them sow the seed, but himself turned back, and led the Pacceka Buddha home, and gave him to eat, and then conducted him again to the Ganges bank. He and his son together made a hut, trunks of fig-trees for the foundation and reeds interwoven for the walls; a door he put to it, and made a path for walking. There for three months he made the Pacceka Buddha dwell; and after the rains were over, the two of them, father and son, put on him the three robes and let him go. In the same manner they entertained seven Pacceka Buddhas in that hut, and gave them the three robes, and let them go their ways. So men still tell how these two, father and son, turned basket-weavers, and hunted for osiers on the banks of the Ganges, and whenever they spied a Pacceka Buddha did as we have said. When they died, they were born in the heaven of the Thirty-Three, and dwelt in the six heavens of sense one after the other in direct and in reverse succession, enjoying great majesty among the gods. These two after dying in that region were desirous of winning to the upper god-world. Sakka perceiving that one of them would be the Tathagata, went to the door of their mansion, and saluting him as he arose and came to meet him, said, "Sir, you must go into the world of men." But he said, "O king, the world of men is hateful and loathsome; they who dwell there do good and give aims longing for the world of the gods. What shall I do when I get there?" "Sir, you shall enjoy there all that can be enjoyed in the world of gods, you shall dwell in a palace made with stones of price, five and twenty leagues in height. Do consent." He consented. When Sakka had received his promise, in the guise of a sage he descended into the king's park, and showed himself soaring above those women to and fro in the air, while he chanted. "To whom shall I give the blessing of a son, who craves the blessing of a son?" "To me, Sir, to me!" thousands of hands were uplifted.

Then he said, "I give sons to the virtuous: What is you virtue, what your life and conversation?" They drew down their uplifted hands, saying, "If you would reward virtue, go seek Sumedha." He went his ways through the air, and stayed at the window of her bedchamber. Then they went and told her, saying, "See, my lady, a king of the gods has come down through the air, and stands at your bedchamber window, offering you the boon of a son!" With great pomp she proceeded thither, and opening the window, said, "Is this true, Sir, that I hear, how you offer the blessing of a son to a virtuous woman?" "It is, and so I do." "Then grant it to me." "What is your virtue, tell me; and if you please me, I grant you the boon." Then declaring her virtue she recited these fifteen stanzas:

I am king Ruci's consort-queen, the first he ever wed;
With Suruci ten thousand years my wedded life I led.
Suruci king of Mithila, Videha's chiefest place,
I never lightly held his wish, nor deemed him mean or base,
In deed or thought, or word, behind his back, nor to his
face.
If this be true, O holy one, so may that son be given:
But if my lips are speaking lies, then burst my head in
seven.
The parents of my husband dear, so long as they held sway,
And while they lived, would ever given me training in the
Way.
My passion was to hurt no life, and willingly do right:
I served them with extremest care unwearied day and night.
If this be true; O holy one, so may that son be given
No less than sixteen thousand dames my fellow-wives
have been:
Yet, brahim, never jealousy nor anger came between.
At their good fortune I rejoice; each one of them is dear;
My heart is soft to all these wives as though myself it were.
It this be true, O holy one, so may that son be given
Slaves, messengers, and servants all, and all about the
place.
I give them food, I treat them well, with cheerful
pleasant face.
If this be true, O holy one, so may that son be given

Ascetics, brahmins, any man who begging here is seen,
I comfort all with food and drink, my hands all washen
clean.
If this be true, etc.
The eighth of either fortnight, the fourteenth, fifteenth
days,
And the especial fast I keep, I walk in holy ways.
If this be true, O holy one, so may that son be given:
But if my lips are speaking lies, then burst my head in
seven.

Indeed not a hundred verses, nor a thousand, could suffice
to sing the praise of her virtues: yet Sakka allowed her to sing
her own praises in these fifteen stanzas, not did he cut the tale
short though he had much to do elsewhere; then he said,
"Abundant and marvelous are your virtues"; then in her praise
he recited a couple of stanzas:
All these great virtues, glorious dame, O daughter of a
king.
Are found in thee, which of thyself, O lady, thou dost sing.
A warrior, born of noble blood, all glorious and wise.
Videha's righteous emperor, thy son, shall soon arise.

When these words she heard, in great joy she recited two
stanzas, putting a question to him:

Unkempt, with dust and dirt begrimed, high-poised in the
sky,
Thou speakest in a lovely voice that pricks me to the heart.
Art thou a mighty god, O sage and dwellst in heaven on
high?
O tell me whence thou comest here, O tell me who thou
art!
He told her in six stanzas:
Sakka the hundred-eyed thou seest, for so the gods me call
When they are wont to assemble in the heavenly judgment
hall.
When women virtuous, wise and good here in the World
are found.

True wives, to thousand's mother kind even as in duty
        bound,
When such a woman wise of heart and good in deed they
        know,
To her, though woman, they divine, the gods themselves
        will go.
So lady, thou, through worthy life, through store of good
        deeds done,
A princess born, all happiness the heart can wish, hast
        won.
So thou dost reap thy deeds, princess, by glory on the
        earth,
And after in the world of gods a new and heavenly
        birth.
O wise, O blessed! so live on, preserve thy conduct right
Now I to heaven must return, delighted with thy sight.

"I have business to do in the world of gods," quoth he, "therefore I go; but do thou be vigilant." With this advice he departed.

In the morning time, the god Nalakara came down and was conceived. When she discovered it, she told the king, and he did what was necessary for a woman in her state. At the end of ten months she brought forth a son, and they gave him Mahapanada to his name. All the people of the two countries came crying out, "My lord, we bring this for the boy's milk-money," and each dropt a coin in the kings courtyard: a great heap there was of them. The king did not wish to accept this, but they would not take the money back, but said as they departed, "When the boy grows up, my lord, it will pay for his keep."

The lad was brought up amid great magnificence; and when he came of years, aye, no more than sixteen, he was perfect in all accomplishments. The king thinking of his son's age, said to the queen, "My lady, when the time comes for the ceremonial sprinkling of our son, let us make him a fine palace for that occasion." She was quite willing. The king sent for those who had skill in divining the lucky place for a building, and said to them: "My friends, get a master-mason, and build me a palace not far from my own. This is for my son, whom we are about to consecrate as my successor." They said it was well, and proceeded to examine the surface of the ground. At that moment Sakka's throne became hot. Perceiving this he at once summoned Vissakamma, and said, "Go, my good Vissakamma, make for Prince Maha-panada a palace half a league in length and breath and five and twenty leagues in height, all with stones of price." Vissakamma took on the shape of a mason, and approaching the workmen said, "Go and eat your breakfast, then return." Having thus got rid of the men, he struck on the earth with his staff; in that instant up rose a palace, seven storeys high, of the aforesaid size. Now for Maha-panada these three ceremonies were done together: the ceremony for consecrating the palace, the ceremony for spreading above him the royal umbrella, the ceremony of his marriage. At the time of the ceremony all the people of both countries gathered together, and spent seven years a-feasting, nor did the king dismiss them: their clothes, their ornaments, their food and their drink and all the rest of it, these things were all provided by the royal family. At the seven years' end they, began to grumble, and king Suruci asked why. "O king", they said, "While we have been revelling at this feast seven years have gone by. When will the feast come to an end?" He answered, "My good friends, all this while my son has never once laughed. So soon as he shall laugh, we will disperse again." Then the crowd went beating the drum and gathered the tumblers and jugglers together. Thousands of tumblers were gathered, and they divided themselves into seven bands and danced; but they could not make the prince laugh. Of course he that had seen the dancing of dancers divine could not care for such dancers as these. Then came two clever jugglers, Bhandu-kanna and Pandu-kanna, Crop-ear and Yellow-ear, and said they, "We will make the prince laugh." Bhandu-kanna made a great mango tree, which he called Sanspareil, grow before the palace door: then he threw up a ball of string, and made it catch on a branch of the tree, and then up he climbed into the Mango Sanspareil. Now the Mango Sanspareil they say is Vessavana's mango. And the slaves of Vessavana took him, as usual, chopped him up limb-meal and threw down

the bits. The other jugglers joined the pieces together, and
poured water upon them. The man donned upper and under
garments of flowers, and rose up and began dancing again.
Even the sight of this did not make the prince laugh. The
Pandu-kanna had some fire-wood piled in the courtyard and
went into the fire with his troop. When the fire was burnt out,
the people sprinkled the pile with water. Pandu-kanna with his
troop rose-up dancing with upper and under garments of flowers.
When the people found they could not make him laugh, they
grew angry. Sakka, perceiving this, sent down a divine dancer,
bidding him make prince Maha-panada laugh. Then he came
and remained poised in the air above the royal courtyard, and
performed what is called the Half-body dance: one hand, one
foot one eye, one tooth, go a-dancing, throbbing, flickering to
and fro, all the rest stone still. Maha-panada, when he saw this,
gave a little smile. But the crowd roared and roared with laughter,
could not cease laughing, laughed themselves out of their wits,
lost control of their limbs, rolled over and over in the royal
courtyard. That was the end of the festival. The rest of it—

> Great Panada, mighty king,
> With his palace all of gold,
> must be explained in the Maha-panada Birth!

King Maha-panada did good and gave alms, and at his life's
end went to the world of gods.

A LOST FRIEND FOUND BY A SONG

Once upon a time, in the realm of Avanti, and the city of
Ujjeni, reigned a great king named Avanti. At that time, a Candala
village lay outside Ujjeni, and there the Great Being was born.
Another person was born the son of his mother's sister. The one
of these two was named Citta, and the other Sambhuta.

These two when they grew up, having learnt what is called
the art of sweeping in the Candala breed, thought one day they
would go and show off this art at the city gate. So one of them
showed off at the north gate, and one at the east. Now in this

city were two women wise in the omens of sight, the one merchants daughter and the other a family priest's. These went forth to make merry in the park, having ordered food to be brought hard and soft garlands and perfumes; and it so happened that one went out by the northern gate and one the eastern. Seeing the two young Candalas showing their art, the girls asked "Who are these?" Candalas, they were informed. "This is an evil omen to see!" they said, and after washing their eyes with perfumed water, they returned back. Then the multitude cried, "O vile outcast, you have made us lose food and strong drink which would have cost us nothing!" They belaboured the two kinsmen, and did them much misery and mischief. When they recovered their senses, up they got and joined company, and told each the other what woe had befallen him, weeping and wailing, and wondering what to do now. "All this misery has come upon us," they thought, "because of our birth. We shall never be able to play the part of Candalas; let us conceal our birth, and go to Takkasila in the disguise of young brahmins, and study there." Having made this decision, they went thither, and followed their studies in the law under a far-famed master. A rumour was blown abroad over India, that two young Candalas were students, and had concealed their birth. The wise Citta was successful in his studies, but Sambhuta not so.

One day a villager invited the teacher, intending to offer food to the brahmins. Now it happened that rain fell in the night, and flooded all the hollows in the road. Early in the morning the teacher summoned wise Citta, and said, "My lad, I cannot go, you do go with the young men, and pronounce a blessing, eat what you get for yourself and bring home what there is for me." Accordingly he took the young brahmins, and went. While the young men bathed, and rinsed their mouths, the people prepared rice porridge, which they set ready for them, saying, "Let it cool." Before it was cool, the young men came and sat down. The people gave them the water of offering, and set the bowls in front of them. Sambhuta's wits were somewhat muddled, and imagining it to be cool, took up a ball of the rice and put it in his mouth, but it burnt him like a red-hot ball of metal. In his pain he forgot his part altogether, and glancing at wise Citta, he said, in the Candala dialect, "Hot, ain't it?" The other forgot himself too, and answered in their manner of speech, "Spit it out, spit it out." At this the young men looked at each other, and said, "What kind of language is this?" Wise Citta pronounced a blessing.

When the young men came home, they gathered in little knots and sat here and there discussing the words used. Finding that it was the dialect of the Candalas, they cried out on them, "O vile outcasts! You have been tricking us all this while, and pretending to be brahmins!" And they beat them both. One good man drove them out, saying. "Away! The blot's in the blood. Be off! Go somewhere and become ascetics." The young brahmins told their teacher that these two were Candalas.

The pair went out into the woods, and there took up the ascetic life, and after no long time died, and were born again as the young of a doe on the banks of the Neranjara. From the time of their birth they always went about together. One day, when they had fed, a hunter espied them under a tree ruminating and cuddling together, very happy, head to head, nozzle to nozzle, horn to horn. He cast a javelin at them, and killed them both by one blow.

After this they were born as the young of an osprey, on the bank of Nerbudda. There too, when they grew up, after feeding they would cuddle together, head to head and beak to beak. A bird snarer saw them, caught them together, and killed them both.

Next the wise Citta was born at Kosambi, as the son of a family priest; the wise Sambhuta was born as the son of the king of Uttarapancala. From their name-days they could remember their former births. But Sambhuta was not able to remember all without breaks, and all he could remember was the fourth or Candala birth: Citta however remembered all four in due order. When Citta was sixteen years old, he went away and became an ascetic in Himalaya, and developed the Faculty of the religious ecstasy, and dwelt in the bliss of ecstatic trance. Wise

Sambhuta after his father's death had the Umbrella spread over him, and on the very day of the Umbrella ceremony, in the midst of a great concourse, made a ceremonial hymn, and uttered two stanzas in aspiration. When they heard this, the royal wives and the musicians all chanted them, saying, "Our king's own coronation hymn!" and in course of time all the citizens sang it as the hymn which their king loved. Wise Citta, in his dwelling place in Himalaya, wondered, whether his brother Sambhuta had assumed the Umbrella, or not. Perceiving that he had, he thought, "I shall never be able to instruct a young ruler; but when he is old, I will visit him, and persuade him to be an ascetic." For fifty years he went not, and by that time the king was increased with sons and daughters; then by his supernatural power, he went and alighted in the park, and sat down on the seat of ceremony like an image of gold. Just then a lad was picking up sticks, and as he did so he sang that hymn. Wise Citta called him to approach; he came up with an obeisance, and waited. Citta said to him, "Since early morning you have been singing that hymn; do you know no other?"— "Oh yes, sir, I know many more, but these are the verses the king loves, that is why I sing no others."—"Is there any one who can sing a refrain to the king's hymn ?"—"No, sir."—"Could you ?"—"Yes, if I am taught one."—"Well, when the king chants these two verses, you sing this by way of third," and he recited a hymn. "Now," said he, "go and sing this before the king, and the king will be pleased with you, and make much of you for it." The lad went to his mother quickly, and got himself drest up spick and span; then to the king's door, and sent in word that a lad would sing him a refrain to his hymn. The king said, "Let him approach." When the lad had come in , and saluted him, quoth the king, "They say you will sing me an answering refrain to my hymn?" "Yes, my lord," said he, "bring in the whole court to hear." As soon as the court had assembled, the lad said, "Sing your hymn, my lord, and I will answer with mine." The king repeated a pair of stanzas:

> Every good deed bears fruit or soon or late,
> No deed without result, and nothing vain:
> I see Sambhuta mighty grown and great,
> Thus do his virtues bear him fruit again.

Every good deed bears fruit or soon or late,
No deed without result, and nothing vain.
Who knows if Citta also may be great,
And like myself, his heart have brought him gain?

At the end of this hymn, the lad chanted the third stanza:
Every good deed bears fruit or soon or late,
No deed without result, and nothing vain.
Behold, my lord, see Citta at thy gate,
And like myself, his heart have brought him gain.

On hearing this the king repeated the fourth stanza:
Then art thou Citta, or the tale didst hear
From him, or did some other make thee know?
Thy hymn is very sweet: I have no fear;
A village and a bounty I bestow.

Then the lad repeated the fifth stanza:
I am not Citta, but I heard the thing.
It was a sage laid on me this command—
Go and recite an answer to the king.
And be rewarded by his grateful hand.

Hearing this, the king thought, "It must be my brother
Citta; now I'll go and see him"; then he laid his bidding upon
his men in the words of these two stanzas:
Come, yoke the royal chariots, so finely wrought and made:
Gird up with girths the elephants, in necklets bright
                                                    arrayed.
Beat drums for joy, and let the conchs be blown,
Prepare the swiftest chariots I own:
For to that hermitage I will away,
To see the sage that sits within, this day.

So he spoke; then mounting his fine chariot, he went swiftly
to the park gate. There he checked his chariot, and approached
wise Citta with an obeisance, and sat down on one side; greatly
pleased, he recited the eighth stanza:
A precious hymn it was I sang so sweet

while thronging multitudes around me pressed;
for now this holy sage I come to greet
And all is joy and gladness in breast.

Happy from the instant he saw wise Citta, he gave all
necessary directions, bidding prepare a seat for his brother, and
repeated the ninth stanza:
Accept a seat, and for your feet fresh water: it is right
To offer gifts of food to guests: accept, as we invite.

After this sweet invitation, the king repeated another
stanza, offering him the half of his kingdom:
Let them make glad the place where thou shalt dwell.
Let throngs of waiting women wait on thee;
O let me show thee that I love thee well,
And let us both king here together be.

When he had heard these words, wise Citta discoursed to
him in six stanzas:
Seeing the fruit of evil deeds, O king,
Seeing what profit deeds of goodness bring,
I fain would exercise stern self-control,
Sons, wealth, and cattle cannot charm my soul.

Ten decades has this mortal life, which each to each
                                        succeed:
This limit reached, man withers fast like to a broken reed
Then what is pleasure, what is love, wealth-hunting what
                                        to me?
What sons and daughters? Know, O king, from fetters I am
                                        free.
For this is true, I know it well—death will not pass me by:
And what is love, or what is wealth when you must come
                                        to die?

The lowest race that go upon two feet
Are the Candalas, meanest men on earth,
When all our deeds were ripe, as guerdon meet
We both as young Candalas had our birth.

Candalas in Avanti land, deer by Neranjara,
Ospreys by the Nerbudda, now Brahmin and Khattiya.

Having thus made clear his mean births in time past, here
also in time past, here also in this birth he declared the
impermanency of things created and recited four stanzas to
arouse an effort:

Life is but short, and death the end must be:
The aged have no hiding where to flee.
Then, O pancala, what I bid thee, do:
All deeds which grow to misery, eschew.

Life is but short, and death the end must be:
The aged have no hiding where to flee.
Then, O Pancala, what I bid thee, do:
All deeds whose fruit is misery, eschew.

Life is but short, and death the end must be:
The aged have no hiding where to flee.
Then, O pancala, what I bid thee, do:
All deeds that are with passion stained eschew.

Life is but short, and death the end must be:
Old age will sap our strength, we cannot flee.
Then, O pancala, what I bid thee, do:
All deeds that lead to lowest hell, eschew.

The king rejoiced as the Great Being spoke and repeated
three stanzas:

True is that word, O Brother! Which you say,
You like a holy saint your words dictate:
But my desires are hard to cast away
By such as I am; they are very great.
As elephants deep sunken in the mire
Cannot climb out, although they see the land:
So, sunken in the slough of strong desire
Upon the Brethren's Path I cannot stand.
As father or as mother would their son
Adomnish, good and happy how to grow:

How happiness after this life is won
Tell me, and by which way I ought to go.

Then the great Being said to him:

O Lord of men! thou cánst not cast away
These passions which are common to mankind:
Let not thy people unjust taxes pay,
Equal and righteous ruling let them find.
Send messengers to north, south, east, and west
The brahmins and ascetics to invite:
Provide them food and drink, a place to rest.
Clothes, and all else that may be requisite.
Give thou the food and drink which satisfies
Sages and holy brahmins, full of faith:
Who gives and rules as well as in him lies
Will go to heaven all blameless after death.
But if, surrounded by thy womankind
Thou feel thy passion and desire too strong,
This verse of poetry then bear in mind
And sing it in the midst of all the throng.
No roof to shelter from the sky, amid the dogs he lay,
But mother nursed him as she walked: but he's a king
to-day.

Such was the Great Being's advice. Then he said, "I have
given you my counsel. And now do you become an ascetic or
not, as you think fit; but I will follow up the ripening of my own
deeds." Then he rose up in the air, and shook of the dust of his
feet over him, and departed to Himalaya. And the king saw it,
and was greatly moved; and relinquishing his kingdom to his
eldest son, he called our his army, and set his face in the
direction of Himalaya. When the Great Being heard of his
coming, he went with his attendant sages and received him,
and ordained him to the holy life, and taught him the means of
inducing mystic ecstasy. He developed the Faculty of mystical
meditation. Thus these two together became destined for
Brahma's world.

KING SIVI

Once upon a time, when the mighty King Sivi reigned in the city Aritthapura in the kingdom of Sivi, the Great Being was born as his son. They called his name Prince Sivi. When he grew up, he went to Takkasila and studied there; then returning, he proved his knowledge to his father the king, and by him was made viceroy. At his father's death he became king himself, and forsaking the ways of evil, he kept the Ten Royal virtues and ruled in righteousness. He caused six alm-halls to be built, at the four gates, in the midst of the city, and at his own door. He was munificent in distributing each day six hundred thousand pieces of money. On the eighth, fourteenth, and fifteenth days he never missed visiting the alms-halls to see the distribution made.

Once on the day of the full moon, the State umbrella had been uplifted early in the morning, and he sat on the royal throne thinking over the gifts he had given. Thought he to himself, "Of all outside things there is nothing I have not given; but this kind of giving does not content me. I want to give something which is a part of myself. Well, this day when I go to the alms-hall, I vow that if any one ask not something outside me, but name what is part of myself,—if he should mention my very heart, I will cut open my breast with a spear, and as though I were drawing up a water-lily, stalk and all, from a calm lake, I will pull forth my heart dripping with blood-clots and give it him: if he should name the flesh of my body, I will cut the flesh off my body and give it, as though I were graving with a graving tool: let him name my blood, I will give him my blood, dropping it in his mouth or filling a bowl with it: Or again, if one say, I can't get my household work done, come and do me a slave's part at home, then I will leave my royal dress and stand without, proclaiming myself a slave, and slave's work I will do: should any men demand my eyes, I will tear out my eyes and give them, as one might take out the pith of a palm-tree." Thus he thought within him:

If there be any human gift that I have never made.

Be it my eyes, I'll give it now, all firm and unafraid.

Then he bathed himself with sixteen pitchers of perfumed water, and adorned him in all his magnificence, and after a meal of choice food he mounted upon an elephant richly caparisoned and went to the alms-hall.

Sakka, perceiving his resolution, thought, "King Sivi has determined to give his eyes to any chance comer who may ask. Will he be able to do it, or no?" He determined to try him and in the form of a brahmin old and blind, he posted himself on a high place, and when the king came to his alms-hall he stretched out his hand and stood crying, "Long live the king!" Then the king drove his elephant towards him, and said, "What do you say, brahmin?" Sakka said to him, "O great king! In all the inhabited world there is no spot where the fame of your munificent heart has not sounded. I am blind, and you have two eyes." Then he repeated the first stanza, asking for an eye:

> To ask an eye the old man comes from far, for I have none:
> O give me one of yours, I pray, then we shall each have
> > one.

When the Great Being heard this, thought he, "Why that is just what I was thinking in my palace before I came! What a fine chance! My heart's desire will be fulfilled to-day; I shall give a gift which no man ever gave yet." And he recited the second stanza:
> Who taught thee hitherward to wend the way,
> O mendicant, and for an eye to pray?
> The chiefest portion of a man is this,
> And hard for men to part with, so they say.

(The succeeding stanzas are to be read two and two, as may easily be seen).

> Sujampati among the gods, the same
> Here among men called Maghava by name,
> He taught me hitherward to wend my way,

Begging, and for an eye to urge my claim.
'Tis the all-chiefest gift for which I pray.
Give me an eye! O do not say me nay!
Give me an eye, that chiefest gift of gifts,
So hard for men to part with, as they say!

The wish that brought thee hitherward, the wish that did
                                                    arise
Within thee, be that wish fulfilled. Here, brahmin, take my
                                                    eyes.

One eye thou didst request of me: behold, I give thee two!
Go with good sight, in all the people's view;
So be thy wish fulfilled and now come true.

So much the king said. But, thinking it not meet that he
should root out his eyes and bestow them there and then, he
brought the brahmin indoors with him, and sitting on the royal
throne, sent for a surgeon named Sivaka. "Take out my eye," he
then said.

Now all the city rang with the news, that the king wished
to tear out his eyes and give them to a brahmin. Then the
commander-in chief, and all the other officials, and those beloved
of the king, gathered together from city and harem, and recited
three stanzas, that they might turn the king from his purpose:
    O do not give thine eye, my lord; desert us not, O king!
    Give money, pearls and coral give, and many a precious
                                                    thing:
    Give thoroughbreds caparisoned, forth be the chariots
                                                    rolled,
    O king, drive up the elephants all fine with cloth of gold:
    These give, O king! That we may all preserve thee safe
                                                    and sound,
    Thy faithful people, with our cars and chariots ranged
                                                    around.
    Hereupon the king recited three stanzas:
    The soul, which, having sworn to give, is then unfaithful
                                                    found.

Puts his own neck within a snare low hidden on the
                                                 ground.
The soul which, having sworn to give, is then unfaithful
                                                  found,
More sinful is than sin, and he to Yama's house is bound.
That which is asked I give, and not the thing he asketh
                                                    not,
This therefore which the brahmin asks, I give it on the
                                                   spot.

Then the courtiers asked, "What do you desire in giving
your eyes?" repeating a stanza:
Life, beauty, joy or strength—what is the prize,
O king, which motive for your deed supplies?
Why should the king of Sivi-land supreme
For the next world's sake thus bestow his eyes?
The king answered them in a stanza:
In giving thus, not glory is my goal,
Not sons, not wealth, or kingdoms to control;
This is the good old way of holy men;
Of giving enamoured is my soul.

To the Great Being's words the courtiers answered nothing;
so the great being addressed Sivaka the surgeon in a stanza:
A friend and comrade, Sivaka, art thou:
Do as I bid thee—thou hast skill enow—
Take out my eyes, for this is my desire,
And in the beggar's hands bestow them now.

But Sivaka said, "Bethink you, my lord! To give one's eyes
is no light thing."—"Sivaka, I have considered; don't delay, nor
talk too much in my presence." Then he thought, "It is not
fitting that a skilful surgeon like me should pierce a king's eyes
with the lancet," so he pounded a number of simples, rubbed
a blue lotus with the powder, and brushed it over the right eye:
round rolled the eye, and there was great pain. "Reflect, my
king, I can make it all right."—"Go on, friend, no delay, please."
Again he rubbed in the powder, and brushed it over the eye: the
eye started from the socket, the pain was worse than before.

"Reflect, my king, I can still restore it."—"Be quick with the job!" A third time he smeared a sharper powder, and applied it: by the drug's power round went the eye, out it came from the socket, and hung dangling at the end of the tendon. "Reflect, my king, I can yet restore it again."—"Be quick." The pain was extreme, blood was trickling, the king's garments were stained with the blood. The king's women and the courtiers fell at his feet, crying, "My lord, do not sacrifice your eyes!" loudly they wept and wailed. The king endured the pain, and said, "My friend, be quick." "Very well, my lord," said the physician; and with his left hand grasping the eyeball took a knife in his right, and severing the tendon, laid the eye in the Great Being's hand. He, gazing with his left eye at the right and enduring the pain, said, "Brahmin, come here." When the brahmin came near, he went on — "The eye of omniscience is dearer than this eye a hundred fold, aye a thousand fold: there you have my reason for this action," and he gave it to the brahmin, who raised it and placed it in his own eye socket. There it remained fixed by his power like a blue lotus in bloom. When the Great Being with his left eye saw that eye in his head, he cried— "Ah, how good is this my gift of an eye!" and thrilled straightway with the joy that had arisen within him, he gave the other eye also. Sakka placed this also in the place of his own eye, and departed from the king's palace, and then from the city, with the gaze of the multitude upon him, and went away to the world of gods.

In a short while the king's eyes began to grow: as they grew, and before they reached the top of the holes, a lump of flesh rose up inside like a ball of wool, filling the cavity; they were like a doll's eyes, but the pain ceased. The Great Being remained in the palace a few days. Then he thought, "What has a blind man to do with rulling? I will hand over my kingdom to the courtiers, and go into my park, and become an ascetic, and live as a holy man." He summoned his courtiers, and told them what he intended to do. "One man," said he, "shall be with me, to wash my face, and so forth, and to do all that is proper, and you must fasten a cord to guide me to the retiring places." Then calling for his charioteer, he bade him prepare the chariot. But the courtiers would not allow him to go in the

chariot; they brought him out in a golden litter, and set him
down by the lake side, and then, guarding him all around,
returned. The king sat in the litter thinking of his gift.

At that moment Sakka's throne became hot; and he
pondering perceived the reason. "I will offer the king a boon,"
thought he, "and make his eye well again." So to that place he
came; and not far off from the Great Being, he walked up and
down, up and down.

"Who is that?" cried the Great Being, when he heard the
sound of the footsteps. Sakka repeated a stanza:
   Sakka, the king of gods, am I; to visit thee I came:
   Choose thou a boon, O royal sage! Whate'er thy wish may
                                                       name.
The king replied with another stanza:

   Wealth, strength, and treasure without end, these I have
                                            left behind:
   O Sakka, death and nothing more I want: for I am blind.

Then Sakka said, "Do you ask death, King Sivi, because you
wish to die, or because you are blind?"—"Because I am blind,
my lord."—"The gift is not everything in itself, your majesty, it
was made with a view to the future. Yet there is a motive
relating to this visible world. Now you were asked for one eye,
and gave two; make an Act of Truth about it." Then he began
a stanza:
   O warrior, lord of biped kind, declare the thing that's true:
   If you the truth declare, your eye shall be restored to you.

On hearing this, the Great Being replied, "If you wish to
give me an eye, Sakka, do not try any other means, but let my
eye be restored as a consequence of my gift." Sakka said,
"Though they call me Sakka, king of the gods, your majesty, yet
I cannot give an eye to anyone else; but by the fruit of the gift
by thee given, and by nothing else, your eye shall be restored
to you." Then the other repeated a stanza, maintaining that his
gift was well given:

Whatever sort, whatever kind of suitor shall draw near,
Whoever comes to ask of me, he to my heart is dear:
If these my solemn words be true, now let my eye appear!

Even as he uttered the words, one of his eyes grew up in
the socket. Then he repeated a couple of stanzas to restore the
other:
A brahmin came to visit me, one of my eyes to crave:
Unto that brahmin mendicant the pair of them I gave.
A greater joy and more delight that action did afford.
If these my solemn words be true, be the other eye
restored!

On the instant appeared his second eye. But these eyes of
his were neither natural nor divine. An eye given by Sakka as
the brahmin, cannot be natural, we know; on the other hand, a
divine eye cannot be produced in anything that is injured. But
these eyes are called the eyes of the Attainment of Truth. At
the time when they came into existence, the whole royal retinue
by Sakka's power was assembled; and Sakka standing in the
midst of the throng, uttered praise in a couple of stanzas:
O fostering King of Sivi land, these holy hymns of thine
Have gained for thee as bounty free this pair of eyes
divine.
Through rock and wall, o'er hill and dale, whatever bar
may be,
A hundred leagues on every side those eyes of thine
shall see.

Having uttered these stanzas, poised in the air before the
multitude, with a last counsel to the Great Being that he should
be vigilant, Sakka returned to the world of gods. And the Great
Being, surrounded by his retinue, went back in great pomp to
the city, and entered the palace called Candaka the Peacock's
Eye. The news that he had got his eyes again spread abroad all
through the Kingdom of Sivi. All the people gathered together
to see him, with gifts in their hands. "Now all this multitude is
come together," thought the great Being, "I shall praise my gift
that I gave." He caused a great pavilion to be put up at the

palace gate, where he seated himself upon the royal throne, with the white umbrella spread above him. Then the drum was sent beating about the city, to collect all the trade guilds. Then he said, "O people of Sivi! Now you have beheld these divine eyes, never eat food without giving something away!" and he repeated four stanzas, declaring the Law:

> Who, if he's asked to give, would answer no,
> Although it be his best and choicest prize?
> People of Sivi thronged in concourse, ho!
> Come hither, see the gift of God, my eyes!
> Through rock and wall, o'er hill and dale, whatever bar
> may be,
>
> A hundred leagues on every side these eyes of mine can
> see.
>
> Self-sacrifice in all men mortal living,
> Of all things is most fine:
> I sacrificed a mortal eye; and giving,
> Received an eye divine.
> See, people! See, gives ere ye eat, let others have a share.
> This done with your best will and care,
>
> Blameless to heaven you shall repair.

In these four verses he declared the Law; and after that, every fortnight, on the holy day, even every fifteenth day, he declared the Law in these same verses without cessation to a great gathering of people. Hearing which, the people after giving alms and doing good deeds, attained to heaven.

THE EVILS OF STRONG DRINK

Once upon a time when Brahmadatta was ruling in Benares, a forester, named Sura, who dwelt in the kingdom of Kasi, went to the Himalayas, to seek for articles of merchandise. There was a certain tree there that sprang up to the height of a man with his arms extended over his head, and then divided into three parts. In the midst of its three forks was a hole as big as a wine jar, and when it rained this hole was filled with water. Round about it grew two myrobalan plants and a pepper shrub; and the ripe fruits from these, when they were cut down, fell into the hole. Not far from this tree was some selfsown paddy. The parrots would pluck the heads of rice and eat them, perched on his tree. And while they were eating, the paddy and the husked rice fell there. So the water, fermenting through the sun's heat, assumed a blood-red colour. In the hot season flocks of birds, being thirsty, drank of it, and becoming intoxicated fell down at the foot of the tree, and after sleeping awhile flew away, chirping merrily. And the same thing happened in the case of wild dogs, monkeys and other creatures. The forester, on seeing this, said, "If this were poison they would die, but after a short sleep they go away as they list; it is no poison," And he himself drank of it, and becoming intoxicated he felt a desire to eat flesh, and then making a fire he killed the partridges and cocks that fell down at the foot of the tree, and roasted their flesh on the live coals, and gesticulating with one hand, and eating flesh with the other, he remained one or two days in the same spot. Now not far from here lived an ascetic, named Varuna. The forester at other times also used to visit him, and the thought now struck him," I will drink this liquor with the ascetic." So he filled a reed-pipe with it, and taking it together with some roast meat he came to the hut of leaves and said, "Holy sir, taste this liquor," and they both drank it and ate the meat. So from the fact of this drink having been discovered by Sura and Varuna, it was called by their names (*sura* and *varuni*). They both thought, "This is the way to manage it," and they filled their reed-pipes, and taking it on a carrying-pole they came to a neighbouring village, and sent a message to the king that some wine merchants have come. The king sent for them and they offered him the drink. The king drank it two or three times and got intoxicated. This lasted him only one or two days. Then he asked them if there was any more. "Yes sir," they said. "Where?" "In the Himalayas, sir," "Then bring it here." They went and fetched it two or three times. Then thinking, "We can't always be going there," they took note of all the constituent parts, and, beginning with the bark of the tree, they threw in all the other ingredients, and made the drink in the city. The men of the city drank it and became idle wretches, And the place became like a deserted city. Then these wine merchants fled from it and came to Benares, and sent a message to the king, to announce their arrival. The king sent for them and paid them money, and they made wine there too. And that city also perished in the same way. Thence they fled to Saketa, and from Saketa they came to Savatthi. At that time there was a king named Sabbamitta in Savatthi. He showed favour to these men and asked them what they wanted. When they said, "We want the chief ingredients and ground rice and five hundred jars," he gave them everything they asked for. So they stored the liquor in the five hundred jars, and, to guard them, they bound cats, one to each jar. And, when the liquor fermented and began to escape, the cats drank the strong drink that flowed from the inside of the jars, and getting intoxicated they lay down to sleep; and rats came and bit off the cats' ears, noses, teeth and tails. The king's officers came and told the king. "The cats have died from drinking the liquor." The king said, "Surely these men must be makers of poison," and he ordered them both to be beheaded, and they died, crying out, "Give us strong drink, give us mead." The king, after putting the men to death, gave orders that the jars should be broken. But the cats, when the effect of the liquor wore off, got up and walked about and played. When they saw this, they told the king. The king said, "If it were poison they would have died; It must be mead; we will drink it." So he had the city decorated, and set up a pavilion in the palace yard and taking his seat in this splendid pavilion on a royal throne with a white umbrella raised over it and surrounded by his courtiers, he began to drink. Then Sakka, the king of the gods, said, "Who are there that in the duty of service to mother and the like diligently fulfill the three kinds of right conduct?" And, looking upon the world, he saw the king seated to drink strong drink and he thought, "If he shall drink strong drink, all India will perish: I will see that he shall not drink it." So placing a jar full of liquor in the palm of his hand, he went disguised as a brahmin, and stood in the air, in the presence of the king, and cried, "Buy this jar, buy this jar." King Sabbamitta, on seeing him standing in the air and speaking after this manner, said, "Whence can this

brahmin come?" and conversing with him he repeated three
stanzas:

Who art thou, Being from on high,
Whose form emits bright rays of light,

Like Levin flash athwart the sky,
Or moon illuming darkest night?

To ride the pathless air upon,
To move or stand in silent space—

Real is the power that thou hast won,
And proves thou art of godlike race.

Then, brahmin, who thou art declare,
And what within thy jar may be,

That thus appearing in mid air,
Thou fain wouldst sell thy wares to me.

Then Sakka said, "Hearken then to me," and expounding
the evil qualities of strong drink, he said:

This jar nor oil nor ghee doth hold,
No honey or molasses here,
But vices more than can be told
Are stored within its rounded sphere.

Who drinks will fall, poor silly fool,
Into some hole or pit impure,
Or headlong sink in loathsome pool
And eat what he would fain abjure.
Buy then, O king, this jar of mine,
Full to the brim of strongest wine...
And after drinking this, I ween,
Andhakavenhu's mighty race,
Roaming along the store, were seen
To fall, each by his kinsman's mace.
Buy then O king, this jar of mine....

The Asuras made drunk with wine
Fell from eternal heaven, O king,
With all their magic power divine:
Then who would taste the accursed thing?
Buy then O king, this jar of mine....

Nor curds nor honey sweet is here,
But evermore remembering
What's stored within this rounded sphere,
Buy, prithee, buy my jar, O king.

On hearing this the king recognizing the misery caused by
drink, was so pleased with Sakka that he sang his praises in two
stanzas:
No parents had I sage to teach like thee,
But thou art kind and merciful, I see;
A seeker of the Highest Truth always;
Therefore I will obey thy words to-day.

Lo! Five choice villages I own are thine,
Twice fifty handmaids, seven hundred kine,
And these ten cars with steeds of purest blood,
For thou hast counselled me to mine own good.

Sakka on hearing this revealed his godhead and made
himself known, and standing in the air he repeated two stanzas:
These hundred slaves, O king, may still be thine,
And eke the village and herds of kine;
No chariots yoked to high-bred steeds I claim;
Sakka, chief god of Thirty Three, my name.
Enjoy thy ghee, rice, milk and sodden meat,
Still be content thy honey cakes to eat.
Thus, king, delighting in the Truths I've preached,
Pursue they blameless path, till Heaven is reached.

Thus did Sakka admonish him and then returned to his
abode in Heaven. And the king, abstaining from strong drink,
ordered the drinking vessels to be broken. And undertaking to
keep the precepts and dispensing alms, he became destined to

Heaven. But the drinking of strong drink gradually developed in India.

THE WHITE SIX-TUSKED ELEPHANT

Once upon a time eight thousand royal elephants, by the exercise of supernatural powers moving through the air, dwelt near lake Chaddanta in the Himalayas. At this time the Bodhisatta came to life as the son of the chief elephant. He was a pure white, with red feet and face. By and by, when grown up, he was eighty-eight hands high, one hundred and twenty hands long. He had a trunk like to a silver rope, fifty-eight hands long, and tusks fifteen hands in circumference thirty hands long, and emitting six-coloured rays. He was the chief of a herd of eight thousand elephants and paid honour to pacceka buddhas. His two head queens were Cullasubhadda and Mahasubhadda. The king elephant, with his herd numbering eight thousand, took up his abode in a Golden Cave. Now lake Chaddanta was fifty leagues long and fifty broad. In the middle of it, for a space extending twelve leagues, no sevala or panaka plant is found, and it consists of water in appearance like a magic jewel. Next to this, encircling this water, was a thicket of pure white lilies, a league in breadth. Next to this, and encircling it, was a thicket of pure blue lotus, a league in extent. Then came white and red lotuses, red and white lilies, and white esculent lilies, each also a league in extent and each encircling the one before. Next to these seven thickets come a mixed tangle of white and other lilies, also a league in extent and encircling all the preceding ones. Next, in water as deep as elephants can stand in, was a thicket of red paddy. Next, at the edge of the water, was a grove of small shrubs, abounding in delicate and fragrant blossoms of blue, yellow, red and white. So these ten thickets were each a league in extent. Next came a thicket of various kinds of kidney beans. Next came a tangle of convolvulus, cucumber, pumpkin, gourd and other creepers. Then a grove of sugar-cane of the size of the areca-nut tree. Then a grove of plantains with fruit as big as elephant's tusks. Then a field of paddy. Then a grove of bread-fruit of the size of a water jar. Next a grove of tamarinds with luscious fruit. Then a grove of elephant-apple trees. Then a great forest of different kinds of trees. Then a bamboo grove. Such at this time was the magnificence of this region—its present magnificence is described in the Samyutta Commentary—but surrounding the bamboo grove were seven mountains, Starting from the extreme outside first came Little Black Mountain, next Great Black Mountain, then Water Mountain, Moon Mountain, Sun Mountain, Jewel Mountain, then the seventh in order Golden Mountain. This was seven leagues in height, rising all round the lake Chaddanta, like the rim of a bowl. The inner side of it was of a golden colour. From the light that issued from it lake Chaddanta shone like the newly risen sun. But of the outer mountains, one was six leagues in height, one five, one four, one three, one two, one a single league in height. Now in the north-east corner of the lake, thus girt about with seven mountains, in a spot where the wind fell upon the water, grew a big banyan tree. Its trunk was five leagues in circumference and seven leagues in height. Four branches spread six leagues to the four points of the compass, and the branch which rose straight upwards was six leagues. So from the root upwards it was thirteen leagues in height, and from the extremity of the branches in one direction to the extremity of the branches in the opposite direction it was twelve leagues. And the tree was furnished with eight thousand shoots and stood forth in all its beauty, like to the bare Jewel Mount. But on the west side lake Chaddanta, in the Golden Mount, was a golden cave, twelve leagues in extent. Chaddanta the elephant king, with his following of eight thousand elephants, in the rainy season lived in the golden cave; in the hot season he stood at the foot of the great banyan tree, amongst its shoots, welcoming the breeze from off the water. Now one day they told him, "The great Sal grove is in flower." So attended by his herd he was minded to disport himself in the Sal grove, and going thither he struck with his frontal globe a Sal tree in full bloom. At that moment Chullasubhadda stood to windward, and dry twigs mixed with dead leaves and red ants fell upon her person. But Mahasubhadda stood to leeward, and flowers with pollen and stalks and green leaves fell on her. Thought Cullasubhadda, "He let fall on the wife dear to him flowers and pollen and fresh stalks and leaves but on my person he dropped a mixture of dry

twigs, dead leaves and red ants. Well I shall know what to do!"
And she conceived a grudge against the Great Being. Another
day the king elephant and his attendant herd went down to
take Chaddanta to bathe. Then two young elephants took
bundles of usira root in their trunks and gave him a bath,
rubbing him down as it were mount Kelasa. And when he came
out of the water, they bathed the two queen elephants, and
they too came out of the water and stood before the Great
Being. Then the eight thousand elephants entered the lake and,
disporting themselves in the water, plucked various flowers
from the lake, and adorned the Great Being as if it had been a
silver shrine, and afterwards, adorned the queen elephants.
Then a certain elephant, as he swam about the lake, gathered
a large lotus with seven shoots and offered it to the Great Being.
And he, taking it in his trunk, sprinkled the pollen on his forehead and presented the flower to the chief elephant,
Mahasubhadda. On seeing this her rival said, "This lotus with
seven shoots he also gives to his favourite queen and not to
me," and again she conceived a grudge against him. Now one
day when the Bodhisatta had dressed luscious fruits and lotus
stalks and fibres with the nectar of the flower, and was
entertaining five hundred pacceka buddhas, Cullasubhadda
offered the wild fruits she had got to the pacceka buddhas, and
she put up a prayer to this effect: "Hereafter, when I pass hence,
may I be re-born as the royal maiden Subhadda in the Madda
kings family, and on coming of age may I attain to the dignity
of queen consort to the king of Benares. Then I shall be dear and
charming in his eyes, and in a position to do what I please. So
I will speak to the king and send a hunter with a poisoned
arrow to wound and slay this elephant. And thus may I be able
to have brought to me a pair of his tusks that emit six-coloured
rays." Thenceforth she took no food and pining away in no long
time she died, and came to life again as the child of the queen
consort in the Madda kingdom, and was named Subhadda. And
when she was of suitable age, they gave her in marriage to the
king of Benares. And she was dear and pleasing in his eyes, and
the chief of sixteen thousand wives. And she recalled to mind
her former existences and thought, "My prayer is fulfilled; now
will I have this elephant's tusks brought to me," Then she

anointed her body with common oil, put on a soiled robe, and lay in bed pretending to be sick. The king said, "Where is Subhadda?" And hearing that she was sick, he entered the royal closet and sitting on the bed he stroked her back and uttered the first stanza:

Large-eyed and peerless one, my queen, so pale, to grief a
          prey,
Like wreath that's trampled under foot, why fadest thou
          away?

On hearing this she spoke the second stanza:
As it would seem, all in a dream, a longing sore I had;
My wish is vain this boon to gain, and that is why I'm Sad.

The king, on hearing this, spoke a stanza:

All joys to which in this glad world a mortal may aspire,
What'er they want is mine to grant, I give thee thy desire.

On hearing this the queen said, "Great king, my desire is hard to attain; I will not now say what it is, but I would have all the hunters that there are in your kingdom gathered together. Then will I tell it in the midst of them." And to explain her meaning, she spoke the next stanza:
Let hunters all obey thy call, within this realm who dwell,
And what I fain from them would gain, I'll in their presence
          tell.

The king agreed, and issuing forth from the royal chamber he gave orders to his ministers, saying, "Have it proclaimed by beat of drum that all the hunters that are in the kingdom of Kasi, three hundred leagues in extent, are to assemble." They did so, and in no long time the hunters that dwelt in the kingdom of Kasi, bringing a present according to their means, had their arrival announced to the king. Now they amounted in all to about sixty thousand. And the king, hearing that they had come, stood at an open window and stretching forth his hand he told the queen of their arrival and said:
Here then behold our hunters bold, well trained in Venery,

Theirs is the skill wild beasts to kill, and all would die
                                                    for Me.

    The queen, on hearing this, addressed them and spoke
another stanza:

Ye hunters bold, assembled here,
Unto my words, I pray, give ear:
Dreaming, me thought an elephant I saw,
Six-tusked and white without a flaw:
His tusks I crave and fain would have;
Nought else avails my life to save.

The hunters, on hearing this, replied:
Ne'er did our sires in times of old
A six-tusked elephant behold.
Tell us what kind of beast might be
That which appeared in dreams to thee.

After this still another stanza was spoken by them.
Four points, North, South, East, West, one sees,
Four intermediate are to these.
Nadir and zenith add, and then
Say at which point of all the ten
This royal elephant might be,
That in a dream appeared to thee.

    After these words Subhadda, looking at all the hunters,
spied amongst them one that was broad of foot, with a calf
swollen like a food basket, big in the knee and ribs, thick-
bearded, with yellow teeth, disfigured with scars, head and
shoulders above all, an ugly, hulking fellow, named Sonuttara,
who had once been an enemy of the Great Being. And she
thought, "He will be able to do my bidding," and with the
king's permission she took him with her and, climbing to the
highest floor of the seven-storeyed palace, she threw open a
window to the North, and stretching forth her hand towards the
Northern Himalayas she uttered four stanzas:

Due north, beyond seven mountains vast,
One comes to Golden Cliff at last,
A height by goblin forms possessed

And bright with flowers from foot to crest.

Beneath this goblin peak is seen
A cloud-shaped mass of darkest green,
A royal banyan tree whose roots
Yield vigour to eight thousand shoots.
There dwells invincible in might
This elephant, six-tusked and white,
With herd eight thousand strong for fight.
Their tusks to chariot-poles are like,
Wind-swift are they to guard or strike.

Parenting and grim they stand and glare,
Provoked by slightest breath of air,
If they one born of man should see,
Their wrath consumes him utterly.
Sonuttara on hearing this was terrified to death and said:
Turquoise or pearls of brilliant sheen,
With many a gold adornment, queen,
In royal houses may be seen,
What wouldst thou then with ivory do,
Or wilt thou slay these hunters true?

Then the queen spoke a stanza.
Consumed with grief and spite am I,
When I recall my injury.
Grant me, O hunter, what I crave,
And five choice hamlets thou shalt have.

And with this she said, "Friend hunter, when I gave a gift
to the pacceka buddhas, I offered up a prayer that I might have
it in my power to kill this six-tusked elephant and get possession
of a pair of his tusks. This was not merely seen by me in a vision,
but the prayer that I offered up will be fulfilled. Do thou go and
fear not." And so saying she reassured him. And he agreed to
her words and said, "So be it, lady; but first make it clear to me
and tell me where is his dwelling-place," and enquiring of her
he spoke this stanza:
Where dwells he? Where may be found:

What road is his, for bathing bound?
Where does this royal creature swim?
Tell us the way to capture him.

Then by recalling her former existence she clearly saw the
spot and told him of it in these two stanzas:
Not far this bathing-place of his,
A deep and goodly pool it is,
There bees do swarm and flowers abound,
And there this royal beast is found.

Now lotus-crowned, fresh from his bath,
He gladly takes his homeward path,
As lily-white and tall he moves
Behind the queen he fondly loves.

Sounuttara on hearing this agreed, saying, "Well, lady, I
will kill the elephant and bring you his tusks." Then in her joy
she gave him a thousand pieces and said, "Go home meanwhile,
and at the end of seven days you shall set out thither," and
dismissing him she summoned smiths and gave them an order
and, said, "Sirs, we have need of an axe, a spade, an auger, a
hammer, an instrument for cutting bamboos, a grass-cutter, an
iron staff, a peg, an iron three-pronged fork; make them with all
speed and bring them to us." And sending for workers in leather,
she charged them, saying, "Sirs, you must make us a leather
sack, the size of a hogshead measure; we need leather ropes and
straps, shoes big enough for an elephant, and a leather parachute:
make them with all speed and bring them to us." And both
smiths and workers in leather quickly made everything and
brought and offered them to her. Having provided everything
requisite for the journey, together with fire-drills and the like,
she put all the appliances and necessaries for the journey, such
as baked meal and so forth, in the leather sack. The whole of it
came to about a hogshead in size. And Sonuttara, having
completed his arrangement, arrived on the seventh day and
stood respectfully in the presence of the queen. Then she said,
"Friend, all appliances for your journey are completed: take
then this sack." And he being a stout knave, as strong as five

elephants, caught up the sack as if it had been a bag of cakes, and placing it on his hips, stood as it were with empty hands. Cullasubhadda gave the provisions to the hunter's attendants and, telling the king, dismissed Sonuttara. And he, with an obeisance to the king and queen, descended from the palace and, placing his goods in a chariot, set out from the city with a great retinue, and passing through a succession of villages and hamlets reached the frontiers. Then he turned back the people of the country and went on with the dwellers on the borders till he entered the forest, and passing beyond the haunts of men he sent back the border people too, and proceeded quite alone on a road to distance of thirty leagues, traversing a dense growth of kusa and other grasses, thickets of basil, reeds and rest-harrow, clumps of thick-thorn and canes, thickets of mixed growth, jungles of reed and cane, dense forest growth, impenetrable even to a snake, thickets of trees and bamboos, tracts of mud and water, mountain tracts, eighteen regions in all, one after another. The jungles of grass he cut with a sickle, the thickets of basil and the like he cleared with his instrument for cutting bamboos, the trees he felled with an axe, and the oversized ones he first pierced with an auger. Then, pursuing his way, he fashioned a ladder in the bamboo grove and climbing to the top of the thicket, he laid a single bamboo, which he had cut, over the next clump of bamboos, and thus creeping along on the top of the thicket he reached a morass. Then he spread a dry plank on the mud, and stepping on it he threw another plant before him and so crossed the morass. Then he made a canoe and by means of it crossed the flooded region, and at last stood at the foot of the mountains. Then he bound a three-pronged grapping-iron with a rope and flinging it aloft he caused it to lodge fast in the mountain. Then climbing up by the rope he drilled the mountain with an iron staff tipped with adamant, and knocking a peg into the hole he stood on it. Then drawing out the grappling-iron he once more lodged it high up on the mountain, and from this position letting the leather rope hang down, he took hold of it and descended and fastened the rope on the peg below. Then seizing the rope with his left hand and taking a hammer in his right he struck a blow on the rope, and having thus pulled out the peg he once more climbed up. In this way he mounted to the top of the first mountain and then commencing his descent on the other side, having knocked as before a peg into the top of the first mountain and bound the rope on his leather sack and wrapped it round the peg, he sat within the sack and let himself down, uncoiling the rope like a spider letting out his thread. Then letting his leather parachute catch the wind, he went down like a bird—so at least they say. Thus did the Master tell how in obedience to Subhadda's words the hunter sallied forth from the city and traversed seventeen different tracts till he reached a mountainous region, and how he there crossed over six mountains and climbed to the top of Golden Cliff:

> The hunter hearing, unalarmed,
> Set forth with bow and quiver armed,
> And crossing o'er seven mountains vast
> Reached noble Golden Cliff at last.
>
> Gaining the goblin-haunted height,
> What cloud-shaped mass bursts on his sight?
> A royal banyan 'tis whose roots
> Support eight thousand spreading shoots.
>
> There stood invincible in might
> An elephant six- tusked and white,
> With herd eight thousand strong for fight;
> Their tusks to chariot-poles are like:
> Wind-swift are they to guard or strike.
>
> Hard by a pool—'tis full to the brim,
> fit place for royal beast to swim;
> It lovely banks with flowers abound
> And buzzing bees swarm all around.
> Marking the way the creature went
> Whene'er on bathing thought intent,
> He sunk a pit, to deed so mean
> Urged by the wrath of spiteful queen.

Here continues the regular story: the hunter, it is said, after seven years, seven months and seven days, having reached the dwelling-place of the Great being in the manner related above, took note of his dwelling-place and dug a pit there thinking, "I will take my stand here and wound the lord of elephants and bring about his death." Thus did he arrange matters and went into the forest and cut down trees to make posts and prepared a lot of kusa-grass. Then when the elephants went to bathe, in the spot where the king elephant used to stand, he dug out he sprinkled on the top of the water, as if he were sowing seed, and on the top of stones like mortars he fixed posts, and fitted them with weights and ropes and spread planks over them. Next he made a hole of the size of an arrow and threw on the top earth and rubbish, and on one side he made an entrance for himself, and so, when the pit was finished, at break of day he fastened on a false top knot and donned robes of yellow and, taking his bow and poisoned arrow, he went down and stood in the pit.

> (The Master, to make the whole thing clear, said:
> The pit with planks he first did hide,
> Then bow in hand the got inside,
> And as the elephant passed by,
> A mighty shaft the wretch let fly.
>
> The wounded beast loud roared with pain,
> And all the herd roared back again:
> Crushed boughs and trampled grass betray
> Where panic flight directs their way.
>
> Their lord had well nigh slain his foe,
> So mad with pain was he, when lot
> A robe of yellow met his eyes,
> Emblem of sainthood, sage's guise
> And deemed inviolate by the wise)

The Great Being, falling into conversation with the hunter, spoke of stanzas:
> Whose is marred with sinful taint
> And vold of truth and self- restraint,
> Though robed in yellow he may be,
> The yellow dress deserves not he.

But one that's free from sinful taint,
Endued with truth and self-restraint,
And firmly fixed in righteousness,
Deserves to wear the yellow dress.

So saying, the Great Being, extinguishing all feeling of anger towards him, asked him, saying, "Why did you wound me? Was it for your own advantage or were you suborned by some one else?"

Then the hunter told him and uttered this stanza:
The king of Kasi's favoured queen
Subhadda told me she had seen
Thy form in dreams, "and so," said she,
"I want his tusks; go, bring them me."

Hearing this, and recognizing that this was the work of Cullasubhadda, he bore his sufferings patiently and thought, "She does not want my tasks; she sent him because she wished to kill me", and, to illustrate the matter, he uttered a couple of stanzas:
Rich store of goodly tusks have I,
Relics of my dead ancestry,
And this well knows that wrathful dame,
'Tis at my life the wretch doth aim.

Rise, hunter, and or ere I die,
Saw off these tusks of ivory:
Go bid the shrew be of good cheer,
"The beast is slain; his tusks are here."

Hearing his words the hunter rose up from the place where he was sitting and, saw in hand, came close to cut off his tusks. Now the elephant, being eighty-eight hands high, like a mountain, was not thrown down. Hence the man could not reach his tusks. So the Great Being, bending his body towards him, lay with his head down. Then the hunter climbed up the trunk of the Great Being, pressing it with his feet as though it were a silver rope, and stood on his forehead as if it had been

Kelasa peak. Then he inserted his foot into his mouth, and striking the fleshy part of it with his knee, he climbed down from the beast's forehead and thrust the saw into his mouth. The Great Being suffered excruciating pain and his mouth was charged with blood. The hunter, shifting about from place to place, was still unable to cut the tusks with his saw. So the Great Being letting the blood drop from his mouth, resigning himself to the agony, asked, saying, "Sir, cannot you cut them?" And on his saying "No," he recovered his presence of mind and said, "Well then, since I myself have not strength enough to raise my trunk, do you lift it up for me and let it seize the end of the saw." The hunter did so: and the Great Being seized the saw with his trunk and moved it backwards and forwards and tusks were cut off as it were sprouts. Their bidding him take the tusks, he said, "I don't give you these, friend hunter because I do not value them, nor as one desiring the position of Sakka, Mara or Brahma, but the tusks of omniscience are a hundred thousand times dearer to me than these are, and may this meritorious act be to me the cause of attaining Omniscience." And as he gave him the tusks, he asked, "How long were you coming here?" "Seven years, seven months, and seven days." Go then by the magic power of these tasks, and you shall reach Benares in seven days" And he gave him a safe conduct and let him go. And after he had sent him away, before the other elephants and Subhadda had returned, he was dead.

When he was gone, the herd of elephants not finding their enemy came back.

And with them also came Subhadda, and they all then and there with weeping and lamentation betook them to the pacceka buddhas who had been so friendly to the Great Being, and said, "Sirs, he who supplied you with the necessaries of life has died from the wound of a poisoned arrow. Come and see where his dead body is exposed." And the five hundred pacceka buddhas passing through the air alighted in the sacred enclosure. At that moment two young elephants, lifting up the body of the king elephant with their tusks, and so causing it to do homage to the pacceka buddhas raised it aloft on a pyre and burned it.

The pacceka buddhas all though the night rehearsed scripture texts in the cemetery. The eight thousand elephants, after extinguishing the flames, first bathed and then, with Subhadda at their head, returned to their place of abode.

And Sonuttara within seven days reached Benares with his tusks.

Now in offering them to the queen, he said, "Lady, the elephant against whom you conceived a grudge in your heart for trifling offence, has been slain by me," "Do you tell me that he is dead?" she cried, And he gave her the tusks, saying, "Be assured that he is dead: here are his tusks." She received the tusks adorned with six different colored rays on her jewelled fan, and, placing them on her lap, gazed at the tusks of one who in a former existence had been her dear lord and she thought. "This fellow has come with the tusks he cut from the auspicious elephant that he slew with a poisoned shaft." And at the remembrance of the Great Being she was filled with so great sorrow that she could not endure it, but her heart then and there was broken and that very day she died.

THE THREE WISE BIRDS

Once upon a time Brahmadatta ruled in Benares and had no heir, and his prayer for a son or daughter was not answered. Now one day he went with a large escort to his park and after amusing himself a part of the day in the grounds he had a couch spread for him at the foot of the royal sal tree, and after a short nap he awoke and, looking up to the sal tree, he beheld a bird's nest in it, and at the sight of it a desire to possess it sprang up in his heart, and summoning one of his attendants he said, "Climb the tree and see if there is anything in the nest or not." The man climbed up and finding three eggs in it told the king. "Then mind you do not breathe over them," he said, and, spreading some cotton in a casket, he told the man to come down gently, and place the eggs in it. When they had been brought down, he took up the casket and asked his courtiers to what bird these eggs belonged. They answered, "We do not

know: hunters will know," The king sent for the hunters and
asked hunters will know.: The king sent for the hunters and
asked them. "Sire," said they, "one is an owl's egg, another is
a maynah bird's, and the third is a parrot's." "Pray are there
eggs of three different birds in one nest?" "Yes, Sire, when there
is nothing to fear, what is carefully deposited does not perish."
The king being pleased said, "They shall be my children," and
committing the three eggs to the charge of three courtiers he
said, "These shall be my children. Do you carefully watch over
them and when the young birds come out of the shell, let me
know." They took good care of them. First of all the owl's egg
was hatched, and the courtier sent for a hunter and sad, "Find
out the sex of the young bird, whether it is a cock or a hen bird,"
and when he had examined it and declared it to be a cock bird,
the courtier went to the king and said, "Sire, a son is born to
you." The king was delighted and bestowed much wealth on
him and saving, "Watch carefully over him and call his name
Vessantara," he sent him away. He did as he was told. Then a
few days afterwards the egg of the maynah bird was hatched,
and the second courtier likewise, after getting the huntsman to
examine it, and hearing it was a hen bird, want to the king and
announced to him the birth of a daughter. The king was
delighted, and gave to him also much treasure and saying,
"Watch carefully over my daughter and call her name Kundalini,"
he sent him away. He also did what he was told. Then after a
few days the parrot's egg was hatched and the third courtier,
when told by the huntsman who examined it that it was a cock
bird, went and announced to the king the birth of a son. The
king was delighted and paying him liberally said, "Hold a festival
in honour of my son with great pomp, and call his name
Jambuka," and then sent him away. He too did as he was told,
And these three birds grew up in the houses of the three
courtiers with all the ceremony due to princes. The king spoke
of them habitually, as my son' and 'my daughter'. His courtiers
made merry, one with another, saying, " Look at what the king
does; he goes about speaking of birds as his son and his
daughter." The king thought, "These courtiers do not know the
extent of my children's wisdom. I will make it evident to them,"
So he sent one of his ministers to Vessantara to say, "Your father

wishes to ask you a question. When shall he come and ask it?"
The minister came and bowing to Vessantara delivered the
message. Vessantara sent for the courtier who looked after him
and said, "My father," they tell me, "Wants to ask me a question.
When he comes, we must show him all respect," and he asked,
"When is he to come?" The courtier said, "Let him come on the
seventh day from this." Vessantara on hearing this said, "Let
my father come on the seventh day from this," and with these
words he sent the minister away. He went and told the king. On
the seventh day the king ordered a drum to be beaten through
the city and went to the house where his son lived. Vessantara
treated the king with great respect and had great respect paid
even to the slaves and hired servants. The king, after partaking
of food in the house of Vessantara, and enjoying great distinction,
returned to his own dwelling-place. Then he had a big pavilion
erected in the palace-yard, and, having made proclamation by
beating a drum through the city, he sat in his magnificent
pavilion surrounded by a great retinue and sent word to a
courtier to conduct Vessantata to him. The courtier brought
Vessantara on a golden stool. The bird sat on his father's lap and
played with his father, and then went and sat on the stool. Then
the king in the midst of the crowd of people questioned him as
to the duty of a king and spoke the first stanza:

'Tis this I ask Vessantara—dear bird, mayst thou be blest—
To one that's fain o'er men to reign, what course of life is
best?

Vessantara, without answering the question directly,
reproved the king for his carelessness and spoke the second
stanza:

Kamsa my sire, who Kasi won, so careless long ago,
Urged me his son, though full of zeal, still great zeal to
show.

Rebuking the king in this stanza. And staying. "Sire, a king
ought to rule his kingdom righteously, abiding in the three
truths", and telling of a king's duty he spoke these stanzas:

First of all should a king put away all falsehood and anger
and scorn:

Let him do what a king has to do, or else to his vow be
                                                  forsworn.
By passion and sin let astray, should he err in the past,
                                                it is plain
He will live to repent of the deed, and will learn not to
                                              do it again.
When a prince in his rule groweth slack, untrue to his
                                        name and his fame,
Should his wealth all at once disappear, of that prince it
                                          is counted as shame.
"Tis thus that good Fortune and Luck, when asked, this
                                        answer have told,
"I delight in a man from jealousy free, energetic and bold."
I'll luck, ever wrecking good fortune, delighteth in men of
                                              ill deeds,
The hard- hearted creatures in whom a spirit of jealousy
                                              breeds.
To all, O great king, be a friend, so that all may thy safety
                                              insure,
I'll luck put away, but to luck that is good be a dwelling
                                              secure.
The man that is lucky and bold, O thou that o'er Kasi dost
                                              reign,
Will destroy root and branch his foes, and to greatness will
                                          surely attain.
For Sakka himself, O King, in energy wearieth not;
In virtue he firmly hath stood, through energy such is his lot.
Gandharvas, the fathers, and gods are refreshed by such
                                          zeal of a king,
And spirits appearing stand by, of his vigour and energy
                                              sing.
Be zealous to do what is right, nor, however reviled yield
                                              to sir,
Be earnest in efforts for good—no sluggard can bliss ever
                                              win
Herein is the text of thy duty, to teach thee the way thou
                                          shouldst go:
'Tis enough to win bliss for friend or to work grievous ill for
                                              a foe.

Thus did the bird Vessantata in a single stanza rebuke the carelessness of the king, and then in telling the duty of a king in eleven stanzas answered his question with all the charm of a Buddha. The hearts of the multitude were filled with wonder and amazement and innumerable shouts of applause were raised. The king was transported with joy and addressing his courtiers asked them what was to be done for his son, for having spoken thus. "He should be made a general in the army, Sire." "Well, I give him the post of general," and he appointed Vessantara to the vacant post. Thenceforth placed in this position he carried our his father's wishes. Here ends the story of Vessantara's question.

Again the king after some days, just as before, sent a message to Kundalini, and on the seventh day he paid her a visit and returning home again he seated himself in the center of a pavilion and ordered Kundalini to be brought to him, and when she was seated on a golden stool, he questioned her as to the duty of a king and spoke this stanza:

Kundalini, of kshatriya birth, couldst thou resolve my quest,
To one that's fain o'er men to reign, what course of life
is best?

When the king thus asked her as to the duties of a king, she said, "I suppose, Sir, you are putting me to the test, thinking 'What will a woman be able to tell me.' so I will tell you, putting all your duty as king into just two maxims," and she repeated these stanzas:

The matter my friend, is set forth in a couple of maxims
quite plain—
To keep whatsoever one has, and whatever one has not to
gain.
Take as consulleors men that are wise, thy interests clearly
to see.
Not given to riot and waste, from gambling and drunken-
ness free.
Such a one as can guard thee aright and thy treasure with
all proper zeal,

As a charioteer guides his car, he with skill steers the
                                            realm's common weal.
Keep ever they folk well in hand, and duly take stock of
                                            thy pelf.
Ne'er trust to another a loan or deposit, but act for thyself.
What is done or undone to thy profit and loss it is well
                                            thou shouldst know,
Ever blame the blame-worthy and favour on them that
                                            deserve it bestow.
Thou thyself, O great king, shouldst instruct thy people
                                            in every good way,
Lest thy realm and thy substance should fall to unright-
                                            eous officials a prey.
See that nothing is done by thyself or by others with
                                            over-much speed,
For the fool that so acts without doubt will live to repent
                                            of the deed.
To wrath one should never give way, nor let it due bounds
                                            overflow;
It has led to the ruin of kings and the proudest of houses
                                            laid low.
Betray none, in that thou art lord, to aught that is useless
                                            and vain,
Nor become thou to women and men the cause of their
                                            sorrow and pain.
When a king from all caution is free, and the pleasures
                                            of sense are his aim,
Should his riches and all disappear, to that king it is
                                            counted as shame.
Herein is a text of thy duty, to teach thee the way thou
                                            shouldst go,
Be an adept in every good work, to excess and to riot a
                                            foe,
Study virtue, for vice ever leads to a state full of suffering
                                            and woe.

Thus did Kundalini also teach the king his duty in eleven
stanzas. The king was delighted and addressing his courtiers
asked them, saying, "What is to be given to my daughter as a

reward for her having spoken thus?" "The office of treasurer, Sire." "Well then, I grant her the post of treasurer," and he appointed Kundalini to the vacant post. Thenceforth she held the office and acted for the king. Here ends the story of the question of Kundalini.

Again the king after the lapse of a few days, just as before, sent a messenger to the wise Jambuka, and going there on the seventh day and being magnificently entertained he returned home and in the same manner took his seat in the center of a pavilion. A courtier placed the wise Jambuka on a stool bound with gold, and came bearing the stool on his head. The wise bird sitting on his father's lap and playing with him at length took his seat on the golden stool. Then the king, asking him a question, spoke this stanza:

We've questioned both thy brother owl, and also fair
                                                    Kundalini;
Now, Jambuka, do thou in turn the highest power declare
                                                          to me.

Thus did the king, in asking a questing of the Great Being, not ask him in the way in which he had asked the others, but asked him in a special way. Then the wise bird said to him, "Well, Sire, listen attentively, and I will tell you all," and like a man placing a purse containing a thousand pieces of money into an outstretched hand, he began his exposition of a king's duty:

Amidst the great ones of the earth a fivefold power we
                                                          see;
Of these the power of limbs is, sure, the last in its degree,
And power of wealth, O mighty lord, the next is said to be.
The power of counsel third in rank of these, O king, I name;
The power of caste without a doubt is reckoned fourth
                                                      in fame,
And all of these a man that's wise most certainly will
                                                        claim.
Of all these powers that one is best, as power of wisdom
                                                        known.

By strength of this a man is wise and makes success his
                                                                own.
Should richest realm fall to the lot of some poor stupid
                                                                wight,
Another will by violence seize it in his despite.
However noble be the prince, whose lot it is to rule,
He is hard put to live at all, if he should prove a fool.

'Tis wisdom tests reports of deeds and makes men's fame
                                                                to grow,
Who is with wisdom gifted still finds pleasure e'en in woe.
None that are heedless in their ways to wisdom can attain,
But must consult the wise and just, or ignorant remain.
Who early rising shall betimes unweariedly give heed
To duty's varied calls, in life is certain to succeed.
No one that's bent on hurtful things or acts in listless
                                                                mood.
In aught that he may undertake will come to any good.
But one that will unweariedly a rightful course pursue,
Is sure to reach perfection in whatever he may do.
To safeguard one's store is to gain more and more,
And these are the things I would have thee to mind;
For the fool by ill deeds, like a house built of reeds,
Collapses and leaves rack and ruin behind.

Thus did the Bodisatta in all these points sing the praises
of the five powers, and exalting the power of wisdom, like to one
striking the orb of the moon with his words, he admonished the
king in ten stanzas:
        Unto thy parents, warrior king, do righteously; and so
        By following a righteous life to heaven thou, sire shalt go.

After uttering ten stanzas about the way of righteousness,
still further admonishing the king he spoke the concluding
stanza:
        Herein is the text of thy duty, to teach thee the way thou
                                                                shouldst go.
        Follow wisdom and ever be happy, the Truth in its fullness
                                                                to know.

Thus did the Great Being, as though he were letting down heavenly Ganges, teach the law with all the charm of a Buddha. And the multitude paid him great honour and raised innumerable shouts of applause. The king was delighted and addressing his councillors asked, "How ought my son, wise Jambuka, with a beak like the fresh fruit of the rose-apple, to be rewarded for having spoken thus?" "With the post of commander -in-chief, Sire." "Then I offer him this post," he said, and appointed him to the vacant office, and thenceforth in the position of commander-in-chief he carried out the orders of his father. Great honour was paid to the thee birds, and all three of them gave instruction in temporal and spiritual matters. The king, abiding in the admonition of the Great Being, by almsgiving and other good works became destined to heaven. The councillors after performing the king's obsequies, speaking to the birds said, "My lord, Jambu, the king ordered the royal umbrella to be raised over you." The Great Being said, "I have no need of the kingdom, do you exercise rule with all vigilance," and after establishing the people in the moral law, he said, "Execute justice," and he had righteous judgement inscribed on a golden plate and disappeared in the forest. And his admonition continued in force forty thousand years.

A KING FINDS HIS FRIEND THROUGH A SONG

Once upon a time, the Magadha king reigned in Rajagaha. The Bodhisatta was born to his chief queen and on his naming-day they called him prince Arindama. On the very day of his birth a son was also born to the royal chaplain, and to him they gave the name of young Sonaka. The two lads grew up together and when they were of age they were exceedingly handsome, in appearance not to be distinguished one from another, and they went to Takkasila and, after being trained in all sciences, they left that place with the intention of learning the practical uses of arts and local observances, and gradually in the course of their wanderings found their way to Benares. There they took up their abode in the royal park and next day entered the city. That very day certain men being minded to make an offering of food to Brahmins provided some rice-porridge and arranged seats, and on seeing these youths approach they brought them into the house and made them sit upon the seats they had prepared. On the seat allotted to the Bodhisatta a white cloth was spread, on that assigned to Sonaka a red woolen rug. On seeing this omen Sonaka at once understood that this day his dear friend Arindama would become king in Benares, and that he would offer him the post of commander-in-chief. After they had finished their meal they returned together to the park. Now it was the seventh day since the king of Benares had died and the royal house was without an heir. So the councillors and the rest after washing themselves, head and all, assembled together and saying, "Thou art to go to the house of the man that is worthy to be king, they started the festal car. On leaving the city it gradually approached the park and stopping at the park gate it stood there, ready for anyone to mount upon it. The Bodhisatta lay, with his outer robe wrapped about his head, on the royal slab of stone, while the lad Sonaka sat near him. On hearing the sound of musical instruments Sonaka thought, "Here comes the festal car for Arindama. To-day he will be made king and he will offer me the post of commander. But verily I have no desire for rule: when he is gone away, I will leave the world and become an ascetic," and he stood on one side in concealment. The chaplain on entering the park saw the Great being lying there and ordered his trumpets to be sounded. The Great Being woke up and after turning over and lying for a while he rose up and sat crosslegged on the stone seat. Then the chaplain clasping his arms in a suppliant attitude cried, "The kingdom, Sire, comes to you." "Why is there no heir to the throne?" "Even so, sire." "Then it is well," he said. So they sprinkled him to be king then and there. And mounting him on the car they brought him with a vast escort into the city. After a right wise procession round the city he ascended to his palace and in the greatness of his glory he forgot all about young Sonaka. But when the king was gone, Sonaka returned and sat on the stone seat, and so it was that a withered leaf of a sal tree fell from its stalk in front of him, and on seeing it he cried, "Even as this leaf, so will my body fall into decay," and acquiring supernatural insight by reflecting on the impermanence of all things he attained to the state of a pacceka Buddha, and at this very instant his characteristic as a layman vanished, and the marks of an ascetic became visible, and making the solemn utterance, "There is no more re-birth for me," he set out for the cave of Nandamula. And the Great Being after the lapse of forty years remembered Sonaka and said, "Where in the world can Sonaka be?" And time after time calling him to mind he found no one to tell him saying, "I have heard of him or I have seen him," And sitting cross-legged on a royal throne upon a magnificent dais, surrounded by a company of minstrels and mime dancers in the enjoyment of his glory, he said, "Whosoever shall hear from someone that Sonaka dwells in such and such a place and shall repeat it to me, to him I promise a hundred pieces of money, but whosoever shall see him with his own eyes and shall tell me, to him I promise a thousand piece of money, and giving expression to this inspired utterance, in the form of a song, he repeated the first stanza:

A thousand crowns for one that sees my friend and playmate
dear,
A hundred lo! I gave if one of Sonaka should hear.

Then a nautch girl, catching it up, as it were, from his very mouth, sang the words, and then another and another took it up till the whole harem, thinking it was a favourite air of the king's, all sang it. And gradually both towns-people and country-folk sang the same song and the king too constantly sang it. At the end of fifty years the king had many sons and daughters, and the eldest son was called prince Dighavu. At this time the peccaka buddha Sonaka thought, "King Arindama is anxious to see me. I will go and explain to him the misery of desires and the blessing of Renunciation, and will show him the way to become an ascetic. And by his supernatural power he conveyed himself thither and took a seat in the park. At that moment a boy seven years old, wearing his hair in five knots, was sent there by his mother, and as he was gathering sticks in the park garden he sang over and over again this song. Sonaka called the boy to him and asked him saying, "Why, my lad, do you always sing the same song and never sing anything else? Do you not know any other song?" "I know others, holy Sir, but this is our king's favourite song, and so I constantly sing it." "Has any one been found to sing a refrain to this song?" "No, Sir." "I will teach you one and then you can go and sing the refrain before the king." "Yes, Sir." So he taught him the refrain "The thousand give" and the rest of it, and when the boy had mastered it, he sent him off, saying, "Go, my lad, and sing this refrain before the king and he will grant you great power. What have you to do with gathering sticks? Be off with you as quick as you can." "Very well," said the boy, and having mastered the refrain and saluted Sonaka he said, "Holy Sir, until I bring the king, do you remain here." With these words he went off as fast as he could to his mother and said to her, "Dear mother, give me a bath and dress me in my best clothes: to-day will I free you from your poverty." And when he had taken a bath and was smartly dressed, he went to the door of the palace and said, "Porter, go and tell the king and say, 'A certain lad has come and even now stands at the door, prepared to sign a song with you." So the porter made haste and told the king. The king summoned him to his presence and said, "Friend, would you sing a song with me?" "Yes, Sire." "Then sing it." "My lord; I will not sing it here, but have a drum beaten through the city and bid the people assemble together. I will sing before the people." The king ordered this to be done, and, taking his seat in the middle of a couch under a magnificent pavilion and assigning a suitable seat to the boy, he said, "Now then sing your song." "Sire," he said, "you sing first and then I will sing a refrain to it." Then the king sang first, repeating this stanza:

A thousand crowns for one that sees my friend and
                                        playmate dear,
A hundred lo ! I give if one of Sonaka should hear.

(Then the Master, to make it clear that the boy with his hair dressed in five knots sang a refrain to the song begun by the king, in his state as perfect Buddha repeated two lines:)

Then up and spake that little boy—five tangled locks he
                                        wore—
"The thousand give to me who saw, who heard a hundred
                                        more:
I'll tell thee news of Sonaka, thy playfellow of yore."

The verses that follow are to be taken in their obvious
connexion:

Pray in what country, realm, or town hast thou a-wandering
been,
And where was Sonaka, my friend, I prithee tell me, seen?
Within this realm, in thine own park is many a big sal tree
With leaves dark green and stems so straight, a pleasant
sight to see;
Their branches densely interlaced, cloud-like, to heaven
they rise,
And at their foot lo ! Sonaka in meditation lies,
Filled with the Arhat's holy calm, when human passion
dies.
The king then started in full force and leveling the road
He made his way straight to the place of Sonaka's abode.
There wandering midst an ample grove within his pleasure
ground,
All passionless, in saintly bliss, his friend at rest he found.

Without saluting him he sat on one side and, by reason of
his being himself given up to evil passion, he fancied he was
some poor wretch and addressed him in this stanza:
His parents dead, with shaven head, clad in monk's robe I
see
A wretched brother in a trance, stretched here beneath
this tree.
On hearing this said Sonaka, "He is no wretched wight
Who is his every action, Sire, has aye attained to right.
Nay rather wretched those who right neglect and practise
ill,
For evil doer evil doom is destined to fulfil.

Thus did he rebuke the Bodhisatta, and he pretending not
to know he was being rebuked, talking in a friendly way with
him, declared his name and family and spoke this stanza:
As king of Kasi I am known, Arindama my name,
Since coming here, Sir, hast thou met with aught deserving
blame?

Then the pacceka Buddha said, "Not merely while dwelling here but nowhere else have I met with any discomfort," and he began to tell in verse the blessings of the monk:

'Mongst blessings of poor homeless monk I ever count it
    one,
In store-room jar or granary he has hoarded none,
But only craves what others leave and lives content
    thereon.
The next of all his blessings this is one deserving praise,
He free from blame enjoys his food and no one him
    gainsays.
Third blessing of the monk I hold is this, that all his days
He eats his food, desires extinct, and no one him gain- says.
The fourth of all his blessings is that wheresoe'er he goes,
He wanders free throughout the realm and no attachment
    knows.
Fifth blessing this that should the town, wherever he may
    be,
Perish in flames, he suffers not, for nought to burn has he.
The sixth of all the blessings he may reckon to his lot,
That if the realm should be despoiled, he suffers not a jot.
The seventh of the blessings that to poverty he owes,
Though robbers should his path beset and many dangerous
    foes
With bowl and robe the holy man ever in safety goes.
Last blessing this that wheresoe'er our wanderer may fare,
Homeless and poor, he journeys on without regret or care.

Thus did the pacceka buddha Sonaka tell of the eight blessings of the monk, and even beyond this he could have told of a hundred, nay a thousand immeasurable blessings, but the king being given upto sensual desires cut short his speech, saying, "I have no need of monkish blessings," and to make it clear how devoted he was to evil passions he said:

Thy many blessings thou mayst praise but what am I to do
Who worldly pleasures, Sonaka, so greedily pursue?
Dear are all human joys to me and heavenly joys as well,
But how to gain both worlds at once, to me, I prithee, tell.

Then the pacceka buddha answered him:

Who greedily on pleasure bent their worldly lusts would
                                                      sate.
Work wickedness awhile, to be re-born in woeful state.
But they who leave desire behind through life all fearless
                                                        go,
And reaching concentration pure are ne'er re-born to
woe. Here tell I thee a parable; Arindama, give heed,
Some that are wise through parable my meaning best may
                                                      read.
See ! borne along on Ganges's flooded tide a carcase vast,
A foolish crow thought to himself as it was floating past,
" Oh what a carriage I have found and goodly store of food,
Here will I stay both night and day, enjoying blissful mood."
So eats he flesh of elephant and drinks from Ganges' stream.
And budging not sees grove and shrine pass by him in a
                                                     dream.
Thus headless and on carrion vile so all intent was he,
The Ganges swept him headlong to the perils of the sea.
But when with food exhausted he, poor bird, essayed a
                                                     flight,
Nor east nor west nor south nor north was any land in
                                                      sight.
Far out at sea, so weak was he long ere he reached the
                                                      shore,
Midst countless perils of the deep he fell to rise no more.
For crocodiles and monster fish, where our poor flutterer
                                                        lay,
Came ravening all around and quick devoured their
                                              quivering prey.
So thou and all that greedily pleasures of sense pursue
Are deemed as wise as was this crow, till ye all lusts
                                                   eschew.
My parable proclaims the Truth. To it, O king, give heed,
Thy fame for good or ill will grow according to thy deed.

Thus by means of this parable did he admonish the king
and, in order to fix it firmly in his mind, he repeated this stanza:

In pity once, nay even twice, utter the warning word,
But keep not on repeating it, like slave before his lord.
Thus in his wisdom infinite did Sonaka the seer
Instruct the king, and then in space straightway did
                                                    disappear.
(This stanza was uttered by the Master as Buddha.)

And the Bodhisatta stood gazing on him as he passed
through the air, so long as he remained within the range of his
vision, but when he had passed our of sight, he was greatly
agitated and thought, "This brahmin, low-born fellow that he is,
after scattering the dust from his feet upon my head, though I
am sprung from an unbroken line of nobles, has disappeared in
the sky: I must to-day renounce the world and become a religious.
So in his desire to join the religious and give up his kingdom he
repeated a couple of stanzas:
Where are my charioteers, dispatched a worthy king to
                                                    find?
I would not longer region; henceforth my crown I have
                                                    resigned.
To-morrow one may die, who knows? I'll be ordained to-day,
Lest, like the foolish crow, I fall 'neath passion's baneful
                                                    sway.

On hearing him thus abdicate his throne his councillors
said:
Thou hast a son, Dighavu named, a goodly prince is he,
By sprinkling raise him to the throne, for the our king shall
                                                    be.

Then, beginning with the stanza spoken by the king, the
verses in due order are to be understood in their obvious
connexion:
Then quickly bring Dighavu here, a goodly prince is he,
By sprinkling raise him to the throne for he your king shall
                                                    be.
When they had brought Dighavu there, their nursing king
                                                    to be,
His sire addressed his darling boy—an only son was he.

Full sixty thousand villages I once did claim as mine,
Take them, my son, to thee henceforth my kingdom I resign.
To-morrow one may die, who knows? I'll be ordained to-
                                                    day;
Lest, like the foolish crow, I fall 'neath passion's baneful
                                                    sway.
Lo! Sixty thousand elephants with splendour all bedight,
With girths of gold, caparisoned with trappings golden-
                                                    bright.
Each ridden by his own mahout, with spiked hook in hand,
Take them, my son, I give them thee as ruler of the land.
To-morrow one may die, who knows? I'll be ordained to-
                                                    day;
Lest, like the foolish crow, I fall 'neath passion's baneful
                                                    sway.
Lo! Sixty thousand horses here, bedecked in bright array
—Sindh horses, all of noble breed and fleet of foot are
                                                    they—
Each ridden by a henchman bold, with sword and bow in
                                                    hand,
Take them, my son, I give them thee as ruler of the land.
To-morrow one may die, who knows? I'll be ordained to-
                                                    day;
Lest, like the foolish crow, I fall 'neath passion's baneful
                                                    sway.
Lo! Sixty thousand cars all yoked, with banners flying free,
With tiger skin and panther hide, a gorgeous sight to see.
Each driven my mailed charioteers, all armed with bow in
                                                    hand,
Take them, my son, I give them thee, as ruler of the land.
To-morrow one may die, who knows? I'll be ordained to-day;
Lest, like the foolish crow, I fall 'neath passion's baneful
                                                    sway.
Lo! Sixty thousand kine so red, with bulls on every hand,
Take them, my son, I give them thee as ruler of the land.
To-morrow one may die, who knows? I'll be ordained to-
                                                    day;
Lest, like the foolish crow, I fall 'neath passion's baneful
                                                    sway.

Here twice eight thousand maidens fair in goodly vesture
stand,
With many a jeweled bracelet decked and rings upon each
hand,
Take them, my son, I give them thee as ruler of the land.
To-morrow one may die, who knows? I'll be ordained to-
day;
Lest, like the foolish crow, I fall 'neath passion's baneful
sway.
They say to me, "Thy mother dear, alas! Poor boy, is dead,"
I cannot live without thee too. All joy from life is fled.
As close behind old elephant a young one oft is found
Moving through mountain-pass or wood, o'er rough or level
ground.
So bowl in hand I'll follow thee, wherever thou mayst lead,
Nor shalt thou find me burdensome or difficult to feed.
As oft some ship of merchants seeking gain at any cost
Is swallowed by a whirlpool and both ship and crew are
lost.
So lest I find a stumbling-block in this unlucky boy,
Instal him in my palace there all pleasures to enjoy—
With maids whose hands caressing him with gleaming
gold are bright,
Like Sakka midst his nymphs divine, he'll ever take delight.
Then brought they prince Dighavu to the palace, home of
joy,
And seeing him these maidens fair addressed the royal
boy.
"Art thou a god, or bard divine, or Sakka known to fame,
Dispensing aims in every town? We fain would learn thy
name."
No god am I, nor bard divine, nor Sakka known to fame,
But heir to king of Kasi, prince Dighavu is my name.
So cherish me and happy be: each one as wife I claim.
Then thus unto Dighavu, their liege lord, these maidens
said;
"Where has the king a refuge gained, and whither is he
fled?"
The king escaped from miry ways is safe upon dry ground,

From thorns and jungle free at last the high road he has
                                        found.
But I am set upon a path that leads to woeful state.
Through thorns, and jungle on I press to reach an awful
                                        fate.
Welcome ᴛᴏ us, as lion is to cubs in mountain lair,
Bear sway henceforth, our sovereign lord, the true and
                                        rightful heir.

And having so spoken they all sounded their musical
instruments and all manner of song and dance took place, and
so great was his glory that the prince intoxicated by it forgot
all about his father, but exercising his rule with justice he fared
according to his deeds. But the Bodhisatta developed the
supernatural faculty resulting from Meditation and passed away
to the Brahmin world.

THE UGLY BRIDEGROOM

Once upon a time, in the Malla kingdom, in the royal city
of Kusavati, king Okkaka ruled his kingdom righteously. Amongst
his sixteen thousand wives the chief was Silavati, his queen
consort. Now she had neither son nor daughter, and the men of
the city and all his subjects assembled at the door of the palace,
complaining that the realm would utterly perish. The king
opened his window and said, "Under my rule no man worketh
iniquity. Wherefore do ye reproach me?" "True, sire," they
answered, "no one worketh iniquity, but no son is born to you,
to perpetuate the race: a stranger will seize upon the kingdom
and destroy it. Therefore pray for a son who can rule your
kingdom righteously." "In my desire for a son, what am I to do?"
"First of all send out into the streets for a whole week a band
of dancing women of low degree—giving the act a religious
sanction-and if one of them shall give birth to a son, well and
good. Otherwise send out a company of fairly good standing,
and finally a band of the highest rank. Surely amongst so many
one women will be found of sufficient merit to bear a son." The
king did as they bade him, and every seventh day he inquired
of all such as had returned, after taking their fill of pleasure,

whether any of them had conceived. And when they all answered, "No, sire," the king was now in despair and cried, "No son will be born to me." Then men of the city reproached him as before. The king said, "Why do ye reproach me? At your bidding companies of women were exposed in the streets, and no one of them has conceived. What now am I to do?" "Sire," they answered, "these women must be immoral and void of merit. They have not sufficient merit to conceive a son. But because they do not conceive, you are not to relax your efforts. The queen consort, Silavati, is a virtuous woman. Send her out into the streets. A son will be born to her." The king readily assented, and proclaimed by beat of drum that on the seventh day from that time the people were to assemble and the king would expose Silavati—giving the act a religious character. And on the seventh day he had the queen magnificently arrayed and carried down from the palace and exposed in the streets. By the power of her virtue the abode of Sakka manifested signs of heat. Sakka, considering what this might mean, found that the queen was anxious for a son and thought, "I must grant her a son," and, while wondering whether there was anyone in the world of gods worthy to be her son, he beheld the Bodhisatta. At this time, it is said, having passed through his existence in the heaven of the Thirty-three, he was longing to be born in a higher world. Sakka, coming to the door of his dwelling-place, summoned him forth, saying, "Sir, you are to go to the world of men, and to be conceived as the child of Okkaka's chief consort," and then he gained the consent of another divine being and said, "And you too shall be her son," and that no man might make a breach in her virtue, Sakka went disguised as an aged brahmin to the door of the palace. The people, after washing and adorning themselves, each being minded to possess the queen, assembled at the royal entrance, but at the sight of Sakka they laughed, asking him why he had come. Sakka said "Why blame me? If I am old in person, my passions are unabated, and I am come with the hope of carrying off Silavati with me, should I get her." And with these words, by his divine power he got in front of them all, and by reason of the majesty that was in him no man could stand before him, and as the queen stepped forth from the palace, arrayed in all her glory, he took her by the hand and made off with her. Then such as stood there abused him, saying, "Fie on him, an old brahmin is gone off with a queen of peerless beauty: he knows not what is becoming to him." The queen too thought, "An old man is carrying me off." And she was vexed and angry, nay disgusted. The king standing at the open window, looking to see who might carry off the queen, on seeing who it was, was highly displeased. Sakka, escaping with her by the city gate, miraculously caused a house to appear close at hand, with its door open and a bundle of sticks laid out ready. "Is this your abode?" she asked. "Yes, lady, hitherto I have been alone: now there are two of us. I will go my rounds and bring home some husked rice. Do you meanwhile lie down on this heap of sticks." And so saying, he gently stroked her with his hand, and causing her to thrill with the divine touch, he then and there laid her down, and at his touch she lost consciousness. Then by his supernatural power he transported her to the heaven of the Thirty-three and set her down on a heavenly couch in a magnificent palace. On the seventh day waking up, she beheld this splendour and knew that this was no brahmin, but must be Sakka himself. At this moment Sakka was seated at the foot of a coral-tree, surrounded by heavenly dancers. Rising from her couch, she approached and saluted the god and stood respectfully on one side. Then Sakka said, "I give thee a boon: choose what it shall be." "Then grant me, sire, a son." "Not merely one, lady. I will grant you two. One of them shall be wise but ugly, the other shall be handsome but a fool. Which of them will you have first?" "The wise one," she answered. "Good", said he, and he presented her with a piece of kusagrass, a heavenly robe and sandal-wood, the flower of the coral-tree and a Kokanada lute. Then he transported her into the king's bedchamber and laid her down on the same couch with the king, and touched her person with his thumb, and at that moment the Bodhisatta was conceived. And Sakka straightway returned to his own abode. The wise queen knew that she had conceived. Then the king, waked, and seeing her said, "Who brought you here?" "Sakka, Sire." "Why! with my own eyes I saw an aged brahmin carry you off. Why do you deceive me?" "Believe me, sire, Sakka took me with him to the world of gods." "Lady, I do not believe you." Then she showed him the kusa-grass which Sakka had given her, saying, "Now believe me." The king thought, "Kusa-grass is to be got anywhere," and still disbelieved her. Then she showed him her heavenly robes. On seeing these the king believed her and said, "Dear lady, granted that Sakka carried you off, but are you with child?" "Yes, sire, I have conceived." The king was delighted and performed the ceremony due to her state. In ten months' time she gave birth to a son. Giving him no other name, they called him merely after the grass, Kusa. About the time that prince Kusa could run alone, a second heavenly being was conceived. To him they gave the name of Jayampati. The boys were brought up with great state. The Bodhisatta was so wise that without learning aught from his teacher, he by his own ability attained to proficiency in all liberal arts. So when he was sixteen years old, the king being anxious to make over the kingdom to him, addressing the queen, said, "Lady, in making over the kingdom to your son, we would institute dramatic festivities, and in our lifetime we would see him established on the throne. If there is any king's daughter in all India you would like, on his bringing her here we will make her his queen consort. Sound him as to what king's daughter he affects." She readily agreed and sent a handmaid to report the matter to the prince and ascertain his views. She went and told the prince the state of affairs. On hearing her the Great Being thought, "I am not well-favoured. A lovely princess, even if she is brought here as my bride, on seeing me, will say, 'What have I to do with this ugly fellow?' and will run away, and we shall be put to shame. What have I to do with household life? I will foster my parents as long as they live, and at their death I will renounce the world and become an ascetic." So he said, "What need have I of a kingdom or festivities? When my parents die, I will adopt the ascetic life." The maid returned and told the queen what he had said. The king was greatly distressed and after a few days again sent a message, but he still refused to listen to it. After thrice rejecting the proposal, on the fourth occasion he thought, "It is not fitting to be in complete opposition to one's parents: I will devise something." So he summoned the chief smith, and, giving him a quantity of gold, bade him go and make a female image. When he was gone he took more gold and himself fashioned it into the figure of a woman. Verify the purposes of Bodhisattas succeed. The figure was beautiful beyond the power of tongue to tell. Then the Great Being had it robed in linen and placed in the royal chamber. On seeing the image brought by the chief goldsmith, he found fault with it and said, "Go and fetch the figure placed in our royal chamber." The man went into the room, and on seeing it thought, "This surely must be some heavenly nymph, come to take her pleasure with the prince," and he left the room without having the courage to stretch forth his hand towards it, and he said, "Sire, standing in your royal chamber is a noble daughter of the gods: I dare not approach her." "Friend," he said, "go and fetch the golden image," and being charged a second time he brought it. The prince ordered the image that the smith had wrought to be thrown into the golden chamber, and that which he himself had made he had adorned and placed in a car and sent it to his mother, saying, "When I find a woman like this, I will take her to wife." His mother summoned her councillors and addressed them, saying, "Friends, our son is possessed of great merit and is the gift of Sakka; he must find a princess worthy of him. Do you then have this figure placed in a covered carriage and traverse the length and breadth of India, and whatsoever king's daughter you see like this image, present it to that king and say, "King Okkaka will contract a marriage with your daughter.' Then arrange a day for your return and come home." They said, "It is well," and took the image and set out with a vast retinue. And in their journeying, to whatever royal city they come, there at eventide wheresoever the people gather together, after decking out this image with robes, flowers and other adornments, they mount it upon a golden car and leave it on the road leading to the bathing-place, and step back and stand on one side to listen to what all such as pass by had to say. The people on seeing it, not dreaming that it was a golden image, said, "This thought really only a woman, is very beautiful, like some divine nymph. Why in the world is she stationed here, and whence does she come? We have no one to compare with her in our city," and after thus praising her beauty, they went their ways. The councilors said, "If there were any girl like it here, they would say, 'This is like so and so, the king's daughter' or like so and so, the ministers daughter' verily there is no such maiden here." And they go off with it to some other city. So in their wanderings they reached the city of Sagala in the kingdom of Madda. Now the king of Madda had seven daughters, of extraordinary beauty, like to nymphs of heaven. The eldest of them was called Pabhavati. From her person stream forth rays of light, as it were of the newly-risen sun. When it is dark in her closet, measuring four cubits, there is no need of any lamp. The whole chamber is one blaze of light. Now she had a humpbacked nurse, who, when she had supplied Pabhavati with food, intending to wash her head, at eventide going forth to fetch water eight slave-girls carrying each a water pot, on the way to the bathing-place saw this image and, thinking it to be Pabhavati, exclaimed, "The ill-behaved girl, pretending she would have her head washed, sent us to fetch water, and stealing a march upon us, is standing there in the road," and being in a rage she cried, "Fie, you are a disgrace to the family: there you stand, getting here before us. Should the king hear of it, he will be the death of us," and with these words she struck the image on the cheek, and a space as big as the palm of her hand was broken. Then discovering it was a golden image she burst out laughing, and going to the slave-girls said, "See what I have done. Thinking it was my foster daughter, I struck it. What is this image worth in comparison with my child? I have only hurt my hand for my pains." Then the king's emissaries took hold of her and said, "What is this story you tell us, saying that your daughter is fairer than this image?" "I mean Pabhavati, the Madda king's daughter. This image is not worth a sixteenth fraction of her." Glad at heart, they sought the entrance to the palace, and had themselves announced to the kings, sending in word that king Okkaka's emissaries were standing at his door. The king arose from his seat and, standing up, ordered them to be admitted. On entering they saluted the king and said, "Sir, our king inquires after your health," and meeting with a hospitable reception, when asked why they had come, they replied, "Our king has a son, the bold prince Kusa: the king is anxious to make over his kingdom to him, and has sent us to ask you to give him your daughter Pabhavati in marriage and to accept as a present this golden figure," and with these words they offered him the image. He gladly agreed, thinking an alliance with so noble a king would be an auspicious one. Then the envoys said, "Sir, we cannot tarry here: we will go and tell our king that we have secured the hand of the princess, and then he will come and fetch her." The king agreed to this, and having hospitably entertained them let them go. On their return they made their report to the king and queen. The king with a great retinue set out from Kusavati and in course of time reached the city of Sagala. The Madda king came out to meet him, brought him into the city and paid him great honour. Queen Silavati, being a wise woman, thought, "What will be the issue of all this?" At the end of one or two days she said to the king. "We are anxious to see our daughter-in-law." He readily assented and sent for his daughter. Pabhavati, magnificently dressed and surrounded by a band of her attendants came and saluted her mother-in-law. On seeing her the queen at once thought, "This maidens is very lovely and my son is ill-favoured. Should she see him, she will not stay a single day but will run away. I must devise some scheme." Addressing the Madda king she said, "My daughter-in-law is quite worthy of my son: howbeit we have an hereditary observance in our family. If she will abide by this custom, we will take her to be his bride." "What is this observance of yours?" "In our family a wife is not allowed to see her husband by daylight until she has conceived. If she will act up to this, we will take her." The king asked his daughter, "My dear, will you be able to act thus?" "Yes, dear father, "she replied. Then king Okkaka bestowed much gear on the Madda king and departed with her. And the Madda king dispatched his daughter with a vast retinue. Okkaka, on reaching Kusavati, gave orders for the city to be decorated, all prisoners to be released, and after sprinkling his son as king and creating Pabhavati his chief consort, he proclaimed by beat of drum the rule of king Kusa. And all the kings throughout India who had daughters sent them to the court of king Kusa, and all who had sons, desiring friendship with him, sent their sons to be his pages. The Bodhisatta had a large company of dancers and ruled with great state. But he is not allowed to see Pabhavati by day, nor may she see him, but at night they have free access one to another. At that time there is an extraordinary effulgence from the person of Pabhavati, but the Bodhisatta leaves the royal chamber while it is still dark. After a few days he told his mother he longed to see Pabhavati by day. She refused his request, saying, "Let not this be thy good pleasure, but wait until she has conceived." Again and again he besought her. So she said, "Well, go to the elephant-stall and stand there disguised as an elephant-keeper. I will bring her there, so that you may have your fill of gazing at her, but see that you do not make yourself known to her." He agreed to this and went to the elephant-stall. The queen-mother proclaimed an elephant-festival and said to Pabhavati, "Come, we will go and see your lord's elephant by name. Then, as Pabhavati was walking behind his mother, the king struck her in the back with a lump of elephant-dung. She was enraged and said, "I will get the king to cut your hand off," and by her words she vexed the queen-mother, who appeased her by rubbing her back. A second time the king was anxious to see her and, disguised as a groom in the horse-stable, just as before, he struck her with a piece and horse-dirt, and then too when she was angry her mother-in-law appeased her. Again, one day Pabhavati told her mother-in-law she longed to see the Great Being, and when her request was refused by her mother, who said, "Nay, let not this be your pleasure," she besought her again and again, so at last she said, "Well, to-morrow my son will be making a solemn procession through the city. You can open your window and see him." And after so saying, on the next day she had the city decked out, and ordered prince Jayampati, clad in a royal robe and mounted on an elephant, to make a triumphal procession through the city. Standing at the window with Pabhavati, she said, "Behold the glory of your lord." She said, "I have got a husband not unworthy of me," and she was highly elated. But that very day the Great Being, disguised as an elephant-keeper, was seated behind Jayampati, and gazing at Pabhavati as much as he would, in the joy of his heart he disported himself by gesticulating with his hands. When the elephant had passed them, the queen-mother asked her if she had seen her husband. "Yes, lady, but seated behind him was an elephant-keeper, a very ill-conducted fellow, who gesticulated at me with his hands. Why do they let such an ugly, ill-omened creature sit behind the king?" "It is desirable, my dear, to have a guard sit behind the king." "This elephant-keeper," she thought, "is a bold fellow, and has no proper respect for the king. Can it be that he is king Kusa? No doubt he is hideous, and that is why they do not let me see him." So she whispered to her humpbacked nurse, "Go, my dear, at once and make out whether it was the king who sat in front or behind." "How am I to find this out?" "If he be the king he will be the first to alight from the elephant: you are to know by this token." She went and stood at a distance and saw the Great Being alight first, and afterwards prince Jayampati. The Great Being looking about him, first on one side and then on the other, seeing the humpbacked old woman, knew at once why she has come, and, sending for her, straitly charged her not to reveal his secret, and let her go. She came and told her mistress, "The one that sat in front was the first to alight," and Pabhavati believed her. Once more the king longed to see her and begged his mother to arrange it. She could not refuse him and said, "Well then, disguise yourself and go to the garden." He went and hid himself up to his neck in the lotus-pool, standing in the water with his head shaded by a lotus-leaf and his face covered by its flower. And his mother brought Prabhavati in the evening to the garden, and saying, "Look at these trees, or look at these birds or deer," thus tempted her on till she came to the bank of the lotus-pond. When she saw the pond covered with five kinds of lotus, she longed to bathe and went down to the water's edge with her maidens. While disporting herself she saw that lotus and stretched forth her hand, eager to pluck it. Then the king, putting aside the lotus-leaf, took her by the hand, saying, "I am king Kusa." On seeing his face she cried, "A goblin is catching hold of me," and then and there swooned away. So the king let go her hand. On recovering consciousness she thought, "King Kusa, they say, caught me by the hand, and he it was that hit me in the elephant-stall with a piece of elephant-dirt, and in the horse- stable with a piece of horse–dirt, and he it was that sat behind on the elephant and made game of me. What have I to do with such an ugly, hideous husband? If I live, I will have another husband." So she summoned the councillors who had escorted her hither and said, "Make ready my chariot. This very day I will be off." They told this to the king and he thought, "If she cannot get away, her heart will break: let her go. By my own power I will bring her back again." So he allowed her to depart, and she returned straight to her father's city. And the Great Being passed from the park into the city and climbed up to his splendid palace. Verily it was in consequence of an aspiration in a previous existence that she disapproved of the Bodhisatta, and it was owing to a former act of his that he was so ugly. Of old, they say, in a suburb of Benares, in the upper and lower street, one family had two sons and another had one daughter. Of the two sons the Bodhisatta was the younger, and the maiden was wedded to the elder son, but the younger, being unmarried, continued to live with his brother. Now one day in this house they baked some very dainty cakes, and the Bodhisatta was away in the forest; so putting aside a cake for him they distributed and ate the rest. At that moment a pacceka buddha came to the door for alms. The Bodhisatta's sister-in-law thought she would bake another cake for young master and took and gave his cake to the pacceka buddha and at that very instant he returned from the forest. So she said, "My lord, do not be angry, but I have given your portion to the pacceka buddha." He said, "After eating your own portion you give mine away, and you will make me another cake forsooth!" And he was angry and went and took the cake from the beggar's bowl. She went to her mother's house and took some fresh-matted ghee, in colour like the champak flower, and filled the bowl with it, and it sent forth a blaze of light. On seeing this she put up a prayer: "Holy sir, wherever I am born, may my body give forth a light and may I be very lovely, and nevermore may I have to dwell in the same place with this lewd fellow." Thus as the result of this prayer of old she would have none of him. And the Bodhisatta, in dropping the cake again into the bowl, put up a prayer: "Holy sir, though she should live a hundred leagues away, may I have the power to carry her off as my bride." In that he was angry and took the cake, as the result of this act of old he was born so ugly.

Kusa was so overwhelmed with sorrow when Pabhavati left him that the other women, though ministering to him with all kinds of service, had not the heart to look him in the face, and all his palace, bereft of Pabhavati, seemed as it were desolate. Then he thought, "By this time he she will have reached the city Sagala," and at break of day he sought his mother and said, "Dear mother, I will go and fetch Pabhavati. You are to rule my kingdom," and he uttered the first stanza:

This realm with joy and bliss untold,
Trappings of state and wealth of gold,
This realm, I say, rule thou for me:
I go to seek Pabhavati.

His mother, on hearing what he had to say, replied, "Well, my son, you must exercise great vigilance; women, verily, are impure-minded creatures," and she filled a golden bowl with all manner of dainty food, and saying, "This is for you to eat on the journey," she took leave of him. Taking it he made a right wise circuit thrice round his mother, and cried, "If I live, I will see you again," and so withdrew to the royal chamber. Then he girded himself with the five sorts of weapons and putting a thousand pieces of money in a bag he took his bowl of food and a Kokanada lute and leaving the city set out on his journey. Being very strong and vigorous by noon-time he had travelled fifty leagues and, after eating his food, in the remaining half-day he made up another fifty leagues, and so in the course of a single day he accomplished a journey of a hundred leagues. In the evening he bathed and then entered the city of Sagala. No sooner did he set foot in the place than Pabhavati by the power of his majesty could no longer rest quietly on her couch but got out of bed and lay upon the ground. The Bodhisatta was thoroughly exhausted with his journey, and being seen by a certain woman, as he was wandering about the street, was invited by her to rest in her house, and after first bathing his feet she offered him a bed. While he was asleep, she prepared him some food and then waking him up gave it him to eat. He was so pleased with her that he presented her with the thousand pieces of money and the golden bowl. Leaving there his five sorts of weapons, he said, "There is some place I must go to," and taking his lute he repaired to an elephant-stall and cried to the elephant-keepers, "Let me stay here and I will make music for you." They allowed him to do so and he went apart and lay down. When his fatigue had passed off, he rose up and unstrapping his lute he played and sang, thinking that all who dwelt in the city should hear the sound of it. Pabhavati, as she lay on the ground, heard it and thought, "This sound can come from no lute but his," and felt sure that king Kusa had come on her account. The king of Madda too on hearing it thought, "He plays very sweetly. Tomorrow I will send for him and make him my minstrel." The Bodhisatta thinking, "It is impossible for me to get sight of Pabhavati, if I stay here: this is the wrong place for me," sallied forth quite early and after taking his morning meal in an eating-house he left his lute and went to the king's potter and became his apprentice. One day after he had filled the house with potter's clay he asked if he should make some vessels, and when the potter answered, "Yes, do so," he placed a lump of clay on the wheel and turned it. When once it was turned, it went on swiftly till mid-day. After moulding all manner of vessels, great and small, he began making one specially for Pabhavati with various figures on it. Verily the purposes of Bodhisattas succeed. He resolved that Pabhavati was to see these figures. When he had dried and baked his vessels, the house was full of them. The potter went to the palace with various specimens. The king on seeing them asked who had made them. "I did, sire." "I am sure you did not make them. Who did?" "My apprentice, sire." "Not your apprentice, your master rather. Learn your trade from him. Henceforth let him make vessels for my daughters." And he gave him a thousand pieces of money, saying, "Give him this, and present all these small vessels to my daughters." He took the vessels to them and said, "These are made for your amusement." They were all present to receive them. Then the potter gave Pabhavati the vessel which the Great Being had made specially for her. Taking it she at once recognised her own likeness and that of the humpbacked nurse and knew it could be the handiwork of no one but king Kusa, and being angry she said, "I do not want it: give it to those that wish for it." Then her sisters perceiving that she was in a rage laughed and said, "You suppose it is the work of king Kusa. It was the potter, not he, that made it. Take it." She did not tell them that he had come there and had made it. The potter gave the thousand pieces of money to the Bodhisatta and said, "My son, the king is pleased with you. Henceforth you are to make vessels for his daughters and I am to take them to them." He though, "Although I go on living here, it is impossible for me to see Pabhavati," and he gave back the money to him and went to a basket-maker who served the king, and becoming his apprentice he made a palm-leaf fan for Pabhavati, and on it he depicted a white umbrella (as an emblem of royalty), and taking as his subject a banquet hall, amongst a variety of other forms he represented a standing figure of Pabhavati. The basket-maker took this and other ware, the workmanship of Kusa, to the palace. The king on seeing them asked who had made them and just as before presented a thousand pieces of money to the man, saying, "Give these specimens of wicker work to my daughters." And he gave the fan that was specially made for her to Pabhavati, and in this case also no one recognised the figures, but Pabhavati on seeing them knew it was the king's handiwork and said, "Let those that wish for it take it," and being in a rage she threw in on the ground. So the others all laughed at her. The basket-maker brought the money and gave it to the Bodhisatta. Thinking this was no place for him to stay in, he returned the money to the basket-maker and went to the king's gardener and became his apprentice, and while making all sorts of garlands he made a special wreath for Pabhavati, picket out with various figures. The gardener took them to the palace. When the king saw them, he asked who had fashioned these garlands. "I did, sire." "I am sure you did not make them. Who did?" "My apprentice, sire." "He is not your apprentice rather is he your maseter. Learn your trade from him. Henceforth he is to weave garlands of flowers for my daughters, and give him this thousand pieces of money"; and giving him the money he said, "Take these flowers to my daughters." And the gardener offered to Pabhavati the wreath that the Bodhisatta had made specially for her. Here too on seeing amongst the various figures a likeness of herself and the king she recognised Kusa's handiwork and in her rage threw the wreath on the ground. All her sisters, just as before, laughed at her. The gardener too took the thousand pieces of money and gave them to the Bodhisatta, telling him what had happened. He thought, "Neither is this the place for me," and returning the money to the gardener he went and engaged himself as an

apprentice to the king's cook. Now one day the cook in taking
various kinds of victuals to the king gave the Bodhisatta a bone
of meat to cook for himself. He prepared it in such a way that
the smell of it pervaded the whole city. The king smelt it and
asked if he were cooking some more meat in the kitchen. "No,
sire, but I did give my apprentice a bone of meat to cook. It must
be this that you smell." The king had it brought to him and
placed a morsel on the tip of his tongue and it woke up and
thrilled the seven thousand nerves of taste. The king was so
enslaved by his appetite for dainties that he gave him a thousand
pieces of money and said, "Henceforth you are to have food for
me and my daughters cooked by your apprentice, and to bring
mine to me yourself, but your apprentice is to bring theirs to my
daughters." The cook went and told him. On hearing it he
thought, "Now is my desire fulfilled: now shall I be able to see
Pabhavati." Being pleased he returned the thousand pieces of
money to the cook and next day he prepared and sent dishes
of food to the king and himself climbed up to the palace where
dwelt Pabhavati, taking the food for the king's daughters on a
carrying-pole. Pabhavati saw him climbing up with his load and
thought, "He is doing the work of slaves and hirelings, work
quite unsuitable for him. But if I hold my peace, he will think
I approve of him and going nowhere else he will remain here,
gazing at me. I will straightway abuse and revile him and drive
him away, not allowing him to remain a moment here." So she
left the door half open and, holding one hand on the panel, with
the other pressed up the bolt, and she repeated the second
stanza:

> Kusa, for thee by day and night
> To bear this burden is not right.
> Haste back, pray, to Kusavati;
> Thy ugly form I'm loth to see.

He thought, "I have got speech of Pabhavati," and pleased
at heart he repeated three stanzas:

> Bound by thy beauty's spell, Pabhavati,
> My native land has little charm for me;
> Madda's fair realm is ever my delight,
> My crown resigned, to live in thy dear sight.

O soft-eyed maiden, fair Pabhavati,
What is this madness that o'ermasters me?
Knowing full well the land that gave me birth,
I wander half distraught o'er all the earth.
Clad in bright-coloured bark and girt with golden zone,
Thy love, fair maid, I crave, and not an earthly throne.

When he had thus spoken, she thought. "I revile him, hoping
to rouse a feeling of resentment in him, but he as it were tries
to conciliate me by his words. Suppose he were to say, 'I am king
Kusa, and take me by the hand, who is there to prevent it? And
somebody might hear what we had to say." So she closed the
door and bolted it inside. And he took up his carrying-pole and
brought the other princesses their food. Pabhavati sent her
humpbacked slave to bring her the food that king Kusa had
cooked. She brought it and said, "Now eat." Pabhavati said, "I
will not eat what he has cooked. Do you eat it and go and get
your own supply of food and cook it and bring it here, but do
not tell anyone that king Kusa has come." The humpback
henceforth brought and ate the portion of the princess and
gave her own portion to Pabhavati. King Kusa from that time
being unable to see her thought, "I wonder whether Pabhavati
has any affection for me or not. I will put her to the test." So
after he had supplied the princesses with their food, he took his
load of victuals and going out struck the floor with his feet by
the door of Pabhavati's closet and clashing the dishes together
and groaning aloud he fell all of a heap and swooned away. At
the sound of his groans she opened her door and seeing him
crushed beneath the load he was carrying she thought, "Here
is a king, the chief ruler in all India, and for my sake he suffers
pain night and day, and now, being so delicately nurtured, he
has fallen under the burden of the victuals he carries. I wonder
if he is still alive," and stepping from her chamber she stretched
forth her neck and looked at his mouth, to watch his breathing.
He filled his mouth with spittle and let it drop on her person.
She retired into her closet, reviling him, and standing with the
door half open she repeated this stanza:
Ill luck is his that ever craves, to find his wishes spurned,
As thou, O king, dost fondly woo with love still unreturned.

But because he was madly in love with her, however much he was abused and reviled by her, he showed no resentment but repeated this stanza:

Whoso shall gain what he holds dear, may loved or unloved
be,
Success alone is what we praise, to lose is misery.

While he was still speaking, without at all relenting, she spoke in a firm voice, as if minded to drive him away, and repeated this stanza:

As well to dig through bed of rock with brittle wood as
spade,
Or catch the wind within a net, as woo unwilling maid.

On hearing this the king repeated three stanzas:

Hard hearted as stone art thou, so soft to outward view,
No word of welcome though I've come from far thy love to
sue.
When thou dost frown regarding me, proud dame, with
sullen look,
Then I in royal Madda's halls am nothing but a cook.
But if, O queen, in pity thou shouldst deign to smile on me,
No longer cook, once more am I lord of Kusavati.

On hearing his words she thought, "He is very pertinacious in all that he says. I must devise some lie to drive him hence," and she spoke this stanza:

If fortune-tellers spoke true words, 'twas this in sooth they
said,
"Mayst thou in pieces seven be hewn, ere thou king Kusa
wed."

On hearing this the king contradicting her said, "Lady, I too consulted fortune-tellers in my own kingdom and they predicted that there was no other husband for you save the lion-voiced lord, king Kusa, and through omens furnished by my own knowledge I say the same," and he repeated another stanza:

If I and other prophets here have uttered a true word,
Save me king Kusa thou shalt hail none other as thy Lord.

On hearing his words she said, "One cannot shame him. What is it to me whether he runs away or not?" and shutting the door she refused to show herself. And he took up his load and went down. From that day he could not set eyes on her and he got heartily sick of his cook's work. After breakfast he cut firewood, washed dishes and fetched water on his carrying pole, and then lying down he rested on a heap of grain. Rising early he cooked rice-gruel and the like, then took and served the food and suffered all this mortification by reason of his passionate love for Pabhavati. One day he saw the humpback passing by the kitchen door and hailed her. For fear of Pabhavati she did not venture to come near him, but passed on pretending to be in a great hurry. So he hastily ran up to her crying, "Crook-back." She turned and stopped, saying, "Who is here? I cannot listen to what you have to say." Then he said, "Both you and your mistress are very obstinate. Though living near you ever so long, we cannot so much as get a report of her health." She said, "Will you give me a present?" He replied, "Supposing I do so, will you be able to soften Pabhavati and bring me into her presence?" On her agreeing to do so, he said. "If you can do this, I will put right your humpback, and give you an ornament for your neck," and tempting her, he spoke five stanzas:

Necklace of gold I'll give to thee.
On coming to Kusavati,
If slender-limbed Pabhavati
Should only deign to look on me.
Necklace of gold I'll give to thee,
On coming to Kusavati,
If slender-limbed Pabhavati
Should only deign to speak to me.
Necklace of gold I'll give to thee,
On coming to Kusavati,
If slender-limbed Pabhavati
Should only deign to smile on me.
Necklace of gold I'll give to thee,
On coming to Kusavati,
If slender-limbed Pabhavati
Should laugh with joy at sight of me
Necklace of gold I'll give to thee,

On coming to Kusavati,
If slender-limbed Pabhavati
Should lay a loving hand on me.

On hearing his words she said, "Get you gone, my lord: in a very few days I will put her in your power. You shall see how energetic I can be." So saying she decided on her course of action, and going to Pabhavati she made as if she would clean her room and not leaving a bit of dirt big enough to hit one with, and removing even her shoes, she swept out the whole chamber. Then she arranged a high seat for herself in the doorway (keeping well outside the threshold) and, spreading a coverlet on a low stool for Pabhavati, she said, "Come, my dear, and I will search in your head for vermin," and making her sit there and place her head upon her lap, after scratching her a little and saying, "Ho! What a lot of lice we have here," she took some from her own head and put them on the head of the princess, and speaking in terms of endearment of the Great Being she sang his praises in this stanza:

This royal dame no pleasure feels Kusa once more to see,
Though, wanting nought, he serves as cook for simple
                                        hireling's fee.

Pabhavati was enraged with the humpback. So the old woman took her by the neck and pushed her inside the room, and being herself outside she closed the door and stood clinging to the cord which pulled the door to. Pabhavati being unable to get at her, stood by the door, abusing her, and spoke another stanza:

This humpbacked slave without a doubt,
For speaking such a word,
Deserves to have her tongue cut cut
With keenest sharpened sword.

So the humpback stood holding on to the rope that hung down and said, "You worthless, ill-behaved creature, what good will your fair looks do anyone? Can we live by feeding on your beauty?" and so saying she proclaimed the virtues of the Bodhisatta, shouting them aloud with the harsh voice of a humpback, in thirteen stanzas:

Esteem him not, Pabhavati, by outward form or height,
Great glory his, so do whate'er is pleasing in his sight.
Esteem him not, Pabhavati, by outward form or height,
Great wealth is his, so do whate'er is pleasing in his sight.
Esteem him not, Pabhavati, by outward form or height,
Great power is his, so do whate'er is pleasing in his sight.
Esteem him not, Pabhavati, by outward form or height,
Wide rule is his, so do whate'er is pleasing in his sight.
Esteem him not, Pabhavati, by outward form or height,
Great King is he, so do whate'er is pleasing in his sight.
Esteem him not, Pabhavati, by outward form or height,
Lion-voiced is he, so do whate'er is pleasing in his sight.
Esteem him not, Pabhavati, by outward form or height,
Clear-voiced is he, so do whate'er is pleasing in his sight.
Esteem him not, Pabhavati, by outward form or height,
Deep-voiced is he, so do whate'er is pleasing in his sight.
Esteem him not, Pabhavati, by outward form or height,
Sweet-voiced is he, so do whate'er is pleasing in his sight.
Esteem him not, Pabhavati, by outward form or height,
Honey-voiced is he, so do whate'er is pleasing in his sight.
Esteem him not, Pabhavati, by outward form or height,
A hundred arts are his, so do whate'er is pleasing in his
sight.
Esteem him not, Pabhavati, by outward form or height,
A warrior king is he, so do whate'er is pleasing in his sight.
Esteem him not, Pabhavati, by outward form or height,
King Kusa 'tis, so do whate'er is pleasing in his sight.

Hearing what she said, Pabhavati threatened the humpback, saying, "Crook-back, you roar too loud. If I catch hold of you, I will let you know you have a mistress." She replied, "In my consideration for you, I did not let your father know of king Kusa's arrival. Well, to-day I will tell the king," and speaking in a loud voice she cowed her. And saying, "Let no one hear of this," Pabhavati pacified the humpback. And the Bodhisatta not being able to get a sight of her, after seven months being sick of his hard bed and sorry food, thought, "What need have I of her? After living here seven months I cannot so much as get a sight of her. She is very harsh and cruel. I will go and see my father and mother." At this moment Sakka considering the matter found out how discontented Kusa was, and he thought, "After seven months he is unable even to see Pabhavati. I will find some way of letting him see her." So he sent messengers to seven kings as if they came from king Madda, to say, "Pabhavati has thrown over king Kusa and has returned home. You are to come and take her to wife." And he sent the same message to each of the seven separately. They all arrived in the city with a great following, not knowing one another's reasons for coming. They asked one the other, "Why have you come here?" And on discovering how matters stood, they were angry and said, "Will he give his daughter in marriage to seven of us? See how ill he behave. He mocks us, saying, 'Take her to wife.' Let him either give Pabhavati in marriage to all seven or let him fight us." And they sent a message to him to this effect and invested the city. On hearing the message, king Madda was alarmed and took counsel with his ministers, saying, "What are we to do?" Then his ministers made answer, "Sire, these seven kings have come for Pabhavati. If you refuse to give her, they will break down the wall and seize your kingdom. While the wall still stands unbroken, let us send Pabhavati to them"; and they repeated stanza:

> Like to proud elephants they stand in coats of mail arrayed,
> Ere yet they trample down our walls, send off in haste the
> maid.

The king on hearing this said, "If I should send Pabhavati to any one of them, the rest will join battle with me. It is out of the question to give her to any one of them. As she has cast off the chief king in all India, let her receive the reward due to her return home. I will slay her and cutting her body into seven pieces send one to each of the seven kings," and so saying he repeated another stanza:

> In pieces seven Pabhavati to hack, it is my will,
> One piece for each of these seven kings, who came her sire
> to kill.

This saying of his was noised abroad throughout the palace.

Her attendants came and told Pabhavati, "The king, they say,
will cut you in seven pieces and send them to the seven kings."
She was in fear of death and rising from her seat she went,
accompanied by her sisters, to her mother's state chamber.

She came into her mother' presence and saluting her broke
into these lamentations:
This face with powder beautified, here mirrored in a glass
To ivory handle deftly fixed, so winsome now alas!
With innocence and purity in every line expressed,
By warrior princes spurned in some lone forest soon will
                                                    rest.
These locks of hair so black of hue, bound up in stately coil,
Soft to the touch and fragrant with the finest sandal oil,
In charnel ground though covered up the vultures soon
                                                will find
And with their talons rend and tear and scatter to the
                                                wind.
These arms whose finger tips are dyed, like copper, crim-
                                            son red,
In richest sandal oil oft bathed and with soft down
                                        o'erspread,
Cut off and by proud kings in some lone forest flung aside,
A wolf will seize and carry off where'er he's fain to hide.
My teats are like the dates that on the palms with ripeness
                                                swell,
Fragrant with scent of sandalwood that men of Kasi fell:
Hanging thereon a jackal soon at them, methinks, will tug,
Just as a little baby boy his mother's breast may hug.
These hips of mine, well-knit and broad, cast in an ample
                                            mould,
Encircled with a cincture gay, wrought of the purest gold,
Cut off and by proud kings in some lone forest flung aside,
A wolf will seize and carry off where'er he's fain to hide.
Dogs, wolves, jackals and whatsoe'er are known as beasts
                                            of prey,
If once they eat Pabhavati, can suffer no decay.
Should warrior kings that come from far thy daughter's
                                        body flay,

Then beg my bones and burn them in some sequestered
way.
And make a garden near and plant a kanikara tree,
And when at winter's close it blooms, mother, recalling me,
Point to the flower and say, "Just such was fair Pabhavati."

Thus did she, alarmed with fear of death, idly lament before
her mother. And the Madda king issued an order that the
executioner should come with his axe and block. His coming
was noised abroad throughout the palace. The queen-mother,
on hearing of his arrival, arose from her throne and overwhelmed
with sorrow came into the presence of the king.

Then the queen spoke this stanza:
With this sword will the Madda king his graceful daughter
slay,
And piecemeal send her mangled limbs to rival chiefs a
prey.

The king to make her understand said, 'Lady what is this
you say? Your daughter rejected the chief king of all India on
the plea of his ugliness, and, accepting death as her fate,
returned home before the prints of her feet were well wiped out
on the road by which she had gone there. Now therefore let her
reap the consequences of the jealousy excited by her beauty."
The queen, after hearing what he had to say, went to her
daughter and lamenting spoke thus:
Thou didst not hearken to my voice, when I desired thy
good,
To-day thou sink'st to Yama's realm, thy body stained with
blood.
Such fate doth every man incur, or even a worse end,
Who deaf to good advice neglects the warnings of a friend.
If thou to-day a gallant prince for thy good lord shouldst
wed,
Bedight with zone of gold and gems, in land of Kusa bred,
Thou wouldst not, served with hosts of friends, to
Yama's realms have sped.
When drums are beat and elephants' loud trumpetings

resound,
In royal halls, where in this world can greater bliss be
found?
When horses neigh and minstrels play to kings some
plaintive air,
With bliss like this in royal hails, what is there to compare?
When too courts with the peacock's and the heron's cries
resound,
And cuckoo's call, where else, I pray, can bliss like this be
found?

After, thus talking with her in all these stanzas she thought, "If only king Kusa were here to-day, he would put to flight these seven kings and after freeing my daughter from her misery he would carry her away with him," and she repeated this stanza:
Where's he that crushes hostile realms and vanquishes his
foes?
Kusa, the noble and the wise, would free us from our woes.

Then Pabhavati thought, "My mother's tongue is not equal to proclaiming the praises of Kusa. I will let her know that he has been living here, occupied with the work of a cook," and she repeated this stanza:
The conqueror who crushes all his foes, lo! Here is he;
Kusa, the noble and so wise, all foes will slay for me.

Then her mother thinking, "She is terrified with the fear of death and rambles in her talk," spoke this stanza:
Art thou gone mad, or like a fool dost speak at random
thus?
If Kusa has returned, why, pray, didst thy not tell it us?

Hearing this Pabhavati thought, "My mother does not believe me. She does not know he has returned and been living here seven months. I will prove it to her"; and taking her mother by the hand she opened the window and stretching forth her hand and pointing to him she repeated this stanza:
Good mother, look at yonder cook, with loins girt up right
well,

He stoops to wash his pots and pans, where royal maidens
dwell.

Then Kusa, they say, thought, "To-day my heart's desire
will be fulfilled. Of a truth Pabhavati is terrified with the fear
of death and will tell of my coming here. I will wash my dishes
and put them away"; and he fetched water and began to wash
his dishes. Then her mother upbraiding her spoke this stanza:
Art thou base-born or wouldst thou deign, a maid of royal
race,
To take a slave for thy true love, to Madda's deep disgrace?

Then Pabhavati thought, "My mother, methinks, does not
know that it is for my sake he has been living here after this
manner," and she spoke another stanza:
No low caste I, nor would I shame my royal name, I swear,
Good luck to thee, no slave is he but king Okkaka's heir.
And now in praise of his fame she said:
He twenty thousand brahmins ever feeds, no slave, I swear,
It is Okkaka's royal son whom thou seest standing there.
He twenty thousand elephants aye yokes, no slave, I swear,
It is Okkaka's royal son whom thou seest standing there.
He twenty thousand horses ever yokes, no slave, I swear,
It is Okkaka's royal son whom thou seest standing there.
He twenty thousand chariots ever yokes, no slave, I swear,
It is Okkaka's royal son whom thou seest standing there.
He twenty thousand royal bulls aye yokes, no slave, I swear,
It is Okkaka's royal son whom thou seest standing there.
He twenty thousand royal kine aye milks, no slave, I swear,
It is Okkaka's royal son whom thou seest standing there.

Thus was the glory of the Great Being praised by her in six
stanzas. Then her mother thought, "She is not speaking in terror.
It must be so," and believing her she went and told the king the
whole story. He came in great haste to Pabhavati and asked, "Is
it true, what they say, that king Kusa has come?" "Yes, dear
father. It is seven months to-day that he has been acting as cook
to your daughters." Not believing her he questioned the
hunchback, and on hearing the facts of the case from her he

reproached his daughter and spoke this stanza:

> Like elephant as frog disguised,
> When this almighty prince came here,
> 'Twas wrong of thee and ill-advised
> To hid it from thy parents dear.

Thus did he reproach his daughter and then went in haste to Kusa and after the usual greetings with folded hands he acknowledged his offence, and repeated this stanza:

> In that we failed to recognize
> Your majesty in this disguise,
> If, Sire, to thee offence we gave,
> We would forgiveness humbly crave.

On hearing this the Great Being thought, "If I should speak harshly to him, his heart would straightway break. I will speak words of comfort to him"; and standing amongst his dishes he spoke this stanza:

> For me to play the scullion's part was very wrong I own,
> Be comforted, it was no fault of thine I was unknown.

The king, after being thus addressed in kindly words, climbed up to the palace and summoned Pabhavati, to send her to ask the king's pardon, and he spoke this stanza:

> Go, silly girl, thy pardon from the great king Kusa crave,
> His wrath appeased he may be pleased perhaps thy life to save.

On hearing the words of her father, she went to him, accompanied by her sisters and her handmaids. Standing just as he was in his workman's dress, he saw her coming towards him and thought, "To-day I will break down Pabhavati's pride and lay her low at my feet in the mud," and pouring on the ground all the water he had brought there, he trampled on a space as big as a threshing-floor, making it one mass of mud. She drew nigh and fell at his feet and groveling in the mud asked his forgiveness.

Then she spoke these stanzas:
My days and nights apart from thee, O king, have passed
                                                          away:
Behold I stoop to kiss thy feet. From anger cease I pray.
I promise thee, if thou to me a gracious ear shouldst lend,
Never again in aught I do will I my lord offend.
But if thou shouldst my prayer refuse, my father then will
                                                          slay
And send his daughter, limb by limb, to warrior kings a
                                                          prey.

On hearing this the king thought, "If I were to tell her, 'This
is for you to see to,' her heart would be broken. I will speak
words of comfort to her," and he said:
I'll do thy bidding, lady fair, as far as lies in me;
No anger feel I in my heart. Fear not, Pabhavati.
Hearken, O royal maid, to me, I too make promise true;
Never again will I offend in aught that I may do.
Full many a sorrow I would bear, fair maid, for love of thee,
And slay a host of Madda chiefs to wed Pabhavati.

Kusa, swelling with princely pride at seeing as it were a
handmaid of Sakka, king of the gods, in attendance upon him,
thought, "While I am still alive, shall others come and carry off
my bride?" and rousing himself, lion-like, in the palace-yard, he
said, "Let all who dwell in this city hear of my coming," and
dancing about, shouting and clapping his hands, he cried, "Now
will I take them alive, go bid them put horses to my chariots,"
and he repeated the following stanza:
Go, quickly yoke my well-trained steeds to many a painted
                                                          car,
And watch me swiftly sally forth, to scatter foes afar.

He now bade good-bye to Pabhavati, saying, "The capture
of thy enemies is my charge. Go thou and bathe and adorn
thyself and climb up to thy palace." And the king of Madda sent
his councilors to act as a guard of honour to him. And they drew
a screen round about him at the door of the kitchen and provided
barbers for him. And when his beard had been trimmed and his

head shampooed and he was arrayed in all his splendour and surrounded by his escort, he said, "I will ascend to the palace," and looking about him thence in every direction he clapped his hands, and wheresoever he looked the earth trembled, and he cried out, "Now mark how great is my power."

Then the Madda king sent him an elephant that had been trained to stand impassive under attack, richly caparisoned. Kusa mounted on the back of the elephant with a white umbrella held over him and ordered Pabhavati to be conducted there, and seating her behind him he left the city by the east gate, escorted by a complete host of the four arms, and as soon as he saw the forces of the enemy, he cried, "I am king Kusa: let all who value their lives lie down on their bellies," and he roared thrice with the roar of a lion and utterly crushed his foes.

The king said:
These foes are rather thine than mine. They all belong to
thee,
Thou only art our sovereign lord, to slay or to set free.

Being thus spoken to, the Great Being thought, "What can I do with these men when once dead? Let not their coming here be without good result. Pabhavati has seven younger sisters, daughters of king Madda. I will bestow them in marriage on these seven princes," and he repeated this stanza:
These daughters seven, like heavenly nymphs, are very fair
to see,
Give them, one each, to these seven kings, thy sons-in-law
to be.
Then the king said:
O'er us and them thou art supreme, thy purpose to fulfill
Give them—thou art our sovereign lord—according to thy
will.

So he had them all beautifully attired and gave them in marriage, one to each king.

THE NINETEEN PROBLEMS

1. "The piece of meat". One day when the Bodhisatta was going to the play-hall, a hawk carried off a piece of flesh from the slab of a slaughterhouse and flew up into the air; some lads, seeing it, determined to make him drop it and pursued him. The hawk flew in different directions, and they, looking up, followed behind and wearied themselves, flinging stones and other missiles and stumbling over one another. Then the sage said to them, "I will make him drop it," and they begged him to do so. He told them to look; and then himself without looking up ran with the swiftness of the wind and trod upon the hawk's shadow and then clapping his hands uttered a loud shout. By his power that shout seemed to pierce the bird's belly through and through and in its terror it dropped the flesh; and the Great Being, knowing by watching the shadow that it was dropped, caught it in the air before it reached the ground. The people seeing the marvel, made a great noise, shouting and clapping their hands. The minister, hearing of it, sent an account to the king telling him how the sage had by this means made the bird drop the flesh. The king, when he heard of it, asked Senaka whether he should summon him to the court. Senaka reflected, "From the time of his coming I shall lose all my glory and the king will forget my existence,—I must not let him bring him here"; so in envy he said, "He is not a sage for such an action as this, this is only a small matter"; and the king being impartial, sent word that the minister should test him further where he was.

2. "The cattle." A certain man who dwelt in the village of Yavamajjhaka bought some cattle from another village, intending to plough when the rains had fallen, and brought them home. The next day he took them to a field of grass to graze and rode on the back of one of the cattle. Being tired he got down and sat on the ground and fell asleep, and meanwhile a thief came and carried off the cattle. When he woke he saw not his cattle, but as he grazed on every side he beheld the thief running away. Jumping up he shouted, "Where are you taking my cattle?" "They are my cattle, and I am carrying them to the place which I wish." A great crowd collected as they heard the

dispute. When the sage heard the noise as they passed by the door of the hall, he sent for them both. When he saw their behaviour he at once knew which was the thief and which the real owner. But though he felt sure, he asked them what they were quarrelling about. The owner said, "I bought these cattle form a certain person in such a village, and I brought them home and put them in a field of grass. This thief saw that I was not watching and came and carried them off. Looking in all directions I caught sight of him and pursued and caught him. The people of such a village know that I bought the cattle and took them." The thief replied, "This man speaks falsely, they were born in my house." The sage said, "I will decide your case fairly; will you abide by my decision?" and they promised so to abide. Then thinking to himself that he must win the hearts of the people he first asked the thief, "What have you fed these cattle with, and what have you given them to drink?" "They have drunk rice-gruel and have been fed on sesame flour and kidney beans." Then he asked the real owner, who said, "My lord, how could a poor man like me get rice-gruel and the rest? I fed them on grass." The pandit caused an assembly to be brought together and ordered panic seeds to be brought and ground in a mortar and moistened with water and given to the cattle, and they forthwith vomited only grass. He showed this to the assembly, and then asked the thief, "Art thou the thief or not?" He confessed that he was the thief. He said to him, "Then do not commit such a sin henceforth." But the Bodhisatta's attendants carried the man away and cut off his hands and feet and made him helpless. Then the sage addressed him with words of good counsel, "This suffering has come upon thee only in this present life, but in the future life thou wilt suffer great torment in the different hells, therefore henceforth abandon such practices"; he taught him the five commandments. The minister sent an account of the incident to the king, who asked Senaka, but he advised him to wait, "It is only an affair about cattle and anybody could decide it." The king being impartial, sent the same command. (This is to be understood in all the subsequent cases,—we shall give each in order according to the list.)

3. "The necklace of thread." A certain poor woman had tied together several threads of different colours and made them into a necklace, which she took off from her neck and placed on her clothes as she went down to bathe in a tank which the sage had caused to be made. A young woman who saw this conceived a longing for it, took it up and said to her, "Mother, this is a very beautiful necklace, how much did it cost to make? I will make such a one for myself. May I put it on my own neck and ascertain its size?" the other gave her leave, and she put it on her neck and ran off. The elder women seeing it came quickly out of the water, and putting on her clothing ran after her and seized hold of her dress, crying, "You are running away with a necklace which I made." The other replied, "I am not taking anything of yours, it is the necklace which I wear on my neck"; and a great crowd collected as they heard this. The sage, while he played with the boys, hard them quarrelling as they passed by the door of the hall and asked what the noise was about. When he heard the cause of the quarrel he sent for them both, and having known at once by her countenance which was the thief, he asked them whether they would abide by his decision. On their both agreeing to do so, he asked the thief, "What scent do you use for this necklace?" She replied, "I always use *sabbasamharaka* to scent it with." Now this is a scent compounded of all scents. Then he asked the other, who replied, "How shall a poor woman like me get *sabbasamharaka*? I always scent it with perfume made of *piyangu* flowers. " Then the sage had a vessel of water brought and put the necklace in it. Then he sent for a perfume-seller and told him to smell the vessel and find out what it smelt of. He directly recognized the smell of the *piyangu* flower, and quoted the stanza which has been already given in the first book:

"Sabbasamharaka 'tis not; only the *kangu* smells;
You wicked women told a lie; the truth the gammer tells."

The Great Being told the bystanders all the circumstances and asked each of them respectively, "Art thou the thief? Art thou not the thief?" and made the guilty one confess, and from that time his wisdom became known to the people.

4. "The cotton thread," A certain woman who used to watch cotton fields was watching one day and she took some clean cotton and spun some fine thread and made it into a ball and placed it in her lap. As she went home she thought to herself, "I will bathe in the great sage's tank," so she placed the ball on her dress and went down into the tank to bathe. Another woman saw it, and conceiving a longing for it took it up, saying, "This is a beautiful ball of thread; pray did you make it yourself?" So she lightly snapped her fingers and put it in her lap as if to examine it more closely, and walked off with it. (This is to be told at full as before.) The sage asked the thief, "When you made the ball what did you put inside?" she replied, "A cotton seed." Then he asked the other, and she replied, "A timbaru seed." When the crowd had heard what each said, he untwisted the ball of cotton and found a timbaru seed inside and forced the thief to confess her guilt. The great multitude were highly pleased and shouted their applause at the way in which the case had been decided.

5. "The son." A certain woman took her son and went down to the sage's tank to wash her face. After she had bathed her son she laid him in her dress and having washed her own face went to bathe. At that moment a female goblin saw the child and wished to eat it, so she took hold of the dress and she said, "my friend, this is a fine child, is he your son?" then she asked if she might give him suck, and on obtaining the mother's consent, she took him and played with him for a while and then tried to run off with him. The other ran after her and seized hold of her, shouting, "Whither are your carrying my child?" The goblin replied, "Where did you get a child? this is mine." As they wrangled they passed by the door of the hall, and the sage, hearing the noise, sent for them and asked what was the matter. When he heard the story, although he knew at once by her red unwinking eyes that one of them was goblin, he asked them whether they would abide by his decision. On their promising to do so, he drew a line and laid the child in the middle of the line and bade the goblin seize the child by the hands and the mother by the feet. Then he said to them, "Lay hold of it and pull; the child is hers who can pull it over." They both pulled,

and the child, being pained while it was pulled, uttered a loud cry. Then the mother, with a heart which seemed ready to burst, let the child go and stood weeping. The sage asked the multitude, "Is it the heart of the mother which is tender towards the child or the heart of her who is not the mother?" They answered, "The mother's heart." "Is she the mother who kept hold of the child or she who let it go?" they replied, "She who let it go." "Do you know who she is who stole the child?" "We do not know, O sage." "She is a goblin,—she seized it in order to eat it." When they asked how he knew that he replied, "I knew her by her unwinking and red eyes and by her casting no shadow and by her fearlessness and want of mercy." Then he asked her what she was, and she confessed that she was a goblin. "Why did you seize the child?" "To eat it." "You blind fool" he said, "You committed sin in old time and so were born as a goblin; and now you still go on committing sin, blind fool that you are." Then he exhorted her and established her in the five precepts and sent her away; and the mother blessed him, and saying, "May'st thou live long, my lord," took her son and went her way.

6. "The black ball." There was a certain man who was called Golakala,—now he got the name *gola* 'ball' from his dwarfish size, and *kala* form his black colour. He worked in a certain house for seven years and obtained a wife, and she was named Dighatala. One day he said to her, "Wife, cook some sweetmeats and food, we will pay a visit to your parents." At first she opposed the plan saying, "What have I to do with parents now?" but after the third time of asking he induced her to cook some cakes, and having taken some provisions and a present he set out on the journey with her. In the course of the journey he came to a stream which was not really deep, but they, being both afraid of water, dared not cross it and stood on the bank. Now a poor man named Dighapitthi came to that place as he walked along the bank, and when they saw him they asked him whether the river was deep or shallow. Seeing that they were afraid of the water he told them that it was very deep and full of voracious fish. "How then will you go across it?" "I have struck up a friendship with the crocodiles and

monsters that live here, and therefore they do not hurt me." "Do take us with you," they said. When he consented they gave him some meat and drink; and when he finished his meal he asked them which he should carry over first. "Take our friend first and then take me," said Golakala. Then the man placed her on his shoulders and took the provisions and the present and went down into the stream. When he had gone a little way, he crouched down and walked along in a bent posture. Golakala, as he stood on the bank, thought to himself, "This stream must indeed be very deep; if it is so difficult for even such a man as Dighapitthi, it must be impassable for me." When the other had carried the woman to the middle of the stream, he said to her, "Lady, I will cherish you, and you shall live bravely arrayed with fine dresses and ornaments and men-servants and maid-servants; what will this poor dwarf do for you? Listen to what I tell you." She listened to his words and ceased to love her husband, and being at once infatuated with the stranger, she consented, saying, "If you will not abandon me, I will do as you say." So when they reached the opposite bank, they amused themselves and left Golakala, bidding him stay where he was. While he stood there looking on, they ate up the meat and drink and departed. When he saw it, he exclaimed, "They have struck up a friendship and are running away, leaving me here." As he ran backwards and forwards he went a little way into the water and then drew back again in fear, and then in his anger at their conduct, he made a desperate leap, saying, "Let me live or die," and when once fairly in, he discovered how shallow the water was. So he crossed it and pursued him and shouted, "You wicked thief, whither are you carrying my wife?" The other replied, "How is she your wife" she is mine"; and he seized him by the neck and whirled him round and threw him off. The other laid hold of Dighatala's hand and shouted, "Stop, where are you going? You are my wife whom I got after working for seven years in a house"; and as he thus disputed he came near the hall. A great crowd collected. The Great Being asked what the noise was about, and having sent for them and heard what each said he asked whether they would abide by his decision. On their both agreeing to do so, he sent for Dighapitthi and asked him his name. Then he asked the wife's name, but he, not knowing what it was, mentioned some other name. Then he asked him the names of his parents and he told them, but when he asked him the names of his wife's parents he, not knowing, mentioned some other names. The Great Being put his story together and had him removed. Then he sent for the other and asked him the names of all in the same way. He, knowing the truth, gave them correctly. Then he had him removed and sent for Dighatala and asked her what her name was and she gave it. Then he asked her, her husband's name and she, not knowing, gave a wrong name. Then he asked her her parents' nae and she gave them correctly, but when he asked her the name of her husband's parents' names, she talked at random and gave wrong names. Then the sage sent for the other two and asked the multitude. "Does the woman's story agree with Dighapitthi or Golakala?" They replied, "With Golakala." Then he pronounced his sentence, "This man is her husband, the other is a thief"; and when he asked him he made him confess that he had acted as the thief.

7. "The chariot." A certain man who was sitting in a chariot, alighted from it to wash his face. At that moment Sakka was considering and as he beheld the sage he resolved that he would make know the power and wisdom of Mahosadha the embryo Buddha. So he came down in the form of a man, and followed the chariot asked, "Why have you come?" he replied, "To serve you." The man agreed, and dismounting from the chariot went aside at a call of nature. Immediately Sakka mounted in the chariot and went off at speed. The owner of the chariot, his business done, returned; and when he saw Sakka hurrying away with the chariot, he ran quickly behind, crying, "Stop, stop, where are you taking my chariot?" Sakka replied, "Your chariot must be another, this is mine." Thus wrangling they came to the gate of the hall. The sage asked, "What is this?" and sent for him: as he came, by his fearlessness and his eyes which winked not, the sage knew that this was Sakka and the other was the owner. Nevertheless he enquired the cause of the quarrel, and asked them, "Will you abide by my decision?" They said, "Yes." He went on, "I will cause the chariot to be driven, and you must both hold on behind: the owner will not

let go, the other will." .Then he told a man to drive the chariot,
and he did so, the others holding on behind. The owner went
a little way, then being unable to run further he let go, but
Sakka went on running with the chariot. When he had recalled
the chariot, the sage said to the people: "This man ran a little
way and let go; the other ran out with the chariot and came
back with it, yet there is not a drop of sweat on his body, no
panting, he is fearless, his eyes wink not—this is Sakka, king of
the gods." Then he asked, "Are you king of the gods?" "Yes."
"Why did you come here?" "To spread the fame of your wisdom,
O sage!" "Then," said he, "don't do that kind of thing again."
Now Sakka revealed his power by standing poised in the air,
and praised the sage, saying. "A wise judgement this!" So he
went to his own place. Then the minister unsummoned went
to the king, and said, "O great king, thus was the Chariot
Question resolved: and even Sakka was subdued by him; why
do you not recognize superiority in men?" The king asked Senaka,
"What say you, Senaka, shall we bring the sage here?" Senaka
replied, "That is not all that makes a sage. Wait awhile: I will
test him and find out."

8. "The pole." So one day, with a view of testing the sage,
they fetched an acacia pole, and cutting off about a span, they
had it nicely smoothed by a turner, and sent it to the village of
East Yavamajjhaka, with this message: "The people of
Yavamajjhaka have a name for wisdom. Let them find out then
which end is the top and which the root of this stick. If they
cannot, there is a fine of a thousand pieces." The people gathered
together but could not find it out, and they said to their
gildmaster, "Perhaps Mahosadha the sage would know; send
and ask him." The gildmaster sent for the sage from his
playground, and told him the matter, how they could not find
it out but perhaps he could. The sage thought to himself, "The
king can gain nothing from knowing which is the top and
which is the root, no doubt it is sent to test me." He said, "Bring
it here, my friends, I will find out." Holding it in his hand, he
knew which was the top and which the root; yet to please the
heart of the people, he sent for a pot of water, and tied a string
round the middle of the stick, and holding it by the end of the

string he let it down to the surface of the water. The root being heavier sank first. Then he asked the people, "Is the root of a tree heavier, or the top?" "The root, wise sire!" "See then, this part sinks first, and this is therefore the root." By this mark he distinguished the root from the top. The people sent it back to the king, distinguishing which was the root and which was the top. The king was pleased, and asked, who had found it out? They said, "The sage Mahosadha, son of the gildmaster Sirivaddhi." "Senaka, shall we send for him?" he asked. "Wait, my lord," he replied, "let us try him in another way"

9. "The head." One day, two heads were brought, one a woman's and one a man's; there were sent to be distinguished, with a fine of a thousand pieces in case of failure. The villagers could not decide and asked the Great Being. He recognized them at sight, because, they say, the sutures in a man's head are straight, and in a woman's head they are crooked. By this mark he told which was which; and they sent back to the king. The rest is as before.

10. "The snake." One day a male and a female snake were brought, and sent for the villagers to decide which was which. They asked the sage, and he knew at once when he saw them; for the tail of the male snake is thick, that of the female is thin; the male snake's head is thick, the female's is long; the eyes of the male are big, of the female small, the head of the male is rounded, that of the female cut short. By these signs he distinguished male from female. The rest is as before.

11. "The cock." One day a message was sent to the people of the village of East Yavamajjhaka to this effect; "Send us a bull white all over, with horns on his legs, and a hump on the head, which utters his voice at three times unfailingly; otherwise there is a fine of a thousand pieces." Not knowing one, they asked the sage. He said: "The king means you to send him a cock. This creature has horns on his feet, the spurs; a hump on his head, the crest; and crowing thrice utters his voice at three times unfailingly. Then send him a cock such as he describes." They sent one.

12. "The gem." The gem, which Sakka gave to King Kusa, was octagonal. Its thread was broken, and no one could remove the old thread and put in a new. One day they sent this gem, with directions to take out the old thread and to put in a new; the villagers could do neither the one nor the other, and in their difficulty they told the sage. He bade them fear nothing, and asked for a drop of honey. With this he smeared the end of this also with honey, he pushed it a little way into the hole, and put it in a place where ants were passing. The ants smelling the honey came out of their hole, and eating away the old thread bit hold of the end of the woollen thread and pulled it out at the other end. When he saw that it had passed through, he bade them present it to the king, who was pleased when he heard how the thread had been put in.

13. "The calving." The royal bull was fed up for some months, so that his belly swelled out, his horns were washed, he was anointed with oil, and bathed with turmeric, and then they sent him to the village of East Yavamajjhaka, with this message: "You have a name for wisdom. Here is the king's royal bull, in calf; deliver him and send him back with the calf, or else there is a fine of a thousand pieces." The villagers, perplexed what to do, applied to the sage; who thought fit to meet one question with another, and asked, "Can you find a bold man able to speak to the king?" "That is no hard matter," they replied. So they summoned him, and the Great Being said— "Go, my good man, let your hair down loose over your shoulders, and go to the palace gate weeping and lamenting sore. Answer none but the king, only lament, and if the king sends for you to ask why you lament, say, This seven days my father is in labour and cannot bring forth; O help me! Tell me how I may deliver him! Then the king will say, What madness! This is impossible; men do not bear children. Then you must say, If that be true, how can the people of East Yavamajjhaka deliver your royal bull of a calf?" As he was bidden, so he did. The king asked who thought of that country-quip; and on hearing that if was the sage Mahosadha he was pleased.

14. "The boiled rice." Another day, to the test the sage,

this message was sent: "The people of East Yavamajjhaka must send us some boiled rice cooked under eight conditions, and these are—without rice, without water, without a pot, without an oven, without fire, without firewood, without being sent along a road either by woman or man. If they cannot do it, there is a fine of a thousand pieces." The people perplexed applied to the sage; who said, "Be not troubled. Take some broken rice, for that is not rice; snow, for that is not water; an earthen bowl, which is no pot; chop up some wood blocks which are no oven; kindle fire by rubbing, instead of a proper fire; take leaves instead of firewood; cook your sour rice, put it in a new vessel, press it well down, put it on the head of a eunuch, who is neither man nor woman, leave the main road and go along a footpath, and take it to the king." They did so; and the king was pleased when he heard by whom the question had been solved.

15. "The sand." Another day, to the test the sage, they sent this message to the villagers: "The king wishes to amuse himself in a swing, and the old rope is broken; you are to make a rope of sand, or else pay a fine of a thousand pieces." They knew not what to do, and appealed to the sage, who saw that this was the place for a counter-question. He reassured the people; and sending for two or three clever speakers, he bade them go tell the king: "My lord, the villagers do not know whether the sand-rope is to be thick or thin: send them a bit of the old rope, a span long or four fingers; this they will look at and twist a rope of the same size." If the king replied, "Sand-rope there never was in my house," they were to reply, "If your majesty cannot make a sand-rope, how can the villagers do so?" They did so; and the king was pleased on hearing that the sage had thought of the counter-quip.

16. "The tank." Another day, the message was: "The king desires to disport him in the water; you must send me a new tank covered with water lilies of all five kinds, otherwise there is a fine of a thousand pieces." They told the sage, who saw that a counter-quip was wanted. He sent for several men clever at speaking, and said to them: "Go and play in the water till your eyes are red, go to the palace door with wet hair and wet

garments and your bodies all over mud, holding in your hands ropes, staves, and clods; send word to the king of your coming, and when you are admitted say to him, Sire, inasmuch as your majesty has ordered the people of East Yavamajjhaka to send you a tank, we brought a great tank to suit your taste; but she being used to a life in the forest, no sooner saw the town with its walls, moats, and watch-towers, than she took fright and broke the ropes and off into the forest: we pelted her with clods and beat her with sticks but could not make her come back. Give us then the old tank which your majesty is said to have brought from the forest, and we will yoke them together and bring the other back. The king will say, I never had a tank brought in from the forest, and never sent a tank there to be yoked and bring in another! Then you must say, If that is so, how can the villagers send you a tank?" They did so; and the king was pleased to hear that the sage had thought of this.

17. "The Park." Again on a day the king sent a message. "I wish to disport me in the park, and my park is old. The people of Yavamajjhaka must send me a new park, filled with trees and flowers." The sage reassured them as before, and sent men to speak in the same manner as above.

18. Then the king was pleased, and said to Senaka: "Well, Senaka, shall we send for the sage?" But he, grudging the other's prosperity, said, "That is not all that makes a sage; wait." On hearing this the king thought, "The sage Mahosadha was wise even as a child, and took my fancy. In all these deep tests and counter-quips he has given answers like a Buddha. Yet Senaka will not let me summon such a sage as this to my side. What care I for Senaka? I will bring the man here." So with a great following he set out for the village, mounted upon his royal horse. But as he went the horse put his foot into a hole and broke his leg; so the king turned back from that place to the town. Then Senaka entered the presence and said: "Sire, did you go to the village of Yavamajjhaka to bring the sage back?" "Yes, sage," said the king. "Sire," said Senaka "you make me as one of no account. I begged you to wait awhile; but off you went in a hurry, and at the outset your royal horse broke his leg." The

king had nothing to say to this. Again on a day he asked Senaka, "Shall we send for the sage, Senaka?" "If so, your majesty, don't go yourself but send a messenger, saying, O sage! As I was on my way to fetch you my horse broke his leg: send us a mule or something more excellent. If he takes the first alternative he will come himself, if the second he will send his father. Then will be a problem to test him." The king sent a messenger with this message. The sage on hearing it recognised that the king wished to see himself and his father. So he went to his father, and said, greeting him, "Father, the king wishes to see you and me. You go first with a thousand merchants in attendance; and when you go, go not empty-handed but take a sandalwood casket filled with fresh ghee. The king will speak kindly to you, and offer you a householder's seat; take it and sit down. When you are seated, I will come; the king will speak kindly to me and offer me such another seat. Then I will look at you; take the cue and say, rising from your seat, Son Mahosadha the wise, take this seat. Then the question will be ripe for solution." He did so. On arriving at the palace door he caused his arrival to be made known to the king, and on the king's invitation, he entered, and greeted the king, and stood on one side. The king spoke to him kindly, and asked where was his son the wise Mahosadha. "Coming after me, my lord." The king was pleased to hear of his coming, and bade the father sit in a suitable place. He found a place and sat there. Meanwhile the Great Being dressed himself in all his splendour, and attended by the thousand youths he came seated in a magnificent chariot. As he entered the town he beheld an ass by the side of a ditch, and he directed some stout fellows to fasten up the mouth of the ass so that it should make no noise, to put him in a bag and carry on their shoulders. They did so; the Bodhisatta entered the city with his great company. The people could not praise him enough. "This," they cried, "is the wise Mahosadha, the merchant Sirivaddhaka's son; this they say is he, who was born holding a herb of virtue in his hand; he it is who knew the answers to so many problems set to test him." On arriving before the palace he sent in word of his coming. The king was pleased to hear it and said, "Let my son the wise Mahosadha make haste to come in." So with his attendants he entered the palace and saluted the king and stood on one side. The king delighted to see him spoke to him very sweetly, and bade him find a fit seat and sit down. He looked at his father, and his father at this cue uprose from his seat and invited him to sit there, which he did. Thereupon the foolish men who were there, Senaka, Pukkusa, Kavinda, Devinda, and others, seeing him sit there, clapped their hands and laughed loudly and cried, "This is the blind fool they call wise! He has made his father rise from his seat and sits there himself! Wise he should not be called surely." The king also was crestfallen. Then the Great Being said, "Why, my lord! are you sad?" "Yes, wise sir, I am sad. I was glad to hear of you, but to see you I am not glad." "Why so?" "Because you have made your father rise from his seat, and sit there yourself." "What, my lord! do you think that in all cases the sire is better than the sons?" "Yes, sage." "Did you not send word to me to bring you a mule or something more excellent?" So saying he rose up and looking towards the young fellows said, "Bring in the ass you have brought." Placing this ass before the king he went on, "Sire, what is the price of this ass?" The king said, "If it be serviceable, it is worth eight kahapanas." "But if he get a mule colt out of a thoroughbred Sindh mare, what will the price of it be?" "It will be priceless." "Why do you say that, my lord? Have you not just said that in all cases the sire is better man the sons? By your own saying the ass is worth more than the mule colt. Now have not your wise men clapped their hands and laughed at me because they did not know that? What wisdom is this of your wise men! Where did you get them?" And in contempt for all four of them he addressed the king in this stanza of the First Book:

You smile, and think that the sire is better than the son, O excellent king. Then is yon creature better than the mule; the ass is the mule's sire.

After saying this, he went on, "My lord, if the sire is better than the son, take my sire into your service; if the son is better than the sire, take me." The king was delighted; and all the company cried out applauding and praising a thousand times—"Well indeed has the wise man solved the question." There was cracking of fingers and waving of a thousand scarves: the four were crestfallen.

Now no one knows better than the Bodhisatta the value of parents. If one ask then, why he did so: it was not to throw contempt on his father, but when the king sent the message, send a mule or something more excellent, he did thus in order to solve that problem, and to make his wisdom to be recognised, and to take the shine out of the four sages.

The king was pleased; and taking the gold vase filled with scented water, poured the water upon the merchant's hand, saying, "Enjoy the village of East Yavamajjhaka as a gift from the king—let the other merchants," he went on, "be subordinate to this." This done he sent to the mother of the Bodhisatta all kinds of ornaments. Delighted as he was at the Bodhisatta's solution of the Ass Question, he wished to make the Bodhisatta as his own son, and to the father said, "Good sir, give me the Great Being to be my son." He replied, "Sire, very young is he still; even yet his mouth smells of milk: but when he is old, he shall be with you." The king said however, "Good sir, henceforth you must give up your attachment to the boy; from this day he is my son. I can support my son, so go your ways." Then he sent him away. He did obeisance to the king, and embraced his son, and throwing his arms about him kissed him upon the head, and gave him good counsel. The boy also bade his father farewell, and begged him not to be anxious, and sent him away.

The king then asked the sage, whether he would take his meals inside the palace or without it. He thinking that with so large a retinue it were best to have his meals outside the palace, replied to that effect. Then the king gave him a suitable house, and providing for the maintenance of the thousand youths and all, gave him all that was needful. From that time the sage attended upon the king.

19. Now the king desired to test the sage. At that time there was a precious jewel in a crow's nest on a palmtree which stood on the bank of a lake near the southern gate, and the

image of this jewel was to be seen reflected upon the lake. They told the king that there was a jewel in the lake. He sent for Senaka, saying, "They tell me there is jewel in the lake; how are we to get it?" Senaka said, "The best way is to drain out the water." The king instructed him to do so; and he collected a number of men, and got out the water and mud, and dug up the soil at the bottom—but no jewel could he see. But when the lake was again full, there was the reflexion of the jewel to be seen once more. Again Senaka did the same thing, and found no jewel. Then the king sent for the sage, and said, "A jewel has been seen in the lake, and Senaka has taken out the water and mud and dug up the earth without finding it, but no sooner is the lake full than it appears again. Can you get hold of it?" He replied, "That is no hard task, sire, I will get it for you." The king was pleased at this promise, and with a great following he went to the lake, ready to see the might of the sage's knowledge. The Great Being stood on the bank, and looked. He perceived that the jewel was not in the lake, but must be in the tree, and he aloud, "Sire, there is no jewel in the tank." "What! Is it not visible in the water?" So he sent for a pail of water, and said, "Now, my lord, see—is not this jewel visible both in the pail and the lake?" "Then where can the jewel be?" "Sire, it is the reflexion which is visible both in the lake and in the pail, but the jewel is in a crow's nest in this palm-tree: send up a man and have it brought down." The king did so: the man brought down the jewel, and the sage put it into the king's hand. All the people applauded the sage and mocked at Senaka—"Here's a precious jewel in a crow's nest up a tree, and Senaka makes strong men dig out the lake! Surely a wise man should be like Mahosadha." Thus they praised the Great Being; and the king being delighted with him, gave him a necklace of pearls from his own neck, and strings of pearls to the thousand boys, and to him and his retinue he granted the right to wait upon him without ceremony.